W9-ATV-657

HELENE DEUTSCH

A PSYCHOANALYST'S LIFE

"The story of a remarkable woman and a remarkable milieu...
unusually interesting and well worth reading."—The New York Times

MERIDIAN

PAUL ROAZEN

"THE LIFE OF ARGUABLY THE MOST IMPORTANT WOMAN IN THE HISTORY OF PSYCHOANALYSIS... THIS CAREFUL STUDY PAYS OFF HANDSOMELY."
—*Psychology Today*

"A portrait of an independent-minded career woman . . . even-handed and candid."—*Publishers Weekly*

"Roazen interviewed her, culls her diary and letters, even shows how she used herself as case material in professional writings. He documents love affairs, marriage, motherhood, analyses with Freud and Karl Abraham, the miscarried treatment of Victor Tausk, and Deutsch's influence in America, where she spent the last 46 years of her long career. Psychoanalytic history, intrigues, and politics appear more vividly here than in Deutsch's own memoirs, making this a worthy sequel to Roazen's *Freud and His Followers.*"
—*Library Journal*

Paul Roazen, a professor of social and political science at York University in Toronto, is the author of *Freud and His Followers; Brother Animal: The Story of Freud and Tausk; Freud: Political and Social Thought; Erik H. Erikson: The Power and Limits of a Vision*, and is the editor of *Sigmund Freud.*

Also by Paul Roazen

FREUD: POLITICAL AND SOCIAL THOUGHT

BROTHER ANIMAL: THE STORY OF FREUD AND TAUSK

FREUD AND HIS FOLLOWERS

ERIK H. ERIKSON: THE POWER AND LIMITS OF A VISION

SIGMUND FREUD (editor)

HELENE DEUTSCH

A Psychoanalyst's Life

PAUL ROAZEN

A MERIDIAN BOOK

NEW AMERICAN LIBRARY

NEW YORK AND SCARBOROUGH, ONTARIO

For Jules and Daniel

Copyright © 1985 by Paul Roazen

All rights reserved. For information address Anchor Press/Doubleday & Company, Inc., 245 Park Avenue, New York, New York 10167.

This is an authorized reprint of a hardcover edition published by Anchor Press/Doubleday & Company, Inc.

 MERIDIAN TRADEMARK REG. U.S. PAT. OFF. AND FOREIGN COUNTRIES
REG. TRADEMARK—MARCA REGISTRADA
HENCHO EN FAIRFIELD, PA., U.S.A.

SIGNET, SIGNET CLASSIC, MENTOR, PLUME, MERIDIAN AND NAL BOOKS
are published *in the United States* by New American Library,
1633 Broadway, New York, New York 10019, *in Canada*
by The New American Library of Canada Limited, 81 Mack Avenue,
Scarborough, Ontario M1L 1M8

Library of Congress Cataloging-in-Publication Data

Roazen, Paul, 1936–
      Helene Deutsch, a psychoanalyst's life.

   1. Deutsch, Helene 1884– 2. Psychoanalysts—
Poland—Biography.   3. Psychoanalysis—History.
I. Title.
RC339.52.D48R63   1986   616.89′0092′4 [B] 85-29184
ISBN 0-452-00803-4 (pbk.)

First Meridian Printing, April, 1986

1 2 3 4 5 6 7 8 9

PRINTED IN THE UNITED STATES OF AMERICA

CONTENTS

PART III CAMBRIDGE, MASSACHUSETTS

INTRODUCTION

Jocasta: Fear? What has a man to do with fear?
Chance rules our lives, and the future is all unknown.
Best live as best we may, from day to day.
Nor need this mother-marrying frighten you;
Many a man has dreamt as much. Such things
Must be forgotten, if life is to be endured.

Sophocles, *Oedipus Rex*

A biography of Helene Deutsch is the story of one of the most famous psychoanalysts, a woman who at her death in 1982 was the oldest survivor of Sigmund Freud's immediate circle. In 1925 she had become the first psychoanalyst to write a book on feminine psychology. Her interest in the subject, along with that of Karen Horney, helped push Freud himself, who did not like being left behind, into writing articles about women. Helene Deutsch is now best known as the author of the two-volumed *The Psychology of Women.* [1] Freud had emphasized that people have bodies, and Helene Deutsch insisted on a further point, which Freud just touched on as a matter of doctrine: she elaborated on some of the essential differences between men and women. The outrage that Freud aroused still surrounds Helene Deutsch's name. To some feminists she is infamous, a traitor to her sex; they have focused their attack against sexism on some of her theories. [2]

Despite how easy it can be to pass judgment by today's standards on the ideas of a woman born over a century ago, Helene Deutsch's writings were the authentic outgrowth of her most intense personal experiences. In social context she herself was a leading feminist; the story of the history of women has had its blind spots. Medicine was an exceptional career for women in the early twentieth century; only seven women entered medical school at the University of Vienna when Helene Deutsch did, in 1907; three of them finally received their degrees. Her unusual talents succeeded in overcoming numerous hindrances to an emancipated woman of that period.

By October 1918, when she went to see Freud as a patient, Helene Deutsch was already an experienced psychiatrist; few women had risen as far as she had in her profession. Psychoanalysis was by then established enough to be a specialty in which she could seek apprenticeship; coming to Freud was a fulfillment of her past as well as a turning point in her life. Helene Deutsch attracted Freud as a potential pupil because of her capacities and professional standing. He knew how much her work meant to her and took her seriously. At the time there was only one other woman in Freud's circle in Vienna.

Within Freud's world Helene Deutsch succeeded in remaining herself. Her humanity led her to expand pre-existing psychoanalytic thinking. Freud was so demanding, and had such high standards for people (she became a favorite of his), that he neglected to realize that in real life human beings can fail to experience emotions described in great literature. From Helene Deutsch's point of view Freud was too moralistic, and she tried to be less a judge and more a helper. She was prepared to become a disciple of Freud's, but as with all great students, the elements of innovation, separation, and devotion were to be mixed together in a much more complicated form than her later reputation as a loyalist might imply. Helene Deutsch was an independent-minded woman who wanted to assert a viewpoint different from that of either traditional psychiatry or conventional analytic wisdom.

By October 1918 Helene Deutsch was concerned that the psychiatric functions she was performing at the University of Vienna would be endangered by the conclusion of the World War. She had been acting as one of Julius Wagner von Jauregg's assistants; he headed the best center for psychiatry in the Hapsburg empire. (In 1927 Wagner-Jauregg became the first and only psychiatrist to win a Nobel Prize.) It had been exhilarating for her to be working on the frontiers of knowledge; the analysts, including Freud, had had little experience with mental patients. But no woman could yet legally hold the position she had been filling, and only the absence of male psychiatrists who were in the war had enabled her to surmount the customary barriers to her sex. Within psychoanalysis, however, she felt she could retain her originality without being threatened by traditionalism.

The legend of Oedipus, which Freud thought was prototypical for human psychology, is a tragedy of recognition. Oedipus's destiny was that of a truth-seeker; his fate, as it had been foretold, was to have slain his father (Laius) and married his mother (Jocasta). But Freud had trouble understanding what the drama of Oedipus meant from a woman's point of view. On a rare occasion when, for example, he mentioned Jocasta's side of things, he referred to her as "the deluded mother and wife."[3] Freud's psychology has often been criticized for its masculine arrogance.

Helene Deutsch took from Freud a way of accounting for her own experience as a woman. She would not just echo Freud, although she has been accused of allowing her loyalty to him to determine her thought, leading to an endorsement of male chauvinist ideas about women. She did accept certain beliefs of her time as to what constitutes healthy maleness and femaleness; she proved flexible, though, in adapting her viewpoint to changing social circumstances. The study of the history of ideas should expand our tolerance for the inevitable limitations of any era's outlook, and help us to acknowledge our own biases. It becomes clear from a close reading of Helene's life, however, that she listened first and foremost to her own heart, as she sought to reinterpret her own most intense conflicts. She remained true to the dictates of her conscience, which sometimes took her in unexpected directions. Her writings were a kind of compensation for her life—in part justification for her choices, in part repudiation of herself as a model. Her practices and work were her own, although she failed to highlight her important and subtle differences with Freud.

In behalf of the broadest meaning of the concept of bisexuality all the early psychoanalysts were trying to criticize previous preconceptions about femininity and masculinity; as with the members of the Bloomsbury group in England, venturesomeness was mixed with snobbery. Helene Deutsch was writing at a time when middle-class women were confined to the narrow lives of their families; she sometimes thought of herself as a freak for pursuing professional goals. Her ideas implied that for each human to be both male and female allows for a richness of potentialities. Her whole life meant a challenge to the prevailing standards of her society.

In her profession she attained freedom and was not just a subject and disciple of Freud's. His genius was the presence which released Helene Deutsch's most creative talents, but in defining who she was Helene Deutsch did not have to rebel against Freud. She inquired into what interested her in her own way; she could transcend Freud without dishonoring their relationship. Her life demonstrated that women need not be victims, but that their special abilities, based on social and biological sources, can be translated into active doing in the world.

Historically Helene Deutsch's career is a leading example of an intellectual woman's problems and triumphs. Few professions in this century can match the receptivity of psychoanalysis to talented women. She wrote, of course, in a society radically unlike ours, and it is unfair to extract her ideas from their proper cultural context. For example, despite all that her detractors say today, she *was* trying to use psychological theory for the sake of female emancipation; she described (1925) how in that era, when mothers rarely worked, an identification with a girl's father could be liberating. Freud's position, in Helene Deutsch's hands, was modified to the conviction that the psychological differences between men and women do not have anything to do with the issue of inferiority. (At the same time she was convinced that women have greater emotional insights than men.) As she wrote with an eye to a professional audience, the terminology was bound to be misunderstood by lay readers. Nonetheless it ought to have been clear that she thought that women are endangered by their unconscious erotic "masochism," and that so-called female narcissism is a vital source of self-protection.

These ideas mattered to her because, like other idealists, Helene Deutsch believed that how we think affects our behavior. One of the attractions of psychoanalysis, like Marxism a surrogate religion for all its initial adherents, was its optimism about the chances of transforming human fate. For all Freud's sense of tragedy, Helene Deutsch, like him, proceeded on the premise that knowledge ultimately means control. As a profession psychoanalysis proved enormously satisfying to her. Freud had created an occupation which allowed her to make use of her own self-knowledge to alleviate the suffering of others. Fascination with her cases, and an appreciation for human diversity, liberated her from the self-preoccupation of grief. Her sedentary calling, spent vicariously sharing the experiences of others, illustrates how exciting an adventure the life of the mind can be.

At the same time Helene Deutsch was able to distance herself from Freud so she could get on with her own concerns; against his wishes but in order to make sure that she would have a life of her own, she left Vienna for a prominent position in Boston, Massachusetts, in 1935. She then relinquished the leadership of the Vienna Psychoanalytic Society's Training Institute, which she had held since its inception in 1924. (Freud's daughter Anna was her successor.) Between 1924 and 1935 Helene Deutsch had had to assess all those who came to Vienna for instruction in analysis.

Whatever she felt to be her personal inadequacies, she knew that she had succeeded in becoming a notable teacher. In addition to her role on international training committees and her reputation as a lecturer, she was much sought after both as a training analyst and a supervisor. Her seminars were remarkable experiences for students, and her classes have been remembered as spectacles. She trained a host of psychiatrists and social scientists, since her students included the next generation of leading analysts. It may be hard to convey any senior teacher's accomplishments, but in Vienna the following taught under her: August Aichhorn, Siegfried Bernfeld, Edward Bibring, Ruth Mack Brunswick, Anna Freud, Heinz Hartmann, Wilhelm Hoffer, Ludwig Jekels, Robert Jokl, Herman Nunberg, Wilhelm Reich, Theodor Reik, Richard and Edith Sterba, and Robert Waelder. In choosing Boston she found such a medical stronghold that her pupils there were a large enough group for her to have made an impact on the development of American psychiatry.

In 1978, when authorizing an account of her life, Helene Deutsch unrestrictively made available to me all her personal papers and letters. These documents will hereafter be deposited for others at the Schlesinger Library for the History of Women in America at Radcliffe College, Cambridge, Massachusetts. Although Freud regretted having told the public so much about himself and advised others against his example, Helene Deutsch had ignored his warning and in 1973 published her own autobiography.[4] She added a separate historiographic dimension by allowing herself to be interviewed by me about her life and work for hundreds of hours. Her family and students cooperated in this project as well. Her clinical papers are also personally revealing (she was immensely cultured and composed with a sense of artistic form).

At one point, in her enthusiasm for our work together, when she was going to her farm for a weekend, she gave me the key to her house. I then found her Polish lover's letters to her. She was excited to go over this material with me, and she was pleased by all the documents I could turn up. She had kept this Polish correspondence in a separate container, at times had read it over, and knew passages by heart. By 1978 she had convinced herself that the Polish letters were long gone. She told me, after her husband had died in 1964 and when I was interviewing her then for research on Freud and the psychoanalytic movement,[5] that she was determined to destroy these letters from a married man. Had she realized she still had these letters, she could have at least used one of his photographs, which were mixed in with the written material she had kept, in her autobiography.

The failure to obliterate historical evidence is a sign of security, in that she more than half-consciously felt able to withstand the closest scrutiny. This affair of hers, with all its pain as well as satisfactions, appears to have been the great love of her life. Had the relationship worked out, her whole life would have been different; probably many have had such precious experiences, although few have been so extensively documented. After discussing with me the contents of these letters, she needed them more than ever; she wanted me to return them to her, although she knew I had made copies; I did so, but before she died—at the age of ninety-seven—she destroyed the originals.

Out of these multiple sources it is now possible to attempt to reconstruct an intimate record of the life of this outstanding woman, a giant in the history of psychoanalysis. But a human being remains mysterious and an enigma, even with the help of the existence of thousands of written private documents. Each kind of self-disclosure has its own way of being misleading, and therefore anyone real will prove elusive and surprising. Only after completing this book did I realize how unlike Freud's views on women were her own.

PART I

Poland

"In general she sees so terribly many faults in me, and she says I'm the most dreadful creature that has ever walked God's earth . . . I have to pull myself together not to hate her."

"Mädi Fournier" about her mother

"They say he acts without feeling, but it's *they* who have no feeling, they have technique, i.e., formal ways of behavior that do not come from their heart and are assumed and artificial—that's something to which I'm terribly opposed."

"Mädi Fournier" on the Viennese actor Josef Kainz

"Haven't you ever heard quiet, mysterious murmurs, almost like cries in the air, or when you are alone in a room, can't you hear a plaintive palpitation of something like a half-dead bird, or can't you hear faint blows against your window? Suddenly in the midst of the night can't you hear something rustling or sighing and beating very, very quietly, as if it were pacing through the room, looking for something, do you hear that Madam? That is my soul searching shelter from life's icy wind."

Herman Lieberman to Helene Deutsch

1

"The Center of the Earth"

Few countries have known as tragic a history as Poland's. At the time of Helene Deutsch's birth, on October 9, 1884, Poland was in one of its saddest centuries. For almost a thousand years Poland had played an important role in European history, and it had developed a rich cultural life. At the end of the eighteenth century, however, it ceased to exist as an independent political entity; its territory was partitioned into thirds by Russia, Prussia, and the Austro-Hungarian Empire. Especially during the first half of the nineteenth century military insurrections were bloodily put down. Even the Polish language was threatened. For long periods Polish schools were not permitted to exist, as the alien conquerors—Russians, Germans, and Austrians—imposed their own conceptions of civilization.

This national martyrdom was, however, accompanied by the greatest outburst of artistic creativity in Polish history. The music of Frédéric Chopin, Helene Deutsch's favorite composer as a girl, she later said, expressed the nation's suffering and exultant hopes. Poland had long endured the shifting of its territorial lines, but the political devastation of the Partitions awakened a burning ideal of patriotic liberation. National pride became a central poetic theme. Poland's mutilation made defiance glorious, and military bravery a commonplace in historical celebration. Although Poland was no longer a nation-state, Polish cultural life achieved new heights of originality and brilliance.

Poles resisted being absorbed into the lives of their conquerors, and dreamed of future national resurrection. For a time the France of Napoleon Bonaparte had held out the possibility of emancipation. Throughout the nineteenth and early twentieth centuries Paris became the haven for Polish émigrés. As Poland's national anthem, composed during the Napoleonic era's hope of freedom, proclaimed:

> Poland is still living
> While we are alive.

Without the normal organization of political independence, Poland's cultural life became the essence of national existence.

Being raised in such a setting left an indelible imprint on Helene Deutsch. She grew up in progressive Austrian Poland, which was enlightened compared to the German and Russian sections; yet the contrast between her oppressed native land of Poland and the relatively benign Austrian Empire of Franz Joseph was appalling. Poland had been partially conquered by the unwarlike, indeed happy-go-lucky, Hapsburgs. But the threat of Germanization still existed; Helene's mother spoke German at home, but the children, out of allegiance to what was to them an invaded country, preferred Polish. Poland retained its symbolic meaning for Helene: whenever in later life she had anxiety dreams they involved a particular policeman from her native town; as a youth she had marched in political protest and the local police would call her father to complain, but they never arrested her. In extreme old age, over seventy years after she had left Poland, she reported that she dreamed in Polish.

She liked to repeat an anecdote about how nationalistic the Poles could be. Eugenia Sokolnicka, another Polish analyst and the first person to practice psychoanalysis in France, was also analyzed by Freud; her husband once woke her up in the middle of the night to ask, "Will Poland ever be free?" She reassured him, until he awakened with another question: "Why do you say 'Yes'?" It would be impossible to overemphasize the loyalist Polish aspect to Helene Deutsch's own character.

Przemyśl (pronounced Chemish), where she was born, was an old fortress town near the Carpathian Mountains; it was founded in the seventh century. On the hillside were the picturesque ruins of a partially preserved castle dating from the fourteenth century. The fort had been badly damaged by the Turks in the seventeenth century; to Helene Deutsch the remains were a reminder of "the glorious time of the Sobieskis and their victories over the Turks." In her day the old fortress grounds were transformed into a fine, vast park (the *Schlossberg)* with extensive walks. As she remembered it at the age of eighty-nine:

> I did not spend many years in Przemyśl in relation to the rest of my life, but it remains for me the center of the earth. To this day I recall every smallest corner of the *Schlossberg* . . . , especially the little hidden benches, which are probably still there, providing the same refuge for lovers that they did in my time. And I remember the surrounding hills and slopes; I wandered there hour after hour. It was an easy walk from our house in the center of

town; either of two roads would take me, past various churches, to the *Schlossberg* in less than half an hour.[1]

Below the town the river San flowed, and during summers Helene rowed and swam long distances there. In wintertime Przemyśl had a lot of snow; when the San froze in November it stayed that way until May. Even before she went to school Helene skated every season. In later years, though she had a personal distaste for the analyst Ernest Jones, Freud's official biographer, she admired him for his breadth in having written a book about skating.

> I have travelled much since then, and experienced with rapture many of the world's wonders, but have never lost my true love for the beauty of my home town. Were the sunsets over the *Schlossberg* hill as fiery red as I remember them? Was the full moon over the San quite as strange and ghostly?[2]

The white world of winter was as memorable as the other times of year; the glow of the different seasons added to the romance of history. Przemyśl remained the time of her youth, a lost paradise, the most beautiful place in the world.

Przemyśl had its many churches, including a fifteenth-century cathedral, and Poland's Roman Catholic Church had traditionally stood for national autonomy. But in her autobiographical reminiscences Helene Deutsch still resented the way, on the death of small children, often a priest would be "congratulating himself that his pious teaching was bearing such goodly fruit."

> I often saw that same priest on the streets, on his way to administer extreme unction to a dying soul. These encounters, so frequent that they should have become a matter of indifference to me, never failed to move me. The sight has lasted in my memory all my life: the priest in his white lace surplice holding before him the viaticum, followed by a hunch-backed altar boy carrying the censer and a shrill little bell, which he shook constantly to remind the faithful to kneel down . . . I alone, the Jew, would remain standing in solemn silence. I felt marked by a stigma, and full of shame. I did not belong.[3]

Jews made up approximately 10 percent of Poland's population, but Polish anti-Semitism was an age-old part of Central European history. Only two synagogues existed in Przemyśl—one for the well-to-do, and the other for the poor. The Rosenbachs, Helene's family, were firmly established and belonged to the former. Her father's family was part of the assimilated intelligentsia. For a Jew to try to share in Polish culture in the late nineteenth century was perfectly self-respecting; it was both tempting and patriotic for one oppressed people to sympathize with another. Oddly enough, to the world outside Poland its Jews became the leading representatives of the national culture, since it was they who were forced to wander to different countries.

The building ("the Gizowski place") in which the Rosenbachs had their apartment was, Helene Deutsch reported, "a microcosm of the Polish-Jewish society of Przemyśl at that time. It was also quite interesting architecturally. In its center was a large courtyard and the three floors went up around it, containing tenants of widely differing social status."

> Standing in the heart of the town, on the *Ringplatz,* the house was separated from the regular traffic by a tiny public garden. Our balcony, in the front, was a box seat where we could observe the flow of the town's life rushing by. Sitting there at twilight we could spy on the love life of maids and soldiers, high-school boys and girls, and sometimes the sinful carrying-on of respectable married men. We could also see from there which tenant was late coming home at night. Sometimes a straggler had to wait outside a long time before the old caretaker, aroused from deep sleep by the doorbell, would appear in his grimy underwear.[4]

Helene was on good terms with this caretaker, who, she wrote, "had learned tolerance: he was a devout Catholic but had two daughters who were full-time prostitutes." If Helene Deutsch had not written about her childhood family, it would be impossible imaginatively to re-create such a background.

As she reported it, early on her father became an inspiration to her. Wilhelm Rosenbach was short in stature, and wore a beard and a closely cropped head of hair; by the time of Helene's birth he had become a prominent lawyer whose services were widely sought. The law was learned not from taking courses and passing examinations, but rather through the on-the-spot study of books and the example of older practitioners. Helene Deutsch said her father was a great reader, although of course most of the law was unwritten; he had to acquaint himself with the required practices and conventions. He was especially well known as a scholar in international law, and for a time represented Galicia before a federal court in Vienna. (His father had also been a lawyer, but as a Jew unable to represent clients in court; when this ruling was rescinded, Wilhelm became the first Jewish lawyer in Galicia to be present in court.)

Helene's father had two places to see clients, one at home and the other at a formal office. His work was central to him: the bathroom in the Rosenbach apartment was situated so that clients could make use of it, which meant that it was rather inconvenient for the family. Wilhelm had a boy to run errands for him, and like others of that generation could never adjust to the use of the telephone. He took Helene with him to court sometimes, and she remembered particular cases for the rest of her life.[5] At his office she often sat in a chair under his desk. Helene at first thought of becoming a lawyer (Freud had shared a similar early ambition himself), but in Vienna the study of law excluded women longer than medicine. Psychiatry turned out to be a suitable compromise for her; on the one hand she would be dealing with concrete cases, like her revered father, and at the same time there was always a human dimension to be taken into account. In one instance, for example, when she was twelve or thirteen years old, she heard the testimony of a hysterical woman; even as a young girl it seemed to Helene that the woman must have had her reasons for being in such a state, which would explain why she could tell such stories.

Although in early adulthood Helene had some difficulties with her father, and even broke with him for a time, she said that even as a child she had modeled herself on him. Nowadays, when women are so much more accustomed to working, it should be less necessary for a young girl to identify with her father in order to have the psychological basis for fulfilling career talents. One of the conclusions Freud came to as a result of Helene's analysis with him was that her tie to her father was the strongest source of her abilities; he did not challenge her bond to Wilhelm as a neurotically "masculine" side to her. Years later, when Helene was an analyst, a rich patient angrily turned on her to say: "Who are you—your father probably was a peddler!" Helene then literally experienced her first heart pain—a patient might accuse her of being a prostitute, but her father remained sacred to her.

Wilhelm had been a poor boy, who waited until he could support a wife and family before he married. His wife, Regina, was nine or ten years younger than he, and in keeping with her times and culture she never sought any profession of her own. Busy with his legal practice, Helene's father was, in her view, too afraid of his wife. He might seem to Helene an important local figure, learned as well as kind, but in his relation to his wife Helene saw him as weak, definitely not a strong man. For the rest of her life Helene retained an unshakable conviction that she had experienced an "oedipal" childhood, consisting in hatred for her mother and love for her father. She could not see any divided feelings or ambivalence in her own experience.

It is curious how children who strongly prefer one parent to the other manage to explain and rationalize the basis of the marital union. Divorce was, to be sure, incomparably rarer then than now. What could such an even-tempered, smiling-faced man—according to Helene—have seen in his wife? Regina was good-looking and her strength meant that her husband remained passive at home; he could not do things of a practical nature, and therefore his wife was the master of the family situation. If Helene ever acknowledged reproachful thoughts about her father it was that he was too obedient to her mother; he loved his wife, wanted peace at home, and therefore remained firmly bound in his marriage.

The central problem of Helene Deutsch's early life, as she later recalled it, focused around the character of her mother, whom she wholeheartedly despised. If we are to accept Helene's version, her own mother was almost unimaginably bad: Regina hated Helene, her youngest child and Wilhelm's favorite, beat her and her siblings when in a bad mood as well as for punishment, and opposed Helene's seeking a higher education. Helene's specific torture had its origins, she thought, in her mother's disappointment in not having borne another son; Helene's brother was unpromising, there already were two girls, so Helene's birth (when Regina was thirty) amounted to a final unbearable frustration.

Regina Fass Rosenbach was strong-minded, distinguished, and socially proud. (Her birthday on August 18 was the same as the Emperor's, so the illuminations in honor of Franz Joseph—witnessed on holiday in Austria— had an added meaning within Helene's family.) Although in Helene's autobiography she traced her mother's status-seeking to the onus of knowing that her own mother had abandoned her family for the sake of another man, Helene could never forgive her conformism. A big, stout woman who nonetheless managed to dress elegantly thanks to her Viennese dressmaker, Regina had an ambition to be invited to the homes of the Polish aristocracy, which was not difficult, since her husband was the lawyer of the local nobles. Regina was such a snob that Helene claimed she once refused to read a novel about the peasantry (who were also clients of her husband) which later won a Nobel Prize for its Polish author, Wladislaw Reymont. Helene resented her mother's cultural insecurity, even though it may have been due to feelings of inferiority; furthermore, the relatives on her side of the family were altogether too money-minded to suit Helene.

Helene said the household of her childhood was dominated by a central concern for social propriety. Regina was an autocrat, and everything in her home had to be perfect. A servant regularly wore foot-brushes on his bare feet to keep the floors mirrorlike. So highly waxed were the floors that once, while Helene was taking a piano lesson, her mother slipped and fell; because of her size it was difficult to lift her up, and Helene succumbed to convulsive laughter at the scene. Although she professed to have been mortified at her uncontrollable laughter, her piano teacher took this occasion to refuse to continue with her lessons; he said he did not want to teach such an unsympathetic daughter.

While Helene adored her father, she hated almost everything about her mother. Freud's concept of the Oedipus complex would later help her understand these feelings, although she considered them objectively justifiable. In politics and religion her father was, from Helene's point of view, at least a patriot; without being especially active he emphasized his nationalism. As a Jew he was more or less indifferent, whereas her mother hypocritically went once a year to the synagogue. (Regina's own father was a particular object of Helene's contempt; his clothing and hairstyle were fainthearted compromises with traditional Jewish custom—he wanted to pass as a modern Jew without daring to abandon openly the safety of religious orthodoxy.) It seemed to Helene that Regina attended services partly to learn the latest gossip, and as a young girl she worried what she might hear; Helene was, for instance, fearful there might be untrue stories about herself and local boys. Her father, although sometimes exasperated by his unruly but talented daughter, remained trusting and a source of support to her.

It was common in that era, and in such a family, for the wife to be a matriarch within the home. A moderately well-to-do lawyer could afford six in help. Servants had to carry water, and there were giant stoves to be lit; *kachedofen* were heating ovens built between bedrooms, and the fires were fed from one end but gave off heat on both sides. In an interview Helene declared she had functioned as the "human bell" for her mother: Regina slapped her, for instance, to get her to the kitchen to tell them to clear the table. Servants were inexpensive and lower class, and Helene's mother would not allow her to learn how to cook. (Helene successfully defied her mother in other endeavors.) It was supposedly beneath a middle-class woman's dignity to be in the kitchen, and the cook also was not pleased to have children around.

It is impossible to know exactly how Helene might actively have irritated her mother; from earliest childhood she must have frustrated her at every turn. As Helene remembered it her very existence was a provocation to her mother. Regina would call for "Hala," Helene's Polish diminutive, but she often refused to come; she liked to play outdoors, and relished hiding. Frequently she stayed away at the cozy home of a surrogate mother, a woman in town who had an illegitimate child; this woman whitened her face with makeup, and was known as "the Pale Countess." The woman's story, which Helene unearthed as a youngster,[6] was of her romantic renunciation of her high-born lover for the sake of the advancement of his career. "The Countess" was very good with her daughter, as well as with Helene and others; she told fortunes with cards, played games, and in the evenings would buy treats.

It is difficult to believe that anyone could have as unequivocally negative feelings for her mother as Helene Deutsch would have us accept.* Only on the rarest occasion could she admit yearning for her mother's love. Instead of traces of affection for her mother Helene remembered being terribly afraid of her. Freud taught that fear and desire go together, and therefore on abstract theoretical grounds there might be reason for thinking that, in addition to her dread, Helene might also have craved for tenderness from her mother. But she steadfastly acknowledged only an unambivalently hostile relationship to her mother. Helene even held that her "devaluation" of her mother had such reality to it that ultimately it made it easier for her to identify with the problems of other women, as they struggled with difficulties in their relations with their own mothers.

The benevolent maternal presence of Helene's older sister, Malvina, made endurable, Helene thought, her unmitigated hatred for their mother. When, for instance, Regina beat Helene with her hand, Malvina was there to

---

* Variations on her feelings are not that uncommon; the anthropologist Ruth Benedict maintained: "I did not love my mother . . ." In 1970 Helene wrote about the extreme example of the socialist revolutionary Angelica Balabanoff.[7]

caution "not on the head," since that might do real damage. Helene later believed that her identification with Malvina had saved her femininity.

Malvina was eleven and Gizela six when Helene was born. The brother, Emil, came between Malvina and Gizela and was almost ten years Helene's senior. There was such an age difference between herself and these three siblings that Helene felt, and evidently was treated, like an only child. Although Helene had many different nurses, Malvina performed various maternal tasks; she was, for instance, in charge of toilet training, and Helene's own childish name for her—"Lincia"—was a sign of their special intimacy.

Helene was to be the only one of the children to have a successful career. Malvina, a painter, also sculpted, and Gizela was musical, but neither of them broke with the expectation that a woman's place was solely in the home. Both sisters married early. Malvina's first romance, with a Gentile, was considered unacceptable by her mother's father, and she eventually—when Helene was ten—found a more "appropriate" husband, a handsome lawyer, Jacob Uiberall. Like others of that time Uiberall was despotic in his belief that women must serve men. The couple moved to Stryj, a small town halfway between Craców and Przemyśl; Malvina ultimately bore four children. She was widowed in 1920 and left in financial difficulties. Although her whole family helped in every way they could, three of her children were to predecease her; she had a terribly hard life.

Malvina was an exceptionally generous and noble person, but she suffered from a neurotic horror of dirt. She had always been puritanical. She obsessively washed her hands, blowing on her fingertips to clean them. At the end of World War I she suffered the tragic loss of her firstborn, a son she especially cherished; he had been slightly wounded at the close of the fighting and succumbed to tetanus. (Just before the war a small child of hers had died.) Malvina suffered a breakdown and was chronically ill thereafter.† Helene said Malvina recovered enough to run a school for local boys, so they would not have to be sent away from home. Like others who have known insanity in their families, Helene later concluded that her sister's illness had been a source of strength to her. Witnessing the worst that can emotionally happen to someone loved liberates some people from undue fears of the full range of human emotions.

While Helene had worshiped her oldest sister, who shared some of the identical conflicts with their mother that she herself experienced, Gizela was too accommodating to win Helene's unqualified admiration. Regina Rosenbach expected a daughter to be married by the age of twenty; when Helene was fourteen, Gizela married a doctor in Przemyśl, Michael Oller. A photograph for the wedding was taken of Helene in a new hat with mountain flowers (edelweiss) in it. Malvina had her children quickly, but Gizela remained childless until after Helene left Przemyśl in 1907. Helene described

† In 1937 Helene used elements of her initial reaction to Malvina's illness in a clinical paper.[5]

Gizela as an unusually sweet person, who seldom went out, altogether less well defended against her strong-willed mother than her older sister. Yet Malvina, hardly a passive personality, was so submissive to her parents that in Vienna once she was unable to sleep at night because she had committed a form of family treason: she had attended an opera with Helene and a married man whom she knew her mother disapproved of Helene's seeing.

Helene's brother, Emil, disappointed his father as a male heir. Emil played cards, bought and sold horses for profit, and did poorly in his schoolwork. Wilhelm Rosenbach then decided to allow his only son, who had not had a bar mitzvah, to be baptized. One could not be a Jew and become a high civil servant in the Austro-Hungarian Empire, and for Emil there was no more likely road to a promising career. He later changed both his names, becoming Henryk Rosborski, and married into the Polish nobility by wedding the daughter of a general in the Austrian Army. Helene's father was embittered that his only son abandoned the family name.

Helene felt that she never had been jealous of her brother, since her father began to regard her as a worthy successor while she was very young. She had a low opinion of Emil, and eventually the whole family lost track of his whereabouts in Europe; it is likely that he, his wife, and their son died during World War II. According to Helene he married an anti-Semitic woman and therefore avoided his relatives.

In childhood, however, Emil played no negligible role in Helene's life; he had in fact inflicted a trauma on his youngest sister through an attempted seduction. She was around four at the time. The girls in the family slept in close quarters, and they kept part of their things in their brother's room, which was next to the kitchen. (Usually one went through the kitchen to leave the apartment.) While her sisters prepared their clothes in the evening for the following day, Helene would go into Emil's room before he was up, to get a dress. The sexual incidents, as she reconstructed them later in her psychoanalysis with Freud, occurred two or three times. Freud was of course most interested in attempted incest; he had once emphasized the widespread reality of such stories of abuse. Painful as these assaults were, as a shy young girl Helene scarcely understood them. In her maturity she later connected her imaginative creativity to attempts to take flight from a childhood reality whose memory she sought to avoid.[9]

Apart from her relationships with the children in the family Helene seems to have been relatively isolated as a child. She played with other girls, but not with boys. As she remembered it she was neither very popular with local children nor particularly adept in activities that build a youngster's self-confidence. At school she did so badly at gymnastics and needlework that she was excused from having to participate in either activity. Although Helene could remember music she could not sing; nor could she learn to play the

piano, which was not only in contrast to her sisters but at odds in general
with what was expected of a Jewish girl from a good family.

Although she was raised in the midst of a traditional extended family,
Helene seems to have derived little conscious benefit from the atmosphere of
a busy household and the presence of a number of relatives. In her later years
she insisted that almost her entire psychic life had consisted solely of her
involvement with her father. One aunt, Frania, did encourage her to be an
intellectual and writer; she came from a poor but intelligent family and was a
distant relative of Joseph Conrad's. (Frania survived the Holocaust and died
in Israel at the age of 104.) Another aunt had read a great deal of
Schopenhauer's work. The rise of the "nuclear" family, in which father and
mother are exclusively responsible for the rearing of children, has often
meant an emotional impoverishment for everyone concerned; aunts, uncles,
and cousins (as well as servants) are not readily available as intimates and
models for the children, nor as allies and intermediaries for the adults. Large
families, moreover, are apt to necessitate the growth of manipulative skills.

Helene Deutsch took Old World family ties so for granted that she did
not think they had on the whole especially enriched her life; perhaps nostalgia
helps account for what is claimed today about the benefits of extended families. Two unmarried uncles in Vienna, on her mother's side, were positively
objectionable to her (actually they were her mother's nephews, but Helene
was so young that she called them uncles); they were engineers, and although
their profession was an unusual one for Jews, their preoccupations seemed
ridiculous to her. They would crudely tease her about the availability of
certain good-looking, marriageable officers. Part of the estrangement came
about because they knew little Polish and spoke in the Viennese German
dialect; as a patriotic Pole she could not accept them and grew up thinking
their language was a joke. Patriotism became a family substitute, as she
sought for the freedom and recognition of a downtrodden people. Feeling
herself the victim of her despotic mother's rule at home, Helene was naturally
inclined to sympathize with oppressed Poland's battle for nationhood.

Most people are apt to cherish certain myths about the past, and at
different stages of life often emphasize some recollections more than others.
Yet Helene thought of herself consistently as a Cinderella child. She did her
best to obliterate any part her mother might have played in her upbringing,
although the fact that she chose a fairy-tale image of innocence might imply
that she knew that her account of her childhood was partly fantasy. To
herself she remained, however, her father's chosen child; and this romance
between them started, in her view, in her earliest years.

If Wilhelm was to Helene the embodiment of the ideal parent, she in
turn was to him the perfect offspring. Intellectually she was so bright that in
their circle in Przemyśl people called her the "old Rosenbach," a chip off the
old block; she was not only his most beautiful daughter but bright enough to

be his son and heir as well. In her years as a psychoanalyst Helene's clinical writings were also a disguised form of autobiography; Freud too concealed self-revelations, even in what purport to be reminiscences of a patient. Helene once mentioned the type of father who wants

> the daughter to replace the son he never had or who was a failure, and to inherit his spiritual values . . . Interestingly enough, such a relation very often obtains with the third daughter, especially if she is also the youngest. It is as though the father's relation to the daughter has got rid of its dangers and freed itself from the fear of incest with the two older daughters. The third one—Cinderella—seems to be particularly suitable for the father's love choice because of her helplessness and apparent innocuousness. The need to save the little daughter from the aggressions of the mother and older sisters certainly plays a great part here.[10]

(At the time Helene wrote these words, she had also witnessed Freud's own relation to his third and youngest daughter, Anna.)

According to Helene, her mother was pathologically jealous, resented Wilhelm's affection for his youngest child, and accused her husband of unfaithfulness with other women. To Helene her father was so perfect that it never entered her head that he might in truth have been something of a ladies' man. He did have to travel a lot for his work, as his clients were widely scattered. In extreme old age she admitted there might actually have been something in her mother's accusations of infidelity. But Helene would never concede that any sexual frustrations might have played a role in Regina's general bad humor.

On occasion Wilhelm would take his youngest daughter with him on a trip, and she cherished the memories of those special periods of intimacy. She felt that he took her with him partly to protect her from her mother's beatings; she, on her side, thought she could save him from her mother's jealousy. Helene's own competitive feelings were mainly directed at her father's affection for her sisters. On one occasion that she bitterly recalled, the whole family had gone on a trip to Switzerland without her; she was still a little girl and would have been a nuisance to the rest of them on their trip. So she was temporarily left at a kind of boarding school/pension. Her father brought her back a very special doll. Although Helene first accepted and loved the doll as her child, she started to hate it; she thought her father had loved her sisters more than her, and out of resentment she broke the doll's feet and legs.

The intimacy between her two sisters reinforced Helene's conception of herself as a Cinderella, and they in turn must have been jealous of their youngest sibling's special status in the eyes of their father. Malvina had once teased her that if she were naughty a terrible, dirty peasant would come and take her away in a bag—just as he had once brought her in the first place. Later in her own analysis with Freud, Helene tried to explain why as a small child she had believed that she was the daughter of this uncouth man she had often seen in her father's office; just because of her idealization of her father she had needed, so she reasoned, to devalue him, and to isolate the coarser aspects of life in the figure of this surrogate father. ("Family romance" fantasies, which more usually raise imagined parents to higher social status, are the more likely in large families with servants; contemporary children, with parents who actively share in child-rearing, are less likely to need such fantasied substitutes for real warmth and love.) In the Poland of that era peasants, like Jews, were often scapegoats, and Helene thought of herself, like her father, as a victim of Regina's tyranny.

All the early psychoanalysts, like other writers (including experimental psychologists) relied on their own introspection for their clinical papers. At the time of her sister's "casual jest" about the peasant "the patient ardently worshipped her father. It was even then a tender, sublimated alliance in which she persisted all her life. She consciously formed her ego ideal after the model of her highly esteemed father, who at that time and later was equal to all her demands."[11] Malvina's "jocular remark" had the paradoxical effect of making Helene love her father all the more; it was as if even so, in spite of her true parentage, her father had thought enough of her to buy her.

By the time she was fourteen, Helene had found the way to initiate her revenge against her mother, denying her any hope for family respectability: Helene began a relationship with Herman Lieberman, a married man in Przemyśl. To Helene this intimacy was a triumph over her mother, for she could use it to get even and strike fear into Regina. To a superconventional mother such a tie was immoral and a shame to the whole family. Regina chose to ignore how Helene suffered in this involvement, unconcerned about the emotional conflicts within her youngest child; Helene felt that only appearances were important to her mother—how it might look to the rest of the small town. Regina was furious at Helene's behavior. She used to sit on the front balcony, and once helplessly watched her daughter rush off to a rendezvous by the San; it was after work and Helene was running.

Just because there is such abundant evidence of Helene's conscious hatred of her mother, one cannot help wondering whether Helene did not also loathe Regina for not having put a stop to the irregular liaison with Lieberman. To be sure, Helene's mother had allied with Lieberman's wife, and they could share their resentment of Helene. For an intelligent woman, Regina did not handle the matter too cleverly. Yet Helene may somehow have taken her mother's ultimate failure to break things up between her and her eventual lover as a final form of rejection. For Helene, much as she resented her mother's attempts to interfere, was also capable of thinking that if Regina had really loved her, she would have succeeded.

In keeping with her early expectations, her father was reluctant to interfere with her romance with Herman Lieberman. Wilhelm was tolerant of her unusual relationship with a much older man. Not only did he appreciate

Helene's difficulties in finding someone appropriately interesting in as provincial a place as Przemyśl, but he had respect for Lieberman as another man learned in the law. Politically Helene's father was more conservative than Lieberman, but Wilhelm did not care what people might think or say about the relationship of his favorite daughter to this prominent man. Helene might have resented her father's passivity in his marriage, but however much he seemed to be dominated by Regina, on the crucial question of the affair of Helene's heart, he was able to think for himself.

Wilhelm Rosenbach obviously had his faults, even if Helene remained reluctant ever to admit it. He had been generous about money matters with her, and in Przemyśl she could always have what she wanted from him without specifically telling him why she needed it; but toward the end of his life he mismanaged his finances and lost many of his assets. Troubling to Helene as a young girl, however, and perhaps in keeping with his later lack of financial restraint, was his drinking. When she was reminded of an illustration in one of her clinical papers that was unmistakably Wilhelm,[12] she would only admit that he drank a little too much, and thereby suffered in her esteem. And even so she blamed his drinking on her mother's tyranny.

According to Helene her father stayed away from hard liquor, but always kept a bottle of expensive wine in his safe. Such a storage space sounds secretive and would encourage the consumption, by her father and/or his clients, of a whole bottle of ordinary wine. In Jewish families drinking was relatively rare; Helene herself as an adult did not drink at all, a sign, according to some psychoanalytic reasoning, of a "latent drinker." If she did not drink herself, it might also be a way of offering a therapeutic example to her father; in a way he was her first patient. An abstainer like Helene might overestimate somebody else's consumption of alcohol; she thought that her brother-in-law Michael also drank secretly. But Wilhelm's motivation, as Helene saw it, was self-protection; if he drank from time to time (as opposed to the alcoholism she mentions in her clinical paper) it was out of depression, and ultimately her mother's fault.

In connection with her affair with Lieberman it is possible to question her father's judgment. Her mother's expectation that things would end badly between her daughter and a married man proved correct. Why did Helene's father sanction such a tie? Wilhelm might, for example, have sent her away from Przemyśl in order to end it all. It sounds self-indulgent of Wilhelm to have said, "Whom should she love here if not this man?" Ideally a parent's love entails self-sacrifice. Helene's father could not bring himself to lose his precious child; he needed too much to keep her a little girl, to fulfill the gratification of his own vanity. Yet if he was too infatuated with her to do what was in her own best interests, she would have been the last to notice.

Helene's father died in 1919 after his return to Przemyśl from Vienna at the end of World War I. While in court Wilhelm had a sudden fatal heart attack. Smoking has been found to be a contributory factor in such seizures;

for years Wilhelm had relieved his tensions by smoking small cigars. Helene was grief-stricken, but between his ill health in the last years of his life and her own concern for her career, they had grown distant; as she recalled it, her mother was too reserved to show much grief. The estrangement between Wilhelm and Helene that began in her youth was never ended. Although she remembered receiving plenty of letters from him, none has survived; one postcard of Wilhelm's exists, and that was addressed to Helene's husband Felix. Helene could be a great letter saver, but there is only one extant letter from her sister Gizela, and none from Malvina. Helene's alienation from her natural family helps explain not only her later need for Freud's circle, but her reluctance ever to risk breaking with this substitute home, an ideal family with its own orthodoxy.

Regina's later years were spent as a lonely old lady living in a large apartment with a single servant. She never soiled her hands with work; she was a great reader of fiction. One of her adolescent grandsons, a child of Gizela's, visited her at least once a week and exchanged her books at the lending library; she read in Polish, French, and German, and left the choice to her helpful grandchild. He brought her Schnitzler, Thomas Mann, Pierre Loti, and Gabryela Zapolska. She had evidently mellowed with age. On the few occasions when Helene visited Przemyśl, with or without her husband, she stayed with her mother, outwardly reconciled.

Regina's own death took place in 1941, but the exact circumstances could never be guessed at from Helene's autobiography or reminiscences. After the invasion of Poland by the Nazis, the Jews were to be evacuated from all the towns; this transfer of population was to start with the old people. Helene's mother was eighty-six and wanted to avoid being expelled from her native town under brutal and barbarous conditions that she had no hope of surviving. Together with a few other old ladies, Regina approached sympathetic doctors to get some lethal injections (her son-in-law, Gizela's husband, was a physician); after deliberating, the local doctors cooperated.

The decimation of Polish Jewry had its effects on the rest of Helene's family. Malvina spent the war in Lublin, living with her daughter and Gentile son-in-law; Malvina finally died in Przemyśl in 1950. Her surviving son had escaped to Warsaw in 1940; earlier he had studied medicine at Craców University and then, before returning to a successful career in Przemyśl, did post-graduate work in dentistry for two years in Vienna with the financial help of Helene. At the beginning of World War II he worked as a dental mechanic in a public hospital under false Aryan papers, until he was fatally denounced by a Jewish co-worker who was cooperating with the Gestapo. Malvina's daughter lived on in Poland until she died in 1981.

During the war Gizela's daughter got her parents out of the ghetto in Przemyśl, and with the help of the Polish underground they managed to get to Warsaw; it was easier to hide in a big city than in any of the towns. Gizela and her husband managed during the war with the help of Aryan birth certificates they bought, but not without having to hide in dramatic circumstances. Their oldest son was killed in 1941 by Ukrainians in the pay of the Germans; another son was a prisoner in Russia, worked as a doctor in labor camps, and then finally settled in England; their daughter moved to Australia, where Gizela herself went in 1952; she died two years later. (Gizela and her husband had been evacuated from Warsaw in 1944 after the collapse of the Polish uprising; they were sheltered in a small country place, where the husband died and was buried as a Catholic in a local cemetery.)

Safe in America throughout these terrible times, Helene was both horrified and guilt-ridden, though helpless, as she watched from afar the destruction of the European civilization she had known. North Americans could understand little of the painful moral dilemmas that touched all those who came from the Old World. Before the war and afterward she helped individual members of her family, both her sisters and their children, with money and parcels. She and her husband might have regarded her brother as a good-for-nothing swindler, but before he, his wife, and his child disappeared without a trace, she was able to respond to an appeal from him for assistance by wiring funds.

In the face of all these dreadful events, it would not be surprising if Helene was relatively disinclined to know all the details of the tragic story of her family, or to re-experience the emotional pains of loss. By the outbreak of World War II she had succeeded in building up a new life of her own, and however much she believed in the power of the past, she did not allow it to undermine her enduringly youthful optimism about the future.

2

Diary of an Adolescent Double

As a young girl Helene Deutsch composed an extensive fictionalized journal. Diary-keeping is in itself hardly exceptional; many adolescents have found consolation in recording their most private thoughts, as they safely express secret wishes and feelings in the security of the written word. Youngsters can feel isolated and therefore greatly desire intimate relationships, even if they have to be in the realm of fantasy. A diary, unlike a real-life friend, does not impose demands of reciprocal understanding. Helene Deutsch, however, kept not a straightforward diary but a novelistic, book-length manuscript of almost sixty thousand words.

Two other pioneer female analysts, Karen Horney (1885–1952) and Hermine von Hug-Hellmuth (1871–1924), also kept accounts of their early years.[1] (They also were both Gentiles, which is striking in a movement that attracted a disproportionate number of Jews.) Karen Horney became a famous revisionist Freudian; first in Berlin, later in Chicago and in New York City, she developed her psychoanalytic concepts in a cultural, "neo-Freudian" direction. For her, adult personality was not just a result of childhood experience but also an adaptation to dominant cultural patterns. Horney's theories of femininity clashed with the more orthodox Freudian approach, which expressed itself in biological-sounding terminology. Although Helene Deutsch and Karen Horney—almost exact contemporaries—took different conceptual tacks, starting in the 1920s, they each had gone for a time to Karl Abraham in Berlin for analysis.

Karen Horney eventually established her own school of followers, whereas Helene remained within the loyalist Freudian fold. Yet both women had had turbulent youths, and in different ways struggled against their family upbringings. And each brought to psychoanalysis her experiences in a psychiatric career, during a period when it was still an unusual profession for a woman. The fact that both of them saved examples of their early writings is telling about the intensity and depth of their commitments as authors, as well as their beliefs as analysts in the importance of youthful experiences.

Although Karen Horney's diary did not appear until 1980, long after her death, Hermine von Hug-Hellmuth's *Diary of a Young Girl* was first published in 1919. Remarkably enough, especially since it was subsequently withdrawn from print in Germany as a fraud,* the book was for years available in English with a preface written by Freud. Like Helene Deutsch (but in contrast to Karen Horney, who had no personal contact with Freud) Hug-Hellmuth had been analyzed by Freud in Vienna. She was the only other woman in the Vienna Psychoanalytic Society when Helene Deutsch joined it in 1918. Hug-Hellmuth specialized in child analysis; her most notable contribution to psychoanalysis was that before her more illustrious successors, Melanie Klein and Freud's daughter Anna, she had originated play therapy as a means of communicating with young children.

The diary which Hug-Hellmuth published purported to be given to her by an unidentified person. But the book so precisely sets forth what Freud had taught about the nature of prepubertal female sexuality that it is generally agreed to have been Hug-Hellmuth's reworking of childhood reminiscences in the light of the psychoanalytic theory then fashionable. Helene Deutsch, however, said she considered Hug-Hellmuth too unimaginative to have recreated a childhood out of whole cloth, and relied on her material for illustrations when, later, she wrote *The Psychology of Women.* Earlier in Vienna her husband, Felix, had satisfactorily checked out certain dates, for example in connection with hospital admissions, in order to help rescue the diary from being treated wholly as a hoax.

Unlike Karen Horney, who became one of the leading post-Freudian theorists, Hug-Hellmuth's career was cut short, and she is remembered as one of the scandals in the history of psychoanalysis.[2] She was strangled to death in 1924 by her sister's illegitimate son, whom she had helped raise. The trial of her eighteen-year-old nephew, Rolf, received international newspaper coverage. He was convicted and imprisoned. Hug-Hellmuth's relationship to the boy seems to have been partly that of a therapist; she made "observations" on him and he provided illustrative material for her articles. After he had served his sentence, he went to the Vienna Psychoanalytic Society demanding monetary compensation as a victim of psychoanalysis. He was referred to Helene Deutsch for treatment, but since a money quarrel had preceded his crime against his aunt, Helene refused to risk stepping into Hug-Hellmuth's shoes vis-à-vis the young man.

---

* Sir Cyril Burt—later himself exposed for fraudulent evidence—had been one of the leaders in the attack.

Helene Deutsch's own diary seems to have been intended as a novel, the journal of a modern Catholic girl—"Mädi Fournier." In carefully correct handwriting, within beautiful leather binding, Helene composed the thoughts and reflections of a Viennese girl from the age of twelve until sixteen. If German was the language of the proprieties of her mother's home in Przemyśl, and if as an adolescent Helene was participating in the politics of Polish nationalism through an involvement with a married man, by entering into the life of a proper young Viennese girl Helene had imagined a means by which she could cover her wayward tracks.

Helene kept this journal in the language of the Hapsburgs, as she realistically yearned to escape from the frustrations of provincial life to the city which was the center of the sprawling empire. Although, as Mädi more than once regretfully noted, it was impossible to write down everything one thinks, this book could be a reliable, because disguised, confidant. Independent of the external world Helene had created an imaginary companion, as she found a better intimate in her writing than any friend who might disappoint her.

On January 29, 1976, when Helene was over ninety-one, in tidying up some of her papers she had glanced at her first piece of written work, saved throughout all those years and geographic moves. She left a note in English (for a future biographer?), Scotch-taped within the back of the book, written on her Cambridge, Massachusetts, stationery: "Has something to do with Burg theater? Daughter of a famous Viennese actress. Author began to write it on the occasion of her 12th birthday." The diary has entries over a four-year period, yet relatively little internal development takes place. Even though the journal is so extensive, one suspects that it was written within a narrower time frame than the dates might otherwise indicate. It is altogether too detailed, marked by sufficient changes in handwriting, for it to have been composed all at once; the drawings, newspaper clippings, and recorded historical events lend the manuscript an air of authenticity. The indications are that she worked on the book over an extended period, although Helene had succeeded at mystification precisely by means of the diary's exact chronology.

The prose with which she begins the diary, although flat and relatively inexpressive, is hardly that of a twelve-year-old. Helene dated the first entry July 26, 1900, when she herself was approaching her own sixteenth birthday. Although the writing seems almost studiedly childish, it possesses the perspective of an older child. Drinking champagne and dancing at balls, even the aspiration to live like that, reported in sentences that are grammatically correct, make one think of someone older than twelve. In Przemyśl there were occasions for dancing, and she was in reality passionately fond of it; in her "family romance" Helene may have turned her father into a peasant, but her dancing partners and associates at parties in the journal were distinctly upper class.

Helene started by setting the human scene around Mädi in Vienna in stark contrast to her own life in Przemyśl, yet some of her characteristic struggles can nonetheless be detected.

> I became twelve years old on May 17, and I think that that is quite a considerable age. My friends agree. But there are people who tell me that I am still a completely inexperienced child who knows nothing about life yet. This I must certainly agree with, as thanks to my beloved parents I have such an untroubled life. The only times I am unhappy are when I have to part from Papa or Mama for some time, and that unfortunately happens every year when Mama has to go to Franzensbad for five or six weeks. But the rest does her such a lot of good that we are always glad to see her come back so refreshed. She is there now, and I was alone with an Englishwoman for some days because Papa is away, on business. I quite like this Miss Slater, only she is more for virtue than for pleasure. In any case I want to learn a great deal from her if I can. She too thinks I'm still a small child. I talked about this recently to Rosa Bell, a friend of mine, whom I'm very fond of. We both said you're only a child if you feel yourself to be one, and I don't feel myself to be a child at all.

Helene had thought of herself as an only child (her sisters were now married, so they no longer shared accommodations); she conceived the life of a girl without siblings. In Przemyśl she was already full of conflicts with her parents, but her journal starts off describing an idyllic account of familial harmony.

Only toward the end of the diary does Helene allow animosity toward her mother, and even her father, to break through. With growing maturity, Mädi sees the shortcomings of her parents, and admits her own misery and unhappiness. In reality, when Helene's parents were away she said they had left her not with an English governess but with a French one, a Miss Deux; and Helene volunteered in an interview that her mother frequented Karlsbad, not Franzensbad. The "friend" in the journal, Rosa Bell, was fifteen and a half, exactly Helene's own age. But the diary is internally consistent as an account of what a thoroughly good young girl might find noteworthy.

In her real life in Poland, Helene was already infatuated with Lieberman; she did as she pleased, and her mother was scandalized. But in her private world of the diary she describes Mädi's apparently harmless crush on a famous Viennese actor, also a married man, in his forties; the age difference was even wider in the journal than that in reality (she was fourteen, and Lieberman twenty-eight, when the relationship between them first began). But Helene went on eventually to have an affair with Lieberman, while Mädi simply experiences the longings and agonies of youthful love.

Josef Kainz was one of the most prominent players on the turn-of-the-century Viennese stage, and a favorite of the mad King Ludwig of Bavaria. (Helene preserved a postcard from Kainz until extreme old age.) In order to make plausible that there be social contact between Helene's other self of the journal and Kainz, Mädi is made the grandchild of a famous Viennese acting couple. Helene was describing how a young girl might be infatuated by a public figure who was real to her through reports of theater performances, which resembles crushes that young women still develop, although nowadays their objects are apt to be motion-picture stars or popular singers. It is typical for young people to find schoolmates too immature, and to prefer to attach fantasies and expectations to leading people who are at one and the same time real and illusory; their emotional presence is unmistakable, thanks to the impact of their profession, yet their unattainability makes them safe as distant objects of affection and fascination. (In the Central Europe of Helene's youth military officers were also in ready supply for a young woman's fantasies.) For Mädi's diary to matter, her beloved had to be a very famous man, although in principle the same literary purpose would have been served had he been notorious rather than celebrated.

The journal fluctuates in its biographical interest. Mädi makes childlike declaration of a burning desire to improve and to delight her parents, in the midst of which she protests—"I really mean all this"—which Helene (in her mid-nineties) pointed out must reflect self-doubts. Mädi reports the pleasure that looking at Kainz's autograph every day gives her, yet is not unaware, at least at times, of how foolish her attachment to him is going to appear in the future. In Helene's 1973 autobiography she mentioned "the tradition of the great actor Kainz" at the Burgtheater, and recalled her youthful passion to be an actress; however long that typical adolescent desire lasted it reflected her ambition to make something special out of herself. (At a similar time in her life Karen Horney had also aspired to be on the stage.) Out of her self-perception and frustration Mädi writes in the diary: "I have a great deal of talent, that I know and everyone knows." She increasingly acknowledges her urgent desire for recognition.

In her praise of Kainz she was also congratulating the possibilities of achievement in her own prospective career. Wilhelm Rosenbach had been interested in theater, but playgoing was exceptional in the household, since to be in Vienna was special. Toward the end of her life Helene could recall that at the age of ten things she had written had been play-acted, and she remembered lines from a play she had authored when twelve. Mädi also writes a play. In the journal Helene's other self confides: "I should very, very much like to go on the stage myself. I really think I have talent. But there is still time for that." Acting, however, was not for her a matter of following formal rules; in a passage that foreshadows Helene's own mature attitude toward the therapist's human approach in psychoanalysis, Mädi defends Kainz's way of identifying with a role: "They say he acts without feeling, but it's *they* who have no feeling, they have technique, i.e., formal ways of behavior that do not come from their heart and are assumed and artificial—that's something to which I'm terribly opposed."

Vienna symbolized the world of freedom to Helene. Her description of

Mädi's absorption with the career of a Viennese actor reflected Helene's real-life obsession with Lieberman. Yet she frequently yearned to break that tie. As she struggled against her liaison with Lieberman it may have helped to forget one forbidden love by the invention of a similar fantasy of Mädi's prohibited involvement with Kainz. By speaking of another she could help distract herself, at the same time as it reinforced her conviction that she was a person of importance.

Helene's alter ego not only spends a good deal of time on holiday away from Vienna, but even gets to travel to Italy. As a youngster Helene must have studied books on Venice to test her capacities as a possible future writer.

> So I've really been to Venice again and I still think I'm dreaming. It was marvelous. We stayed at the Hotel Angleterre, where it was quite good. We often took the one-hour trip to the Lido and walked on the beach. The blue sea with the foaming waves, the perpetually blue Italian sky, the good air and the infinite expanse of the sea, which one can't imagine if one hasn't seen it, all these things made such a shattering impression that it would be impossible ever to forget it. And the town itself. It's so magnificent that one thinks it a miracle of nature. There are many towns, and in essentials they are all more or less alike. But Venice is an exception, it is so unique that it is utterly bewildering. The singing at night, the serenades on the Grand Canal, the feeding of the pigeons in St. Mark's Square, all those things are so original that one will see nothing like it again. We went to the Palace of the Doges; Mama had bought a book with descriptions of every picture and of the whole palace. Those marvelous rooms, and the pictures! The whole palace, like the whole town, is sublime. Only the prisons are bad dreams. They are grim and horrible, and you can see plainly where heads were put before they were cut off. There are three holes in the floor through which the blood flowed, and it was then channeled into the canal spanned by the so marvelously hewn Bridge of Sighs. That's quite dreadful, but to make up for it the upper rooms are the more splendid. There's a magnificent picture there by Titian. It represents the Doge Antonio Grimani at prayer. There are also pictures by other great and famous artists which are the most splendid one has ever seen. Also there's a lovely fountain in the courtyard of the Doges' Palace.
>
> We also went to see St. Mark's, the beauty of which cannot be described. How marvelously the floor of the whole church is inlaid.

Her use of picture books of Venice may help explain why her style here was more lively than her literary criticism of plays, by Shakespeare and Schiller for example, that she supposedly had attended in Vienna. Neither her reading of plays (Mädi also studied Schopenhauer, and Helene read Nietzsche as well), nor newspaper accounts of Viennese productions, were enough to re-create the atmosphere of theatergoing.

On rare occasions Mädi actually exchanges a few words with her beloved Kainz. She finds him capable of speaking with a "charming" Viennese accent. Mostly she attends his performances, follows his acting career, speculates about the state of his marriage, and watches for him in his carriage. She has to stop walking by his house only because her presence was once observed by his wife. Yet there is something enduringly human about the kind of childish infatuation Helene had recounted. All love involves a merging of souls, and to the extent that we become involved with another we invest that person with attributes of our own. Love is a mysterious emotion, but it often has a component of being entranced with one's own conception of the other; and this can be especially true for people of imaginative power. An adolescent crush is, to be sure, more self-involved, as well as more naïve, than what happens in later life, but not all so different as we might like to think.

The romantic attachment Helene undertook to describe omits almost all reference to sexuality. A proper young woman might suitably attend classical theater in Vienna, but ought not to go if "indecent things" were going to be read. Even Shakespeare's *Measure for Measure* was so unseemly that Mädi could not go and see it. She feels no inner conflicts about being automatically excluded from such performances.

Yet Helene allows Mädi to express traces of sexual understanding. When in a play Kainz says something in a woman's ear, Mädi notes: "I felt a little uncomfortable at this point." When she thinks about adult romantic misbehavior, Mädi thinks: "It is a man's greatest pleasure." She imagines Kainz embracing her, and reports vivid dreams of his kisses, "as distinctly as if it were real." In reality Helene, though still a virgin, was sexually knowledgeable for her age. She had first menstruated at fourteen; she already knew about it and had been impatient. (Her mother had not told Helene anything about her periods beforehand; even her sister Malvina had been too shy to discuss it.)

As the story of Helene's double, Mädi, unfolds, gradually the family picture begins to resemble that of Helene's own experience. "In general," Mädi writes of her mother, "she sees so terribly many faults in me, and she says I'm the most dreadful creature that has ever walked God's earth." Mädi's animosity toward Kainz's wife opens the way to Helene's giving a lifelike account of her own feelings for Regina Rosenbach. The external reason for Mädi's bad behavior, which is the occasion for the worst of her mother's reproaches, has to do with Mädi's attitude toward a gentleman admirer of her mother's who poses a threat to the family harmony. (In reality Helene suspected her mother of having had an affair with a Gentile associate of her father's.) Although Mädi had liked him at first, "Herr Suess" becomes a "disgusting creature," a monster who is responsible for her father's suffering. She confesses her sadness for her mother's situation, but the life of a young girl afraid of her mother begins to emerge. "I have to pull myself together in order not to hate her."

Only toward the end of the manuscript does Helene permit her disappointment in her father, a university professor in Mädi's story, to become part of the diary. (Lieberman, a father figure for Helene, was an exceptionally eloquent lecturer.) Mädi's father had kicked up a fuss and shouted over some household trifle, and she comments in an imaginary letter to Kainz:

> He, the man whom I admire (I've just had to cry so terribly, and I long so much for a look, a word, a loving act on the part of my Josef), the man whom I love and value more highly than everyone else (except you, of course), the man whom I've defended whenever I could, is as crude, as ruthless and selfish as the commonest drunk. It was for his sake that I was disloyal to my mother, formed the blackest opinions of her and had to force myself not to hate her.

Wilhelm Rosenbach's drinking must have fed Helene's family-romance fantasy about a peasant father.

As far as can be reconstructed, Helene was eighteen but describing the feelings of a fourteen-year-old; enmeshed in an unsatisfying family life, they both yearned for the fulfillment of creative work; once Helene could write about wanting to be an actress, the possibility of becoming an author seemed an alternative. Mädi knew that she lacked the literary ability properly to communicate her feelings: "empty words can't express what I feel, and that's my trouble."

Whatever happened, Mädi did not want to turn into the goose that Helene's mother seems to have expected her, too, to become.

> I'm not satisfied with myself, I must either study or go on the stage or something of the sort. I must, I must, be something different from all these silly girls. Yesterday evening I wrote an essay on "The Life History of a Dachshund." It wasn't at all bad; Papa and Mama said so too. So perhaps the muse of literature will leap into my brain, who knows?

And again, in defiance of an anticipated social role, Mädi writes:

> I shall never get married . . . Because I don't want to be like all these silly creatures, first dancing around in the world terribly stupidly, then getting married, being more or less happy, having children, etc. I feel I'm quite different; that's terribly conceited, I know, but I can't help it.

A hopeless love affair confirmed Helene's sense of detachment from conventionality. Mädi's contempt for social narrow-mindedness reflected one of the bases for Helene's whole life and career.

Mädi finds the idea of marriage repellent. A fortune-teller had predicted she would marry a man and go overseas at the age of twenty, the age by which Regina had thought a young girl ought to have found a husband. When Mädi encounters a young happily married couple, however, she is filled with remorse: "Shall I ever be with a man who means everything to me, who is my whole world, whom I love so much with all my heart and who will be my companion through life?" For Mädi, to know the joys of "normal" love

would first mean abandoning Kainz, "my beloved who possesses my heart."
Helene's relationship with Lieberman left her feeling trapped, like Mädi.

The last portion of the diary becomes transformed into letters to Kainz,
"to him who is my all, my life." As she day-dreams about him, Mädi is
convinced that he alone understands her. The language becomes more explicit and intense: "You live inside me and with me, you're my real self . . .
We press close to each other, I feel your body resting on mine, we are inter-
twined into one." Mädi feels beset by all the emotional furies of great literature, as she struggles for calm and peace. The inner chaos of her feelings can
only be appeased by creative work:

> . . . when am I happy? Only when I'm working, working is the only thing
> in the world, I can immerse myself in my books and forget the gloomy
> present, immerse myself in the ideas of a man or of a nation, try to under-
> stand why this or that step was taken or how an artist felt when he created
> some work.

One can imagine the solitary, joyous hours Helene spent on this journal.
Mädi looks for salvation through identifying with others. However miserable
she might sometimes sound, she was convinced of the splendor of human
effort: "I think the attraction of life lies in the will to search and find."

Mädi becomes so absorbed with Kainz that she creates his double, a
version of the loved one who fully reciprocates her feelings: "he's exactly like
that Herr J.K., with the sole difference that he loves me and that I can serve
him . . . He's always with me . . . we build castles in the air and laugh
and weep and are happy." If she worships this double of her imagination, she
also finds she needs the real Kainz as well. It is no wonder that Mädi stops
knowing what was true and what was untrue.

From Helene's point of view, however, Mädi's story was in itself a protection against reality. Mädi's life might be full of turmoil, but as a self-
creation of Helene's the story was free of conflict and anxiety. Mädi's sorrow,
however, was expressed in language which covered Helene's own tormented
relationship with Lieberman: "Heavens, to be young and to be able to enjoy
something, to enjoy it with all one's heart." Mädi writes to Kainz: "It's a
shame about my youth, because I was made to be happy and to enjoy things.
Don't think it's your fault . . ." Eighty years later Helene would—without
having reread her journal—echo the same words as she reflected back on her
own adolescence.

As a psychoanalyst Helene reported the "case" of a young girl undergoing a "remarkable experience" between the ages of thirteen and seventeen.

> She is an attractive girl, intelligent and of ardent temperament. She does not
> lack opportunities for amorous relations, but always avoids them with the
> greatest reserve. A high-school boy of about seventeen, rather unattractive,
> whom she knows only by sight, becomes the hero of her erotic fantasies.

These have an extremely passionate character—consuming kisses, ardent embraces, sexual ecstasies, the young girl's imagination creating everything that reality can give to a sexually mature woman. She becomes so absorbed in this fantasy that in her seclusion she leads a life full of joys and sorrows: her eyes are often swollen with tears because her lover turns out to be tyrannical, covers her with abuse, and even beats her; then, overflowing with love, he brings her flowers that actually she buys herself. She manages to get a picture of him and on it she writes a loving dedication in her own hand, distorted for the purpose. She has dates with him in forbidden places, they become secretly engaged, etc. For three years she keeps a detailed diary about all these imaginary experiences; when her lover goes away she continues her relations with him by writing him letters that she never mails, and to which she replies herself.[3]

Helene interpreted the girl's behavior in terms which nail down the incident as a version of her own autobiography; as an adolescent she was taking flight into fantasy, according to her psychoanalytic thinking, from a childhood memory of an attempted sexual seduction by an older brother.[4]

Looked at more positively, however, Helene's journal had been a temporary haven, as she created a world which no one could detect or touch. By being defiantly good she had made up an imaginary world, one which not only released her from day-to-day tensions but prepared her for her future career as an author. As she worked at Mädi's diary, she sought to replace realistic troubles with the beauty of an imaginary world.

Helene stopped Mädi's journal in November 1904, just after her own twentieth birthday. She would not fulfill her mother's expectations about making a socially acceptable marriage; in contrast she became more publicly associated with Lieberman. His political fortunes became her concern, and she also had to think more in terms of preparing herself for a career of her own. In the small town of Przemyśl they were locked into a secret bond. As they looked forward, however, to a busy future, a life in Vienna became the great solution for them both.

3

Political Activism

The passionate longings, desires, frustrations, and despairs of Mädi's diary were not concocted out of whole cloth. For throughout the period 1900–4, which are the dates in the journal, she was involved with Herman Lieberman. It is not possible to be certain when she first became enamored of him other than that he was importantly figuring in her life as early as 1898. Throughout this whole period Lieberman does not need to have been aware of the overwhelming significance he had acquired in this young woman's life. Mädi's diary ends the year Lieberman first holds elective office; he became an alderman on the Przemyśl city council in 1904. Helene increasingly shared in his political career; 1905 marked when the first general elections in Galicia were held, and then in 1907, the same year Helene chose to start medical school in Vienna, Lieberman was elected as a deputy from Poland to the parliament in Vienna.

The active love affair between Helene and Lieberman began, according to her, in 1906; she was by then twenty-two and he thirty-six. In a 1911 letter, written just after they had finally broken up, Lieberman wrote her of their seven years together. But from Helene's point of view she had put far more time into their relationship, and those years formed a disproportionately large part of her young life. Her love for Lieberman remained not only her sexual initiation and the romance of her youth, but a central turning point in her existence. Lieberman encouraged her professional ambitions, helped her undertake university studies, and on and off remained a real (as well as a fantasy) figure in her life until he died in London, England, in 1941, the Minister of Justice in the Polish Government-in-Exile.

The evidence for what was going on between these two people comes from both sides, yet it is necessarily of a different nature. Publicly Lieberman never wrote about Helene. Even in unpublished memoirs, deposited after his death in a Polish institute in London, England, he did not refer to her by name or implication. Yet over a hundred of his letters to Helene, some quite lengthy, still exist. Mail service in Europe was efficient; postal delivery within Vienna, for example, was twice daily, and one could expect a letter to reach someone on the same day. He sent his letters mostly by express and often telegraphed.

Only one short postcard from Helene to Lieberman has survived; somehow it got included among the letters of his that she saved. (Mädi's letters had had to remain unsent.) The postcard expresses a playful and mischievous spirit, in keeping with the underlying conception behind Helene's journal. Undoubtedly if Helene's letters to Lieberman still existed the aura of their commitments to each other would be far less somber. She was someone who, in all her other letters, succeeded to an unusual degree in putting her thoughts and personality into writing.

Entirely aside from the military and political upheavals in Central Europe, and Lieberman's exile from Poland in 1933, it was dangerous for him to keep Helene's letters. His wife might have come across them. Even in his autobiographical reflections, he would have been obliged to be discreet about Helene; at the time he wrote them she was a married woman. When she published her own autobiography, nine years after her husband's death, she could discuss Lieberman. The only one capable of being hurt by the revelation was her own son, and she hoped that the full story of her life might help reconcile him to the nature of her marriage.

Lieberman was born on January 3, 1870, in Drohobych, and attended public schools. According to a historian of the Polish socialist movement, as a young man of fourteen Lieberman was already converted to the cause of socialism and national independence.[1] His father was a rich paraffin and petroleum magnate, whom Helene recalled as terrible and money-grasping; Lieberman did not get on with him. Through his father's work he became aware of the existence of social exploitation. After having been thrown out of high school because of his activities at secret meetings in behalf of freedom for Poland, Lieberman graduated from high school in Stryj in 1888. Although he loved his mother, his hatred of his father meant that as a student he was going to be impoverished. For a couple of months he attended the University of Vienna, where he began to study law.

The workers' cause was an international one, and Lieberman left for Zurich, Switzerland. He was cooperating with others who were dedicated to the Polish labor movement. It is important to realize the specific socialist phase in which Lieberman was living. Karl Marx had died only in 1883, and Friedrich Engels lived on until 1895. V. I. Lenin, who was later to lead the

first socialist victory on a national level, was born the same year as Lieberman.

Lieberman spoke French well and wanted to go to Paris, the symbolic
home of Polish freedom fighters. (As late as 1924 he proposed a rendezvous
in Paris with Helene.) He had gone to Vienna in the first place partly because
he had no money; then, in Zurich, someone offered him a trip to Paris in a
cattle wagon, and in exchange for taking care of the animals he arrived in the
French capital. Whatever France might have continued to mean in the minds
of Polish revolutionaries, the country which originally proclaimed the ideals
of liberty, equality, and fraternity was now powerfully conservative. While a
student, Lieberman lived in Paris from 1889–91, associating with Polish and
Russian political immigrants; but in November 1889 he was imprisoned there
for three months by the French police because of his radicalism.

Lieberman returned to Poland in 1891 and enrolled in law at the University of Craców. In 1892 he joined the Polish social democratic party. After
getting his diploma as a doctor of laws in 1894, he was a lawyer's trainee first
in Rzeszów and then in Przemyśl (1896). He soon became a prominent criminal lawyer in Przemyśl, and politically active as well. He was one of the
founders and co-editor of *The Przemyśl Voice,* and a leader in cultural and
educational matters. Mainly, however, he was known as a lawyer willing to
defend socialists and workers in court, whether as individuals or as party
members; and he was willing to help organize demonstrations and meetings.

Helene's father was a liberal, certainly no socialist; but he too was a
lawyer, practicing in civil rather than criminal cases. He and Lieberman had,
she said, great professional respect for each other, although in deference to
Helene's mother's authority in family matters Wilhelm Rosenbach ultimately
supported his wife's determination to break up the affair. Helene's sister
Malvina had married a lawyer also, but they had moved away to Stryj. Lieberman was a political lawyer with an immense practice, yet he did not
perform his services for money; so to an idealistic young woman he might
appear not just a hero of her fantasy, but realistically a participant in the
cause of human emancipation.

Helene did not meet Lieberman by chance, but at the home of her sister
Gizela, who had recently married. In Malvina's absence Gizela, whom Regina Rosenbach especially loved, could be an alternative mother to Helene.
Compared to Lieberman's own background, Helene's was an intellectual one.
Her brother-in-law in Przemyśl, Michael Oller, was a physician who had
studied in Craców with Lieberman; as school friends they both had then been
active socialists. (In later years Helene's nephew, Edward Oller, did a caricature of Lieberman for a local paper, *The Colorful Pajama.*) Oller's medical
field was dermatology, and Lieberman was a bit hypochondriacal; he often
worried about his lungs, and frequently sniffed to see whether he could
breathe properly. Oller specialized in venereal diseases, and Lieberman might

have contracted something harmless and been concerned about it. Whatever the specific reason, Lieberman often came to the Oller's house. It would not be the first occasion when a family has discovered to its surprise that a romance unexpectedly began between a much older man, a social friend, and a young woman whom he often saw in an apparently harmless setting.

To women Lieberman was a handsome, attractively masculine man, something of a Don Juan; in a letter to Helene he once referred to his "little romances." She thought his photographs did not do him full justice; she said it was his "burning disposition," the life in his face, that was the main source of his appeal. His eyes were not big but they were black and fiery. He spoke with eloquent indignation about all the injustices to the workers, as he fought in behalf of human equality. Helene remembered his strikingly beautiful gold-brown hair, which still retained a reddish tint. And she recalled him wearing a debonair mustache and smiling frequently. Lieberman may sound sentimental and melodramatic in his letters to Helene, but the overall charm of his temperament was such that he could be thoroughly captivating.

As a socialist, Lieberman gave first consideration to the party, not to his private life. Politicians have so often been associated with many shifting tactical positions that public figures, at least in North America, have been apt to acquire an unsavory reputation. But Lieberman was a dedicated member of an international movement, an idealist in the cause of humane values. As an exponent of radical social change he was thoroughly identified with socialist ideology. While he worked within pre-existing electoral systems, and was therefore at odds with all those on the Left who wanted to ignore bourgeois parliamentary forms, Lieberman had absorbed an intellectual framework of ideas.

He was absolutely devoted to democratic socialism. Helene said that every single worker, organized or unorganized, was a personal concern of his; his emotions went out not just abstractly to the masses, but to each laborer as an individual. He was so involved with the socialist movement that his friends were almost all socialist party members. It would have been impossible to share troubles with people outside the cause of the workers, and Helene and he came to have many friends in common within the social democratic party. Lieberman once gave her the calling card of the famous French socialist Jean Jaurès, who had sought his help. (A correspondence between Lieberman and Jaurès did not survive World War I.) Lieberman was a proud member of an international group of adherents. At odds with his own father, Lieberman found in socialism a welcoming family.

As an extremely popular figure Lieberman was widely known outside Przemyśl. Although Helene said that he was adored by the workers she also reported how he frequently complained about them. Perhaps all the sacrifices he made meant that disappointment was inevitable. He devoted himself to working in behalf of the needs of individual workers, yet more often than he cared to think, noble organizational issues deteriorated into mere demands for money. In terms of socialist theory the proletariat might have a historic task ahead of it, but in reality workers could be stupid and dishonest, as apt to try to drink their problems away as to turn to their party for help.

In such a situation Lieberman felt lonely and isolated, inadequately appreciated by those he struggled for. He did not allow Helene to become a formal party member; she was too good for them, he said, as the morale of workers was in his view terrible. He thought she should not have to listen to gross sexual jokes, nor to see too close up how the laboring class failed to live up to ideal standards of behavior; the adherence to socialism, even on the part of party members, could at best be transitory. Of course it was also less than impeccable for himself as a leader of the working masses and also a married man to have a relationship with this beautiful young woman from a good local family; so there were several reasons for Lieberman's desire to keep Helene at some distance from all his party activities.

Although he gave himself unstintingly to the party, and was so busy politically that he did not have the time to earn much money, Lieberman could be highly critical of Polish social democrats. Left-wing parties have always experienced this phenomenon: radicals who prove organizationally difficult to unite. Within his own party were those he could not approve of, and Lieberman was a rebel. In any event he was bound to be beset by political troubles. Politically he may have been a powerful man, but he came to ask Helene for her advice on party matters.

When he was elected as a deputy to the parliament in Vienna a new set of issues arose. All the delegates from Poland formed a special parliamentary section, as they wanted a united front in behalf of their homeland; but there were questions on which they would split, since they were themselves divided by social classes. Lieberman then knew class conflict not only as a social reality in the outside world but politically had to deal with those who represented the aristocracy and the middle classes.

Polish socialism, although part of an international movement, was at the same time committed to the principle of national independence. Not until 1918, with President Woodrow Wilson's thirteenth point, did the necessity of creating an independent Polish state finally win recognition. Jews have always had a curious relationship to modern nationalism, since traditionally they have been among the first to suffer from the nonrational emotions that go with nation building. Lieberman, like other emancipated Jews, had wanted to assimilate to Polish life.

In her youth Helene shared with Lieberman a distaste for Jews, if not a streak of anti-Semitism. In Mädi's diary she had allowed herself to refer once to "the whole unpleasant tribe of Israel." To be a Galician Jew was, at least to German Jews, almost a disgrace; but the problem was more complicated than the simple desire to emphasize Polishness as a way of escaping from a socially reinforced pattern of inferiority. Helene later stressed that Polish Jews, especially rich ones, could be conservative, unwilling to adjust to a "modern" environment. Such Jews isolated themselves in groups, and lent no support to the patriotic desire for freedom. Furthermore, within socialism Jewish separatist elements played a part; and Lieberman had to combat those Jews, Zionists as well as others, who would have weakened the social democratic party by forming their own splinter groups. So for Lieberman there were religious divisions, as well as nationalist and class barriers, to be politically surmounted. (Curiously, Lieberman's socialist breadth led him to escape the Nazi Holocaust: his principled opposition to the reactionary Polish regime in the 1930s led to his early expulsion, while those more strictly concerned with questions of import mainly to Jews stayed on to be trapped by the outbreak of World War II.)

Lieberman succeeded in awakening Helene politically as well as intellectually. She came to share his political life, and they both participated in the same ideology; the Polish social democratic party was their cause. Mädi's journal stopped when Lieberman succeeded in becoming a member of the Przemyśl city council (1904); she was also active in the first general election of 1905. Helene was so involved in the political part of her relationship to Lieberman that she once even led a strike of women working in a shirt-collar factory in Przemyśl; it was badly timed in terms of then current market conditions, but Helene had a chance to begin to learn how to speak in public. Although Lieberman felt he had to hide the growing relationship between them, he listened to her and was proud of her public-spirited activities. But he could be in despair over her naïveté, and instructed her—often belatedly—on tactics in class warfare.

Lieberman became Helene's mentor, especially as she prepared to get the *Abitur,* the certificate which would allow her to study at almost any European university. As she had identified with his political struggles, he in turn helped encourage her that she had talents worth developing. At the age of fourteen she had finished whatever official schooling she, as a middle-class girl, could be expected to receive. A smattering of art history was supposed to be sufficient intellectual preparation for the kind of future her mother had in mind for her: marriage and domestic concerns.

Helene exerted herself to break free of what seemed to be expected of her at home; the existence of Lieberman in her life helped reassure her that there was a world beyond the narrow concerns of middle-class Przemyśl. It was partly out of boredom that she first got involved with Lieberman; but he was also an unforgettably fine speaker, the greatest orator she had ever heard in her life, and she always remembered his leadership at meetings. He got her a job helping with advertisements on *The Przemyśl Voice,* hard work for which she got paid; and she even wrote some short articles.

Her parents did what they could, by their own standards, to protect their youngest child. Helene finally had to threaten to run away unless her father

agreed to support her efforts to attain her *Abitur;* she made him sign a written
contract to that effect, lest he subsequently relent under pressure from her
mother. Although Helene had spent a few months in Switzerland, where she
came in contact with socialist theoreticians and revolutionaries, her main
means of education was through independent reading and private tutoring.
Poor young students, often in exchange for meals, would help her prepare for
her exams, which had to be taken in German.

While Lieberman was supporting Helene's efforts to get an education, it
was not long before she was trying to broaden his cultural horizons. As a
young man trying to earn an independent living, he had condensed some
classics into little pamphlets that students could use when studying for their
exams; even then, unlike Helene who as a young woman had followed her
father's example, he was not a great reader and therefore felt no special
respect for the sacredness of a text. He was well educated in philosophy and
knowledgeable about subjects like military or political organization, but not
well versed in general literature. Helene therefore undertook to look after his
education in Polish cultural life.

From Helene's perspective Lieberman had little sense of art, and there
too she tried to be his guide; but he could never take her artistic interests
seriously. For music, as for painting, he had no time, although later in Vienna
she continued to bring him culture in, as she put it, "small doses." In contrast
to the man she ultimately married, Lieberman had only the slightest understanding of music; he could tolerate light music, whereas Helene preferred
operas. He was too busy for concerts, and when he went to theater he was so
tired that it was mainly for amusement and relaxation.

Lieberman had a great love for nature, however, and was a passionate
traveler. For the sake of his practice he often had to travel, but that was one
aspect of his career that he did not need to complain about. Lieberman's
devotion to his party work was single-minded and consumed all his energy;
although he liked short hikes, he had no sport and was good, as Helene once
recalled it, "from the head up." There was no time in his life even for dancing, and when Helene danced, Lieberman, like her father had before him,
would sit and watch her admiringly.

As a writer, however, Lieberman could teach Helene; he was also such a
good speaker that she could not help learning from him when it came to the
use of words. In any relationship between two people an exact accounting as
to what one gave the other is bound to be misleading. There was a genuine
mutual exchange between them which flowed naturally, all the more surprising in view of the differences in their realms of experience. Physical consum-
mation was a gradual outgrowth of their spiritual union. When Helene finally
put an end to the relationship in Munich in 1911, their earlier identification
with one another made severing the bond all the more painful.

4

Forbidden Romance

Given the times and her family background, it had required courage on Helene's part to make plans for formal higher education. She fought hard in order to begin the pursuit of a professional career; but she was endowed with a gift of the inner conviction that she was somebody of creative capacity. Although she lived on into an era when it was possible to take for granted the earlier efforts for female emancipation, she had had to be educated independently of preparatory schools, since none of them yet existed for women in Przemyśl. However, when she left Poland for the University of Vienna in 1907, it was simultaneous with Lieberman's first undertaking his parliamentary duties. He was by then thirty-seven, still married, and the father of a daughter, so the relationship between them was irregular for both.

Lieberman was hardly someone who in general had difficulties in getting on with women. His calm exterior only highlighted the inner intensity. He was, while being fully masculine, capable of moving tenderness, gallant and chivalrous; and in feminine company compliments came readily from him. He was so used to treating the workers, however, as children, incapable of knowing their own best interests, that it may have contributed to his initial attraction to Helene.

Although at the beginning he could not have realized how extensively he had filled the inner world of Helene, someone of his age and experience ought to have appreciated what a mistake he might be making in encouraging her in any way. In her last years she sometimes thought of herself as having been a helpless child of fourteen, innocent and full of fantasies, and she resented the way he had taken advantage of her; but she admitted she also could be aggressively flirtatious, and she herself volunteered the idea that Lieberman's attentions might have been intended to pacify her.

Throughout all their years together Lieberman bought Helene only one gift, a green bag that she found in terrible taste. Of course he worked hard, laborers were his company, and he was often tired during the time he spent with her. On rare occasions, for example when they were walking together in Vienna, he might buy her some roses sold by a young woman on a street corner. But his reserve in this sphere may have also been tactful; since she had so little money, anything he gave Helene might put her in an embarrassing position. He preferred the cheapest restaurants. In hotels, or when they ate out together, she tried, as a poor student, to keep track of what he spent on her, although she never paid him back. At the outset of her studies in Vienna she was not getting much money from home, and she was doing her best to be self-sufficient. (During her first year in Vienna her father had suddenly arrived on the instigation of her mother, to persuade Helene to return home; instead her father had given her more money.) She did, however, make little gestures for Lieberman; she woke him up one morning with strawberries. And when his daughter in Poland wanted an umbrella, she bought it for him in a Viennese store.

In Poland, however, the contact between them had had to be very restricted. She vividly recalled a public meeting at which he had, from her vantage point, made his declaration of love to her: he had been speaking about how life had begun to be empty and sad for him, until he met someone who had rekindled his revolutionary enthusiasm. Stifled by small-town existence, she was entranced by each glimpse of the outside world. Lieberman was the first man in her life, and Helene was determined to fulfill every ideal of feminine devotion and faithfulness.

Under the circumstances they always had to be circumspect in how they saw each other, and this was especially true in Przemyśl. It was not safe for him to write to her, since she lived with her parents, nor she to him, because his wife might intercept a message; but they did manage to communicate, sometimes by code. One such message from him to her reads, when deciphered: "Wait Tuesday at 12:30 P.M. or at 2:30 P.M. in the second-class waiting room. Don't go out on the railway platform." In their later years in Vienna, although he could obviously see her more freely, there was still the obstacle of his being a well-known figure within certain political circles. When in 1910 he took her along with him to an international meeting of socialists, she heard whispers of impropriety. All the secrecy must have had its attractions. Even in her autobiography Helene only once mentioned Lieberman by his full name, regularly referring to him instead as "L." Yet by the end of their time together she had had her fill of romantic hiding.

In spite of the difficulties connected with their being together, letter writing became an essential element of the tie between Lieberman and Helene. While she was a student in Vienna he often had to go back to Przemyśl, either for his political career or his legal practice. But he wrote regularly and copiously; it sounds as if she were as avid a correspondent as he. For those of a literary bent letters can be a superb outlet for exercising a talent for language. They shared a need to objectify their thoughts and feelings in writing. Even though only his letters are available for scrutiny, the general picture of an ecstatic, yet unhappy love becomes clear.*

   The position of Lieberman's wife, Gustawa, however, is not easy to reconstruct. The inarticulate tend to be historically neglected, and since she was unintellectual, Gustawa's side of things has to be pieced together mainly from bits and snatches that Helene, her rival, remembered about her. No independent documents enable one to verify commonsense assumptions about the likely emotions and behavior of a betrayed wife in the social setting of that era in Poland. But just as it is possible to make some inferences about what was going on between Helene and Lieberman from an examination of one side of their love letters, material does come up in that correspondence on the nature of his marriage.

   Gustawa's maiden name was Brinjs. As a young woman she had been beautiful, but although she was the same age as her husband, by the time Helene knew her she had grown stout and looked older than he. They had married young, at a time when he was still an impoverished student; she supported him financially, and Lieberman felt permanently obligated to her. He did what he could for her family; she had a crippled younger sister whom he helped take care of, and an unpromising brother for whom he managed to get a job. Lieberman tried to be as decent as possible to his wife's relatives.

   The romantic attachment between Lieberman and his wife was over quickly. They had little in common and he had soon tired of her. Although he acquired the reputation of being a "ladies' man," there are no signs that she was anything but loyal. He did not take her with him on his trips, since their life together was joyless. No doubt one reason he was bored with her was that she knew so little about his political convictions, and therefore could not imaginatively participate in that crucial part of his life.

   When, however, he was briefly put under arrest in Przemyśl in 1910, as his wife she was allowed to visit him; and in keeping with her expected social role, it was she who brought him extra food. The more Gustawa continued to take care of him, the more obligated he felt to her. When he was imprisoned, for example, he could not readily turn aside her help; he was badly treated in jail, as bourgeois society had a chance to take its revenge on him. The workers marched around the prison, exultantly singing revolutionary songs. For them his imprisonment meant one more stage in the prophesied collapse of reactionary power. Whatever Lieberman's political thoughts might have been, his acceptance of Gustawa's assistance reinforced his conviction that he

* In 1910, another future analyst, Sabina Spielrein, was struggling with identical feelings about an affair with a married man, Carl G. Jung.[1]

was not going to escape from his wife. The lesson was not lost on Helene
either, since she was prevented from seeing him.

However humiliated Gustawa may have felt by her situation, society
reinforced her position. She was Lieberman's wife, as well as the mother of
his child, and she could not bear to lose him. He managed his best to be good
to her, and she in turn was kind. From an abstract theoretical point of view it
may seem like the worst thing she could have done to herself, but she was
functioning within the social order of her time. Even after Helene became an
open threat to the marriage, Gustawa was determined that another woman
was not going to succeed in formally taking away her husband. Lieberman
developed a physical aversion to his wife, claimed to have ceased having
sexual relations with her, and in the end spoke of Gustawa with disgust.

In one letter Lieberman sent to Helene, written after one of their early
separations (probably in 1905), he felt called upon, after an extensive account
of all that Helene meant to his life, to give a version of his relation to Gustawa. It sounds as though Helene had expressed her own hesitations toward
Lieberman in terms of her guilt feelings over his wife.

> And now I will answer the question that is bothering you. Your worries
> about my wife are baseless. If we are to speak about injustice, then she must
> have done you wrong several times.
>
> Our relationship has always been of a formal and conventional nature.
> Over all it is a very sad thing. After my high school graduation, I spent two
> years travelling through Western Europe; when I returned back to Poland
> shocked by the great depravity present everywhere, I decided to start work-
> ing with great energy toward my ideals. It seemed at that time that my goal
> could only be achieved with the help of a woman who shared the same ideas
> as myself.
>
> Because of an unfortunate and strange fancy of mine, it seemed that this
> woman would be the one I had just met by chance.

Lieberman was so wrapped up in his work that he could completely
mislead himself on such an important personal issue; he was just the kind of
man who, especially in his youth, might allow his political fantasies to deceive
him about whom he was marrying. As with Helene's own powers of invention, his self-involvement was a necessary component of his strengths, but
also a potential source of weakness. On his return home to Poland, moreover,
Lieberman felt that his male vanity had misled him into thinking that Gustawa was worth pursuing.

> Because she avoided me, I felt that my youthful pride was hurt, and I
> decided either to die or to submit her to my will. I succeeded in accomplish-
> ing the latter, but at that time when I realized how wrong I had been, I was
> already engaged.
>
> Because I knew how much she would have suffered if I had broken up
> with her, I entered marriage out of pity, this union that has me stuck until

the end of my life. I had some feelings, however, when entering this union, and this can be confirmed by a living witness—Dr. Spitzman who was at that time my confidant and friend.

At the time Lieberman was writing, Helene had no special knowledge of psychiatry.

Two hours after the wedding I was overcome by a spell of insanity, so that Spitzman had to take me to a doctor, and keep me under his eye for days and nights to prevent any misfortunes from happening to me.

I overcame my pain under the influence of some strange body and soul reactions—my temporary madness went away—and I have lived for so many years with this pain.

It was in keeping with Lieberman's personality that he should express himself so passionately. If his immediate reaction to the marriage sounds improbable, he was in reality one of those people whose emotional and somatic lives are especially intimately connected.

Before meeting you . . . my morale was low, but that was a good side of my personality, that I never let my wife know how much I was suffering and what a misfortune this marriage was for me. I was always directed by compassion when dealing with her, and I have tried to spare her all the sadness in life. I never refused any sympathy and I always gave her plenty of it. It has been like this until the present days. I would not be worthy of you if I could brutally ridicule someone else's pain.

So you should not ever think about it . . . , because if you are still worrying about it I would rather disappear and die.

I do not want to take your time with writing letters to me, but I would like to ask you to let me know as soon as possible if you still have any doubts concerning this problem.

Helene was busy studying for her examinations, and it would seem that Lieberman's letter did succeed, for the time being at least, in allaying her misgivings. Lieberman's misery was one source of his appeal to a young woman, and although his tale may have also touched others, his attachment to Helene was genuine. Twice in the course of his story about himself Lieberman had used the formal word "Madam" to Helene, a sign that this letter precedes their full intimacies together.

Like other accounts of unhappy marriages, Lieberman's was bound to be considerably biased. Even disregarding Gustawa's side of things, Lieberman was guilty of some striking omissions in writing Helene. As a youth he had made Gustawa pregnant, and accordingly felt obliged to marry her. But it is also likely that marriage offered him at least the prospect of peace and security.

Since in our own time divorce has become so commonplace, and in certain circles even fashionable, it requires an effort to try to understand Lieberman's full dilemma. In a Catholic country, where religion forbade divorce, and in an era when every social standard encouraged the maintenance of marital unions, even on terms which might now seem demeaning to both parties, the choice Lieberman made was hardly exceptional. Legally, if he had really wanted a divorce, he could have obtained it. Perhaps he was afraid of so bold a step toward freedom. Certainly he was restrained by guilt feelings toward Gustawa; the more he wronged her, the more obliged he felt to pay for his conduct through his own unhappiness. While he might seem almost in quest of his marital misery, the genuineness of his feelings for Gustawa ought not to be forgotten.

In the context of their society, divorce would have been crueler than sexual and emotional infidelity. Gustawa was, in terms of social status, wholly dependent on Lieberman. As his wife she had the title and income that came from the security of her marriage, even if he no longer loved her. If Lieberman had openly left her, it would have been an even bigger scandal. As a Jew in politics, and a socialist to boot, Lieberman already had enough problems to contend with. The voters would be looking for a man they could trust. Although this was a point that did not need to be explicitly mentioned by Lieberman to Helene, in the circumstances of the times it was better for his Polish political career for him not to abandon Gustawa; yet his public activities were not opportunistic but were founded on social idealism.

From Helene's point of view, the Lieberman marriage reminded her consciously of the union between her parents. Like her father, Lieberman seemed afraid of his wife. Perhaps she was indulging in some wishful thinking here, but to her, Gustawa's determination to hold on to Lieberman was reminiscent of her own mother's domination of her father. Helene's attraction to Lieberman was built on her affection for her father, as well as an attempt to free herself from him; Gustawa's existence must have been part of the excitement. Although an affair with Lieberman would not be incestuous, such a bond flew in the face of all other social rules that Helene knew. Ecstasies and guilt feelings reinforced each other. It gave Helene an enormous sense of how emancipated she was in her own right for her to be able to function in a situation of normlessness, to experience love without limits.

According to Helene her involvement with Lieberman lasted her whole life. In a chapter of her *The Psychology of Women,* entitled "Eroticism: The Feminine Woman," she gave an account of her own childhood family story; she was writing about some

> very trivial and fully conscious fantasies of the normal young girl that relate to the father. In one he is a great man who deserves a better fate, a victim of the prosaic mother who has tied him to the gray business of earning a living. She, the little daughter, would be a more suitable object for him, though he must painfully renounce it.

Then Helene went on to try to account for her love for Lieberman, which she could now interpret in the light of Freud's system of thought.

> In a large number of instances, a psychologically sound woman may have as her first love object—an object to which she often remains attached for life— an unfree man, often a married man, who fans her love and responds to it, but cannot break his old tie. Such a man reproduces the situation described above. The fantasy of his painful love yearning and the woman's own suffering, shared with him, often prove stronger motives for faithfulness than the fulfillment of love.

Helene even illustrated how the fate of young love could play a part in her own relation to Freud.

> There is another type of adolescent love that continues throughout life in some women and that may occur in women who are excellently adjusted to reality. For instance, a happily married woman who has children and a career, and who is in every respect an adult and mature person is constantly entangled in a painfully blissful and platonic love for some man who is usually a father figure for her, such as her working superior, or an important man in a field in which she is interested, etc. One woman called this love her "Sunday happiness"; for only on Sundays did she have time to indulge in fantasies relating to it.
>
> In *Much Ado about Nothing* (Act 2, scene 1) we find an interesting illustration of this division of emotional life into everyday gratification and Sunday high seriousness.

> Don Pedro: Will you have me, lady?
> Beatrice: No, my lord, unless I might have another for
>   working days;
>   your grace is too costly to wear every day.[2]

Emotional knowledge, though, can lag long behind experience, and Helene published these words almost a decade after she had left Vienna, and five years after Freud's death.

In the midst of all Helene's own youthful emotional fantasies and conflicts, however, the cold reality was that Gustawa obviously still loved her husband. In that social setting, so different from our own, the varieties of marital feelings are bound to be hard to understand now. According to Lieberman's account to Helene, he had stopped loving Gustawa long ago; on strictly rational grounds Helene did not have to feel as though she were breaking up a happy home. Traditional European life was more formal than what we are used to, so this arrangement among these three people could persist, in different forms, for years. It was therefore possible for Lieberman to be kind to Gustawa in his own way, since he did not want her to suffer; yet he could at the same time indulge his desire to be with Helene.

Gustawa was no fool, however, and did not simply passively accept the presence of a younger woman in her husband's life. She could not help knowing about Lieberman's involvement with Helene in Przemyśl, and she was furious with Helene for threatening her marriage. The fact that Lieberman was trapped in his own guilt feelings, and blocked from divorce politically, emboldened Gustawa's will to fight. Gustawa's jealousy meant that even if she had not wanted to keep him, she was not going to participate in giving him to Helene. She would have had to give her consent for a divorce; although part of her wanted a divorce, since it was no kind of marriage for her either, once Helene was in the picture Gustawa, from sheer hatred of a rival, would not agree to a divorce. According to one of Helene's memories, if Gustawa had granted the divorce there would have had to be a condition: he would have to stay in Przemyśl and be a father to his daughter, Misia.

The relationship between Lieberman and Helene was forbidden by all the standards of their society, and the difficulties in their path helped contribute to the furtive attractiveness of the union. The liaison was not just a violation of abstract social norms, but such a shame to correct Jewish circles in Przemyśl that both families sought to intervene. Gustawa became an intimate friend of Helene's mother, who had already been jealous of her in relation to her own husband; both women joined forces to disrupt the illicit relationship. Wilhelm Rosenbach might have liked to think that everything Helene did was perfect, but his need for family peace, and his fear of Regina, pushed him into opposing his youngest daughter. Helene now felt there was a growing hostile alliance against her in Przemyśl.

Lieberman was under pressure too because of the situation, and he suggested that he go away on a trip to Spain, and that Helene meet him there. Such a proposal was obviously attractive to her, but it also reminded her what a demanding lover he was capable of being, and how precarious was her own position. If she went to Lwów, and concentrated on her studies to pass her university entrance exam, she might succeed in breaking free of what seemed a hopelessly painful entanglement. On one level Lieberman accepted her refusal to travel with him, as well as the impending separation; but the more he missed her the more annoyed he got.

Yet Lieberman's appeal to Helene became one which she treasured more than ever. In the same letter in which he gave her an account of the circumstances of his marriage he had also written:

> In the first moment after our separation, I thought that I would be able to break away completely and be able to live with my precious memories about you, Madam. But the silence in the first few days was terrifying and full of horror. I imagine that a similar feeling is present in the souls of the families of fishermen, who after the storm, stand at the shore, listening into the distance for the sounds of the people dear to them, who trusted their fate to the storming sea. But no voice of a living creature answers to their cries, only silence, interrupted by the mournful roar of the waves.

When Helene wrote to him, he had second thoughts about the separation he had initiated.

> I am convinced that I already cannot live in total isolation from you, Madam. That is why each one of your letters brings great joy to me. In reality they increase my longing and grief, because in every word written by your hand I see what I have lost in you, Madam. At the same time, however, this great force of emotion which emanates from these words and especially the moral power of your thoughts, has in itself so much soothing strength, it lifts my spirits. I do not consider myself to be unhappy at all.

Helene's absence fanned Lieberman's passion for her; he declared that it was for her sake that he had tried to renounce his own personal happiness. In trying to bring Helene peace, Lieberman assured her he was not to be worried about: her memory inspired him in his work. She strengthened him when he was tired, and she was his "horizon" for his doing something good for other people.

> At other times, when I err, and try to hurt other people, then you stand between me and my victim looking so dangerous and frightening, that everything dies of great grief inside me. At moments like that I miss you the most, I feel my loneliness so painfully then, and a gentle cry comes from my soul.

Lieberman had a poetic streak in him.

> Haven't you ever heard quiet, mysterious murmurs, almost like cries in the air, or when you are alone in a room, can't you hear a plaintive palpitation of something like a half-dead bird, or can't you hear faint blows against your window? Suddenly in the midst of the night can't you hear something rustling or sighing and beating very, very quietly, as if it were pacing through the room, looking for something, do you hear that Madam? That is my soul searching shelter from life's icy wind.

At the same time Lieberman did not want to alarm Helene: "But these are rare moments. Sometimes I have such feelings and then I am sure that you are thinking about me and perhaps missing me as well." Doubtless he was touched by her inexperience; as a young woman, showered with such words from a man she had admired at a distance for years, Helene was not able to muster the critical judgment of a woman of the world. He was writing in the romantic vocabulary that she, like others of that time, treasured. She must have given him encouragement beforehand for opening up so to her.

Shared Madness

In early 1905 a crisis arose between Helene and Lieberman over the death of his son. The boy, about a year old, fell acutely ill, probably of meningitis, in the course of an infectious epidemic in Przemyśl. Lieberman was on his trip to Spain. He was in Barcelona when he received the telegram with the news of his son's serious illness. Although he hurried back to Poland, the boy was already dead by the time he arrived.

This baby had played a curious role in the romance between Helene and Lieberman. Gustawa's pregnancy should have reinforced Helene's jealous suspicions. Even though Helene was not yet actively sexually involved with Lieberman, his wife's so recently having given birth cast a shadow over the exclusivity of Helene's spiritual union with him. But somehow he and she worked Gustawa's baby into their shared fantasies, and the boy served to support rather than threaten their tie.

For Lieberman had proposed the idea that while his older child, his daughter, would stay with Gustawa, in some way this precious male heir would come with him and Helene. It is hard to believe that a man of thirty-five and a woman of twenty-one could be so naïve as to build such a castle in the air. But as Freud liked to quote from Shakespeare's *Hamlet,* "There are more things in heaven and earth, Horatio, than are dreamt of in your philoso-phy." No rules exist that define the limits to the humanly unusual. (As a psychiatrist Helene later wrote more than once on the phenomenon of *folie à deux,* and touched on its relation to normal love.)

Lieberman and Helene were passionately involved with each other, and to that extent were fully capable of thought processes that sound infantile; they both were highly emotional and derived satisfaction and autonomy from self-creations. It was of the essence of the intimacy of their involvement to exclude the outside world. Under a cross in Przemyśl they once swore undying fealty to the permanence of their relationship. In the real background of this whole picture, however, was Gustawa. At one point she had, in anger, threatened to kill both children if her husband did not mend his ways. Lieberman himself, like other Jewish fathers of that time, was deeply attached to his little boy; the child's existence held out the hope of another life for him, a second and renewed self, which he somehow thought he might share with Helene.

At the same time Lieberman had guilt feelings toward Helene, since what he was offering her of himself was less than perfect by middle-class standards. That she was credulous enough to accept the idea that this child would somehow belong to her is one sign of how wildly in love with Lieberman she was. (In terms of Freud's theories, her blindness could also be interpreted as an unconscious desire for a child from her father.) Her own guilt feelings, however, about the dishonesty of what was being done to Gustawa, may have been assuaged by the fancy that she was not really taking away the father from two children.

The death of the boy was terrible for Helene and Lieberman. (The rate of infant mortality is different today, but this small child was exceptionally sensitive.) Both of them were forced at least partly to face the realities of their situation. It had been all along fanciful to think that Gustawa would ever give up the child, especially to a woman she had reason to hate. Helene and Lieberman might have had their wish for a child of pure love, but the magic of their romance was confronted by the painful realities of his marriage. The loss of the child reminded them of Gustawa's justified animosity, which seemed to be magically fulfilled by the boy's death. If Gustawa had wanted to hurt Lieberman, nothing could have been worse for him than what had happened; her threats against his children had been partly carried out, by nature, and it seemed a cruel form of revenge.

Gustawa's health was poor; she suffered from a circulatory disorder, Raynaud's disease, which meant that she was hyperreactive to cold. Her extremities, fingers and toes, were affected by the illness. The disorder afflicts women more than men. In serious cases the pain and loss of dexterity may lead to serious disability. Attacks have been known to be triggered by emotional stress. The illness still has no known physical cause; but when the small arteries in the digits go into spasms in response to cold, circulation is cut off and the fingers and toes turn white and numb. The child's death reminded them all of mortality; they had wondered whether Gustawa would live to see the boy grow up. Helene and Lieberman felt remorseful that the whole idea of the child coming to them was a reflection of an unspoken longing on their part that the mother no longer exist.

Lieberman's desire for a son was so strong that the idea of the boy being with Helene may have been also a way of trying to insure its safety. Gustawa's illness caused him anxiety, and Helene was thinking in terms of a medical career. While the child still lived Lieberman could therefore in some sense trust Helene with it. Somehow in his thinking Lieberman was willing to allow his daughter, who did not seem promising, to remain with Gustawa. The death of his beloved son, however, took place before the child was old enough to have been in any way a disappointment.

Lieberman had enjoyed traveling alone, and was too estranged from Gustawa to think of taking her on the trip to Spain. However, having interrupted the trip because of his son's illness, he now took pity on Gustawa and proposed that she join him on a trip to a warm climate. Although Helene knew that this was an act of charity, she was also angry with him for leaving like that. The boy's death, far from allowing Lieberman greater freedom to be with Helene, forced him to comfort Gustawa. Gustawa knew she had obstructed his romance and may have felt some guilt over interfering with his happiness; in her grieving she may have reproached herself that she had not cared for the child properly. Gustawa's sorrow brought her the support of her circle of family and friends; Helene thought that both she and Lieberman were now obliged to take care of Gustawa.

Helene was treated as something of an outsider to these events, although she went to the railroad station in Przemyśl to see Lieberman and Gustawa off. All the members of her own family were there too, including her brother-in-law. At the station Helene was so swept up in contradictory emotions that she was tactless enough to take his hand to say good-bye. Not only were her closest relatives present, but Gustawa, whom Helene had forgotten about, saw it all from the train window.

Most of Lieberman's letters to Helene are undated. Since, in contrast to the letters from her husband which she saved inside their envelopes, Lieberman's letters have been reread and removed from the envelopes, it is usually only possible to establish their sequence from internal evidence, the stationery, or the handwriting. One letter from Nice, France, however, dated April 26, 1905, helps establish part of the course of events. Lieberman wrote Helene about his exhaustion and sense of oppression; in the past, whenever he had been tired, traveling had been a way of his resting. "I am rushing to write a few words in reply. You understand, Madam, that it is difficult for me to find a moment of free time to write you a more detailed letter. I am never alone." It was a knotty point, reminding Helene—who had earlier refused to travel with him—that Gustawa was with him now.

> After reading your letter I cried so dearly. Only you understand why I cry so much about the death of the poor baby.
> I cannot find peace. Among the greatest noise and clutter of many towns, I see before me this little angel and the wound in my heart bleeds. I

try to control my pain—I am sure I will overcome it and I will submit my
fate to you, Madam.

Whenever Lieberman used the word "madam," translated from the Polish *pani,* it meant a sign of formality between himself and Helene. It was not a
word used to express love, but an index of estrangement. Since intimacy was,
as she later expressed it, the music of their relationship, "madam" also had a
teasing connotation; under the circumstances, the word had a hostile tinge to
it, since it meant she was something of a stranger to him. And he would not
have used it without being irritated if not angry; out of his guilt feelings he
had the need to put her in the wrong. He did not feel free as a man, yet he
resented that Helene was not even more a part of his life.

Still he felt he could open his heart to her. In another letter from this
period, which may have been his first on leaving Przemyśl, he wrote:

> I have not had a moment of solitude yet, which I could have spent
> writing you.
> And I was so anxious to tell you that I still feel the same way about you
> as I did during our last parting, in spite of my great misfortune.
> And now, when I am so torn apart, your feelings will be like a rock,
> against which I wish to lean my aching head in order not to perish.

Lieberman may have been a party man, but now he was not living in his
world of political strife.

> I am in Florence now, everything is so beautiful here, but my thoughts
> and my soul are breaking far away from here, they wander through the
> cemetery in Przemyśl where the being which I loved so much was buried.
> My soul spends days and sleepless nights with this poor and unhappy child,
> thanks to whom I have experienced many moments of relief and soothing
> from my suffering. I see before me its small white arms, stretching out from
> the grave toward me begging me to save him from the underground worms.
> And I hurry to the grave and spend the whole day with this little angel in a
> coffin, and it seems to me that in this way I am preventing him from rotting.

Lieberman had a visual mind, and he characteristically expressed himself
to Helene in pictorial language, for her visual sense was the most important
one of all to her. (Her cat's eyes throughout her life struck people as extraordinarily expressive.) In 1905 Helene left Przemyśl to study for her *Abitur* in
Lwów, where she had some cousins; it was four hours by train from her
home, and one of the two places in Poland where, she recalled, a woman who
had not attended a regular high school could be given special permission to
take her college entrance exam.

In the midst of Lieberman's grief over the death of his son, he sounds
angry over Helene's partial withdrawal from his life. The naïveté of his conception of the child's future strengthened the bond between himself and Helene.

> If you are ever in Przemyśl, Madam, I would like to ask you to plant
> some flowers on this grave so dear to me. Believe me, this unfortunate child
> deserved this, it belonged on *our* team—with its great sensitivity of heart and
> its extraordinary intuition which I admired so much. Had it lived, it would
> have loved you very much, it would have belonged to both of us.

According to Helene, Gustawa was aware of her husband's intentions for the
child, but was so vain that she thought he would relinquish the fantasy of
taking it from her. In another sense, however, he was proposing to treat
Helene as someone who takes care of another woman's baby.

Politically a hero, at heart Lieberman was a soft person; he could seek to
win Helene through an account of his suffering. Continuing on about the
dead child, he wrote:

> it has flown away to an unknown land, and it will not return. I was
> racing against time for four days and three nights from Barcelona just to find
> it alive, I was full of despair and doubt, because I thought that I would save
> it with the strength of my great and unearthly love for it. But at home I
> encountered an already made grave for what was a part of my soul and my
> heart.
>
> Please forgive me for writing only about my loss, but I experience a
> great relief by writing you. Who will understand me and who will share my
> feelings better than you? Will I ever raise my head up again in order to face
> the sky with a bright look, desiring to see luminous horizons? Will my soul
> ever shake off this heavy cloud of sadness and doubt, in which I am so
> absorbed now, will it find its old hardness and faith in the world?
>
> I only know that now, more than ever, I need the pure, holy feelings
> from my beloved person, in order to dissipate this dark, black night which is
> approaching me, spreading over my dark head.

Lieberman gave Helene, as a postscript, his next address near Genoa, Italy, as
well as the one in Switzerland where he planned to be in a week's time.
(Despite their separation, he turned to her to help arrange for money of his to
be telegraphed under a fictitious name from Lwów to Lugano, even if it
meant a trip to Przemyśl for her.)

Throughout his journey with Gustawa, Lieberman continued to exchange letters with Helene in Lwów; away from Przemyśl they could write
more freely to each other, without the same fear of family inspection. Yet he
made no mention of his wife's suffering, nor of his daughter back home in
Poland. In another letter he showed signs of realizing the extent to which he
had been selfishly self-absorbed; he asked her to write him in Switzerland
about "what is happening to you, how you are spending your time in Lwów,
who you have been seeing—but mostly write about yourself."

He had planned to be back in Przemyśl by May 6, and evidently Helene
wrote him there through an intermediary, "J." (This middle person may have
been Jodka, an ardent socialist who was Lieberman's teacher and closest
friend.) Shortly thereafter he had left for Vienna, and on May 13, 1905, back

at his party work, he wrote: "I got the letter from J. just before leaving. Right now I am in Vienna taking part in a session of the Austrian party council which will make a decision regarding the creation of a new Jewish party." But before recounting his political struggles, Lieberman wanted to reassure her about their personal relationship.

> Your fears are completely baseless, Madam. Nothing has changed and you have not ceased to be the star of my life, my only confidante, who with her bright love and friendship will support my painfully bleeding soul. The fact that I am living and that I wish to continue living is thanks to you, Madam, and if it was not for her, then an eternal darkness would surround me.
>
> I came back from the trip very tired, almost broken down and so terribly exhausted . . .
>
> From my children I encountered only one alive, and instead of one party, for which I fought and worked so much, I encountered two.

The extent to which Lieberman had recovered from his grief can be seen in his account of his struggle against the new splinter group. Political activity also helped him forget his troubles. He could count on Helene to have followed the developments in Polish socialism, which were at that time necessarily connected to the Austrian socialist movement.

> Surely you must already know about this terrible confusion which reigns among the party members. During my absence, the so-called leaders committed so many malicious, brutal and stupid mistakes, that a split must have occurred. For a few days now I have been very active, and I have been making every effort to repair the situation.
>
> Yesterday we had a very stormy meeting of the central council, there were many sudden occurrences between me and [Victor] Adler and a few other members of the Polish party.
>
> Today it continues.
>
> The split of the party has hurt me beyond words. You will understand, Madam, what a misfortune it is to see people leaving the party ranks, together with them I have suffered so much, fought and shared the rare moments of joy and triumph.

However preoccupied he might be by public matters, he was concerned about himself and Helene.

> I was very depressed that you did not write me either to Lugano or to Lucerne, Madam. You must have had much time to do that. I was looking forward to it. I thought that you must have decided to break off with me because of your conscience or bad news about me.
>
> Tonight I am going home—I am asking you to write me about yourself, through J.

Politics had resumed its central place in Lieberman's life, and he freely wrote Helene about his struggle to reunify the social democrats. But the dead boy was still a central issue for them; as he began another letter around this time:

> Your letter strengthened me very much. I have never cried so dearly as when reading your letter about my deceased child.
> You knew his soul so well, Madam. You know how to pluck so gently those strings that cry secretly in the bottom of my heart, being afraid of the world, so that their painful sounds would not be muffled by the brutal human tumult.

He sounds relieved, yet also irritated, that Helene is able to work hard at her studies. The party, he is able to report, has now been reunited, and the Jewish faction had ceased to exist as an independent entity.

From Lieberman's point of view the creation of a Jewish party would have been "a truly reactionary, anticultural and pro-zionistic deed." He was disillusioned by the disloyal behavior of one of his supporters. But Lieberman did not want to dwell on how hurt he felt, preferring instead to continue harboring "illusions about the idealism of some chosen souls." Far from joining others in depriving his former ally of his party position, Lieberman declared that he

> would prefer to smash the whole party to smithereens than to allow someone to be deprived of his daily bread because of different beliefs. I not only prevented his removal from his position, but I also forced them to raise his salary as well. I convinced his most embittered enemies to vote for him.

Lieberman yearned to see Helene again. "I am waiting with a mad longing . . . for the moment when I can look into those eyes that accompany me like two stars in my dreams and in reality." Apart from her his life was gloomy.

> Really I have been born out of sadness itself, I have grown up from what hurts me. Since my boyhood there has not been anything but fights, sufferings, disappointments. Ah! Sometimes I feel such a mortal exhaustion. The atmosphere in which I live now is so heavy, like lead . . . Before the sound of my dear, divine child had soothed my grief for moments—but today there is only a grave silence everywhere.

Helene was far away, and Lieberman feared the separation would last for years; when she returned there was no certainty that everything between them would not have changed. Yet her proposed career as a pediatrician seemed to follow naturally from what had recently happened.

> Do you know, Madam, that your plan for the future literally amazes me? It would be so nice if you carried out your intentions of finishing medicine and of choosing the field of childhood diseases.
> This profession would suit your nature, it would be so beautiful! And at

the same time it would be so practical, which is not an unimportant thing, if you desire to be self-sufficient.

Helene admired Käthe Kollwitz, now remembered as an artist, and wanted to be a physician like her. Helene could not yet know, however, that treating children would never be her primary interest, but she soon became fascinated by psychiatry. In later years playing with children on a regular basis, not to mention the possibility of trying to help them psychotherapeutically, would have taxed her patience intolerably.

Although Lwów was far enough away from Przemyśl to distress Lieberman, his professional activities sometimes took him there. Somehow, Helene's family got wind of the fact that the tie between Helene and Lieberman was not being weakened by her absence. Her declared intention to go to medical school at the University of Vienna did not seem to indicate that there would be sufficient distance between her and her persistent suitor. Before he had left for his earlier trip alone to Barcelona he had written her that "two hours before my departure I had a very unpleasant conversation with one of your family members about your leaving." Now, once again, pressure was brought to bear on him.

Lieberman was frank with Helene about her mother's intervention.

> I am going through terrible times. I feel so shattered that I cannot concentrate my thoughts to write more than just a few words. Your mother paid me a visit.
>
> It was awful! If it were possible to die and finally find peace and put an end to this miserable life.
>
> I was given an awful choice. It is impossible to die, you know why. We have to separate—don't give up hope, we have been through so much sadness together that we deserve some peace and happiness. Maybe we will come together sometime again. But now, only limitless sadness, loneliness and separation. It must be so. Obey their will, leave Vienna and go to the University of their choice.
>
> It would be good too, if you came to Przemyśl and made peace with them. I promised not to see you anymore, until destiny will allow for our permanent union and be accepted "by people and the world."
>
> Don't be sad and carry this burden with courage. I will always remember you through my tears—I will live with thoughts of you.

As Lieberman was proposing a separation, he at the same time was promising to write again the next day. For the time being he was, in part, bending under the pressure of her family. He entreated her to "undergo a medical examination to show them that you are pure and that you were holy for me."

> Once again, don't be sad—you are mine for ages and I will be yours forever until my heart explodes from grief. Be well—it is terrible to have to separate from you—what a life is waiting for me. Do not be sad and do not lose your courage or hope.

Helene's position was growing worse rather than better. For the first time she was living away from home, planning a professional future, yet she was far from free. She had tried, even if only half heartedly, to break away from Lieberman, and yet found herself still firmly attached to him. Her anger that he remained with his wife did not help her; after the loss of the boy Gustawa's hold on Lieberman became unbreakable, even though emotionally she had lost him.

Helene had been strong enough to defy social convention, pursue the requirements for a career, and carry on a seemingly hopeless love; now she reacted with a depression. Although she had been capable of hard work, she could spend hours lying on one of the couches in her family's home. She was not consciously acting, yet she was aware that she was to a certain extent simulating sickness, as she exaggerated her dreary and hopeless feelings. She always had had a theatrical sense and dramatic flair; but she so lost track of time that her father grew alarmed. He did not like the idea of leaving her with her mother, so he decided to take her to Vienna for a medical consultation.

The recommendation her father received was that he place his favorite daughter in a sanatorium, and one at Graz was chosen. The sanatorium Maria Grün was located in a small Austrian town, and was presumably far enough from Przemyśl to insure Helene's separation from Lieberman. (In 1885 Baron von Krafft-Ebing had applied for the license to set up Maria Grün. The sanatorium was to treat diseases of the spinal cord, and all kinds of nervous disorders, with the strict exception of mental illnesses. It was to be open in winter as well as in summer; cold-water and fresh-air treatment were to be available; and for the benefit of the public a large park was to be built. Dr. Hugo Gugl was appointed medical director; in 1906 Dr. Herman Albrecht succeeded to Krafft-Ebing's post. No records from this institution have survived.) Helene's father was obviously upset about the way things were going. The so-called social disgrace that so exercised his wife did not directly affect him, except that she was capable of making his life miserable because of it. Helene remembered how Wilhelm had cried on the train to Graz, as he thought about leaving Helene there; but the tears may have been a reflection of mixed emotions—relief that Helene was going, as well as resentment at her leaving.

The sanatorium was expensive, designed for rich people, and by modern standards did almost nothing. It offered a rest cure, as well as a regime of baths. It was also possessed with electrical equipment that warmed by massage. Undoubtedly, though, the sanatorium had been chosen mainly for the purpose of enforcing Helene's separation from Lieberman.

Lieberman felt considerable moral responsibility for what had happened to Helene, and he immediately wrote her from Przemyśl.

Depression shows in your letter, but as far as I am concerned I am sure about your future.

It is good that you are in a sanatorium under strict discipline, which exists in such institutions, and that you have now the possibility of curing your nervous disposition.

I admit openly that I am even glad that it happened so. I am sure that you will return to us healthy and completely stabilized, with a firm plan for your future, that you have needed so much until now.

And if the sound of my voice has any meaning for you, then I ask you to forget about everything, to stop worrying about the future or the past. Think only about the present and about yourself. Take advantage of the time and recuperate your health. I send you my warmest greetings and no matter how worried I was about you before your trip from Przemyśl now I can look encouragingly into your future. I know that because of your treatment now, your instability will go away, and a strong desire, to do seriously all the important tasks that await you, will remain.

I am leaving Przemyśl on the 18th, through Vienna to Abbazia, where I am taking my family. Probably I will be going through Graz.

In Przemyśl the party was already preparing for the 1907 general elections. For Lieberman it was the calm before the storm, and he wanted to take the trip to Spain that had been interrupted by the death of his son. He left Helene with a list of his addresses, inviting her to write him only about herself, for the sake of relieving her feelings.

Although Maria Grün was a well-intentioned institution, midway between a hotel and a hospital, Helene found her stay there a terrible experience. Yet it was to provide the background for a set of ironies. Lieberman was writing to Helene about his love for her and at the same time reported taking his family on a trip. He came to Graz alone; as she later expressed it, he found a way to do his duty with a relatively clear conscience, and then he could turn to his happiness. When Lieberman came to see her she told the officials in charge that he was her uncle. He took her out to the opera, where they saw a performance of *Carmen*. It was the first time they had been able to spend the whole night together, and nobody at the sanatorium even noticed.

Once again Lieberman wanted her to go to Spain with him. But Helene was uncertain of her capacities, and in her depression not prepared to break with her family. Her father had been acting under her mother's orders in bringing her to Graz in the first place; if she had used that occasion to defy them by running off with Lieberman, she thought her mother would have blamed her father. Lieberman, usually of quick temper, could hardly be really angry at Helene, and may have realized how demanding he was being. There were limits to how emancipated he could expect her to be, and if they bided their time they might be lucky. In February 1907 she finally passed her exams, which cleared the way for her to study medicine in Vienna; later that spring Lieberman won the election that would regularly take him to the same city.

On his trip Lieberman wrote Helene regularly; from the period between April 10 and May 6, 1906, five letters and six postcards still exist. Although he gave her specific instructions about where he could be reached by mail, she was not able to match his letter writing. As a sightseer, it was easier for him to find things to recount. During this period when she was recuperating in Graz, it might not have seemed desirable to rehash all their well-known difficulties.

Only Lieberman's initial letter, dated April 10, was intensely personal. For the first time he addressed her with an intimate Polish diminutive, "Halusia." All his earlier letters had started without any salutation at the beginning; in his one letter before visiting her at Graz he had begun on a more intimate, yet still rather stilted note—"Miss Hala." But now their relationship had changed.

> My dear Halusia,
> After a few days of unusually tiring travel, I have finally arrived in Bordeaux.
> I had a very sad trip. I was in such a gloomy mood as never before. I am overcome by fear all the time. It seems that the cause of it is the passionate and as strong as death feeling that links us.
> My soul keeps on asking itself a question: what is the reason for this journey through foreign lands and seas, when I leave behind me everything that contains all the charm and beauty of life?

Up till then Lieberman had liked to travel alone on vacation, especially to escape the tensions in his life. He was a lonely person who, in an apparent paradox, did not like company on a trip. Now that he was involved with Helene, however, he no longer enjoyed being a solitary traveler, and finally he ceased his globe-trotting. But he had a more immediate issue to address himself to with Helene—his reputation as a Don Juan.

> My dear Halusia, after what you have heard about my "romances" it may seem to be a paradox to you—but I think that for the first time I am loving in a pure, true and noble way.
> My thoughts are always with you, and really you are within me, I feel you in my blood, in my nerves and in every heartbeat.

All of Lieberman's letters to Helene had a sentimental air, which may sound overcompensatory but more likely reflects the cultural conventions of that time. Any love letters are apt to be relatively boring to outsiders; these, however, were to be enduringly touching to Helene.

> In the train I kept looking at the photographs that you gave me. You do not have any idea what a wonderful pastime these photographs were to me during the trip, and how well you have done by giving them to me before leaving.
> I relive in my imagination hundreds of times those moments that we

have spent together recently, my divine girl. How I wish to have you by my side, here where I am surrounded by strangers, lonely and sad. I have decided never to travel without you again. We should take all the forthcoming trips together. I am so intoxicated by your love, my good and passionate dear, my one and only you, Halusia, that I cannot bear being alone any more.

My soul is too eroded by my longing for you to live away from you.

Lieberman's political mind could not help making its observations about the history of social revolution.

Bordeaux is an extremely beautiful city, where—as it can be seen—the Girondists from the French Revolution are thriving. It is the capital of Gironde. A magnificent monument has been erected for the Girondists, of which these brave people are in my opinion worthy.

The next day Lieberman crossed the border into Spain at Biarritz, then a fashionable resort. A purpose can be detected in his careful dating of letters and postcards to Helene, in contrast to his usual practice when writing her; he wanted answers, and when he did not stick to his travel schedule he let her know. On April 12 he wrote her a postcard from Biarritz.

I am sitting on a high cliff detached from the mainland. The ocean roars at my feet, blue and shining in the sun and boundless. The sadness and longing in my heart are as great as this roaring sea.

Through the Pyrenees which disappear in the mist of the sky, my mind flows toward you. At my feet the ocean roars and moves me with its music.

This morning I got your letter. What a joy this was for me! And now I am reading your words. If you were with me! Biarritz is a very beautiful place just on the Spanish border—a place for rest for kings!

Unrestricted luxury reigns here. This afternoon I am going to San Sebastián.

Lieberman was dazzled by the seashore at San Sebastián, and headed on to Madrid. "Yesterday, because of lack of attention of the royal palace guards, I sneaked into the private royal chapel, where a cardinal was celebrating a mass. The Queen Mother was there, the prince Bourbon and a princess. I stayed until the end of the mass and felt strengthened afterward." He planned to see a major bullfight, as a national celebration not to be missed. He found the city "full of temperament, the life is nervous, upsetting, full of fleeting impressions, it is full of life all day and night." He was heading for Andalusia, but his letter was personal.

I have been alone all the time during my trip. I have not made any acquaintances yet—it is not the same as before.

I avoid it on purpose.

I do not have any news from Poland.

And how is it with you, Halusia? I imagine that with every day you

grow stronger, and I remind myself frequently of when we were in Graz
feeling so truly and childishly happy.

How different it would be if we could have taken this trip together!

As he headed for the romantic south of Spain, he wrote: "I feel that I will
take this trip once again in my life, and then I will be an excellent cicerone for
someone, whose figure accompanies me now through many countries and
cities."

The bullfight in Madrid made a terrifying impression on him, but the
drama was such that, although he was upset, he was going again in Seville: "I
am attracted by something to see this awful duel of people and animals
against death." Frenchmen and Englishmen were in Seville, but the city reminded him of the world of opera—the settings for *Carmen, The Marriage of
Figaro,* and *Don Giovanni.*

> The city has not lost yet its romantic nature famous from the operas. It is
> true that the European culture has left its leveling-out mark here, but in spite
> of that everything here looks like a fairy tale. The city is full of roses, orange
> blossoms, palm trees, the smell of balsam rises from the ground. Much of the
> Mauritanian culture has been preserved here, but everything pulsates with
> the hot southern life which is still unknown to us. Everything here causes
> day-dreaming: the nature, the people and their customs, the ancient Arab
> castles . . .

He had had no news from Helene. The more glorious his trip, the more
reason she might have had for resenting that he had gone without her. But he
still addressed her in the same way: "How are you, my beloved goddess?"

The romance between Lieberman and Helene had had a fairy-tale quality
to it from its beginnings. She had set her cap for him years before he began to
notice her as a woman. One source of the mutual attraction, for each, had
been the unattainability of the other. Then in Graz they had entered a different phase. Especially for Helene, but for Lieberman as well, it was the fulfillment of years of fantasy. Now, on top of the seeming unreality of what had
happened to them both, Lieberman was adding to the glow of their love his
accounts of this glorious and exotic trip.

He sent a postcard from Cádiz, and then a note about a stormy crossing
to Morocco. Tangier was entirely different from anything Helene had ever
seen; North Africa was such a contrast to Europe that Lieberman tried to
capture the spirit of the place.

> When I set my foot on land I saw an image which no human imagination
> could create. I was in Turkey—but what I saw there was a poor imitation of
> this sea of colors and sun rays, which seemed to flow through the whole
> country. The real, wild, barbarian and fantastic Orient immersed in warm
> colors surrounds me. There is nothing more enchanting than studying the
> life and habits and movements of this great mass of half-naked people, wear-

ing colorful turbans, fantastically draped burnooses over their shoulders and walking with awe-inspiring grace through the streets and fields. You can see here human faces of all colors—from the white skinned Arabs to the shining black skin of Negroes.

In the midst of this civilization Lieberman was struck by the dignity of the Jews: "what noble, knightly figures! How gracefully they move! How beautiful are their attires!" He felt reborn under the impact of the stream of new impressions.

Lieberman then crossed back to Gibraltar and Algeciras in Spain, in order to see the Alhambra in Granada.

This masterpiece cannot be described, it must be seen. The person who built it was really a landscape painter, because with the aid of perspective incorporated in the arcs and columns above the windows, he was able to show everybody the marvelous views of living Nature, which surrounds Alhambra with a circle of snowy mountains and green hills.

On his way to Algeria, Lieberman was unexpectedly forced to spend four days in Cartagena; it was a boring hole of a town, but he wrote Helene, after expressing his frustration, a bit about the history of the place: in 1873 the socialists had seized the war fleet docked in the port, and then spent months under siege from the English. The spot had therefore its one deed in "a great style," but otherwise was without the charm of other Spanish towns.

He had met an interesting woman, an American journalist, with whom he had gone mule riding in Morocco; and also an Englishwoman. Stuck in Cartagena, he wrote Helene about the people he had spent time with. He hated the company of Germans, "a boring, gluttonous and stupid people." After four weeks he was homesick and filled with longing to be back in Poland. But before returning home, he went to Algiers, Constantine, the Sahara desert, and then returned to Europe through Tunisia. Lieberman said he had gone without any word from Przemyśl, nor been able to read anything in the newspapers about Austria. He had received a postcard from Helene in Granada, but evidently her letter to him in Seville had gone astray. Unsure that his feelings for her were fully reciprocated, he planned to be back in Poland by the middle of May.

Once he was home he threw himself into the political campaign that ended in his victory. With a restricted suffrage, and although he was stigmatized as anti-Polish because he was a Jew, Lieberman polled 58.5 percent of the vote; he got 3,533 votes to his opponent's 2,496. Evidently he did not burden Helene at this time, either with dissatisfactions over his political conflicts or with his personal loneliness. The important issue in her life now was passing her exams.

He encouraged her to finish with her preparations for the *Abitur.* At one point she had been worried about his health, since a mutual friend had reported he looked sickly. Despite his self-preoccupation, he briefly reassured her and then went on:

> Don't let these sad thoughts detach you from your work. I'm expecting with great anxiety the day when you take your exam and if you pass then it will be the biggest reward for me, for all the sadness I felt. I count on you to do everything to achieve your goal and then that would be a great day of happiness. I'm looking eagerly forward to it. You should forget about me, about my fate, all your strength and energy should be put into your studies and then I'll have a bright moment in my lonely life. Nothing else is more important for me than seeing you free, joyful and happy. Please forget about me until you pass the exams.

Lieberman had confidence in Helene's talents and confirmed her own faith in her future. Her own father was too subservient to her mother to be able to propose suitable plans. However much her relationship to Lieberman had threatened the stability she needed as a setting for her work, at the age of twenty-two, after three years of preparation, she got her *Abitur*. Now she could move to the city of her imagination.

PART II

Vienna

"Don't let anybody read this letter. It will not be a lie if you don't show this letter. A lie is sometimes a human deed. If one of your patients will have a deadly heart disease, would you tell him that openly in order to avoid lying? Halina, respect my pain. Maybe you think that such a pain is not a sacred thing. Only you may look upon it, nobody else has the right to."

Herman Lieberman to Helene Deutsch, early spring 1911

"I know that I have long been remote from life—I find my soul just as proud and ready for a fight as back when I expressed my hatred and my 'outsiderness' by means of unkempt hair and a dirty dress . . . Fel, in my failures I find myself again! My good, good comrade, how I need you now, how near you are to my soul! The two of us remain *we*—we will not yield even for a kingdom—in misery and in foolery—but not in 'adaptation-conformism'—we will be together. Do you understand me? To strive —yes—and how!—even with elbows, if need be."

Helene to Felix Deutsch, September 18, 1913

"You have been here and I know nothing of it. Everything I had to say to you disappeared. All the kindness and tenderness I wanted to show you dissipated, and when the train was gone I wanted to run after it and make up for what I had missed. Thus one lives within oneself, besides oneself, past oneself."

Helene to Felix Deutsch, early spring 1923

1

"Storm-free" Existence

In 1907 Vienna was in its heyday. During the late nineteenth century and before the outbreak of World War I, the city underwent a cultural Renaissance. Striking new developments took place in music, philosophy, mathematics, economics, as well as in art and psychology. A spiritual unity existed within the intellectual elite, much of it composed of emancipated Jews. People in different fields knew each other, and sometimes even changed professions; the leaders in each area were aware of innovations elsewhere. The circle immediately around Freud had had its formal inception in 1902; by the time Helene moved to Vienna Freud's influence on the younger generation of intellectuals there was immense.

Adolf Hitler also came to Vienna in 1907, where he stayed until leaving for Munich, Germany, in 1913. The Austrian capital was a maelstrom of conflicting ideologies, as the Hapsburg empire teetered on the edge of extinction. Nationalist forces pressed from a bewildering number of directions. The gulf between reality and official ideology stimulated a general revolt of the intellect, a search for the actualities beneath pious public formulas of the truth. This rebellion was led by those ideally placed to see the discrepancy because they had nothing to gain from accepting the official view: the educated Jews. Mordant irony was a key weapon for piercing the structure of formal beliefs.

Vienna's cosmopolitan intellectual life was the vortex of the vigorous cultural conflict between East and West that enlivened the last days of the Austro-Hungarian political system. The intensity of the social forces, as well as the sense that liberal culture was on the verge of being undermined, are reflected in the work of many Viennese writers and thinkers. The Viennese

intelligentsia were to be the first to have to face one of the central perplexities
of twentieth century history: the erosion of liberal beliefs. Pre-World War I
Vienna foreshadowed the collapse of the traditional values of humane civilization. It can be no accident that it was then that so-called Victorian commonsense notions about human psychology were to undergo the most searching scrutiny.

It has been tempting for some to think that history has a progressive
tendency, and that as time passes people grow more emancipated from social
prejudice. All too often, however, technological improvements are confused
with cultural gains; we are apt to be at least as intolerantly narrow as any
previous era. The Vienna Helene came to was expressive and creative, yet
highly civilized. It was characteristic of old Vienna that some of its leading
representatives were talented people who had moved from the provinces.
Helene had admired the Viennese spirit since at least the days of Mädi's
diary, and she retained its special cultural vitality for the rest of her life.

Helene had had to struggle for her freedom, and to a remarkable extent
her achievement was an individual one. Had her education simply been the
result of conformist pressures, doubtless she would have lacked the drive to
make as much of herself as she succeeded in doing. Intellectual women were
rarer then than now, and Helene had received a grab-bag education. The
Swiss traditionally had facilities for educating women, and her parents had
sent her to a school in Zurich for a few months of study; she was already
deeply involved in socialist doctrine, and encountered theoretical debates
among Marxists of a kind she was not to experience again until she came
upon psychoanalysis. But in whatever context she found herself there was no
doubt of Helene's determination to make the most of her abilities. In the end
the whole of her family in Poland, including her mother, were immensely
proud of her professional achievements.

Although early on Helene had abandoned pediatrics for psychiatry, her
interest in a medical career was constant. She needed to take no special
premedical requirements at the university; under the system as it was established then, she could start her medical studies immediately. Helene did not,
however, ignore the barriers that existed to women's pursuing a legal education, and she and two friends spent hours lobbying a cabinet minister in order
to get him to allow women to study law. Law might have been her father's
profession, but psychiatry had a continuing human interest for her; it also
allowed Helene to fulfill her early ambition to be a writer.

Hard as she found her medical work, Helene remembered no special
difficulties as a woman. With an individual professor there might be prejudices against her sex, but on the whole she had no complaints. Unlike in
North America even today, once one had passed the entrance examination to
a university the assumption was that one was competent. Education was not
intended for the masses. The antidemocratic premises of elite education

meant that students were expected to work at their own pace, and within broad limits could choose when they sat to pass various required examinations for graduation. European education needed few distinctions between good and best; competitiveness for grades was therefore superfluous.

At first Helene's parents were reluctant to support her financially; they did not want to help underwrite a continuation of her liaison with Lieberman. Since she was under no immediate pressure to fulfill academic requirements, she earned money as a secretarial assistant for an author of popular adventure stories. She lived frugally, eating at places for poor students; she recalled mainly goulash, or sausages and ham. When she had prepared for her *Abitur* her parents had borne all the extra expenses of her premedical education. Medicine was expensive as a career, and therefore unusual for women, mainly because of the time it required and the difficulty of holding any kind of job while studying.

Helene passed her first examination (Rigorosum) on March 15, 1910, with the level of attainment marked "excellent success." As soon as her parents had realized how serious she was about completing her formal medical education, they started to help her more generously. Although it might seem that for the first time Helene was forced to function within a bureaucratic setting, it would be hard to overemphasize the degree to which she— like others in Vienna—relied on informal sources of intellectual support. In retrospect she thought she would never have succeeded in passing her medical exams without the existence of the mutual exchanges at Viennese coffeehouses.

Helene had no special interest in medicine itself. Medicine as a career, however, was one of the most likely to ensure her independence, and she was good enough to be able to master what she needed to know. The suffering associated with her attachment to Lieberman helped convince her of the advantages of satisfying work. The prospects of her future profession served to still any doubts about the long-range nature of her love for Lieberman. Helene's conviction that through productive work she could reach personal fulfillment coincided with Lieberman's plans to come to Vienna as a parliamentary deputy. As a representative from Poland he was obliged to attend parliamentary sessions, although he kept his legal office in Przemyśl; there was no conflict between his continuing to practice law and his serving in public office. Many of the letters from Lieberman to Helene concern dates when he planned to be in Vienna; train schedules were critical, since he was so busy that to save time they often met in railway stations, and then headed off to eat. Considering all the prior obstacles, their romance had now been blessed by good fortune; for the next four years Vienna was to be the happiest setting for them, as they enjoyed their best years together there.

At the beginning of her stay in Vienna, Helene had an inexpensive attic room; but before too long, with her parents' help, she could afford an elegant, expensive little apartment with central heating in the center of the city. When she first had looked for a place to stay (she was to have many different addresses in Vienna), one potential landlady had inquired what nationality she was; when Helene explained, the woman asked her what religion the Poles were: "Mostly Jewish" was Helene's gentle, teasing answer to a plainly anti-Semitic line of thought. Jews were hardly a novelty in Vienna, and she had her pick of where she chose to live.

One of the advantages of the apartment in Vienna where she spent most of her time was that it qualified as "storm-free." That expression meant that you could receive a member of the opposite sex without anybody's storming at you. Helene's flat, which overlooked beautiful gardens, was near to both the university's hospital, where she worked, and the parliament buildings. She had put a good deal of effort into finding a suitable place to live; "storm-free" accommodations were much easier for a man to find. Lieberman was more casual about where he lived in Vienna; his real home was in Przemyśl, and he was sometimes willing to rent a room without any kitchen facilities.

Lieberman continued to take short holiday trips without Helene, aside from his traveling back and forth to Poland on political business; but he did so without enthusiasm and for limited periods, accompanied by colleagues. Sometimes he and Helene took trips together, once to the Adriatic; usually he left first, and then she joined him. Throughout their separations they wrote to each other regularly. He sounds demanding and moody, but evidently she appreciated how much he expected of her. She knew that on behalf of the workers, as well as in relation to her, he could also be giving; no sacrifice of his time seemed too much for him. He worked until he was exhausted, and his idealism could leave him disappointed.

> People are getting worse, ruder, one cannot count on them. Little by little I come to a conclusion that my whole life and my work were a failure until now. I suffered so much in my life, everything that was noble and good in me, all my youthfulness, my dreams and longing of my soul I gave everything to the workers, but I do not see any results. The hearts and the minds of the people that I worked for so honestly are just as empty as before.

The frustrations of his career highlighted the purity of his affections for Helene. In one letter he referred to her as his "beloved girl," but more frequently he reversed the age difference between them, making more of their intimacy, and wrote as if she were the parent, the loving mother, and he her child. He might have been older and, within his circles, a famous man, but he still appealed for her help. Without her he was sad, often complained of being troubled by sleeplessness, and was concerned about his health. Yet she could be whimsical and they both were unquestionably happy.

Occasionally there were purely political events to report, as when he went to a "peace" meeting in Berlin in 1908. As he wrote on September 21:

I am the only social democrat from Austria. You will understand that this role is somewhat awkward, because, the way I see it, the "peace" conference is being boycotted by the social democrats. I was preparing myself emotionally for the party's court and I was thinking: here is a new conflict with the dogmas of our officially recognized church, but luckily I have found two Swiss social democratic deputies and two Norwegians. I will have something to defend myself with.

Long before Helene joined Freud and his psychoanalytic movement, her association with Lieberman had acquainted her with the ways in which secular ideologies could replace traditional religions; she admired Lieberman's independence, and at the same time she was intrigued by the world he was able to move in.

As he wrote in that same letter from Berlin:

The conference itself is an empty and boring comedy. We gather everyday at Reichstag and some old political mummies babble about some old ideas about the European peace and about arbitrational tribunals. One can die of boredom if one takes it seriously. When someone . . . wanted to carry a motion of sending a letter of recognition to Tolstoy as an apostle of peace, the presidium decided to reject it, because such congratulations are only sent to kings, and not to "private people." I imagine that such behavior toward Tolstoy will not worry you, because, if I remember correctly . . . you do not like Tolstoy either.

Helene was more literary than Lieberman; although she admired Tolstoy's artistic genius, and later as a psychoanalyst quoted from his novels, as a feminist she objected to the contrast between his high-sounding words and his contemptuous treatment of women (and serfs) in real life.

But international politics were far away from the life of a university student in her second year.

Every evening we have banquets and receptions, given by the heir to the throne or by Prince Bülow, etc. Because I wanted to get acquainted more closely with everything and despite the unpleasantness, I went to one of these receptions. Of course I did not go to Bülow's—I only took part in the banquet given by the German deputies. Sitting beside me was a very happy German woman, the daughter of some German deputy. I had to bear through the toasts in honor of "all the kings," which amused very much all the Austrian deputies who were with me. I drowned my sorrow in champagne and left. Probably I will not be going to official banquets any more.

Berlin did not strike Lieberman's fancy, any more than the national character of its people; as he wrote Helene, "it is a very noisy city, without any charm or enchantment which makes Vienna so agreeable."

From Berlin he was scheduled to go back to Przemyśl; except for a day or two stay in Vienna in early October, and short trips within Poland, he had to spend the next month there. Whatever reservations he might have had about what his life was like politically, the prospects at home were exceptionally bleak.

> I think with horror about the possibility of being thrown back into this mud, without any hope of freeing myself—it would be so terrible! I do not have any energy left to live like this in this uninspired place for many years, like before. And now, it would be even worse, because I would be living far away from you.

Aside from his career away from Przemyśl Helene was his one ray of hope. Lieberman felt that his parliamentary and public life did not leave him enough time for reading, so he thought Helene could help him endure Przemyśl by sending him a list of Polish books.

Lieberman's letters from Przemyśl over the next few years are filled with accounts of his misery there. He recalled the ruined fortress, and how they had strolled together on its grounds: "Our castle is so marvelous, it is more beautiful every day, you would be delighted to see it. But it is a meeting place for all the backward people, and I have to sneak in at night in order to avoid them. I feel disgust for them." Without her, Przemyśl was a "deserted" city; once he missed her in Vienna, and his memories of her made it seem like a "desert" to him: "In no town do I miss you so much as here." But Przemyśl seemed the intractable problem in his life.

> It is so sad here today in Przemyśl. The sky is gray and cloudy. Everything is so mournful, monotonous and boring, that in despair which penetrates my heart deeper and deeper, I wander through the city in the evenings and ask: how long will it be before I leave this hole!
> By the second day after returning from Vienna I was already tired and worn out from staying here, and to think that I will have to return here several times! I do not see anybody socially, not even the people from the party, I make a speech here and there and I disappear to sink in my loneliness. Life hurts me more and more and I turn away from it so that I will not see it, because the more I look the more it hurts and the more sadness enters my heart.

At times Lieberman welcomed the solitude in Przemyśl. He had to "work like a horse," and postpone thoughts of going away for a rest. But he could see how the vacuum around him in Przemyśl could be a welcome time in which to reflect: "I have problems and troubles, may God have mercy on me, but at least it is good that I am surrounded by total silence. During moments off work I can at least remain at freedom with my thoughts. That is when my heart is with you."

On the whole, though, Lieberman found Przemyśl a dreadful place; he felt irritable, nervous, and exhausted. It took all his strength to overcome his feelings and stay for a while in that town. Repeatedly he yearned for Helene, recalled their time together, and contrasted life away from Przemyśl with his sadness and bitterness there.

> I think about those last moments that we spent together in Vienna . . . You were lying on the grass, flooded with the green of the trees, facing the sky and the sun. Do you remember, how I stared speechless into your luminous eyes for a long moment? Then I was saying to myself how dear you are to me, and how difficult it is to live without you. My Halusienka, my dear mother, how sad I feel now in this desertlike Przemyśl, without your caresses, without your warnings, without any arguments with you and without your thundering morals.

Away from Przemyśl he enjoyed the beauty of nature, which he always associated with thoughts of Helene.

Lieberman never mentioned his wife or daughter in these letters to Helene, nor made any references to mutual friends. On one occasion he reported seeing her family on the street, and that they looked well; he continued to dine with the Ollers. Once Lieberman had some words about her father, who had tried to curb her but at the same time had the feeling that she was determining her own destiny.

> I saw your father in court. He greeted me very warmly and tenderly. It moved me very much, and made me glad. I looked sincerely into the old man's eyes, and I think he read what they had to say: "Why do we need this mutual grievance and coldness? We both love her dearly and adore her. Wouldn't it be better if we could get together and have a long talk about our dear Halusia?"
>
> I saw him in court again the next day. I couldn't help myself and I told him a few heartfelt and sincere compliments. Your father blushed, probably he was pleasantly surprised, because he talked to me for a long time afterward. But each one of us felt that this was not the right topic to talk about, and we would read in each other's eyes one word and one name: Halusia!

No matter how despairing he might sound about the troubles of his own life, Lieberman was generally thinking of others. At one point Helene's father fell seriously ill, and Helene and Lieberman both were worried; Helene went home to see him, and when he had recovered she telegraphed the news to Lieberman. It was another occasion on which he could express his admiration for her father.

> Send my greetings to your sister and tell your father that I wish him a speedy recovery. I know that I must hide these greetings in my heart and that I am not allowed to say them out loud, but at the same time they will join together with yours at the bedside of your father, whom I love and respect just as sincerely as you.

The main recommendation Helene could make to alleviate Lieberman's unhappiness was to suggest that he devote himself to serious reading. She sent him lists, and gave him copies, of books that mainly had a social and historical interest; it was part of her effort to broaden him. She might now be in the midst of her medical studies, but she knew how much solace books could be; so she suggested the comfort of great literature. Books could offer both of them an escape from troubles; sadness was so much his "essence" that to re-experience it strengthened and encouraged him.

At his worst Lieberman claimed scarcely to have time to keep up with the newspapers. But, at least when he visited her in Vienna, he kept promising to reform his life by getting to bed earlier, and to start reading "systematically." But as he failed in his good resolve, he joked about Helene being his "mentor," and that he needed her rules and teachings in order to overcome his own lack of self-sufficiency. Nevertheless he sent her his reactions to various books, as part of an effort to share in her intellectual life. For both of them the life of the mind was a critical means of self-fulfillment.

It is hard to evaluate how realistic Lieberman's depressed moods were. His talk of suicide to Helene may have been partly a pose. But he felt especially burdened by his obligations as a socialist leader. He had to be "a spokesman for others, a messenger of life and hope for thousands! Try telling people about the future joy and victory, when having inside yourself a soul which is torn and defeated and stripped of all worldly happiness." He also worried about what he was doing to Helene by involving her in his life. He may sound neurotically self-involved, but she shared his existence, and he feared that he might destroy her chances for happiness. "I think that by loving me, you sentence yourself to an eternal state of sadness, eternal pain and problems." However given to hyperbole he might be, the era was one which expressed itself in exaggerated terms; the mastery of intense emotions takes place within a cultural context. Helene was in danger of being consumed by her involvement with him. He may well have been not far wrong in sensing from each of her words "a despairing pain."

It is also hard to disentangle Lieberman's real health problems from his hypochondria. He often used to worry about his lungs, which he sometimes strained from too much speechmaking; but then, his younger brother was tubercular. Lieberman was also bothered by heart palpitations; he did eventually die of heart failure. Even if Helene had not been studying to become a physician, his concern about his health would have been a normal way of appealing for her sympathy. Traveling as much as he did was genuinely tiring; considering the age gap between them it would not be surprising if his talk about his physical state was an unconscious way of being sure he could hold on to her.

Lieberman's self-absorption and Helene's patient sharing in his life can be documented from the letters he sent her; but her own health anxieties have to be pieced together from his concerned comments to her. He was fully capable of being tenderly worried about her. It had been for her sake that he temporarily separated from her while she was still living in Poland; but his guilt feelings were not great enough to allow him to break off with her permanently. They were locked together, in love and in suffering, although he did try to encourage her to overcome what he thought were her nervous sensibilities.

In the summer of 1908, and evidently during subsequent seasonal vacations from her university work, Helene suffered periodic physical and emotional disorders. It was unthinkable that she return to her mother in Przemyśl, but her sister Malvina's house in Stryj was a welcoming haven for recuperation. From Lieberman's point of view she never wrote enough about how she was recovering, and he sounds jealous about how she spent her time; but he repeatedly warned that she had been careless about her health. Malvina accepted the relationship between Lieberman and Helene. But their parents' attitude made it impossible for him to visit her in that small town. There was no hotel, and Malvina and her husband would not have allowed Lieberman to make a secret visit.

The nature of Helene's illness was not clear, but it is likely that a good portion of her problems were psychological. Lieberman's peace of mind was upset when he did not hear news of her, especially since she could be so sad and depressed when he left her. He once wrote her that he remembered her eyes as "always full of tears," and her "always painful soul." He reproached her, when she was again sick in the summer of 1909, for not having kept her word, and for having once more behaved "light-mindedly" about her health. From his point of view she had only to pull herself together to be strong again. When she went to Malvina's in 1909 he said he wanted to hear from her every day, or at least every other day.

Once at least she seems to have been seriously ill. She was afraid she was going to die, which Lieberman attributed to a temporary depression as a result of her being a lonely convalescent. He insisted that she go away for at least two months. First she must consult a good doctor, and then he offered to take her wherever she wanted to go. He undertook to pay the expenses, although to overcome her "scruples" he promised that they would try not to spend too much. If her parents would not send her more money, he wanted to take care of her: "This is my *right,* of which you cannot deprive me, not mentioning that it is my duty."

Evidently Lieberman failed on this occasion, although at another time they spent a few days together in the sunshine at the seashore in Abbazia. When they traveled they did so with party friends; but Helene later said her medical duties prevented her from going as often as she might have liked. Whatever Lieberman's real money troubles may have been there was never any sign of stinginess on his part. When she was sick on one of her vacations in Stryj, he wanted her to get the best doctor, even one from Craców, and he would send the money. The prospect of taking money from him only made her feel worse about their relationship. To his amusement she gave him I.O.U.s for some of their dinners. If she ran short of money, he would be available for a "loan" if it were spent while they were together, and a couple of items of correspondence refer to what seemed to them both as a mundane side of things.

Helene and Lieberman were usually together only for short periods. It is all the more remarkable that they managed to keep in such close touch by mail. He could, however, more easily reach her than the other way around. When he went on one of his frequent trips, he would send her his itinerary; but aside from the safety of his travels, Przemyśl was so small a town that he always had to be careful where her letters went. On one occasion, when he was troubled about her health, he suggested she adopt a subterfuge.

> If you are well, write: The committee won twenty seats. If you are not well, write: The session has been delayed. Sign: Seitz.
> I ask you, please do it, however I know how you are—you will find it disagreeable to use such maneuvers. Do it for my peace of mind—I am so upset.

(Seitz was, although not a socialist, a considerable political figure in Vienna.) The secrecy that had characterized their romance from the outset continued. On another occasion he asked her to send him a telegram with a specified and urgent-sounding political content, so that he would have an excuse to avoid a silly trial and be free to leave for a rendezvous with her in Vienna.

It was not overcautious of them to be discreet when they were together, even in Vienna. If Lieberman had been a less important figure there would have been less of a problem, but there always was a furtive atmosphere to their meetings. Sometimes they were able to get away from Vienna to an elegant hotel on the Semmering, which was a three-hour train ride from Vienna; it had beautiful views, and was a favorite resort for what Helene termed "intellectual workers." Such a brief holiday would offer them both a chance to relax from their respective obligations. Yet sometimes they took separate rooms. There was no way of being certain they might not run into people who knew them both; from Galicia one went to the Semmering, and somebody from Przemyśl might even be vacationing there.

They both had to go to considerable lengths to keep straight the day and hours of his planned arrivals. Sometimes Lieberman could not be certain of his plans for arrival in Vienna, and he gave her alternative possibilities. Once he announced that he would be at the railroad station at seven in the morning; another time he expected to come at eight, and hoped she would be waiting for him even though, if something unexpected happened, he would not be able to arrive until the next day at the same time. If he was not absolutely certain of the date of his arrival he would still expect her to wait for him in a cafe in the evening. Even when he was staying in Vienna, unanticipated events like a legislative session could prevent their meeting. Although patients might delay her, she recalled that the interferences, usually parliamentary struggles, came mainly from his side. Mail delivery was so prompt, however, that there was never a mix-up in their arrangements.

Objectively, it looks as though Lieberman was treating Helene in a high-handed, peremptory fashion. It is true that in his letters she is referred to as an angelic presence; she always remains his "golden Halusia." But when he sends her telegrams with train schedules, he appears domineering. The relationship sounds, at least from reading his side of their correspondence, fundamentally one-sided. He set the lunch appointments, and it was he who was detained by political meetings. For her sake, though, he would get opera or theater tickets, although he would have preferred to relax at a cabaret.

For a trip to the Semmering he expected her to pack his things as well as her own. The details of their arrangements for living together reflected the overall atmosphere of their lives. He would specify which books that he left behind she bring him, as well as some "first class" fiction.

> Bring me my vest that I wore on the last day, and buy me five collars (size thirty-eight) and also two pairs of white cuffs (size twenty-two). One pair of underwear and one shirt. My shoes are on the night-table, if they are in good shape, bring them.

Although they were not married, he expected from her—and she complied—everything he would have from a wife according to the cultural standards of that time. Helene must also have liked the idea of taking care of him, a form of pseudodomesticity. Of course what looks like infantile behavior patterns are readily accepted by a couple in love; the necessity for all the complicated meeting plans was taken for granted by both of them.

Lieberman spent time in Vienna during parliamentary sessions. It made sense therefore, given his limited means, for him often to switch living accommodations. Since Helene regularly resided in Vienna, he expected her help. On one occasion he could not remember whether he had paid rent in advance, or owed money when he moved out of an apartment. Another time she was expected to find him a place to stay, as well as see about the transfer of his things from a fellow deputy's rooms. In general he relied on her help with his landladies, as well as her advice on where he should stay in Vienna. However, she never regarded looking after him as work.

Meanwhile Lieberman's political work in Przemyśl increasingly bore fruit. The social-democratic party activities there grew over the years. A cooperative store, which before had operated secretly, was publicly opened. Lieberman proceeded to buy a bookstore for the party, which was growing richer and turning into a local financial and political power. A big undertaking was planning the construction of a House of Workers: the cornerstone was laid, and construction started, on September 10, 1911; the building was opened on December 8, 1912 and destroyed during the German occupation in World War II. This institution was intended to be a place where workers could read, take courses, and hold their meetings; if they were homeless they could sleep there. The erection of this huge facility took far more of his time than he had anticipated. (Today a street in Przemyśl is named for Lieberman.) But whatever his public activities, inwardly he remained disappointed in the human character of the workers.

From the point of view of his party, however, Lieberman was one of its most popular leaders, and while he entertained fantasies of withdrawing from politics his fellow socialists were urging on him new electoral struggles. He resisted running for office in Stryj, but for a while gave in to pressures that he try for a parliamentary seat in a hitherto unpromising area for his party. Temporarily he allowed himself to be trapped into a visit to Stryj, where he was so pressured that he had to accept the candidacy; but victory seemed impossible, and he managed to withdraw from that race. Even in Przemyśl he thought of not running again for parliament; after listening to Helene, for a time he decided not to run for office. He saw in it "a moral slavery." He claimed he had had enough of political ambition; and the most doctrinaire wing of his party was not too sympathetic about his running. But personal unhappiness left his public life an area of service and of satisfaction.

When the parliament was dissolved in 1911, Lieberman relented.

> I was so discouraged during the last few days, that I decided not to run for office any more. You will smile skeptically, but my intentions were sincere. I fought with the party committee and other institutions for three evenings until at last I gave in.
>
> A superhuman job awaits me now, a fight against everything that is dirty and vile, a fight not with ideas and trends, but with the dirt. I cannot think about that without horror.
>
> Before starting the fight, I ask you, my only beloved and adored being in this world for your blessing. Since I have known my Halusia I have gotten used not to start a work of any importance without your blessing. In 1907 you blessed me from far away and I won.
>
> When I went to the parliament for the first time you predicted that I would not get lost in the dull crowd and this proved true. And now again, my Halusia, I ask for your blessing.

Nothing, Lieberman might like to think, had changed between himself and Helene; she remained his inspiration. Yet she had decided to go from Vienna to Munich for a while. Lieberman may have detected in this supposedly professionally motivated move on her part an important shift in her attitude toward him. His expressions of love reached a new pitch. "Do you know, my Halusia, when I die? Not when *my* heart stops beating but only when there is no room for me in *your* heart."

2

An End in Munich

The turning point in Helene's relationship with Lieberman came late in 1910 and early in 1911. From his point of view, her decision to break with him was sudden and shattering; for years he had worried that she might find someone who was younger as well as free. Miserable and depressed though he might sometimes be, basically he was content with their arrangement. He had this intellectually stimulating woman to share his life, a beautiful companion who understood his work. From Helene's point of view, she had halfheartedly been trying to escape for years. The irregularity of their relationship, a source of the initial attraction, also imperceptibly eroded it.

Outwardly their relationship continued smoothly throughout 1910. During the summer holiday they traveled together in Scandinavia; she was accompanying him to an international socialist congress that had originally been scheduled in Stockholm, but was ultimately held in Copenhagen. Even though Helene's interest in studying at Munich was fully justified by its fame as a psychiatric center, it is probable that Lieberman had perceived it as a sign that she was slipping away from him, and therefore tried to display their relationship publicly. On the trip, however, when she saw young people happy together, she regretted the way her own youth—supposedly years of happiness—had been spent. At the conference she also admired the independent position of a leading woman delegate, Rosa Luxemburg, who had originally come from the Russian part of Poland. (In her mid-eighties Helene was still fascinated by Rosa Luxemburg, read a long biography of her, and wrote some thoughts about her life.)

Lieberman was so self-preoccupied, and she so identified with his inner conflicts, that it had been hard for him to appreciate the deterioration of their relationship. Helene was beginning to realize the harm she had suffered as a result of her love for Lieberman. They bickered during the trip, and she had regularly been seasick; on the voyage she remembered feeling it was their last holiday together. He could acknowledge to Helene the deeper issue: "I too suffer terribly when I think about the tragedy of your young life, it is my fault that it took such a turn." She later said she was always busy with him, her heart heavy with his problems. If he felt he could not make a change in their lives together, Helene was willing to try something different; in the fall of 1910 she started her year of medical training at Munich.

One key element in her turning away from him can be detected in letters from Lieberman that deal with her health. They both worried about the possibility of Helene's becoming pregnant; that this possibility had not materialized, however, made her begin to wonder whether there might not be something wrong with her. On one occasion, when she thought she was pregnant and first told him so, he was horrified, and his reaction wounded her. She wanted him to share her own desire for a child of their own. Helene believed having a child by Lieberman would have been a way of getting him to break with his wife.

Her general health was excellent. She was never sick enough in Vienna to miss a lecture. So when she had reported to Lieberman on her "dangerous illness," his fears of her pregnancy were aroused; an abortion, what she once described later as a "planned miscarriage," helped crystallize her feelings toward him. For Lieberman to offer to pay for her recuperation was the least he could do to assuage his guilty feelings. She herself had not for a moment been prepared to have an illegitimate child; it would have wreaked havoc on the career she had been planning. Other rebels have wanted to have their cake and eat it too. But there were limits to how emancipated Helene was prepared to be in defying her family and the social rules of her upbringing. In spite of the way she had lived her life, she also wanted the advantages of the conventional order; she craved a legitimate child.

In full agreement with the advanced feminist thinking of the time, Helene thought women had a right to their own bodies, and in terms of her ideology she had not hesitated about getting an abortion. To the extent that abortions were medically more difficult then than now, sex had proportionately more guilt attached to it; if done properly, an abortion in Europe before World War I was not necessarily risky. Although Lieberman was aware of some of the implications for Helene of her becoming pregnant, the full nature of her reaction was beyond her conscious control. Whatever her animosities toward her mother, in some primeval way she had also identified with her. Her pregnancy meant that she was now paying for her involvement with Lieberman; it would be galling for Helene to have to conclude that her mother had in any way been right all along.

The long period in which she had failed to become pregnant only reinforced the fears in Helene of the folk wisdom, which held that an abortion might render her sterile, or cause injury to some future child she might bear. Her guilt feelings, as well as her fears of bodily injury, were exacerbated because she was not in a position even to think about conceiving a child legitimately. In the individual circumstances between Helene and Lieberman, however, a more or less standard situation was rendered unique by the death of his son in 1905. For now it seemed once again that she would not be able to have a child, and she was directly complicit in the death of a foetus. Although Helene was a woman given to imaginative exaggeration and fancy, in her case it did turn out that she did subsequently—after marriage—have at least two miscarriages before the birth of her son in 1917.

Although in Munich Helene could not expect to find the circle of friends she had known in Vienna, a change of scene was what she needed. The Bavarian capital was new to her, but she had been only a visitor in Austrian Vienna as well. As a Pole she could expect to find, like other émigrés in similar situations, that her fellow countrymen would stick together. Poles who were culturally or educationally ambitious might go either to Vienna or Munich, but especially in Germany they would feel alienated and in need of each other's support.

Joseph Reinhold, a Polish student of philosophy as well as a neurologist, was also in Munich in the fall of 1910. He was a year younger than Helene, and his parents were from Stryj. Later he obtained a doctorate in philosophy in addition to the one in medicine, and became the director of a sanatorium; to Helene he was one of the most knowledgeable people she ever met in her life. In the spring of 1911 he was making his appearance as a guest at the Vienna Psychoanalytic Society. (Although he later drifted away from Freud's immediate influence, a *Festschrift* in honor of his fiftieth birthday contained articles by prominent analysts, including Helene.) It was Reinhold who in Munich gave her a copy of Freud's greatest book, *The Interpretation of Dreams.* At the time she was working with schizophrenics. When she used Freud's concepts to help understand an especially confused case, a nurse wondered which of them was the crazier; but for the first time she felt she could comprehend her patient's conflicts.

For someone as involved with her work as Helene, it was impossible to segregate intellectual and personal friendships. For that fall of 1910 Reinhold was a genuine friend to her. When she was unhappy over Lieberman, she could go to Reinhold and tell him her troubles; he was a good listener, and she could allow herself to cry in his presence. Reinhold was also an acquaintance of Lieberman's. When Lieberman, for example, earlier had needed someone to straighten out money matters in Vienna, he had turned to Reinhold, whom he knew as an intimate acquaintance of Helene's.

Helene often went on walks or spent relaxed evenings with Reinhold; Munich was then as outstanding in the world of art as Vienna was in music. Although she considered him a handsome man, the nature of her sorrow was enough to dampen any sexual interest he might have held for her. On the whole her problems were too complicated for Reinhold, but he did what he could to protect her from Lieberman; he was concerned about her reputation as well as her unhappiness. (Later he would be one of the two official witnesses at her wedding.) Reinhold was then mainly interested in philosophical problems, as well as painting, books, and music; although he was a kind person, Helene found him passive when it came to women.

Throughout the fall of 1910 Lieberman's letters indicate some concern, but no alarm, over what was going to happen between himself and Helene. He might seem all along to have been too selfishly concentrated on his own problems, but he was a creative and talented leader who had reason to be self-absorbed. Then Gustawa's health appeared to take a serious turn for the worse. As Lieberman wrote Helene in Munich: "I am home by myself. Misia is not back yet, her mother is very sick and as I found out—seriously. So because of this a new great trouble awaits me."

Lieberman thought that if Gustawa died that that would solve the problem for himself and Helene. To a lay person her white fingers appeared alarming. But medically Helene was sophisticated enough about the nature of Gustawa's illness to know that it was unlikely to be fatal. (Gustawa in fact lived on until December 2, 1940, when she died of a heart attack during the Russian occupation of Przemyśl.) As far as Helene could see, Lieberman was kind and did everything to help Gustawa; although he no longer loved her, he did not want to be responsible for any harm coming to her. He asked Helene to be patient.

As their relationship turned sour, everything seemed to encourage its dissolution. The prospect of Gustawa's death did not have the effect on Helene that Lieberman had anticipated. Much as Helene wanted him to be free for her, she did not want to build her happiness on someone else's death; she was afraid of further guilt feelings, since the death of his son had been burden enough for her to bear. But she was shocked by his conscious hope, or preference, that his wife die. If she *had* died, Helene would have felt like her killer. The child's death had inhibited Lieberman, at least for a time; Gustawa's dying would have been disabling for Helene. A live opponent was more bearable than the prospect of a dead one. Helene did not want to wait around for any dread eventuality. For years she had resented the control Gustawa had over Lieberman's life, and fantasied that he might betray their secrets to her. Helene now decided never to go back to Vienna.

In Munich she was spared all the domestic details of her life together with Lieberman; although they had never actually lived together in Vienna, various possessions of theirs inevitably got mixed up. Helene started to detach herself from Lieberman; if she had squandered her youth on a hopeless love, she had to reassess each aspect of their life together with regret. The childlike intimacy they shared had been too close to incest. (Unconsciously the affair may have expressed how she had wanted to be loved by her father.) Despite all the passion, for one reason or another Lieberman had not created a decent situation for them both; Helene was forced to conclude that if he could only be free of Gustawa through her death, he would never opt out of his marriage. But her courage was limited, as was his; she had run away to Munich rather than face the dilemma any other way. Once again, just as she had done as a young woman—and would do later during her marriage—she was acting on what she later wrote about as one typical woman's fantasy, "the need to drive herself from home in order to become a freezing and starving Cinderella."[1]

Lieberman continued to write to Helene in the same spirit as before: the burdens of his work, his inability to read, as well as his loneliness and ill health. He asked her to buy him a brochure about the parliamentary activities of his party in the last session. Even though she was a medical student, he knew she had time for reading interesting books. Despite the complaints about life in Przemyśl, there is no hint that she had become any less attentive as a correspondent.

Then, on November 4, 1910, Lieberman was arrested in Przemyśl. A Russian officer had slapped him in the face, and he had broken his own umbrella in the course of a scuffle; laborers had attacked other officers, and a curfew been put into effect. The morning before his imprisonment, Lieberman had telegraphed Helene in Munich that things were well. But he was rounded up, along with others, and put in a jail. The political prisoners were not well treated; it was then that Gustawa—regardless of the state of her health—and not Helene was allowed to bring him food. Helene was both furious and jealous that in such a situation she could not come to his aid. The legal case was transferred from Przemyśl to Lwów, where it was quickly dismissed.

Lieberman found Vienna dull without Helene, and he made elaborate plans to come to see her in Munich. In the meantime he sent her a shorthand account of a speech of his on inflation. It took about twelve hours by train to get from Vienna to Munich; there was a night train but not an express. Lieberman arranged for them to spend at least a week together around Christmas. Before visiting Munich he had mentioned how hurt he had been by "the malicious taunts and the disbelief" of Helene's "last laconic letters." What he called her "cruel bitterness" may have been temporarily appeased by their time together, but the bulk of the remainder of his correspondence with her is filled with reproaches and grief.

For example, on January 24, 1911, he wrote her, still with the intimate salutation of "My Dearest Halusia," about his own decision to separate. When couples come apart, in the maelstrom of conflicting emotions the participants can be confused about who has initiated what. Lieberman's breaking with Helene was a reaction to her struggle to handle her perception that he did not fundamentally want her.

You understand that after what happened yesterday I could not come back
to you. You insulted me (and from now on I consider you to be a liar in
whom I trust no longer) which means that you have lost respect for me, and
in order to come back to you I would have to be contemptuous of myself. I
will come back to you, only if I regain respect from you in an honest and
certain way. Anyway, what kind of a life would it be? Every few weeks, these
violent changes that destroy us so much.

Getting away from Lieberman meant everything to Helene; she felt that if she
were to succeed, she had to break completely with him. A little bit of distance
was too dangerous, in terms of undermining her resolve. By calling her a liar
he was trying to wound her in a sensitive spot—her imaginative powers; he
was, however, able to acknowledge that she must be suffering even more than
he.

Lieberman was so emotionally caught up that he could not realize what
was happening. Once again he appealed for her compassion.

You do not understand the awful tragedy of my life, which is much worse
and dreary than you could have ever imagined. And now, when I am going
to lose you, when we are going to separate, an image of the one that I love so
immensely, the one who was the joy and the guiding light of my life, appears
before me in my soul.

She could not brush aside the genuineness of his feelings for her. Although he
described himself as desolate and miserable, he expressed his confident belief
in Helene's own "great future." As she felt she had suffered enough, she
blamed him; yet he portrayed himself as the victim. He still did not appreciate her own determination to put an end to their relationship; her ambivalences, even if unexpressed, as well as his natural wish to deny what was
happening, gave him false hope.

That February and March of 1911 Lieberman did not let up; he proposed they meet; he wanted to come see her, even though he knew it might
disturb her peace. On another occasion he expected her to come, but instead
she sent a letter. In Przemyśl he was preparing for another parliamentary
election, but there is no mention of politics in these last appeals to Helene.

My Halusia,
    I was sick for three days—and now that I am writing it is not to get an
answer from you. I am writing because during our parting the desperate
tears and sobbing prevented me from telling you everything that I had in
mind.
    Halusia, if I have done you wrong, then I have already paid for it with
those two days and nights, that I spent in Munich last time.

Lieberman had thought he had given himself to Helene; a born idealist, he
was disappointed in himself, and also resentful. He knew he had done nothing
to hold Helene.

She had now told him of a new man in her life, Felix Deutsch, and this fresh attachment of hers to a recent "acquaintance" still had to be absorbed.

> And now when I think that my, my, my holy and adored Halusia was and will be in the embrace of another man, a terrible fear and horror overcomes me, and I feel as though I was falling into a bottomless abyss. Perhaps you will never understand how hurt is even the smallest nerve in my body and how poisoned is every drop in my blood.

Like many other civilized people, Lieberman savored his own suffering too much; but he felt he had to answer her accusations; as her commitment to him evaporated, he looked like a changed personality. "It is not true that I am a different person than the one you loved. It is the same, sad, lonely, excitable and full of pain Herman. . . ." In not divorcing Gustawa he was, in his own eyes, refusing to be egocentric, as he remained faithful to his ideals of self-sacrifice; the scandal of divorce would mean he could do nothing for the cause of Polish socialism. It did not help Helene that she had to some extent shared his concern, and guilt, for Gustawa's prospects as a divorced woman; nor that his political goals had been her own as well.

> Think about it—as you have said—"philosophically," and you will understand that this social instinct growing inside me since childhood or maybe also an ideological one is stronger than my will. Think deeper, Halusia, about all this, and you will understand that I would be hurt if I were to be reproached for that, especially that I myself suffer and have suffered tremendously under this inherent burden.

He reminded her how much she had meant to him, and assured her that he would never forget her. He asked her not to think about him, but to prepare herself for a new life. She had his blessings for the future: "We have had so many holy bonds between us, that in spite of everything we have mutual indestructible duties for each other."

Another letter of his communicates her own accusations against him, as well as the intensity of his love for her; he could accept her decision with dignity and eloquence. Perhaps their mutual love of words had undermined whatever chance they had.

> I heard terrible words from you yesterday: "You have behaved lightmindedly about me, it is your own fault, you did not think about the outcome." It was a death sentence. You did not see, you did not feel the tears that I cried after those words, and with which my whole happiness went away. I acted "light-mindedly" about you. When I fell in love with you I was young, I did not make any calculations, I did not make decisions, I did not know that I would not be able to be together with you and marry you as soon as I would have wanted. I was being directed by my emotions and by the bright look that appeared in your eyes. The youth in my heart was in full swing, and I did not think about the past or about the future, I found my goddess after

which I have longed so much, without which I have been feeling so sad and so oppressed until now.

He might have been immature when he married Gustawa, but that hardly could excuse his conduct toward Helene; he was full of guilt feelings.

You also told me: "I cannot give anything to you, and neither can you." You were so sincere and open yesterday! And when I was listening to your confessions, I had the impression of having some cold ironlike hand tear my bleeding heart out of my chest and throwing it at my feet all mutilated and covered with mud. You have taken away my faith in my worshiped Halusia, you have broken the last link between all people and me.

Lieberman's anger and resentment, more properly directed at himself or Gustawa, could not help boiling up against Helene and humanity.

Now I hate you all so much, you scoundrels. Now everything is over! Now I want to live alone. To love? I would rather embrace a stone, the hard and gray ground, hissing snakes, than love you, living people, who in return for my sadness and tears, my pain and the holiest dreams, pay me with filthy words, insults, scoffing, and cruel disdain. Scoundrels!

From Helene's point of view she was not so much rejecting Lieberman as trying to save herself. She was still only twenty-six years old. Lieberman was so guilty toward her that he had to accuse her of guilt too.

Although their letters over the years had been concerned with planned meetings, times and places, that spring of 1911 he showed up in Munich unannounced. In the midst of her medical studies, while she was on her way from one lecture to another, Lieberman appeared. Although, objectively speaking, she should have allowed herself more time, she had defended herself by becoming engaged to be married. Now he learned that it was over between himself and Helene. He addressed her more officially as "Halina": "I spent the whole night without sleeping and today I'm walking through the mountains and I think about my unhappiness and it seems to me that the only solution for despair and suffering is death." Neither she nor he took a suicide threat seriously; he immediately went on:

But the call of life which is almost dying beats inside me like a wounded bird and cries for help. I'll follow this call and I'll try to live. I have decided to follow your advice, I'll overcome the pain and lead a dead-like existence.

But you, Halina, will not disappear from the horizon of my life. This is the only thing that I ask of you. I have to be near you and I must see you from time to time, talk to you even about meaningless things. And after that I'll go away strengthened to continue overcoming my suffering.

I'm asking just for your friendship, nothing else, without any hidden thoughts, I give you my word of honor. I'm not asking for any pleasure, any sweetness, any caresses from life. I want to live upon your friendship, a miserable crumb. I know that I am a nothing in your life. You have your own little place, your happiness and your quiet, gentle love. But in spite of this don't reject my friendship. Don't be afraid of it and your fiancé should not fear it as well. You will be convinced what a great soul I possess. No human creature has been able to get such a wonderful, pure and divine feeling from his heart, as is my friendship. Don't be afraid of it, I won't use it foolishly as the other feeling. All the crimes and wickedness of my broken feeling will be repented for by this enormous, pure and holy friendship, which I'll always have for you.

This friendship will not be temporary, its fate will not depend upon the chance of our meeting or not. It will be half the content of my own life, touchingly it will look onto your happiness, your peacefulness and your little lovely place, which you will create for yourself. Over your happiness my friendship will rise like a rustling tree above lovers heads. I don't ask for anything in return for my friendship. Just be good for me.

Yesterday, probably without intending this, you told me a few rude things which hurt me to the marrow.

Helene later said she had had to do that, she had waited so long before breaking from him. "We will *never* talk about the past, but when talking with me always remember that you are talking with a very poor person whose whole soul is one big wound."

She knew how hurt he was. His lament was different from his habitual complaining.

You will respect my shocking unhappiness and my holy but rejected feelings. I'm not asking for any warmth nor for any mutuality in the friendship, because I will nourish it in my heart for you and that will be the sweetness of my life and my source of strength.

Still he had a demand for her.

Just come over to see me for a few hours so that we will talk about it, I have to ask for much advice from you. Do it for me. It is your fault that today I'm facing the future helpless. You showered me with caresses, you spoiled me and today I'm not able to make a step on my own without you. You threw me from the heights to an abyss and if you don't take my hand and save me I'll not get out. This will last for a few days more, my Halina, and this will help me a little bit to get used to my life.

I beg you, come to see me for a few hours, immediately after receiving this letter. I have much to talk about, nothing about the past, everything about what I intend to do with myself in the future. You have to be patient with me. I know that you don't have any time, that you are busy, but find the time, break away, please do this.

Lieberman was staying outside Munich, and during an interview in 1978 Helene said she had then gone to see him. For years he had been appealing for her help, but now he needed something specific from her.

Halina, dedicate one day of your studies to me, come to me as a doctor, I'll be the patient. Nobody but you is able to save me from madness or suicide with your goodness and wisdom. If you knew that somebody is very sick and depends upon your help and advice for life, wouldn't you leave the clinic behind and hurry to help? But here a man, who however has no rights to you, is begging you for it, a man to whom you were closely associated before.

Yesterday I heard from you about the disgust and horror with which you look behind you upon the years spent with me. But believe me that there were times not rare, when I gave you a lot of happiness, euphoria and we shared many happy moments. I remember them, they stand vividly before me.

Helene too recalled their good times, at least later on. Lieberman's most poignant letter to her continued:

I even remember the words which you whispered into my ear and your big eyes that were filled with indescribable ecstasy, opening bottomless depths for me. Remember during those times our hearts moved toward each other and we were truly like one soul. So come here, I'm expecting you. Here in the mountains the wind blows strength and health. These mountains know us from those happy days, when the sun was still clear and bright over me, let's start our friendship right here, you will be convinced that from now on I will live from your happiness without jealousy and I want to bury for ages the biggest pride and happiness of my torn life. I only want to live for you. My only reward will be a heartfelt word of discreet compassion, which possibly I will hear from you. Believe me it's true. This dreadful misfortune which struck me like lightning tore from my soul all the sordidness which poisoned your life for almost seven years. But do come to see me, my sweetheart. It's even your duty to do so.

Lieberman had encountered Helene and Felix together on a street corner, and he saw with his own eyes that she had chosen someone else in her life. On Helene's initiative, Felix—a member of a dueling society—had threatened to fight Lieberman if he did not leave them alone.

I was trembling like a poplar leaf in the wind, I was sobbing inside and at the same time I felt joyous: here is my sun, here for a short while a sunbeam will warm up my cold heart. But both of you kept turning away from me and chasing me away. Believe me, Halina, there are short-lived sufferings which equal oceans of pain. Believe me, believe me, when you both sent me with your looks underneath a street wall, there I bought back with my immeasurable unhappiness all the sordidness and crimes committed against you.

Please come over, Halina . . . One more favor. Don't let anybody read this letter.

Lieberman obviously had Felix in mind, and at the same time wanted to atone for his accusation about her untruthfulness.

It will not be a lie if you don't show this letter. A lie is sometimes a human deed. If one of your patients will have a deadly heart disease, would you tell him that openly in order to avoid lying? Halina, respect my pain. Maybe you think that such a pain is not a sacred thing. Only you may look upon it, nobody else has the right to.

Lieberman respected Helene's capacity to cushion the truth as a human asset, not a moral liability, and she respected his plea as well as Felix's delicacy of feeling.

Do you remember what you said in Munich at the railway station: "I only love you, and if you become sick, write to me, I'll come." Time has denied your first assurance, but the second doesn't require much trouble on your part. Send me a telegram about your visit. I'm very, very sick. Bring me something for headaches and sleeping pills. Also bring me something for a sore throat because I caught a cold yesterday.

He had failed, lost Helene, and his longest letter to her ended with himself as almost a little boy in relation to her.

As far as one can tell, Lieberman was as good as his word; although it is not entirely clear from the handful of remaining letters of his from 1911, it seems unlikely that Helene visited him. Her physical presence would only have prolonged both their suffering. She could communicate the warmth of her feeling through letters, although she may have feared that even letter writing might unintentionally mislead him, and disturb herself. He was grateful for her "warm tears," but on the whole was able to leave her alone. Once, in August, when she had returned alone to Vienna, since Felix had had to stay on in Munich for a while longer, Lieberman telephoned her; and then in September he wrote her, again hoping for a short chat. He had a free day in Vienna, on the way back to Przemyśl, and tried to arrange a meeting. He was full of faith in his capacity to transform his own suffering into service in behalf of the misfortune of others.

Twice in the 1920s Lieberman turned to Helene for medical help in Vienna for his daughter, Misia; although he was cautious about interfering with her life, he knew he could count on her. Earlier, when Misia had married, Lieberman and his wife sent Felix and Helene an official announcement. Misia later became emotionally disturbed, and Felix, although not a psychiatrist, had the necessary hospital affiliations to help take care of her. During early 1924, while Helene was in Berlin apart from Felix, Lieberman met her; they exchanged confidences, wrote letters to each other, and then failed to agree on when they might see each other again. In 1925 they saw each other by chance in Venice, where Helene had gone on holiday with her eight-year-old son, Martin.* Lieberman, according to Helene's memory, consulted with Felix about Gustawa's health, and saw Felix in late November, 1935, about his own medical problems (high blood pressure).

In his final letter to Helene in 1911 Lieberman had promised to live in

* Cf. chapter 12, pp. 223–27.

such a way that she would, unlike then, remember "with emotion and blissfulness" the years in which she had loved him. She could hardly have done otherwise; as active as she continued to be, she also possessed the memory. Helene later fully appreciated the spirit of a 1929 letter of Freud's,[2] written to a Swiss follower after the death of a son.

> Although we know that after such a loss the acute state of mourning will subside, we also know we shall remain inconsolable and will never find a substitute. No matter what may fill the gap, even if it be filled completely, it nevertheless remains something else. And actually this is how it should be. It is the only way of perpetuating that love which we do not want to relinquish.

Breaking apart can be as mysterious and unfathomable as falling in love itself. Perhaps the couple had been too accepting of each other's imperfections, in addition to their other similarities. In a famous clinical paper of hers, "Hysterical Fate Neurosis" (1930), Helene tried to re-examine some of the themes of her love for Lieberman. Psychoanalysis was a system of thought which emphasized the significance of the past; but to concentrate on childhood traumas can be a defense, an evasion of how much more acute adult suffering can be. Had she married Lieberman, or borne children by him, her career would have been entirely different. Some of her later theories about feminine psychology can be interpreted as regret that she broke with him. Anybody is apt to romanticize the past; but after 1911 Helene felt like a different person. She had made her decision, and then obsessed over it for the rest of her life. She was to interpret her suffering over Lieberman as part of a general feminine tendency toward "masochism."

No matter how tortured Lieberman's private life may have been that spring of 1911, in April he accepted the candidacy for re-election to parliament. On June 19 he again won. (His victory was narrower—3,432 out of 6,753 votes—but there were over five hundred canceled ballots, most of them apparently rightfully belonging to Lieberman.) His success gave him a foundation on which to endure the loss of Helene. His political career continued along idealistic lines. In December 1912 the Workers' House was finally opened in Przemyśl; whatever his complaints about them, the workers stuck by him.

During World War I he served in the Polish Legion. Once Poland was again an independent country, thanks to the Treaty of Versailles, he was elected to the new parliament in Warsaw. He rarely visited his wife in Przemyśl, although he sent money and gifts; their relations remained the same. As an opponent of the right-wing strong man General Josef Pilsudski, who staged a coup d'état in 1930, Lieberman was arrested and spent three months in a military prison. After being sentenced to two and a half years in prison, in September 1933 Lieberman emigrated from Poland to Czechoslovakia and then to France. He took only a small suitcase with him from Poland.

Przemyśl had been occupied by the Russians during World War I, and they had searched his quarters then; his Jaurès correspondence, along with other papers, got lost at that time. At the beginning of World War II the Russians again occupied Przemyśl, and then later the Germans; the Nazis robbed Polish culture in addition to devastating the country.

Misia died in a tuberculosis hospital on July 19, 1940, a few months before her mother. By then Lieberman was the Minister of Justice of the Polish Government-in-Exile in London. Although Gustawa died in Przemyśl on December 2, 1940, the news did not reach London until the end of June 1941. Lieberman, on September 27, 1941, married—almost secretly—Stefania Sigalin,† a much younger woman who was a party worker; the anti-socialist press in Poland had gossiped about his possible divorce, and in remarrying he sought to avoid a sensation. His mission in life remained his political career. Lieberman himself died in London on October 21, 1941; on the way to a meeting he suffered a heart attack (he was being treated for heart problems), got himself into a car, but died on the way to the hospital.

---

† She later became involved with Stanislaw Mikolojzyk, Premier of the Polish Government in London between July 1943 and November 1944; she went back to Poland with him after the war, and remarried after he fled in the summer of 1947.

3

Felix Deutsch

From Lieberman's point of view he had behaved as honorably as he could toward Helene. If Helene suffered, so did he; he was doing his best. He had sacrificed the harmony of his home life for her, remained faithful to her, and paid a price in terms of his reputation. They had had plans to move to Paris, where he proposed to become a newspaperman. Helene was, however, skeptical, as they both shared the conviction that his calling lay with the cause of Polish socialism. Any way he tried to turn meant a painful dilemma. No one ever has unlimited options, and as best he could he accepted the responsibility for his own life. If he sounded depressed a good deal of the time, there were objective grounds for unhappiness.

Helene's position was no more enviable. After having first pursued Lieberman, for years she had passively submitted to an untenable situation. Later, in 1924, he reproached her that her devotion to him had made it harder for him to contemplate breaking with his wife; but by then Helene too was married.

It is possible to be harder on both Lieberman and Helene. On Lieberman's side the self-indulgence was clear; he loved Helene but chose to remain helpless about a divorce. In politics he could be strong, but with her he acted weak; he could not have been pleased that she was the witness of his incapacity. She too had tried to take a short cut to happiness; even though she was so young when she first was entranced by him, long before the age of twenty-six she might have awakened to the impossibility of what she had had in mind. Her hesitation must have been one of the sources of her appeal to him.

Although it was easy for them to idealize their relationship, they had also succeeded in bringing out the worst in each other. Lieberman, an active man, was reduced to being a chronic complainer with Helene. He could rarely laugh about himself, but accused life, and the workers in particular, for his inability to find space to breathe in. Yet he also enjoyed his predicament too much. Helene too had shared his pleasure in suffering. She later said she had contributed to the problem by never demanding that he make a choice; by spoiling him, she helped take away his forcefulness. She too was punished by her own guilt feelings. Realistically, however, no matter how much it took from her to break with him, she was too young to allow herself to be trapped.

It had been very positive for them to have given each other all their love, yet the love was too tainted with pain and worry. Although Helene still loved Lieberman, her instinct for self-preservation gave her the strength to break with him. Both of them had all along felt there was something wrong about their relationship; each had trembled at the prospect of losing the other. She made the final choice, and although they both suffered the consequences, it was her life that was to be completely transformed.

Certain tragedies can be an asset, not just a liability. The need to suffer may be one of the curses of creativity. Losing Lieberman was to be a central trauma of Helene's life; yet she had done her best, and the failure was not attributable to any lack of effort on her part. What happened with Lieberman might have been heartbreaking, yet it was in some sense worth while. Helene had never sought respectability and contentment; she thought she deserved more than that from life. For some people such a tragedy can deepen understanding and feelings; it expanded Helene's tolerance, and also enhanced her outlook on life. She could not regret the positive uses to which she could put her whole experience with Lieberman. Consciously having decided made it more painful, yet it broadened her; and Helene, like others, was convinced that one has not quite lived life without experiencing tragedy.

Although an undercurrent of grief and mourning about Lieberman persisted for the rest of Helene's life, at the time of the break she managed to deny to herself the loss she had suffered. In 1933 she published a paper on the role of denial in "chronic hypomania." And in 1937 she wrote an article entitled "Absence of Grief," something she was familiar with; her mourning for Lieberman was piecemeal and delayed. That same spring of 1911 she had become engaged to Felix Deutsch.

At the time she could throw herself into her work. Helene now was determined to fulfill her final requirements for her medical degree. Professional ambitions could help replace the private failure of her life. The more she had suffered, the more she demanded of herself that she find work that would satisfy her creative needs. She had her career ahead of her. Felix Deutsch could help her, humanly as well as in her profession.

The whole atmosphere of Helene's relationship with Felix was different from her involvement with Lieberman. Felix was just a few months older than she, although, since he had gone to medical school without the delays she had experienced, he had become a doctor in 1908 and was further along in medicine than she. Above all, however, she experienced a sense of relief now; there was no reason for hiding with Felix. He was unmarried and unattached; for the first time in her life Helene felt free with a man. She always remembered having gone hiking ("mountain-climbing" as they called it in Central Europe) with Felix in the countryside outside Munich, and on the crowded train coming back remarking to his temporary incomprehension that "the air is clean." She meant that she no longer had to fear that someone —her mother, Lieberman's wife, a chance acquaintance—would not allow her to find her own way. Her relationship with Felix was a legitimate one, without guilt and anxiety. She could look forward to marriage and children with a man who, as it happened, was a Jewish physician her family could not object to.

Felix, a native Viennese, was spending a year in Munich on staff; he had made internal medicine his specialty and went there to study under a famous Professor, Friedrich Müller. Munich was not just the capital of Bavaria and a major artistic center but altogether a cosmopolitan place. In psychiatry, Helene's field, Munich's medical school could boast of Emil Kraepelin's famous clinic; it was such a renowned center of psychiatric training that the most famous Swiss psychiatrist, Eugen Bleuler, often came to lecture. Felix first saw Helene as a student in a large classroom; he asked one of his assistants who this attractive woman was. A mutual friend introduced them.

In her autobiography Helene called it love at first sight; she recalled how he had been sitting in his white doctor's coat. Love is infinite in its variety; since Helene was still not extricated from Lieberman, her feelings for Felix were bound to be different from anything she had experienced before. In extreme old age, as she contrasted these two men in her life, in moments of exaggeration she denied ever having been truly in love with Felix. He had been very kind to her, the ally who helped her most in a time of great trouble. Their early letters, however, indicate how dear to her heart he was then. They both were talented and unusually gifted people, so the relationship between them was bound to be subtle. Within a year they married, and lasted as a couple for fifty-two years. Their union was not founded on passionate erotic feelings; Lieberman had referred to her new "quiet, gentle love." Helene and Felix mutually respected each other, and had minimal jealousies; liking may be different from what many mean by love, yet it is an essential component of a stable union.

With the security of her attachment to Felix, Helene felt able to return to Vienna in late July, 1911. After accompanying her on the journey, Felix went back to Munich for another month's work, sacrificing a holiday with her. Their letters communicate the spirit of their emotions. His first letter is typical.

Unfortunately Munich, July 27, 1911

My dear Hala!

So I remain here! I remain with a heavy heart and an even lighter body.
I remain for opportunistic reasons, not because I want to, and hope to do a
decent job of sweating it out through August. In his lecture Müller has
frequently mentioned my experiments with praise, and Neubauer has promised me that however much I redo, it will be published. So it came about that
I unpacked my suitcase again, and caused my landlady to jump for joy,
corpulent though she is. My Baedeker and my dictionary look at me sadly
from their shelf on account of this arrogant betrayal; and I took them longingly in my arm and put them in the suitcase.

Felix spent his first evening playing the piano and reading. The next day he
found time for swimming with an English colleague, and then laboratory
work in the afternoon. He naturally wondered how Helene was getting on. He
regretted having left her before his plans for the next month were decided.

. . . and you yourself made no gesture, even though you generally have so
much initiative. But be penitent and make your unhappy pear-face, because
you have arrogantly cheated me concerning your picture. I had forgotten it
in a hurried moment—which is inexcusable. Please, make it up to me.

Many kisses of the usual sort,
and some special ones as well.

Your,

Fel.

When Lieberman went to Spain she had made sure to give him a photograph
of herself.

Helene went to Stryj to see her sister Malvina, and Felix sent her mail
regularly. He missed her but felt sentimental, as he had to pass by her former
quarters in Munich:

you don't come to the window as you used to, so that I am reminded of the
days when I always looked up to see if you were home for me. Now, however, I am no longer facing the uncertainty as then, and never want to get in
that situation again, do you hear? Never again, not even in my thoughts, for
the test of power was too great. Write words to me that let me forget the all
too present past, write the way you used to speak to me and what I always
listened to "so coldly." Write stupidly, naïvely and comically, and exuberantly, but in such a way that I feel your joyfulness and do not have to be
despondent. "Be good for me," as your proverb went.

His laboratory work did not flourish, because there was an insufficient number of the appropriate clinical cases of gout. But he had bibliographic work to
do, as well as some critical reviews to write.

Despite all his letter-writing attentiveness, it was not until August 1 that
he received a reply from Helene. An earlier trip to Paris had started him on

the project of French lessons three times a week in Munich (he never got far with his French); maybe if they could converse in a neutral language she would be less distant from him. He had explicitly asked her not to speak Polish with him, since he did not understand it. Mail should have taken only a day to reach him; for all Lieberman's complaints, he had never scolded her for not writing to him. Nor did she send Felix a photograph. (He sent her one of himself.)

> My good darling,
>
>   At last, a card! I can't explain to myself this twenty-four-hour journey around the world—is this unspeakable place totally in the wilderness? Just don't get too acclimatized—I mean this only in a linguistic sense. I think with horror of your twisting of words. I am going to hurry up with French, so that we can communicate in at least one language, in which neither of us will notice the other's errors.

In Poland, Helene, like Felix in Munich, was going on excursions, and he was supportive about her decision to spend the next year in Vienna passing her final examinations to become a doctor.

    He recounted his weekend diversions. A trip to a castle made an impression on him, despite the summer heat.

> All expectations were exceeded—great glory and riches were packed together in small spaces—so that even without wanting to, one had to overlook half of it—besides the fact that the guide spoke incomprehensible gibberish and boasted of the very least significant items, while busily hurrying us through the rooms. And yet: the man who collected all this art about himself must have been an artist—but must also have been a sick spirit—there is nothing personal which speaks out of the whole, no inner connection with the possessor—merely a museum, merely the illusion of forgetting the shallowness of the world through splendor.

He also went to a weird lecture about an educational system supposedly derived from Zarathustra.

> . . . a priest in red robes between evergreen plantings, who had announced himself fearfully in the dark auditorium by means of mystical Indian-sounding music, talked some . . . nearly idiotic nonsense about Zeitgeist, old railway locomotives, and electric laundry-wringers—he finally proclaimed that he didn't want to argue about whether God had created mankind or whether mankind is the "polarization object of natural forces"—and that he was not trying to make converts—at this moment I left the room, almost nauseated . . . The audience was made up mainly of ladies as old as Methuselah, and men in formal attire but—barefoot!—with sandals. I believe that only sane people are locked up in madhouses, and that the crazies are allowed to run at large.

Felix wanted Helene to be less reticent about herself, but he did not complain; his own sense of raptures gave him a physical sense of well-being, and of being close to her.

Somehow Helene felt neglected by Felix, and he had to coax her into becoming aware of the possible reasons for his ignoring a telegram from her.

Steel your heart in the fire of love and don't let it despair! Don't let little spirits of revenge nest in a breast which feels annoyance toward me who am innocent, but rather show forgiveness toward—the post office, which is slower than my thoughts which fly toward you. Then don't take revenge on me for what I'm not guilty of, and write as often as you must, and as I want you to. So—a Sunday without receiving a word. And I had been so happy to see your letter in the evening, lying on my briefcase when I came back tired from Nürnberg. Do I have to explain to you that I was not at home through the day on Saturday, but found your telegram in the evening, but could not send you a telegram in the night and was of the opinion that you must anyway have received my earlier message by then?

Felix claimed that his peaceable and conciliatory mood could be traced to his visit to Nürnberg, but his account of that old city communicates some of his own natural kindliness.

. . . that emblem of past centuries, with its narrow, crooked, quiet, mysterious streets which wind and twist, turn and bend as if unsure where they want to lead, until they all strive upward to the great, old, proud, protecting castle. And the little houses, shaky and rickety, they beckon us so kindly and invitingly, and nudge one another's corners with a smile as if they want to say: "It's good to see you, you new human, you inconstant one—just look at us in astonishment—hi, hi!—even if we're old and ramshackle, old-fashioned and crochety—we aren't longing for modern times; what we were, that we were totally—and thus we shall endure, but you will perish—hi hi!" I left the place with a pious shudder.

Although a Viennese, Felix appreciated the best of German culture; on returning to Munich he also wrote Helene:

I have looked around in all the nooks and crannies of the town, seen the knightly castles and the torture chambers; then I have landed safely here. A thousand-year-old, well-known past greets us from every corner. Hans Sachs, the Meistersinger, Albrecht Dürer etc. A homely, symphonic picture.

Felix's spiritual peacefulness contrasted with Helene's temperamentality. Despite her shifting moods, at bottom he was secure about her feelings for him. Once he referred to her as *"my girl,"* closing the letter: "if you wish it, I shall remain your boy." However she might sulk, he knew they shared a common point of view. Even though he was an internist and she was planning to specialize in a different medical field, they both had similar psychological interests. The 1911 letters contain no specific reference to Freud, but nothing

Felix wrote her implied anything other than sympathy for the psychoanalytic world view. For example, he had been reading August Forel's book on hypnotism; Felix was critical and dissatisfied with a writer he considered a windbag.

> . . . fundamentally it is difficult to explain psychological matters somatic-physiologically, to account purely materialistically for the processes of consciousness, even though we know that they have only this origin. However, rather than remaining consistent to the extreme point, i.e., to the point where we must say "we don't know," there he begins using phrases and theories, which make any sober-thinking person's hair stand on end—this is where one must draw the limit with the contemplation of these seemingly metaphysical matters. It is a fruitful area, worthy of measuring one's mind on it.

A little over ten years later Felix would himself enter the field that became known as psychosomatic medicine. In 1911, like a Freudian, Felix would use images of labor pains to describe the completion of his current work project. (Because of their having been in Munich, both Felix and Helene missed hearing at firsthand of the struggle over Alfred Adler's ideas within Freud's psychoanalytic society in Vienna.)

On his twenty-seventh birthday, alone in a foreign city but the recipient of birthday greetings, Felix was in a "solemn" mood as he contemplated his stage in life. It was an exceptional letter for him, in contrast to all the others.

> And even if you see me with your eyes dazzled by the shimmer of your feelings—yet what I am, I am totally for you. And only for you I will try to make my assets increase in the currency of the world—not outward honors, not the quest for outward recognition—for myself I unfortunately have too little ambition. If it weren't for the question of—why?—to what purpose?! Once, when I was sixteen—I lay in the grass and dreamed—there came a kindly old lady and congratulated me. "On what?" I asked—after all I am nothing. "You will become something." At that time I racked my brains to try to figure out what I could become, why anyone would congratulate *me.* At most, I could become what would mean that *others* should be congratulated. I didn't want to become anything and certainly not anything for myself.—I just wanted to feel, to have a good feeling for people.

Felix thought that at the age of sixteen he had had capacities for faith which had been eroded by the succeeding years. As enthusiastic as he was about his work, restless at inactivity, in moments of depression his newly gained knowledge seemed hollow. But even in moments of great eagerness for work he longed for something beyond pure perception: "I would like to be active and to become tired with gaining satisfaction. Knowing is much, but being able is more."

Felix's somber thoughts must have been also related to how he felt about what was going on between himself and Helene. At least Helene interpreted his letter that way, but he had recovered his normal self to reassure her about his need for her, and her significance for him.

> The holy fire that is burning in me for you will consume all the cinders of the past, and I shall come out of this metamorphosis, even if not young, yet so pure and strong. The cinders are still glowing—they burn with difficulty— but by the time I return they will be burned up without a trace and turned to ashes—and then we shall get to work, with laughter and jubilation. So, no more introspection . . .

Together, with their mutual strengths, he was sure they could turn "shabby existence" into "a festival day."

Even before Felix could correct the impact of his low feelings, Helene had returned from Stryj to Vienna, where she had to find a place to live. She would not have much more time for work left in August, and Felix teased her about what Reinhold would think of that. As she left Stryj for Vienna, Felix wrote her he was "really glad to see you returning to the civilized world." But he was concerned about how they would do together back in Vienna. "The circle of your friends will have closed tightly around you by the time I get there—the newcomer, the outsider, the intruder. I don't think I can get close to them—too many possibilities of comparison, too many memories. But we shall see." Helene had the added responsibility of a visit of her parents to Vienna. Although she had no fixed address in Vienna, she complained of lack of contact from Felix; while he was writing daily, he had the distinct impression she was the neglectful letter writer.

Only one letter of Helene's to Felix from that month they were apart has survived; although she saved his conscientiously, as she had Lieberman's, he may have been less self-consciously writing for posterity. In later years there is less of a discrepancy, as they both may have sensed that they might be writing for more than just each other. Just before he left Munich for Vienna Helene wrote him on August 28, 1911:

> Dearest! So it will be soon! Everything in me is just one anticipation. Please, don't delay anymore, it is really beginning to be distressing.
>
> Today I'm not writing much, because I am saving everything to say to you orally.
>
> Yesterday I wrote an angry letter in answer to the enclosed card—I destroyed it, because in the end I became convinced that the bit of anger that I keep in my heart is but a drop in the sea of heart-feeling and warmth which I have for the bad boy, and that the momentary protest would be a lie tinged with pride. And I know that the card too was an expression of a momentary mood and of a misunderstanding. Is that not so? We're too much friends, too earnest in feeling and too upright, to allow the possibility of petty quarrel- ings to arise between us. We will always be able to understand each other because we pursue no other purposes and aims against each other other than the demands of our feelings.

Helene was hoping to settle down to work in Vienna, and wanted to dispense with a boat trip Felix had proposed. She told him she had been reserved toward her friends in Vienna, and was looking forward to being alone with him. "Our further friendships we will pick out mutually." Felix was unhappy with the "piecework" he had undertaken in Munich; his delay in returning to Vienna had been caused by his characteristically being full of ideas. Helene too wanted her thinking to be more systematic.

> I am being visited, which robs me of much time—I can't shake off many conventional social courtesies, and thus I fall victim to these little lies. But when it gets too hard I become ruthless. I'm doing almost no work. Everything is splintered and dilettante. My boy is going to help me get order and system.

Felix was not jealous of Lieberman; he sympathized with the "unpleasantness" to Helene of Lieberman's efforts to renew contact with her in late August. There were never any secrets between Felix and Helene; he might quietly be perplexed how she could have gotten into such a relationship with Lieberman, but he was tolerant and understanding. Felix and Lieberman came to know and respect one another. Although female virginity was still an important issue then, and Helene had the reputation of a woman with a past, Felix accepted her without reservation. He had a maternal side to him that took pity on her suffering. If Helene's relationship with Lieberman had foundered partly because they were too close, almost incestuously involved with each other, in a sense her love for Felix was threatened by a different kind of absence of limits.

For a man like Felix, inexperienced with women, Helene's involvement with Lieberman served to reassure himself. He was in part drawn to her because she was so attractive to other men; her beauty and intelligence made her, in his eyes, a dazzling catch. He was never especially concerned with money, but he always thought in terms of presents for Helene; at a time when they both ate frugally, he found the wherewithal to buy jewelry for her.

The contrast with Lieberman could not have been greater, and in choosing Felix, Helene was going in an entirely different direction. He was, although an active person, more passive in relation to Helene. Felix was less threatening and not as moody; he did not ask as much of Helene as Lieberman had. Lieberman was demanding, and thought in terms of all or nothing; it could reasonably seem to Helene, when she reflected on him in her midnineties, that either he was in ill humor or in ecstasy. Life with Felix would be more ordered. His love was more tender, warmer, more human, in that it imposed less pressure on her. Helene remembered Lieberman in terms of "fire," while the image she used of Felix was that of "good water." Lieberman had given her a lot because she took it; with Felix she thought that humanly she got more from him than he from her. But Felix had wanted it that way, and the relationship between them was what both needed.

For years Helene had been identified with Lieberman, a soldier in his ideological army. When she lost him it would not be surprising if one way she handled her grief was by becoming more like him. She was much younger than he, but still, his treating her as his "beloved girl" was psychologically significant; he had expected her to be weak and yielding. Helene's love for him had been filled with pain, while with Felix she could be linked in joy. She knew Felix, a gentle person, was not going to hurt her. He was a giver, not a conqueror; and Helene could treat Felix as her "boy."

Felix's artistic personality was attractive to Helene. He painted and composed, was a bit of a poet and an excellent piano player—it would be hard to imagine a greater contrast with Lieberman. Felix was also well read in literature—in a letter to Helene in 1911 he refers to "your Ibsen"—and was altogether culturally well rounded. If he did not go to more concerts it was because he preferred to play himself. (His musicality played a role in a contribution to psychotherapy he made years later in America: he learned a great deal about patients by provoking associations through repeating words, since tone had such meaning for him.) Felix's mind was full of fantasies, and he fully shared Helene's early interest in art.

Felix was exceptionally good with small children; he loved to play with them, and they responded to his attentiveness. He had an emotional openness and a naïveté that he retained to the end of his life; as a therapist he learned to use his natural directness, and childlike inquisitiveness, to become an excellent interviewer. Helene said she found that Felix had an extraordinary "cleverness of heart"; he could be both receptive and intuitively wise at the same time. In contrast to Helene's tendency to imaginative flights of fancy, Felix was more securely down-to-earth, a motherly, not very masculine, man.

Felix was exceptionally neat about his own person, a dandy. Only a relatively narcissistic man would have been so pleased with Helene's being attractive to other men. At the time he met her he was already completely bald, and he was sensitive to his baldness all his life. Many of his photographs show him wearing a hat; and during his last years he would even wear a beret during an analytic hour.

Like Helene's own father, Felix came of a poor family. His father, a minor bank official, was a hunchback who had died while Felix was still a small child, so that Felix never really knew him. Felix's mother suffered from scoliosis (curvature of the spine), with which Felix was also afflicted. A rich unmarried uncle subsidized Felix's education; he felt torn between studying music or going to medical school but decided to become a doctor, since it was so hard to make a living as a musician. Nonetheless Felix tried to combine music and medicine, and in later years in America after supper he could disappear and play the piano for hours. He had a younger sister, Else, whom he was very much attached to. His mother lived in Vienna. A brother, Armin, a hotel manager, was about two years older than Felix. Unlike Felix, Armin was handsome, with a full head of hair; he married several times but had no children. Although Felix was devoted to his mother, Armin was her "spoiled" boy. Armin was unreliable about money, and married more than one rich widow, so Felix was the steady earner in the family; in later years they were not on speaking terms.

One of the sharpest contrasts between Lieberman and Felix, and a new element in Helene's life, was Felix's Zionism. He was one of the founders of Kadimah, a Zionist student organization in Vienna, and Helene maintained that Felix had been one of Theodor Herzl's pallbearers. In an effort to counter anti-Semitism, the members of Kadimah imitated the fighting Gentile world; so they were a dueling society as well as a social group. Felix, who was also a good swimmer, had suffered an eye injury in a duel, although it did not impair his vision. Through Kadimah Felix met Freud's oldest son, Martin, and therefore had informal social contact with the Freud family. (In later years Freud chose Felix, who did not much care for cards, as one of his card-playing companions.)

As a Viennese Jew it was impossible for Felix to be an Austrian patriot; the political regime was corrupt and backward, and an obstacle to the growing nationalism of the various peoples that made up the empire. Helene, as a Pole, could be patriotic; but the only nationalist political engagement open to a self-respecting Viennese Jew was Zionism. Although their backgrounds and attitudes toward Jewishness were completely different, Helene and Felix respected each other's beliefs.

4

Two Careers

Both Helene and Felix shared the conviction that their work was a sacred vocation. They did not have the mentality of those who look on an occupation as a job, a mere means of livelihood, or an index of social status. For some unlucky people work can be a way of consuming time and escaping boredom. For the Deutsches, however, medicine was the avenue through which they sought to fulfill their yearnings for creative achievement, a basic aspiration for them both. The calling of medicine, however, meant something different at that time than it does in North America today; in the years before World War I the Deutsches had a financial struggle. Although they lived modestly, they did not have an easy time of earning their living. Nor did they have the support of any widely accepted attitude about women as professionals, or previous models of couples who both pursued successful careers. Helene and Felix were married on April 14, 1912, before she began finally qualifying for her degree; Felix had wanted to be sure to have his last name on her diploma. She passed her second examination on November 13, 1912, with a "sufficient," and her third—again with a "sufficient"—on March 11, 1913; grades were not important to her then. She received her degree on March 13, 1913.

Except for psychiatry and neurology Helene had not felt any special interest in medicine and did her studies in internal medicine only at the end of her university career. By then Felix was able to encourage, if not coach, her in an area which remained foreign to her. He left Vienna at least twice, in June and then in October, partly in order to allow her to concentrate all her energies on passing the required examinations. She was not then on good terms or in regular contact with her family in Poland. At the wedding cere-

mony, the two official witnesses, Reinhold and Felix's actor friend Paul
Barnay,* joined the couple in sending telegrams to her parents to make sure
they understood that the relationship between Helene and Felix was now
legitimized. Although her father did not come to her graduation, an impres-
sive ceremony at the University of Vienna, Lieberman did; he lined up with
university officials and the families of graduates to shake her hand.

Felix was an optimistic man, apt to overlook minor troubles; his health
could be uncertain, but he was inclined to minimize his suffering. In the
spring of 1913 he contracted jaundice; out of dedication to science and the
desire to help others he had taken a medicine, autophan, which had not yet
been tested. He had been suspicious of the drug, and he used himself as a
guinea pig before prescribing it for patients. The drug poisoned his system,
and he suffered permanent liver damage; his complexion and eyes were thereafter a bit yellow.

In September 1913 Felix went to Karlsbad to spend his vacation and
recuperate; the letters he and Helene exchanged provide a good account of
their career preoccupations then as well as an insight into their early married
life. Their love and concern for each other are evident, as they affectionately
reported about their own lives, inquiring about the other's. Felix is addressed
as "Papuschkerl," Helene as "Mamuschkerl," and they later devised variations on these diminutives of endearment. (Helene later defined Papuschkerl
as a cozy name for a father—"my little father.")

Felix liked to treat Helene as his "queen," so she could couch her anxieties about his health in terms of an obligation he owed her; as she wrote on
September 16:

> I think with ardent, heartfelt joy of my convalescent boy—I see him exuber-
> ant with strength, returning home and I believe I shall never again have to
> feel my anxious concern at the sight of a gray, sunken face. Isn't it true, Fel,
> you'll do everything to give back your wife her joy and calm. For you have
> no idea what a torture that is, this fear for a beloved being. I want to make
> your conscience heavy, my Fel—as prophylaxis against any recklessness
> which may come upon you.

As she thought about their future happiness together, she had every confidence how free and joyful they could be; although she did not dwell on his
"cure" at Karlsbad, it could never be far from her mind. Two days later, in
the midst of other concerns, she returned to the problem of his physical state.

> Are you going to get well for me? My boy, my boy—how afraid I am for
> you, how I would like to pray faithfully only for this one grace of Heaven:
> for your health. If you have it, the world belongs to us! Write to me the
> truth, I beg you: how do you feel? What do you think of your body? Are you
> going to become strong again, and in full possession of your health? Have

* For more about Paul Barnay, cf. chapter 7.

you reflected upon your ailment at all? Is it going to get better, completely better? *Write lots and lots to me about it!*

She would not hear of the possibility of his cutting short his stay at the spa. Much as she longed for him, she wanted Felix to make "this sacrifice of patience to our future."

From mutual acquaintances, and his sister who had visited him, she found out how he was getting on. Financial considerations did not permit Helene to make such a trip herself. She could make light of their economic situation: ". . . as far as money is concerned, we'll sing for it if need be. If it's all gone you will go piano-playing by night and I'll do massage by day—hurrah!" In her mid-nineties the affection she had had for him surprised her.

> How gladly I would take all the suffering from your poor sweet body upon me! How free I am of worries about myself, knowing only the one worry about you! Is my Fel all right? It is frightening how all my knowledge extends to only one thing: the tenderness I feel toward you. This makes me so shameless as to write down everything, which perhaps I would never say to you . . .

One purpose of Helene's letters was to amuse her husband, to distract him from the inevitable tedium of his stay at Karlsbad. Felix, however, minimized the treatment he underwent: mineral water, mud baths, "and that sort of humbug." He had to eat regularly, sleep, and take walks—but he felt that medically it was mostly hocus-pocus. Letter writing also gave him a chance to put into words how he felt about his spouse.

> How much I recognize you, so far away—see you as a crystal-clear soul-mirror, as truth itself, as my power and will, the smithy-fire of life has welded me firmly to you—I cling to you and you'll never be rid of me, poor you.

With all the happiness in his heart, the separation had been useful: "for me to find out how much you love me, how much you are to me."

Just after he left she had "a day full of cares, spent in utter loneliness." As she wrote him on September 14, 1913:

> I wandered around in the Vienna Woods until near evening, when I met up with a fat, corpulent citizen, whom I used as temporary therapy for my "complex"—he declared he was "for internationalism, more or less a social democrat, but have no fear of me, Miss—others are people too, and we don't carry bombs."

"Complex" was then a fashionable psychoanalytic term; it stood in stark contrast to her past with Lieberman. In quoting the socialist she had met, she had tried to reproduce his dialect.

I felt a strange need to go to his country and said: "I'm one too." And we
talked about internal party matters until we came upon a large congregation
of comrades, among them a female comrade from Vienna whom I knew
well. I was greeted cordially and with such respect that I turned quite red—
and with deep, deep sorrow I thought of my childhood dreams where every
worker was a proud god holding the red victory flag in a sinewy hand,—
every social democrat an ascetic with a halo, and with fire in his soul.

The world of socialism now seemed very far away.

For a few minutes I participated in the silly, ignorant nonsense, then chose
the lesser evil—being alone . . . at the approach of darkness. I went—I ran
—through the black, lonesome forest, fearing for my life and thinking of that
evening when as a young thing I was accosted by a drunk. It became clear to
me for the first time that this . . . trauma from my childhood has made me
into a slave. I have undertaken to use the time of your absence for a systematic self-treatment. And if one day you should read in the newspaper: "A
woman has been arrested for aimless nocturnal wandering around"—think
of me.

She cherished her autonomy, and throughout her later work was interested in
investigating the origins, especially in women, of a lack of self-determination,
which she would one day write about in psychoanalytic language as "passivity" and "masochism."

However she liked to dramatize her life, her career now was in the world
of ideas; political action and social rebellion were over. But she still regarded
herself as a feminist, however disillusioned she might be with her earlier
hopes. She was chosen by her female medical colleagues to represent their
protest against women being denied the right to appear in court. She did not
like the task, but felt indignant at the sexual inequality. She wanted to demand of men the freeing of the sanctuary of all scientific endeavor from
medieval, degrading subjugation. "The scandal is not *our* not going," she told
them, "but that the others *do* go." As she wrote Felix in frustration: "I
wanted no further discussion, only longed to have the power to command and
to forbid."

Part of Helene's lack of enthusiasm for the role her female colleagues
would have thrust upon her was that the issue as they had drawn it up was
too bread-and-butterish. She had grown up in an ideology which saw the
emancipation of women as part of a general human awakening. A trade-
union mentality embarrassed her, and her revolutionary idealism still sought
satisfaction.

Oh, Fel! How low down we still are! Into what sad caricature are sacred
things distorted! How do I see the trail-blazer of freedom, whom I once
wished to esteem over my personal happiness, dragged into the mud! Liberation of woman! Bursting the fetters! And poor, dead Bebel, how have his

words been obliterated: "Woman and worker, in your hands lies our future."
What should the women's movement have become, and what has it become!

Despite her medical profession and her marriage, Helene felt she had remained loyal to her early aims.

> How fortunate I consider myself, to have remained true to my youth, forever immune to the spirit of the surroundings, with the strong feeling of inner enmity toward cowardly, enslaved society in which we live, with the profound hatred for the order of society which subjugates us. I feel myself as much as ever prepared for the battle of liberation . . .

Her union with Felix, a dedicated Zionist, could not help but remind her that she had not escaped burning some of her old bridges: "Ach, Fel, why is the way to your ideals found elsewhere?"

Felix liked it best when Helene wrote him with her natural exuberance and her high-spiritedness expressed itself through her idiosyncratic command of German. (A colleague later said of her that she spoke "five languages, all in Polish.") In response to her first letter to him from Vienna, Felix wrote back from Karlsbad:

> Nice talk, coherent and incoherent, just as I like it, lots of it and good to listen to. Twice a day this pearl of the German language, as no one speaks it, is taken out of my pocket and I laugh and chat with you, as if you were here.

On occasion Helene might find herself annoyed at her own twisting of German. She still wanted to talk to Felix in Polish, and hoped that while he was away in Karlsbad he might learn some; but by the end of his stay he wrote that he still did not understand a word of it.

The bulk of Helene's letters to Felix in Karlsbad are not about his health or their feelings for each other but rather concern her dedication to her work. Now that she was finished with her medical studies she was preparing herself for a career that would give suitable scope for her capacities. Psychiatry offered her the best chance of uniting her humanistic interests with her scientific objectives; so she set about systematic reading, in Kraepelin as well as the French neurologist Pierre Janet, in order to prepare herself for her calling. As she wrote Felix on September 14:

> Today I am sitting in our nest and reading anything and everything—I am conversing mostly with noble hearts—and I find it very nice to live with such a still, sweet longing, with the comforting knowledge that somewhere in the world there is a little, worthless Papuschkerl—and to live in such an impersonal way—all intellect, all thought. Napoleon-Ibsen-Kraepelin: deed-soul-thought:—I love Napoleon as I loved him as a child and hated him as a party man. I have a horror of Ibsen and I reproach him for giving us so little in the way of ideas and that for us his truths are old-fashioned and ordinary.

> But tomorrow I am going to "Pillars of Society" at the Burgtheater. But not expecting much.

Her love of art, music, and literature preceded her political commitments, and she pursued her new profession with the faith that the past discontinuities in her experience would be resolved.

Helene had many clinical irons in the fire in Vienna, and one of the places she worked at was a hospital for mentally retarded children; mongolism was the specialty of the head physician, Erwin Lazar, but other kinds of deficiencies were also being studied. Yellowish children without nails would have emotional problems as well, but these were secondary to their cognitive weaknesses. For the time being Helene wanted to master the various techniques that had been devised, although she sought some general theory which would lend coherence to her clinical experience.

> My whole activity so far has consisted of listening, and of coming to the conclusion that I have no inkling of the subject. For the time being I am learning the various methods (even, I believe, the quite coarse ones) of investigating the state of mind and intelligence, deficiency of particular qualities, differentiations of relationships of psychological functions to particular areas of the mind, etc. At the moment it is sufficient to satisfy me—however, I already feel the apprehensive concern within myself 1) that I will be permitted to take absolutely no steps of my own 2) that I ought to have prior suitable training in a proper suitable training institution. There is a jumble of topsy-turvy testing . . .

She did not find the atmosphere a congenial one, and disapproved of a younger figure Lazar had picked to promote.

> But what pleases me and gives me the uplifting feeling of free striving is the reading which I am now carrying on systematically and scientifically . . . I study with a hot head and come to the conviction that every other piece of so-called scientific work I have "more or less" done was a slavish self-desecration. I now have a feeling of freedom in my work and I rejoice that there is still so much to learn. But the practical utilization (I don't mean materially) and clinical supplementation—what tribulation!—I am testing in the dark and feel that I need a boss, a school, or complete freedom and disposition of the material.

Lazar's clinic was unsatisfactory, although she was looking forward to a psychotherapeutic congress to be held in Vienna.

> At the clinic things are pitschi-patschi. Lazar is very much occupied with congress preparations and seldom comes to the department. Moreover his activity and his efforts are less directed to the clinic than to various outside institutions, punitive institutions, etc.—his inseparable pupil Roth accompanies him everywhere and seems to hope, for the hard money, to acquire the means directed toward psychiatry. The atmosphere stinks, and there is an anarchistic mood toward the milieu.

If she was bored by the clinical material, offended by the clinic, and at sea without a theory, Helene was more sure of herself than ever. Her marriage to Felix had been to a kindred spirit, whatever the differences in their backgrounds. She felt a new sense of security and was at the height of her powers.

> I now know that I have long been remote from life—I find my soul just as proud and ready for a fight as back when I expressed my hatred and my "outsiderness" by means of unkempt hair and a dirty dress . . . Fel, in my failures I find myself again! My good, good comrade, how I need you now, how near you are to my soul! The two of us remain *we*—we will not yield even for a kingdom—in misery and in foolery—but not in "adaptation-conformism"—we will be together. Do you understand me? To strive—yes —and how!—even with elbows, if need be.

Neither of them would settle for conventional definitions of success, and this shared conviction underlay their entire married life. Helene was determined to make her own way; her work had to be an extension of her struggling, creative self.

> I have been doing a lot of thinking and my way lies clearly before me: I shall never pay with my life-blood for self-delusions and quixotic phantasmagoria —what I fight and win for my own development under most difficult conditions, that will be my own proud possession. But for my personality I will not give up the most personal part of my soul, my life-joy. It really doesn't matter in what form one creates for oneself the lie of life—and I don't intend to let my soul wither for the sake of the problematic possibility of augmenting the potency of my brain by an atom. And I won't let little bubalas tell me what to do.

> Lazar's clinic was not the environment she needed.

> My ways have not yet found firm ground. The work with Lazar does not bear the deep, serious sign I would like to have. The material is very scanty, a fumbling and searching—the whole thing is decentralized, and corresponds to some personal interest that Lazar got out of his study of psychiatry together with an interest in the care of youth, but it doesn't bear the sign of a strong personality that could be an authority to the seeker.

Helene knew that for the sake of her future development, she needed a broader framework than Lazar could offer.

> His tendency is clear to me, the matter is very beautiful, new and interesting, but I have the feeling that one must first learn psychiatric thinking, one must see a great deal of clinical material, have observed the great psychoses *en masse,* and only then turn to this special area of psychiatry.

Psychiatric categories then were different from nowadays, but Helene knew enough already to realize that she needed more exposure to clinical material before settling down to any specialty. She lacked the appropriate institutional setting in which to continue her education.

> If I am to be interested in children's hysteria, must I not first have seen the many manifold faces of hysteria? Have studied its mechanism in a great body of material, and only then apply this experience to children? Or Dementia Praecox? This massive area of children's psychoses, which clinically shows as many thousands of variations as hysteria? With Lazar, I won't see as many dementia praecox cases in ten years, as in one month in a big clinic. On the other hand, I would not like to lose contact with Lazar and with the clinic.

To go on with Lazar, though, meant that, to use one of her Polish sayings, she would have to try to wash her elbows without getting wet.

In the midst of her involvement with psychiatry, however, Helene did not contemplate becoming a psychoanalyst; if she was uncertain about her future course of training, for the time being she was determined to continue her education as a psychiatrist. Freud was a neurologist at odds with academic psychiatry in Vienna, although for a time Carl G. Jung had been a link between Freud and official Central European psychiatry. (The private split between Freud and Jung had already taken place in 1912, although it did not become public until 1913.) Lazar had given Helene a case for psychoanalysis, and she found the etiology of a typical hysteria in her subject; but she did not know what sort of therapeutic results would follow. Freud's followers within Vienna were not very promising. Yet it is apparent that Helene already understood a great deal about Freud's teachings, and Felix did as well.

One of Felix's first postcards from Karlsbad had been misaddressed to Helene under her maiden name, and in clipping the evidence of his mistake to return to him with her next letter, Helene teased him with her knowledge of psychoanalysis.

> One of my old admirers who well knows that I have been miserably married for one and a half years writes me a card which is addressed by mistake to Dr. H. Rosenbach—through a fortunate intuition of the letter carrier the card reaches the addressee. One need know no more psychoanalysis than my stupid Papuschkerl in order to be able to get the correct interpretation of this "slip of the pen" . . . . : "if she were unmarried, I could call her by her maiden name." Inwardly not in agreement with my marriage, the writer "wishes" to himself that my name should be Rosenbach. The case is clear.

The joke on Felix could be amplified by Freudian reasoning.

> If the writer were not my admirer but my spouse, I would not like to change anything in this interpretation, only the sentence would have to be formulated a bit differently: "if she were unmarried = if I were a bachelor." Isn't that so? What is the name of *her* at whose sight your subsconscious would dare . . .

In the same letter Helene announced that the psychiatric meetings were about to open in Vienna.

> Tomorrow the Psychotherapeutic Congress begins—extremely interesting program—I'm already looking forward to it. I will report about it. I didn't take a participant's card—I'll try to swindle my way through the congress, and only get a card if necessary. My darling, write to tell me exactly what interests you, and with what I ought to mistreat my psychiatric ears.

Despite her expectations, the congress turned out to be far less stimulating than she had imagined. It took up so much of her time that it was some days before she wrote to Felix again.

> I am all involved in the congress. On my breast I proudly bear the Pallas Athena as symbol of the taken-for-granted wisdom of the mighty Reichs-German provincials. From my self-confident expression no one is likely to suspect that I wangled this ornament and smuggled myself in. But I listen to the lectures with the same boredom as the "paid-up" participants. With a busy and important expression on my face I run from one section to the other, and make clever observations and comments about the martyrs of their ambition and malice.

Otto Marburg was a famous Viennese neurologist, who led one of the centers where Helene had worked; as she wrote Felix with pride, "Marburg almost kissed me in view of the public and almost proclaimed me a professor. At any rate he regards me as a colleague for the near future—he has 'great plans' for me." But even in the midst of momentary good spirits in Vienna, Helene saw her future in the context of her life with Felix:

> My dear, I am building castles, towers up to heaven, divine ideas, earth-shattering plans, all on our work together. I have had enough of abstinence and want to be together with you a lot. We have to divide up our time properly, and even if our tendencies in work diverge, we will build a life together in it. On the floor of the Neurological Institute I plan to "set up the German flag and from there proclaim to the astonished nation" (your favorite expression) that such as we two, we two etc. . . .

However dissatisfied Helene may have been with her career in Vienna, outwardly her work was going well. Her first scientific paper appeared, a report on findings with a dialysis process on the decomposition of thymus tissue by normal serum.[1] She was also preparing to join the staff of Wagner-Jauregg's Clinic for Psychiatry and Nervous Diseases at the University of Vienna; she was supposed to serve on the women's and children's wards, although she still hoped to remain in close contact with Lazar. Wagner-Jauregg's clinic was the best source of psychiatric material in the Austro-Hungarian Empire, but Helene's future still seemed a source of frustration to her. She regretted losing the material at Lazar's clinic: "small in quantity but quite unique in quality." If she were to try to follow Wagner-Jauregg, as well as Lazar and Marburg, wouldn't she be spreading herself too thin?

> And then the practical use of my future knowledge? If I should be silly enough to forego material success, I still don't want to lead my life as a fifth wheel with Wagner. I want to have my position a serious, responsible, leading one. I see no possibility of becoming a somebody in psychiatry.

Helene did not need to make the point explicitly to Felix: women could not then hold important clinical positions within psychiatry at the University of Vienna.

> Moreover the need to earn is now playing an important role. For first of all, my whole "I" protests against rolling the whole serious problem of a living onto you, and moreover a healthy social instinct is awakening in me, making me want to answer socially for my hard-achieved vocation. Besides intellectual satisfaction, I want to see the exchange fulfilled between my output and the corresponding remuneration.

After a week of the psychotherapeutic congress, Helene concluded that her work called for her to leave Vienna. Psychiatry either in Munich, under the leadership of Kraepelin, or in Zürich, under Bleuler, would be far more rewarding than anything she could anticipate in Vienna.

> I'm so tired from the sessions of the psychotherapeutic congress, as if I myself had personally contributed much . . . I heard much that was dull, little inspiration. One positive gain—the insight that I can do nothing, that in me the great possibility would be to have ability and to produce in this area, and that I face ruin in Vienna.
>
> I made observations and acquaintances. I became convinced—and this was confirmed by experienced people—that in no field so much as in this one, which I want to choose, *one concept* must serve as a guideline, without which everything must remain dilettantism, cheap stuff on the marketplace of science. That key word is: *school.*
>
> What I find in Lazar is a ridiculous caricature. I haven't been there for two days, and must *force* myself to go. Books are now my world—but where will that lead?

Helene felt blocked, but knew that for Felix Vienna was home; his career in internal medicine was already under way, and it would be nearly impossible for him to get away.

> Fel—I won't and I can't leave you. Is this strength or weakness? I don't know. I only know that I could only make this sacrifice to my feelings if I were willing to go not as a seeker, but only as one standing before the certainty of fulfillment. But as things are? Come with me, let's flee this wretched town, which I hate more than I once hated my poor, gray native town. I came here with glowing expectation, hot youthful hopes—and experience only desperate disappointment.

Viennese psychiatry seemed to her not an independent source of learning, but a provincial appendage to German knowledge: "disgusting—mainly medical 'petit-bourgeois,' knowing more or less."

Part of the earlier correspondence had been taken up with Felix's career uncertainties. No sooner had he gotten to Karlsbad than he began to entertain the thought of becoming a physician there. At first she had responded positively.

> We could live through the whole long wintertime in Munich, in our beloved native city of Munich, in the cradle of our happiness—we could rebuild freedom and joy—we could grab life with strong arms, work with all the momentum of youth, measured with happy maturity—spend jubilant Sundays on the snowy peaks and take a run at workaday Monday with the sweet and strong powerfulness of our limbs—Fel, that would be living!

Their joint Munich plan was only dismissed when Helene heard on her own that his prospects at Karlsbad were discouraging. (He even contemplated moving to Egypt, although he knew any such proposal would interfere with Helene's "whole life plan.") Felix was proud of Helene's professional standing, and confident about her future. He joked with her about a conversation on marriage at Karlsbad, in which "someone said that when the wife achieves more than the husband, the marriage goes on the rocks. So, don't frighten me." In almost no time she would shoot ahead of him professionally, and it caused a permanent strain on their marriage.

When Helene wrote about her need to leave Vienna, however, Felix responded with self-assurance and tact.

> You don't want to leave me, but you don't want to remain. The cry of fate knocks hard on the gate of life. You have to choose. You must somehow put an end to this rift. You feel in yourself that you are ordained to a higher goal which however must ever remain unattainable, as you believe, if you are not led by a knowing hand through the dark paths to the open road.

He understood her grounds for wanting to leave Vienna, without raising a hint of real objection.

> . . . against all these weighty arguments of the danger of a ruined career there is nothing that falls into the balance except the highly unfortunate love for a highly pitiable Papuschkerl, who—moreover—is expected to give you advice! My conscience would not let me falter, and, prepared for any sacrifice I would set you free—this would separate us for months, and the example of others would be small consolation; the thought of 180 love letters from a Mamuschkerl in half a year seems to me like a grand consolation—and yet, I am not a strong man, and my heart would bleed to let you go. And together? A hundred hindrances would have to be cleared out of the way, and in the meantime the most favorable time could have passed. I find no solution, but I am not in despair.

If self-fulfillment in her work meant a temporary separation, Felix understood its necessity, as well as the danger of trying to interfere in any way.

> There is no rift, there must be no wavering; hesitation means weakness. Later years would distort this untimely sentimentality, and the burden of one-time unfreedom could turn against me as a reproach, and nothing but bitterness and resentment would remain. Do you believe you must get away? Then go, but go with strength not in tears and sorrow—I can't even guarantee for you. But Mamuschkerl, what harsh words I send you from afar! I wouldn't have the strength to say it to you.

Long before it became commonplace for a married couple to have to try to juggle two separate careers, almost at the outset of their marriage Felix and Helene started to face the conflicts that are inevitably involved. It would not be the last time they would encounter the dilemma, and as the years passed it could at times be excruciating for them both.

Regina Fass Rosenbach, Helene Deutsch's
mother, was strong-willed and socially proud.
As a child Helene,
fearing and resenting Regina's autocracy,
rejected her values.
Helene's antagonism
toward her mother never ceased.

Wilhelm Rosenbach,
a leading lawyer in Przemyśl, Poland,
was an early inspiration to Helene.
She became his chosen child,
not only his most attractive daughter
but gifted enough to amount
to his son and worthy heir.
Helene always minimized
any of his failings,
except for what she saw
as his weakness toward his wife.

Helene, fourteen years old,
wearing a new hat for
her sister Gizela's wedding.
Helene soon became involved
with Herman Lieberman.

Herman Lieberman (1870–1941),
a prominent criminal lawyer in Przemyśl.
He was dedicated to the cause of socialism
and Polish independence,
and as a young woman
Helene shared his politics.

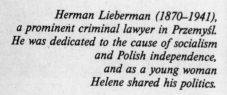

Helene Deutsch and Lieberman
on shipboard as they spent
their last holiday together in 1910.
They traveled in Scandinavia;
she accompanied him
to an international socialist congress.

Felix Deutsch, a native Viennese,
was meticulous about his dress.
He became a doctor in 1908,
and specialized in internal medicine.

Paul Barnay, Felix's best friend, was a
well-known actor, director, and theater manager.
In addition to her description
of their intimate friendship,
Helene alleged there had been
a sexual relationship between the two men,
and she herself may have had an affair with Paul.

Victor Tausk during World War I.
He was analyzed by Helene in early 1919
while she was still in analysis with Freud.
After Tausk killed himself on July 3, 1919,
Freud wrote Lou Andreas-Salomé:
"His farewell letters . . . attest his lucidity,
blame no one but his own inadequacy
and bungled life—
thus throw no light on the final deed . . .
I confess I do not really miss him;
I had long taken him to be useless,
indeed a threat to the future."

5

Kraepelin's Munich

It took some months for Helene to make the arrangements, but by February 8, 1914, she was settling into her renewed studies in Munich. Her work there in 1910–11 had taken place under the cloud of her unsettled private life; now she had come as a specialist, determined to try her hand at one of the world's great centers of psychiatric learning. Bleuler's school in Zürich was more psychologically oriented, but Kraepelin had been recommended to Helene by Wagner-Jauregg. Kraepelin was already famous for his classification and descriptions of mental illness.

Pre-Freudian psychiatry is often now underrated. R. D. Laing, for example, has taken one of Kraepelin's textbook illustrations in order to show how the patient could be understood as making subtle fun of even one of the greatest of old-fashioned psychiatrists.[1] But it is easy to overlook the achievement of classical psychiatry in encouraging case histories which are ample enough to allow for such later self-correction. By now the pendulum, thanks partly to the psychoanalytic revolution, has swung so far that throughout the literature individual patients tend to get lost in abstract speculations.

Kraepelin, whom Helene later said Freud regarded as a "coarse fellow," had been professor of clinical psychiatry at Munich since 1903; his textbook first came out in 1883, so that by the turn of the century he was one of the most famous authorities in his field. Out of his careful study of thousands of patients came "a system of descriptive psychiatry that is still used to classify patients on the basis of manifest behavior."[2] He distinguished between dementia praecox and manic-depressive insanity, as he looked on psychosis as a series of disease entities. His work was the crowning achievement of the neurophysiological line of thought; his organic approach lifted psychiatry to a new scientific level.

In coming to Munich, Helene wrote Felix (February 8) that she had made "great heart-sacrifice to my brain." However much she missed him, she felt

> strong, hard and equipped. The time of my exile will be very rich in work and intellectual gain . . . I have a great and earnest zest for work—I am already breathing in the scientific atmosphere which Munich had for me before my unexpected good fortune caught up with me here in the blessed city, and I see before me the great reward for the terrible sacrifice which I made to myself.

She was confident that Felix's tolerance for her need to fulfill herself intellectually would ultimately enrich their relationship.

> My Fel, it is good for both of us that my instinctive will drove me off like this. You know how I thirst for knowledge, and you know how little satisfaction and stimulation I found in Vienna. When I return, rich—not in positive skill, time's too short for that—but in inward discipline, in reliable acquired discipline in work—only then will we be united by great harmony, longed-for release, earnest optimism, joyful relaxation, the glorious freedom of my love for you. I couldn't say no to the great demands of my past—so I made you into one who is patient—and if it were not for the spirit of your great heart and the boundless goodness of your understanding, I don't know whether the great inner possibility of our mutual happiness would not be destroyed by me.

Her friend Reinhold was in Munich too, but she did not dally in getting started on her work. Wagner-Jauregg had specified that Helene should find out what Kraepelin was doing psychologically along experimental lines. Although she had come to Munich with the endorsement of her Viennese mentor, she and Kraepelin did not hit it off. She described to Felix her initial encounter with the great psychiatrist, stressing what she called his "comic-German standoffish bearing."

> I believe I'd have been booted out, without recommendations. "So! You want to do psychological work. What knowledge do you have of the subject."— "None at all, Herr Professor"—"So! Then it will not be possible for you to work here."—"I just wanted to learn, Herr Professor."—"So! how long do you want to stay?"—"Half a year."—"Too short a time, far too short."— Silence—"Where have you studied?"—(my story)—"I'll speak with Isserlin, and ask him if he has work for you to do; come back and inquire on Monday."

Helene was not discouraged by her encounter; within hours she had spoken with Max Isserlin (Kraepelin's assistant) herself, and he found work for her immediately. She wanted to learn the newest technical methods of investigation, using the rich clinical material at her disposal. She later acknowledged that Kraepelin was a great theoretician, clinically accurate, but dry and boring; someone severe and correct, and at the same time without fantasy, did not appeal to her.

Her first reaction to Munich was so favorable that Helene proposed spending two or three months working in a sanatorium during the summer; she and Felix could then afford to have a few months together in Munich. The city had unusual museums, art exhibitions, and enjoyable trips could be taken on weekends.

> Munich is glorious—more so than we used to see it in our longing for it. The weather is magnificent, warm, lots of sun. Life pulsates, misery goes and hides in some corner, and what one sees is pure joy, fun and laughter, and if you were here we'd tip the cup . . . One thing is certain—you must come here. It's work I'm thinking of. In Vienna one sinks in the bog and only realizes it once one is here. It is not true that one can work anywhere—one exhausts oneself so much in the difficulties of outward conditions that one brings only scraps of strength and energy to one's work. How different it is here!

Felix's first letter had been waiting for her on her arrival. He repeatedly encouraged her to write spontaneously: "Just write a lot of dear, sweet, dumb stuff—write just as it flows from your heart" (March 2); "write incautiously and unreservedly" (July 14); "Send me strokes of the pen, incoherent words —no thoughts, but write" (July 12). At the outset Felix hoped to be able to join her in working in Munich. She replied to his first letter on February 11 (they wrote to each other almost every day).

> If I once thought I had felt everything there was of joy and pain, I was wrong. I didn't know there was a desire that fills the soul in excruciating anguish, and gnaws in the brain and makes joy impossible. I am very sad and always think "what is my faraway darling doing?" and this thought accompanies me inseparably in all that I do. And at the same time I am filled with a rosy shimmer of happiness, that you are mine and that you await me and will come to me, and that then there will be years in which we always remain together. How sweet in its suffering is a longing, the fulfillment of which one is approaching with certainty!

At her beginning work, however, Helene was forced to be more realistic about the nature of her training in Munich. It turned out that her activity would have to be "splintered," and she proposed to concern herself, at least for the first few weeks, with what was known as experimental psychology. Kraepelin's interest in psychopharmacology, the effects of various drugs on the brain, led to the devising of different tests of mental functions. Helene's topic was to be "Influence of feelings upon the ability to remember," which was supposed to be published while she was still in Munich.

I'm up to my ears in the literature, and am learning a lot, but don't expect that much will come of my work. It's not original; Peters has already written on the same subject here, and my work is a kind of checkup on his results—however, that is how one begins. I will see what I can get out of it on my own, and I have an odd feeling: I am supposed to do something which is against my good conscience and my bad knowledge. I am supposed to talk about memories, search out complexes, and, completely neglecting my psychoanalytic convictions, I am supposed to act as though I did not know that there is a subconscious, and finally bring evidence against Freud!!

In Vienna Freud was well known in humanistic circles, especially among the younger generation, even if he was ignored or rejected within academic psychiatry. But in Munich it was possible for Helene's superiors to think in terms of gathering evidence against psychoanalysis. (According to a letter from Ernest Jones to the Professor of Psychiatry at Johns Hopkins, Adolf Meyer, in 1911 Kraepelin "made the following interesting admission from his unconscious: 'I suppose the Freudians would say the reason why I did not accept their views is that I am suffering from auto-erotic . . . megalomania.' Whether they said it before or not, they will certainly say it now, for it is impolite to contradict such a great authority."[3]) In Kraepelin's domain Helene decided

to attempt the art of producing a Janus-job, with two heads, one official and one of value; whatever more I see and experience than is prescribed by the Order of Experiments imposed "from above" will be placed as "something of greater value" in the treasury of my attainments—and later, weapons against myself will be hammered out of these.

Her task was to find out how people react to word tests, designed to get at the emotional experiences of life. If she was dissatisfied with the ideological framework in which her research had to proceed, her strictly medical work seemed a waste of time. Neurology and psychiatry were separate disciplines, but she acknowledged that as a psychiatrist she needed to know about neurology too.

I can see neurological cases in greater multiplicity in Vienna, also the medical atmosphere is much too boring for me; the visits which stretch on endlessly, where one is only a silent figure, trials of sensitiveness, writing, stool, stomach complaints—etc.—in one word, adjustment to medicine does not suit me; clinically, there's only one thing for me—*psychiatry*. One day I shall take care of neurology as a necessary evil in Vienna—here I want to learn that which I do not have in Vienna: *experimental* psychopathology.

Her attraction to psychiatry and psychoanalytic thinking had been fed by her interest in other people. If the depth of Helene's involvement with Freud can be detected in her astonishment at what might be expected of her research in Munich, Felix's letters to her there are a sign of their mutual interest in Freud's teachings. Psychoanalysis was not yet an established profession. It was not until 1924, under Helene's own leadership, that the Vienna Psychoanalytic Society had its own training program. In 1914 Freud was holding small Wednesday evening meetings at his apartment and delivering Saturday night lectures in Wagner Jauregg's auditorium at the University of Vienna. Only adherents of Freud's came on Wednesday, but the Saturday gatherings were larger and made up of a diverse audience. As a psychiatrist in Wagner-Jauregg's clinic, Helene was automatically eligible to attend Freud's public lectures, while others needed his personal permission. He did not hold a regular professorship, and needed a minimal attendance of three in order to be allowed to continue with his lecturing.

In February 1914 Felix was attending Freud's Saturday night presentations, which he assumed Helene would be interested in. As he wrote on February 15:

> Yesterday I heard Freud—as lovely and elevating as ever: child rearing and psychoanalysis. The subject didn't seem to suit him, for during the lecture he didn't warm up, but perceptive is perceptive. The quintessence: the parents have three great renunciations to make in child-rearing: (1) Renunciation of secrecy. Not only in the sexual sphere, but in the whole system of desires. Sexual enlightenment should take place gradually, according to the intellect. (2) Desist from threats and punishment. (3) No transference of narcissism-love-egoism to the child. I believe you can fill in the rest from this sketch yourself.

On March 18 Felix was reading some case histories: "If one has read Freud's analyses and then looks at this stammering, then criticism will surely hinder one's progress." Even if Freud had not yet been successful in establishing a profession in which others could expect securely to join, he already had created a system of ideas which was comprehensive in scope.

In Munich Helene had, in addition to Reinhold, another psychiatric colleague, a woman physician she had met in 1910–11 who specialized in nervous and emotional disorders; she was married, had children, and was hospitable to Helene. But another woman, a psychiatrist who had been working in Vienna and was an especially intimate friend of Helene's (and of Felix's), decided to come to Munich at Helene's suggestion to expand her professional knowledge too; Helene changed her living accommodations in order to be more conveniently located for this (unmarried) friend, although by the end of Helene's stay in Munich she was disenchanted with her.

Felix was the center of Helene's emotional life while she was in Munich, and when he fell ill (bronchitis and a touch of influenza) she was filled with concern for him. He had had to miss hearing Freud, "a sacrifice not easy to take." He went to the Semmering to recuperate. On March 6 he wrote her: "I have received an invitation to Przemyśl from your mother, and your father asked for immediate word about my state of health. Did you tell them any-

thing?" It was sheer coincidence. In one letter of hers (February 26) she tried
to explain what he had brought to her.

> . . . you are my youthful friend, with the great, unspoilt, untouched-by-life
> readiness of spirit to take as your own everything great and sublime, with a
> great drive toward lofty goals and ideals. With a peculiar, incredible strength
> you have conserved in yourself that which—after a certain period of life and
> experience—has remained to us as a glorious memory of youth, as a syn-
> onym for past youth. That we become thus is the necessary way of our
> development; the great tragedy of our life is that we feel our aging so pain-
> fully as a departure from our youthful striving—the better and more uncon-
> sumed we are, the more firmly we cleave to that which passes away—until
> finally we are swallowed up by the gray workaday world, by the battle for
> existence, and we have become "so completely different" and really have
> remained completely ourselves, only that we have gone through the natural
> evolution that inheres in us and in the universal law.

According to her Felix had rekindled her youthfulness.

> You, my boy, by virtue of a certain infantilism—blessings upon it—have
> brought into my life that which was beginning to be the past—not through
> disappointment, that is a phrase but through my overmaturity, which I
> reached without wishing to, through the early beginning and intensity of my
> experience. It is you that have prolonged my youth, and have thus renewed
> the drying-up well of my enthusiasm and my life-possibilities.

After intensive reading, as much as eight hours a day, on February 27
Helene began her experiments. She wanted to carry them out on normal
subjects as well as on cases from the clinic. But she had already found out
that Isserlin was not interested in independent work, and that she would have
to restrict herself to the boundaries that he drew for her. Equally disturbing
was the expected loss of support of Kraepelin's daughter, who had been
providing Helene with cases.

> Although she is very nice with me, yet I feel that she has allowed a bit of a
> strong impression to be made on her (which was very easy) and now I feel
> the hatred and envy of the limited and powerless person arising in her heart.
> She confessed to an acquaintance of mine, from whom she had received
> information about my intellect, that she was the one who had prevented our
> admission to the clinical work, and was the direct author of the letter in
> question. I think it's supposed to mean that I'm expected to court her favor.
> I won't dream of it. In any case, I wouldn't work in the clinic if I had to have
> her as my boss.

Kraepelin's daughter took care of her father, and saw that the clinic was in
order; in later years Helene had parallel difficulties working with Freud's
daughter Anna.

In spite of the problems Helene encountered, she continued with her experiments, and gained access both to the outpatient and clinic departments of the psychiatric hospital. In the back of her mind was the possibility of psychoanalytic practice, although she was uncertain what city she would end up in. She knew that ultimately she would benefit from the wide clinical exposure of the Munich facilities. On March 2 she wrote:

> I see and learn a lot I will be able to use in private practice: the beginning of psychoses which have not developed, neuroses, depressions, headaches, epilepsy, mental retardation, etc. And I see that one must know a lot not directly related to psychoanalysis, including therapy, even if you are convinced that there is only one therapy for neuroses: psychoanalysis.
>
> I saw twelve cases today, of the type that come to see a specialist for psychiatric disorders—but *only one* was a suitable subject for psychoanalytic treatment. None of the patients suffered from actual nervous disorders, they do not come to see us.

("Actual" was a technical term Freud had devised for those suffering from complaints stemming from current sexual difficulties.) She said she was even beginning to practice psychoanalysis in Munich, although not in the strict formal sense.

Throughout her stay in Munich, Helene was concerned that Felix might doubt her love for him. It would not be the last time in their marriage that she would leave home for the sake of her work, but she felt she had to be explicit with Felix, reminding him of her motives.

> I went away because I said to myself one day "I must make a last sacrifice for my career," and I left although it hurt and although my heart is with you and with our house. I went knowing full well that I would never experience greater happiness in life than at your side. I have never underestimated what I have, but the more I cherished it, the more I wanted to make this sacrifice to improve my knowledge; to do what seemed most reasonable to me, no, to us. If I was inconsiderate toward you, I was so because I was suffering as much as you did from this separation. Believe me, Fel, there was more masochism in what I did than you seem to know. That's what I call the great and endless pain which I have caused myself by leaving you.

Although Felix's letters were without reproaches about his loneliness, Helene feared what might be going on inside him unconsciously.

> You think I left to enjoy myself, you are convinced deep down that by leaving I disturbed the natural order of things and whatever makes up our life—my studies were a matter of self-deception, a bridge to the far more exciting life elsewhere. No, my boy, this I am not guilty of. In you I have found what I want most from life and whatever revelations will come my way, I will share them with you.

It is likely that Felix's temporary ill health made her justify her decision to herself. Her ambition temporarily seemed empty, and she longed to be with Felix and have a child.

Helene was shaken by Felix's renewed bout with illness, and surprised by the depth of her need for him. She wrote (March 9) as a reformed feminist.

> Oh weakness! I, the emancipated one, I who once preached "wide horizons" —and who regarded it as woman's greatest dishonor—the absolute dependency on feelings, and as the foundation stone of the whole edifice of liberation trumpeted out freedom from and negation of these "slave" feelings—I am soon going to shake the dust off my wandering feet and return in happiness and joy to my husband, and regard the inner necessity of my return as the greatest triumph of my development!

It seemed to her that her emancipation as a woman had followed, rather than preceded, her liberation as a proud individual: "now I am a *free woman*—in order to become that, I had to be a *free human being.*"

In her work Helene was still trying out different techniques. She wanted to stop undertaking hypnotic treatments (March 11) "because I am doing it against my will and don't feel honest about it." Away from Vienna, and in the midst of diverse cases at the psychiatric clinic, she found that whenever her material got interesting she needed psychoanalytic concepts. The attitude around her, however, was hostile to Freud: " 'it is a sacred duty to fight these dangerous and fateful teachings.' " Wagner-Jauregg may have made jokes about Freud, but he genuinely respected him as well; Wagner-Jauregg did not consider Freud an advocate of dirty sex, as was common in Munich. The attitude toward psychoanalysis in Munich was less subtle than in Vienna, leading Helene to exclaim about "these thick-headed Germans!" Although she had not yet become a follower of Freud's in Vienna, she felt in Munich that "somehow the tremendous personal influence of Freud is missing."

By mid-March she was increasingly preoccupied with the practical side of her life with Felix. He had been working on a long paper on kidney functioning, but he also had been toying with the idea of establishing a sanatorium outside Vienna, or getting a post at an existing institution; the same idea had come up during his convalescence at Karlsbad in 1913. It would have restricted his practice to rich people. Helene now encouraged him to get out of private practice, in the hope that there would be two positions available, one for him as an internist and one for her in neurology. Any publication arising from her work in Munich could, she thought, be completed after she had got back to Vienna. In sticking to her plans for a summer job at a sanatorium, perhaps at the one in Gräfenberg where Reinhold was going, Helene still had in mind the possibility of being with Felix in Munich in the autumn of 1914.

Felix was more worried about her being short of money than she was. One course was too expensive (sixty marks) for her to enroll in. She scarcely went out; Munich's *Fasching* seemed vulgar to her. Felix complained: ". . . your sealing yourself off from all but scientific interests cannot spring from lack of desire for or interest in art, theater, etc. In the burden of your work you lack the spice of nonprofessional activity . . ." As she put it on February

28, however, "I *am* twenty-nine years old and really I have no right to parasitize."

Helene reported the progress of her research regularly. Her investigation on feelings and memory gave her a focal point; she used a stopwatch, eliciting pleasant and unpleasant associations to words. Comparing the responses of depressive and other patients, she found that depressed people more often gave pleasant thoughts or memories than the others.

> If further tests prove what I am only assuming now but cannot prove because I do not have enough material, then God help Schopenhauer! For man remains an utter optimist even when he is deeply depressed. For depressions are also based on memories and seem to tie in with what meant happiness, even if it results in a sad event. It still was based "in that time."

Outside of Reinhold, however, Helene was not pleased with the personal acquaintances she had made. "Some talented young Poles, some stupid German scientists, nothing else." As she began to anticipate winding up her work in Munich and returning to Vienna in another month or so, Helene was especially conscious of what Felix had come to mean in her life. To her they had become one; he was "my friend, my lover, my comrade." (March 17) Her stay in Munich had been as she had expected: "loneliness but the knowledge of belonging to someone. And sure of this: we will get together and stay together until death do us part. Only a one-to-one relationship is of value; we both know it."

Then, on March 20, Helene conceived a remarkable proposal for their future.

> . . . an important matter! You must help me. The following plan was made —no—experience and observation have made me think of this: young girls suffering from neuroses and psychoses are the unhappiest creatures in the world. They are sent to unsuitable places, places which make their illness worse. If they have a neurosis, they are in real trouble. They are sent to sanatoria where instead of real psychiatric treatment they are given hydro-electric therapy. Flirtations with doctors and affairs with other patients spoil these girls for life. Where real medical care could bring about a miracle in dealing with the complaints, unscientific approaches cause havoc.

Helene did not allude to her own experience in Graz, or anything she might have seen there; but she did take for granted, thanks to her psychiatric training, a distinction between neurosis and psychosis that Freud would only come formally to accept in the 1920s.

> And psychoses: all these schizophrenics, these split personalities who could live peacefully until they succumb entirely in their insanity! And all those in an observation period when we don't know if we are dealing with a hysteria or a dementia praecox? The many who are at the borderline and who are crying out for help while they can still feel their individuality and their

being. I know already: only a woman can understand and help them. That is
the most wonderful aspect of my profession—I can feel my power and I
know what I can do!

I want to establish an institution near Vienna for neurotic and psychotic
girls aged 14–20. Not a school for the mentally retarded or impossible cases,
no. But: real neuroses and psychoses. This means: hysteria, psychopathy,
different neuroses, "disappointed love"—also: the large number of unclear
emotional problems which signal the beginning of psychoses—also: an observation ward and a place for real psychoses (mainly: dem. praecox), epilepsy,
etc. But only for young girls!

Although Helene had acquired a facility for using the latest psychiatric terminology, she had not lost touch with her common sense; and therefore in the
midst of clinical diagnoses she listed the phenomenon of "disappointed love."

Even now few such specialized institutions exist to treat young people as
a distinct entity.

I am also thinking about all the foreigners who consult the professors and
have nowhere to stay: I am thinking about the sweet young Roumanian girl
who came to see Wagner and who had to look with her innocent eyes at an
old vile and masturbating woman: what can we do, where can we take her?

She had in mind an institution where a free choice of doctors would be
allowed. She could take care of the cases of neurosis. She proposed to begin
on a small scale with about twenty beds, in two houses, one closed for
psychoses and the other open for neuroses. The therapy would consist in
"whatever can be done now—and I think I know." She wanted Felix's help
raising the money in Vienna and in speaking to an authoritative figure like
Marburg.

Tell him how much psychiatry means to me, how enthusiastic I am about it
and how necessary I think this institution is. For neurotic girls where a
change of atmosphere is important and a *female doctor* above all! For
psychotics, especially in unsolved cases—epileptics with consideration of
parents—for foreigners seeing professors (important!) mention the free
choice (of doctors)!

Her naïve hopefulness about what Felix might accomplish by a talk with
Marburg was partially fueled by the evident failure of his own sanatorium
plans. She always thought he was inadequately energetic in his own behalf.
She had in mind for her own institution that Felix would be a consultant on
internal medical problems.

In the meantime, Professor Bernard von Gudden—a famous
neuroanatomist—was going out of town for a few days, and appointed Helene
as director of his clinic. It meant she could expect to see fifteen or twenty
patients daily. As she wrote (March 24):

> For two days I have borne the burden of the outpatients department on my weak shoulders. As if out of spite, there prevails a rush of patients such as I have never seen, and I am the only doctor—what do you say to that? It is a pleasant feeling for me to bear the responsibility and to perceive that I have the necessary authority—though I be lacking in knowledge, I'm not worried, I'll manage to pick up the necessary knowledge—authority is what must sit right. And the fact that I seem to have it, that I find very fine!

Differential diagnoses were then, as now, a key issue.

> I fish out patients who interest me particularly and schedule them for the afternoon, in order to explore them. Today for example I fished out a hysteria case which had been treated by Gudden for a long time, and after a two-hour conversation with her, I recognized for certain an incipient schizophrenia—I'll give my head for this diagnosis. A "psychopath" turned out to be a chronic hallucinous, the class of which I was not able to determine—and much more . . .

Helene was able to laugh at her growing sense of self-importance. "Am I going to end up as a megalomaniac? I have long had myself under suspicion —like old 'talented' (!) psychiatrists." If Felix could smooth the way for her plans in Vienna for an institution for young girls, she was prepared to fight for her proposal. Helene was convinced she could bring a fresh approach to Viennese psychiatry.

> . . . it is a matter of creating a "milieu" for neuropsychopathic girls—as far as I am concerned, with electricity and massage as the main treatment. Moreover, the courage is needed to transplant psychotherapy to Vienna— it's not so bad—all the neurologists practice it in Vienna as suggestion, hypnosis, etc.

A couple of days later, however, after Reinhold had returned to Vienna, Helene was able to see how discontented she had grown in Munich. He then seemed "the greatest scientific attraction" for her in Munich. As she wrote Felix earlier, "Reinhold remains my old love . . . he bears in himself a calm, comforting intellectual atmosphere—with such wonderful naturalness." She had, however, joked with him about a shopgirl in Vienna (Annie), whom Helene teasingly recommended as his wife—and ultimately, to Helene's horror, he was to marry her.

> As soon as she is gone, Reinhold is a different person altogether. I have used my right of our friendship and spoken against the affair, after Reinhold told me how unhappy he is with it. We agreed that he will see little of her in Vienna and tell her that a break-up is inevitable. What a coward of a man.

Helene grew actively discontented with her training in Munich. Otto Pötzl, one of Wagner-Jauregg's assistants, had not been in favor of her choosing that city in the first place.

> I get little support and initiative from Isserlin, and my profit is only from
> books, and from patient-material for the experiments. I can get the former in
> Vienna, and the latter I can get even more abundantly than here. Systematic
> knowledge of exp. psychology cannot be achieved here. Pötzl was right.

(Pötzl later wrote on experimentally induced dreams, became Professor of
Psychiatry at Prague, and finally came back to Vienna as Wagner-Jauregg's
successor;* for a time he was a member of the Vienna Psychoanalytic Society.) Helene thought she had already gained enough new knowledge, so that
the rest would be up to her. She now longed for the responsibility that might
be accorded her once she returned to Vienna.

Helene decided to leave Munich, and made up a tragic story to tell
Isserlin: an aunt with a tumor was the reason for her departure. (In fact, she
did have a dying aunt in Poland.)

> Isserlin regretted with profound sympathy that I am not completing the
> work. I would have to leave the records there—he would try to see that I
> could work on the remainder in Vienna, but it is not practiced here and the
> article couldn't appear in Kraepelin's publications.

If she had wanted to write it Isserlin's way, the paper could be completed in a
couple of weeks.

> However, I have a strong resistance against publication of a flat piece of
> work which could become very fine, given greater psychological knowledge
> and immersion in the subject. So much the more because the subject goes
> deep into Freud's area and would certainly produce a lovely selection for
> psychoanalysis, if one went deeper into the arrangement of experiments (as-
> sociations, analysis of every memory)—that won't be possible here.

She stayed on in Munich to make a duplicate of her records, and to round off
her experiments. If Isserlin agreed with what she produced, that would be
fine, but otherwise she was willing to forego publication. On April 4 Felix had
tried to dissuade her from her decision: "It would nevertheless be good to
publish the work—you know how that is valued here—a few printed pages.
Hopefully it will not be terribly compromising."

In the end Helene had kept records of twenty tested persons, although
she was unsure how to evaluate the material. In February she thought that
Isserlin had agreed with her "severe criticism" of the work to be re-examined.
Now she fully realized that Isserlin wanted her merely to corroborate Peter's
prior investigation, which had been carried out on normal test people, while
her own was done on psychotics. She proposed to do further reading and
writing in Vienna, in order to produce a more mature piece of work. Isserlin,
however, wanted nothing to do with her continuing on in Vienna; he had
found her results striking, but wanted further confirmation carried out on
cases. From her point of view there were no properly coordinated laboratory

* Wagner-Jauregg was Professor of Psychiatry from 1893 to 1928.

facilities in Munich; Isserlin himself was "shallow," and she had failed to find the school of "plan governed learning" that she had sought. Furthermore, as a foreigner she was now in principle excluded from work at the clinic. (Felix was supportive: "You are coming back disappointed, and poorer by many a hope, and richer in suffering, that must not be! I want to bring my Hala through the gates of Vienna as the same old happy, gay, life-exuding Munki that went away.")

Helene wanted her work published only if Isserlin absolutely insisted on it; it went unpublished, and she returned to Vienna in the first part of April, 1914. She looked forward to joining the Neurological Department with Wagner-Jauregg, but wanted to continue looking at psychiatric cases. Also, she planned to attend Victor Tausk's "seminar" on psychoanalysis in Vienna.

Tausk, an intimate friend of Reinhold's, was one of the few adherents of Freud's who was also a psychiatrist; he was five years older than Helene and had been attending meetings of the Vienna Psychoanalytic Society since 1909. Originally a lawyer in Yugoslavia, Tausk was one of the brightest lights in psychoanalysis. When Lou Andreas-Salomé, friend of Friedrich Nietzsche and Rainer Maria Rilke, came to Vienna in 1912, she found Tausk "the most prominently outstanding"[4] of Freud's disciples; they had a brief affair the year of her stay in Vienna.

Tausk already had a secure niche as one of Freud's followers; and he and Helene were friends. He had only started in medicine in 1908, and finished in 1914; so they were fellow students. In both psychiatry and psychoanalysis, however, Tausk was her senior; from Munich Helene had asked Felix to send someone to Tausk to borrow Jung's book on association experiments; he was the most knowledgeable person in the field in which she herself was becoming involved. Felix also shared her friendship for Tausk, and while Helene was away went to the opera with him a couple of times.

In her letters from Munich Helene would inquire whether Felix had been seeing Tausk, and whenever Felix had something to report about him he would pass it along to Helene. When Felix spent an evening at one of Freud's Saturday lectures, and Tausk was absent, it would be striking enough to mention. Tausk was such a devoted follower of Freud's that his missing a lecture would be a presumption of ill health. But Felix's reports about Tausk could not encourage Helene about the prospects of psychoanalytic practice in Vienna. Tausk's case load was stagnating, and he had to struggle to get enough paying patients; since he was such an established pupil of Freud's, both Felix and Helene knew that their own problem of finding a productive livelihood was shared by others.

Felix also kept Helene informed about the antipsychoanalytic bias in Viennese neurology. Frankl von Hochwart had an outpatient clinic ("clinic" was then the equivalent of our academic "department"), and Tausk worked there in an official capacity. Helene, along with Tausk and Reinhold, had spent many hours together discussing professional problems with Frankl-Hochwart. But on the subject of Freud Frankl-Hochwart was adamant. Although the younger people might be fascinated by Freud's ideas, the leaders in Viennese neurology were by no means friendly to psychoanalysis. Felix reported (March 18) on having run into Frankl-Hochwart one evening:

> he got onto psychoanalysis, talked himself into a fury, cursed, took Freud and company's name in vain, and didn't stop until I left; disgustingly senile.
>
> He particularly castigates Freud for his high honoraria. He has just rescued two youths from Freud, who had fought with their parents in the consequence of a treatment by Freud. He reconciled them and—sent them to Gräfenberg . . . to get "ironed out." It was really terrible to hear. He sends his greetings to you.

When Helene made her proposal for an institution for young girls, Felix replied (March 21):

> do you believe the private doctors will press forward so readily to an understanding as to make a psychological treatment—which is perhaps also psychoanalytic—better than cold water cures and electric procedures; at the moment there are not yet many of a better nature. What harm is there in a little hysteria or neurasthenia? A little change of surroundings . . . will patch up the trouble perfectly well! And the neuroses?! Are not the majority of nerve doctors just like the type of Frankl-Hochwart! Embarrassment is so much in flesh and blood in Vienna that the gentlemen could hardly afford to change saddles suddenly.

Reinhold had specifically spoken to Frankl-Hochwart about Helene's project; Felix reported (March 29):

> . . . of course his answer was senile; if psychoanalytic treatment were to take place, there would be no use in it; in general, he said he hoped he would live to see the end of this aberration; I too seemed to him psychoanalytically infected—etc., etc. But otherwise he would think such an institution very necessary. Well, that's the kind of people you want to work with. His practice is currently somewhat on the rise, and as far as he is concerned that means that psychoanalysis is losing ground.

Helene, unlike Felix, had known what it was like to be alienated from her own family. Throughout her stay in Munich she was out of contact with her relatives in Poland. Her sister Malvina, as well as her father, thought she had decided to go to Zurich. Felix undertook to mend Helene's family relations; when Malvina's little girl (brain-defective at birth) fell fatally ill, she wrote to Felix for advice. He told Helene (February 19):

> Since *your* sense of family was stirred in *me* through this new contact with relatives, I drafted an epistle to your parents and Ollers, to enlighten them about the fact that you and I no longer share one roof. I take it you have not

yet found sufficient time for this task; rest assured that I took up the connections in diplomatic fashion.

Felix had not wanted to break the bad news to Malvina, and only gradually informed her of his prognosis. When one of Helene's Polish aunts (Celina) died, Felix was told, not Helene. Malvina felt desperate; as Felix put it, "the poor girl is losing her loved ones one after another." Although Helene felt sorry for her aunt's daughters, the loss had made "no strong impression" on her.

When Helene heard that her father planned to be in Vienna on business, and would be coming to see Felix, she wanted her greetings sent to him. Felix seemed more concerned about her father than she did; Wilhelm was busy, and the first day he saw Felix (then still convalescing) he stayed only a few minutes, then left for the ballet. The next day he came with Helene's brother, Emil. Felix was impressed with Wilhelm's "work-energy," but wrote (March 1):

> I have gained the impression that he has become even more egocentric than we observed during his last illness. It may well have contributed to his at least outward, apparent indifference, that our life goes on with such complete exclusion of his person—and perhaps he is miffed at his favorite daughter, whose whereabouts he didn't even know exactly. This seems to concern him, for with a certain purposefulness he avoided asking about or showing much interest in our family state, and when I told him your address he did not even note it down.

Felix suspected that his mother-in-law, along with Helene's brother and sister-in-law, had helped alienate Wilhelm.

> I don't want to go into details. I am only sorry that the uniquely decent, truly just-minded man was dragged down into the swamp of innuendo and slander, and low-down mean thoughts. It pains me to have to withdraw the share of respect and love that I had held out for him when he came at one time before. There is no longer any use in it: thus one step closer to misanthropy. Is it perhaps even a bit of homosexuality, that I had been glad to have been permitted to love him, or is there even such a thing as a . . . father-in-law complex?!'

Helene was distressed by Felix's report.

> The news about Papa hurts a great deal. I knew it would come this way. But in the end, the forces that sustain a person do give way. Even so, he had held on for such a long time. In the next few days I will try to make up for that which could be my fault.

Evidently Felix had been accurate about Wilhelm. Shortly thereafter Helene got what she described to Felix as a "nice tender letter" from her sister Gizela in Przemyśl. Helene didn't usually write, but had remembered Gizela's birthday; and her older sister was moved by Helene's warm, loving letter. Gizela offered to send Helene money and also wanted to read her work. Wilhelm had told the family about Felix's latest sickness; Gizela sensed that Felix might have been put off by her father's behavior in Vienna. She explained that Wilhelm loved Felix very much but that their father was now old, tired, and sick and therefore not able to show the proper emotion over Felix's own illness. During her stay in Munich, however, Helene was so caught up in her career and with her marriage that she was barely in contact with her family in Poland.

By July 1914, however, Helene was several months pregnant and went for a ten-day visit to her sister Malvina in Stryj. In Munich Helene had neglected her family, but they understood how important her work was for her and felt secure in her feelings for them. She naturally turned to her sisters at this time; Gizela came to Malvina's with her young daughter. As Helene wrote on July 7:

> A few words to you out of this dull, stifling atmosphere. I am being pampered and coddled, yet I look at the calendar with longing and count the days I am still obliged to spend here.
>   All my Jewish-Galician melancholy and joylessness weighs like a ton on my shoulders, and the gray, hopeless monotony of workaday tightens upon my thought, and doesn't give me freedom to look up. There is no thought of reading, and even less of contemplation. Not a moment of solitude—but instead a strange sultriness that makes me listless and tired.

Felix was looking around for yet another place for them to live in Vienna; he had moved to smaller quarters when Helene had gone to Munich, and then they had taken a different apartment on her return. Helene was eager to return to the joy of her work. She felt somewhat queasy and had divided feelings about "the choral talk of the surroundings and the mad racket of children." Although she wanted the baby more than she dared think, in Stryj, at any rate, she felt less than content.

> I am so much like a mere shadow, so far estranged from myself, like a lethargic instrument of nature, soul-less and unsublimated, in fear for the future and longing for the past, just wandering about. Will I endure this animal-somatic existence until the date of return? Think: not a moment alone, corroded, and heavy as a fattened pig, a well into which all cares and slaveries are swept—nearly desperate from pity and nearly hating from contempt.

Although she felt no longer herself "but a vessel," she was confident of being able to draw herself "back to life on the ladder" of her feelings for Felix.

Helene had complained about her pregnancy, but could not have fully anticipated the possibility of a miscarriage. In July 1914, however, during her stay at Malvina's, Helene began to doubt the wisdom of having left Felix for her family. Her desire to become a mother had played its part in their relationship from the beginning; she knew her going to Stryj had its incongruous features: "Ought I to be the one that tears away from my boy that which led me to him?" Before going back to Felix in Vienna, Helene went to Przemyśl; on July 14 she wrote him:

> I have been here since last evening. For the first time in many, many years I am breathing home air, deeply conscious, and filled with pain and love. I am wandering around aimlessly, wetting with hot tears the places of the dreams of my youth, of my bold hopes and resolutions.
>
> How strange everything is—I have a home after all. I find my past on every tree, on every stone. Everything is filled with memories. How good it is that I have come here—how good it is that I can feel the sweet pain, just at this time! How sunny and clear is my future with you, you one-and-only.
>
> I'll soon be with you.

In keeping with the spirit of their mutual projects throughout 1914, the letters between Felix and Helene the summer of 1914 are filled with their plans and hopes. Neither of them so much as hinted at the existence of an outside world of politics. The Archduke Francis Ferdinand had been assassinated on June 28. Like so many others at the time they assumed their lives would go on as usual. Even when Austria declared war on Serbia on July 28, few realized what was happening. A complicated set of diplomatic alliances set in motion the events that were to pull Europe into World War I.

6

World War I and Motherhood

The outbreak of the war meant that almost one hundred years of relative international peace had come to an end, and a new era was ushered in that disappointed those who had had faith in progress. The nineteenth century's advances in science and technology had not succeeded in bringing a new age of beneficence. Instead, a skein of political and military ties led to a bloody conflict, a catastrophe for every European country involved. World War I was a watershed in Western history, and the twentieth century as we have known it can be said to have started from that summer of 1914.

The weakened Austro-Hungarian Empire could not withstand the forces that the prolonged stalemate unleashed; the Hapsburgs' dynastic hold on legitimacy had been undermined by nationalist aspirations, and the power politics by which the Treaty of Versailles divided up the spoils of war was the final force that dissolved the empire. While for some Americans the war rekindled democratic idealism, for Central Europeans it confirmed the worst fears of its more cynical skeptics. Civilization proved to be an even more fragile entity than pessimists had anticipated; human barbarism disillusioned those who had naïvely thought well of mankind.

It took a while for the full moral effects of the war to sink in; but the impact on Helene's career began to be felt almost immediately. Unlike her male colleagues she was not liable to military service. She had earned a foothold in Wagner-Jauregg's clinic since 1913, although she had been frustrated by an insufficient access to psychiatric cases. At that time women at the University of Vienna only had appointments in theoretical subjects. With the war, however, physicians were needed by the military; and Helene gradually found that new and welcome clinical responsibilities were being thrust upon her. Before long she was functioning as one of Wagner-Jauregg's assistants, a high post to which, as a woman, she could not legally be entitled.

Wagner-Jauregg's clinic was the stronghold of psychiatry in Vienna, which was one basis for a rivalry between himself and Freud. They had a complicated personal relationship, and as contemporaries they had known each other since their school days. During the period Helene was a student at Wagner-Jauregg's clinic, he held the most prestigious psychiatric position in the Austro-Hungarian Empire. (He was Krafft-Ebing's successor.) It is no wonder that Freud always resented never having been a regular faculty member at the University of Vienna.

One of Wagner-Jauregg's innovations was malarial treatment for general paresis, which by itself earned him his Nobel Prize. Syphilis was now treatable. (Wagner-Jauregg jokingly used to cite, as an example for diagnosing progressive paralysis in syphilis, a waiter adding a bill who makes a mistake to his own disadvantage.) Although Helene was still uncertain about the therapeutic results of his fever therapy, she found beginning cases for him from the clinic. Wagner-Jauregg also helped cure cretinism by treating iodine deficiencies. His work might be psychologically meager, but his discoveries were to prove humanly important.

Wagner-Jauregg and Freud each felt he had claim to fame. Although Wagner-Jauregg is now almost forgotten, at the time Freud was commonly considered the lesser figure. In 1909 Freud had gone to the little-known Clark University in Worcester, Massachusetts,[1] to accept an honorary degree; although America had already started to respond to Freud's ideas before the war, his world fame did not come until after the Armistice in 1918.[2]

Relatively little is known about Wagner-Jauregg's personal history. Helene reported that he had an unhappy family life; she said he was married to a Jewish woman who had once been his patient, and he did not present her socially. Wagner-Jauregg was one of those people who never spoke about himself to his students, although eventually he wrote a formal autobiography. Kraepelin had been an uninspiring teacher to Helene, but Wagner-Jauregg was such a warm, fatherly man that he became a great figure in her life. Yet once she became a member of Freud's movement Wagner-Jauregg was so mentally lost to her that she was not even interested when his posthumous autobiography appeared in 1950. (He had died in 1940.)

Wagner-Jauregg was a sensitive psychiatrist; it was possible to be humane though not a Freudian. On rounds he remembered which patient was suffering the most and went there first. He was as much a clinician as a scientist. In cases of depression, for example, Helene recalled how he put great emphasis on constitution; since it was important for such patients to have their bowel movements, he would inquire whether they had had their enemas. This is an example of one of Wagner-Jauregg's practical observations, the way depression can be a body problem; but he did not try to make a large-scale theory out of his good clinical insight.

Ideology aside, everything in psychiatry can depend on the personality of the practitioner. Psychiatrists then, without sharing today's emphasis on treatment, were concerned more with the custodial care of psychotics. Yet these old-time psychiatrists did not "know" enough to realize that they could not do what they in fact sometimes accomplished. Wagner-Jauregg, for example, had a deep, quieting voice that had a great therapeutic impact. Rude though he could be in externals, he was very human; Helene thought he was very goodhearted. He had come from the countryside, originally of peasant stock, and he cared about his patients. Such a psychiatrist was able to help patients, even though it might not have been possible for him to explain why he had had his successes. As a matter of principle Wagner-Jauregg was organically, rather than psychologically, inclined; but any psychiatrist, if only as a matter of professional practice, has to be more than a pure scientist.

As a young psychiatrist Helene was trying rationally to understand psychotic phenomena which had hitherto been incomprehensible. It was exciting to be able to explore new areas of knowledge; the psychoanalysts, including Freud, had little experience with hospitalized mental patients, who were seen only by psychiatrists. (The early distinction between psychiatrists and analysts persists today throughout most of Europe.) The suffering of the patients Helene saw was, according to the line of thinking she wanted to pursue, meaningful. She, like others who have been psychiatrically trained, retained for the rest of her life the memories of some of her earliest cases.

She wrote about one of her patients to her husband in 1923.

A small experience from the early period of my psychiatric (pre-analytic) activity just occurs to me.

I saw a catatonic stupor for the first time. I was overcome by a passionate curiosity to discover what lives and goes on in the souls of these wretches in such bouts.

I courted the (female) patient for weeks—until one day it happened. She received me with a smile, and looked at me warmly and tenderly, and she pronounced a sound for the first time. I came toward her joyfully, but at the same moment she plunged toward me, punched me in the face, and only the fact that Nunberg happened to walk in saved me from worse.

I did not doubt for a moment that this behavior was an unconditional consequence of what was going on in her—I never accepted the psychiatric view of "sudden"—I also knew that her loving reception belonged to the punch that was delivered. But I never again went in, not only out of self-defense.

One of the attractions of Freud's outlook was the proposition that love and hate are intimately interconnected, and that in patients who are seriously disturbed one can expect to find primitive mixtures of affection and aggression. Helene was both moved and appalled, as a human being as well as a psychiatrist, by the clinical material she encountered at the University of

Vienna's psychiatric facilities. (Herman Nunberg was a fellow Pole and already a disciple of Freud's; Helene remembered being distressed at his detachment about a self-blaming female melancholic at Wagner-Jauregg's clinic. Preoccupied more with theory than clinical reality, Nunberg wondered aloud: "But where is her libido?")

Though he was humanly interested in patients and respected Freud personally, Wagner-Jauregg was critical of psychoanalysis. He objected that Freud thought that analysis could do everything. As a psychiatrist in Vienna Wagner-Jauregg had to take a stand against Freud. Yet he was more mocking than aggressively hostile; he maintained a tolerant but sarcastic attitude toward psychoanalysis. His skepticism was also a result of his doubt that nonsense like psychoanalysis could cause any harm. Although he could be biting, he was fair, and let his staff do as they wanted about Freud; most of them were antagonistic to psychoanalytic work. Freud felt that the clinic at the University of Vienna was in enemy hands, and that anyone studying under Wagner-Jauregg was not likely to acquire a friendly attitude toward psychoanalysis. Wagner-Jauregg could ridicule Helene for being so interested in Freud; for example, he might say to a patient of hers: "Has Dr. Deutsch put in your mind that you want a child from your father?" But despite his teasing he respected her as a psychiatrist.

Under the exceptional circumstances of wartime, Helene rose to the place of assistant in charge of the women's division. Otto Pötzl was in charge of the men's section. Throughout the war Helene was responsible for diagnosing cases. Once they had decided they could do nothing for a patient, he or she was committed to an asylum. Because of her heavy responsibility in this situation, Helene had had to learn fast, and by and large on her own; she later thought she had benefited from there being no one to teach her.

Pötzl was sympathetic to Freud and did work that anticipated later psychoanalytic research. But he was harsh with war neurotics, considering them draft dodgers; if they were paralyzed and could not walk, he might kick them as malingerers. Someone like Pötzl had little patience for psychogenic disorders.* Hysterical reactions, especially when there was realistic though unconscious gain in the illness, could be contagious; and Pötzl grouped his cases so that there were rooms filled with patients suffering from similar organic expressions of psychological conflicts.

Helene remembered in particular one peculiar type of war neurosis, in which patients lost a reflex in their eyes so that the cornea dried up; suffering from the symptom of blinking constantly, these patients were sent home from the front. Although there were those who deliberately simulated psychiatric disorders, Pötzl thought that they all were malingerers, and his reaction was typically sadistic; for example, for those patients with the cornea problem he

* In 1920 the Austrian War Ministry conducted an investigation of the electrical treatment of war neurotics; Freud was asked to submit a memorandum, and testified orally as well, exonerating Wagner-Jauregg of any personal responsibility for excesses which might have occurred.[3]

put matchsticks under their eyes. This kind of conversion symptom has not been seen since then, but it may have further helped persuade Helene about the reality of unconscious mental forces. These patients characteristically had no conscious knowledge of their desire to evade the fighting. Both world wars stimulated an enormous interest in psychoanalytic thinking.

Helene's own clinical tasks were of a more traditional psychiatric nature. But she also had to treat cholera patients who suffered from high fevers; they could not read, lay in their own feces, and had no idea of what the war was about. No scientific treatment was possible for these cases, except to try to keep them from losing too much fluid. In addition to her clinical work, she also did some scientific writing. She published a neurological paper on brain damage in monoxide poisoning; the bleeding in the gray matter was part of the effect that coal dust could have in damaging a portion of miners' brains.[4]

She also wrote a psychological study of "induced insanity,"[5] in which she described some cases observed during the war at Wagner-Jauregg's clinic. She was interested in the emotional strains of the wartime situation, and how whole families could join in hysterical confabulations in order to cope with emotional distress; she was tolerant in her willingness to suspend judgment about the sources and fate of morbid thinking. She concluded that the nature of familial love may leave everyone "normal" prone to disturbances that ought not necessarily to be treated as a psychiatric illness. Not all "castles in the air" deserve the approach appropriate to delusions. Her fascination with "induced insanity," which she followed up in her later clinical writings, may have been directly related to her own shared madness in her earlier relationship with Lieberman and Gustawa.

When Helene left Wagner-Jauregg's clinic in the fall of 1918, in order to undertake her analysis under Freud, she had attained considerable standing within Viennese psychiatry. She had gone further than a woman could ever have expected to, except under special wartime circumstances. The testimonial Wagner-Jauregg wrote for her is a good summary of what she had achieved.

> The undersigned certifies hereby that Frau Dr. Helene Deutsch has been employed without interruption from August 1913 until today as Secondary Doctor and War Doctor in the Clinic for Psychiatry and Nerve Diseases.
>
> From the beginning of the war, since almost all of the assistants had entered the armed forces, Frau Dr. Deutsch has actually performed assistant duties, and has led the psychiatric women's clinic, almost entirely on her own, to the complete satisfaction of the undersigned, during the greatest part of the wartime.
>
> Frau Dr. Deutsch has conducted the duties entrusted to her with great diligence and self-sacrifice, and as she, in the course of time, has undergone thorough training both in psychiatry and in neurology, she has provided valuable services to the clinic. She has also displayed scientific interest in an

active way, and from the clinic she has published several pieces of scientific work.

Prof. Wagner v. Jauregg

Vienna, Nov. 12, 1918

When Helene had returned to Vienna from Munich in the spring of 1914, she was about to turn thirty years old; for a young person thirty can seem a venerable age, and she was distressed at still not being more established professionally; 1914 was a turning point for her, for she discovered through her work at the clinic, at least during wartime, that she could approach the professional standing that she expected of herself.

In 1914 she also had the first miscarriage of her married life; as a woman she also felt the pressure of her age. Her pregnancy is still mentioned in a letter from an intimate to Felix in October 1914, so she had managed to carry the child for some time before the miscarriage occurred. Before (and after) her son Martin was born, on January 29, 1917, she had more miscarriages. During each of her pregnancies she worried terribly; in spite of her fear of giving birth to an abnormal child, she was determined to become a mother. Each miscarriage was bound to cause an upheaval, stirring up guilt feelings (she wrote about it anonymously in one of her later papers[6]); Helene may also have doubted the wisdom of her marriage. In the midst of her wartime psychiatric duties, however, she found it easy to blot out the full emotional reaction that the miscarriages might otherwise have entailed.

By the time she gave birth in early 1917, the problem of childlessness had been weighing on her mind for years. When in 1945 she published Volume 2 of *The Psychology of Women,* she used her own experience to illustrate the principle of how the processes of a woman's identification with her mother can determine the course of pregnancy:[7]

In every instance the capacity for motherhood is related to this identification. The ego of the pregnant woman must find a harmonious compromise between her deeply unconscious identification with the child, which is directed toward the future, and her identification with her own mother, which is directed toward the past. Wherever one of these identifications is rejected, difficulties arise. In the first case the fetus becomes a hostile parasite, in the second the pregnant woman's capacity for motherhood is weakened by her unwillingness to accept her identification with her own mother.

The case Helene used to illustrate this theory was that of herself.

The patient, whom we shall call Mrs. Smith, was the youngest in a family with many other children, one boy and several girls. After this boy had disappointed the ambitious hopes of the parents, they wanted to have another son, but instead my patient was born. Her mother never concealed her disappointment over this fact, and her attitude toward the girl was unmistakably: "It would have been better if you had not been born." The patient

was saved from traumatic reactions to this attitude by two compensations—
her father's deep and tender love for her, and the maternal affection of one of
her sisters, twelve years older than herself. Her father's love aroused in her
the wish to become a substitute for his son and she successfully turned her
interests and ambitions toward this goal. She was saved from the dangers of
the masculinity complex because her father's love for her emphasized and
encouraged her femininity. The two tendencies frequently conflicted but did
not lead to a neurotic result.

Helene's own childhood beginnings are unmistakable, even if she was using a
Freudian framework to describe her emotional conflicts.

As she reported "Mrs. Smith's" case:

Only after she had married and conceived an ardent desire for a baby did her
childhood difficulty come to the fore. As a little girl she had reacted to her
mother's rejection with conscious hatred and devaluation. The idea of identification with her aggressive mother had filled her with almost conscious
horror. Up to her pregnancy she had been able to be feminine by disregarding her mother problem; but this method no longer worked when she herself
was about to become a mother.

Malvina had been, in Helene's view, a surrogate mother. But even this tie was
subject to tension.

Her identification with her older sister, her childhood substitute mother, was
also disturbed. During her early puberty Mrs. Smith had discovered that her
sister, like herself, was engaged in a hate-filled conflict with her mother, and
perhaps unconsciously sensed that this sister had many children not because
she was motherly but because she was sexually subjected to her husband.
With whom, then, could she identify herself, in order to become a mother?
Her tragic feeling that she would never achieve motherhood was intensified
when she gave birth one month before term to a stillborn child.

It may have been that Helene's difficulties were exacerbated by her
mother's presence in Vienna; both her parents had come to live there for a
good part of World War I, and she had helped support them. According to
Helene's account of Mrs. Smith, the solution lay in a friend's mother. "Mrs.
Smith"

soon . . . was again pregnant; and her joy was now even more mixed with
fear of loss than during her first pregnancy. By this time she had come into
close relation with a former friend of hers who was also pregnant and expected her first child in joyful, undisturbed tranquillity. Thanks to this
friendship, Mrs. Smith felt relieved; only from time to time she aroused the
friend's laughter by remarking, "You are the luckiest person in the world,
you will have a child"—thus expressing her doubts as to the fulfillment of
her own wish. In her full identification with her friend she nevertheless
began to feel more hopeful.

Helene's friend was a dermatologist, Dr. Marianne Bauer, whose husband, also a doctor, later received an appointment at the University of Southern California Medical School; the Bauers remained the closest nonanalytic couple to the Deutsches. Marianne's mother served as a surrogate for Helene's own, and helped cushion her pregnancy. According to Helene's narrative about "Mrs. Smith":

> Only later, during her analysis, did she realize that the success of her identi-
> fication with her friend was not due to the latter's inner harmony but to
> another motive. The friend had a mother who was the opposite of her own.
> While her own mother was tall, domineering, cold, and aggressive, her
> friend's mother was very small and full to the brim with maternal warmth.
> She spread her motherly wings both over her own loving daughter and Mrs.
> Smith, who was thus able to achieve motherhood by sharing in this benign
> mother-daughter harmony.

"Mrs. Smith's" friend was due to be delivered a month before her, but did not have her child at the expected time; instead she

> gave birth to a boy overdue by a whole month on the very day that Mrs.
> Smith expected her own delivery. A few hours later, Mrs. Smith began to
> have labor pains and thus fulfilled her seemingly hopeless wish that both
> babies be born on the same day. The children were later referred to as twins
> of different parents.

Helene thought that a psychogenic factor, "simultaneous loving identifica-tion," helped account for the delay in Marianne Bauer's giving birth. Martin Deutsch always considered Franz Bauer his twin; a second son, Klaus, was later born. After Franz had died, Martin named his younger son for Klaus.

Helene reported that "Mrs. Smith" and her friend consciously agreed on another pregnancy, and they conceived in the same month. "Mrs. Smith" was without fear or doubts; during the third month, however, her friend told her that her husband had been offered a position in another city, and that the family would probably move there.

> Mrs. Smith felt panicky and asked her friend what would happen to her own
> pregnancy. The friend replied laughingly that this time she would have to
> struggle through it alone. That very day Mrs. Smith started on a miscarriage
> and the physician who was summoned was unable to do anything about it.
> The clinical diagnosis was that of overexcitability of the uterus.

"Mrs. Smith" never succeeded in having a second child. And Helene's description of her tells something about her own conception of herself.

> She was very motherly and greatly enjoyed motherhood in relation to the
> one child she had, though with an admixture of fear. Psychoanalytic treat-
> ment did not remove her difficulties. She ironically called herself an "appen-
> dix mother" who could bring her pregnancy to a successful conclusion only
> by leaning on another woman. Beyond this she was not neurotic, and could

solve all the other problems of her life. It was only to the heavy task of pregnancy that she was unequal, for reasons of which she herself became aware. After her friend had failed her she could no longer chase away the shadow of the mother she had rejected.

In defiance of her mother, Helene had liked to think that her real parent had been her father. She was passionate in her wishes, and had tried to eradicate her mother's influence on her. In part because of her intellectuality, Helene also believed in the magic of her impulses; having had evil thoughts about her mother, she had to worry about becoming a bad mother herself. At times Helene would not be as confident, as when writing about "Mrs. Smith," about having unambivalently enjoyed the rewards of motherhood; she could not help identifying with the mother she had rebelled against. Nonetheless Helene interpreted her miscarriages entirely in terms of her relationship to Regina; she did not touch on any criticism of her father, nor mention insecurities about her husband, and evidently Freud's analysis of her did not extend in these directions.

Helene chose the name Martin for her son; in a paper published in 1930[8] she mentioned a "case" which was once again herself; the mother rationalizes the choice of a name on the grounds that it was that of "an energetic, capable peasant." In Polish Martin was a peasant's name, and she consciously wanted him to be a simple, natural person, not an intellectual son. She "really wanted her son to be well adapted to the harsh realities of life." In a much later publication[9] Helene interpreted the woman's decision about a name in terms of a conflict with her "ardent wish to have a son who would resemble her revered father—who would be intellectually distinguished, of lofty morality, etc." But Helene never wanted to admit that her choice of a name had anything to do with a possible future father figure in her life; for Freud's eldest son was also named Martin. Although she had not yet entered Freud's circle, Helene may have guessed his pleasure at her boy's receiving the same name as his first child. (Freud's close pupils frequently named their children after his, as part of their becoming members of his extended psychoanalytic family.)

Throughout her pregnancy Helene remained a full-time member of Wagner-Jauregg's staff. Food grew scarce, and the housekeeper at the hospital secretly gave Felix and Helene packages of supplies. Helene nursed her infant because there was, she feared, no secure supply of milk available; she kept two goats grazing in the clinic's garden. First she had breast-fed Martin at home, and although she did not like it at the beginning, before long the nursing became a pleasure for her. Breast-feeding was an interference with her professional life, but she kept it up as long as possible because of the wartime shortages. People joked that even the rats at the old insane asylum had trouble finding enough food.

Eventually Helene took a room in the clinic for her baby and a nursemaid. As a woman she was a rarity in Wagner-Jauregg's clinic, and he teased her about the baby. "Oh, Dr. Deutsch," he once said, "I did not know you were pregnant. Where did you carry it?"

"The usual place," she replied, and he quietly laughed.

In Poland servants had been cheap; her family had had many in help, and she brought a similar attitude to her life in Vienna. Before 1914 she had not earned money from the clinic, but during the war she was highly paid; she had, however, new obligations toward her parents. Helene made more money than Felix, even though he had been further ahead of her professionally. His chronic liver disease meant that he could not perform military service; as a civilian he worked at several hospitals, becoming a *Dozent* at the University of Vienna in 1921. Besides the nursemaid for Martin, Helene hired a cook, a chambermaid, and a cleaning woman. In Vienna a wood stove in the cellar provided heat, so that conditions were better than in Poland; it was not necessary, for example, to hire someone to carry water.

One of Helene's first psychoanalytic papers, published late in 1919, was entitled "A Two-Year-Old Boy's First Love Comes to Grief." Freud had encouraged her to publish the paper, an account of Martin's ("Rudi's") loss of his nurse, Paula. "Because of his mother's heavy professional schedule and because of the pressure of external events, this nurse had been a mother surrogate . . . for two years."[10] Freud had put some observations about his daughter Anna into print, and Helene was writing about her child's mourning reaction to the loss of his nurse. Paula was illiterate and a dwarf, but excellent with Martin; she grew so possessive of him that Helene used to slip her extra money to be allowed to spend time with her son. As she wrote, as a result of all that his nurse did for him Martin "disregarded his mother," and the nurse "well knew how to make little Rudi's object choice even more exclusive, for she did not allow anyone else to perform the tasks of love."

By most people's standards, including her own, Helene had neglected her boy. In later years Martin resented the way in which throughout his childhood household help whom he loved were periodically discharged. In addition to hiring good servants, Helene also gave Martin a great deal of herself, especially on vacations. A batch of letters exist from the summer of 1918, when Helene took him (with Paula) away to the countryside for several months' vacation. They rented a little barn without electricity in Seebenstein, near Vienna. Certain foodstuffs were easier to get there. Helene managed to get reading done, professional as well as literary, yet the letters from her to Felix confirm how important Martin was to her. Felix made regular trips to see them, and brought various provisions, including needed books. Helene kept him informed of their life.

"He" is totally indescribable: already a few more nuances darker, the hair possibly still lighter. His eyes shine like the sun—all in all he looks like a ray

of sunlight—or like a flower steeped in sunshine—like a ripening peach—like a symbol of life and joy. Nothing but gaiety and laughter, fun and glee.

His knowledge grows surprisingly from day to day—he already says whole sentences, repeats every word he hears, enjoys new characteristics of words—he speaks to me in a loud voice as if he knew how my heart beats with joy . . .

Martin was genuinely precocious as a child, and later became a nuclear physicist at the Massachusetts Institute of Technology. One letter is particularly touching, since at the bottom of it Helene disguised her handwriting and wrote a short note to Felix as if she were Paula.

Once, Martin fell ill and Helene became highly anxious. She was worried about the danger of diphtheria, and sent regular medical bulletins to Felix, who had undertaken to have Martin's urine analyzed in Vienna. The boy was feverish, lost his appetite, and vomited. She reproached Felix: "I expected that worry about the sick child would bring you here." Yet she retained her sense of humor:

The point of view that I am suffering from a "psychosis" is a little too helpful in getting over the situation. Nobody can describe the torments that I am suffering, but my mind is still clear enough to see that Junior is severely ill with an unknown sickness. Yesterday he cried all day, until completely hoarse.

She was tired and worried, sought medical help, until she grew agitated. Helene (July 4) sounds almost hysterical: Martin was "visibly getting worse. I beg you—come—but not just for a few hours—I can no longer remain alone. My child is perishing before my eyes. Help!"

Helene was so apt to worry about Martin not only because it had taken her so long to bear a child, but because he was to remain, despite her conscious wishes, without siblings. Afterward she sought to find psychological reasons for her having had only one child. She enunciated the principle that in raising her own child, a woman necessarily repeats her own mother-child history.[11] If she had been unwanted by Regina, then that would explain why she was rejecting of Martin. So many years had come between her and her own older sisters and brother that she had had the fantasy that she was an only child, and her father had supported this conception of herself. According to Helene's psychoanalytic thinking, some women can "put too much, often their whole rich emotional world, at the disposal of this one child."

One such woman succeeded, after many years, in solving the riddle of why she had had only one child, although motherhood was in her eyes the highest value. She had identified herself with her child to such an extent that the idea of giving birth to another, who would compete with him for her motherly love, seemed unbearable to her.

Out of identification with her child's jealousy, then, she had therefore had only one child.

> This woman was experienced and shrewd, and *consciously* she wanted to protect her child from the unfavorable situation of being an only child; but unconsciously she yielded to the power of her identification with him and remained monogamous as a mother just as she was in all her other relations.[12]

Realistically Helene's own child took up all the motherly energy that she could summon; even when, many years later, she had two grandsons, she chose one of them as her special favorite. During World War I, however, she felt as though she had joined the ranks in war service; her professional work took so much of her time and capacities that her other emotions were overtaxed. She might overcompensate her neglect of Martin by spoiling him, or through getting overwrought at his falling ill; she could exaggerate her motherliness when she wanted more of the child, and get Paula out of the way. But her disappointment in herself as a mother went hand in hand with a heightened creative spurt. In the last years of the war, and during the beginnings of Martin's childhood, she made the commitment to Freud that was to be decisive for her life as a psychiatrist. In her teaching she could succeed in being maternal. Yet these upheavals in her took its toll on her relationship with Felix. When in 1920 she published a case about the psychology of a woman whose love for her husband had begun to fade, it is evident that she was describing a problem which had become acutely troubling to herself.

The Friendship of Paul Barnay

Felix had one exceptionally intimate male friendship that had started when both boys were five or six. Paul Barnay, one of the two witnesses at the wedding of Helene and Felix, was already a well-known actor, director, and theater manager. Felix's personality would be impossible to understand apart from the warmth of his affection for this old friend; and Paul Barnay came to play a notable part in the early years of the marriage between Felix and Helene. She remembered having gone on walks with Paul in the final part of her pregnancy with Martin. He was the Viennese son of a physician (the Deutsch family doctor), and his mother, a piano teacher, gave Felix free music lessons as a child. The Barnay household was a deeply cultured one, filled with books and art, and Felix found himself a second home there.

Unlike Felix, Paul was only marginally Jewish; and much of his family lived in Germany, not Austria. While Felix chose a career in medicine, Paul pursued a life in the world of art; a posthumous novel of his was published. Acting was hardly a secure means of earning a living, but Paul was good enough to take his chances. Once he and Felix were apart, they exchanged letters and postcards.

In an unpublished paper[1] that Helene gave before a psychoanalytic audience in December 1965, she wrote a paragraph about Paul that would have been hard for her to deliver if Felix had still been alive (Felix died in 1964, Paul in 1960); Felix might have been annoyed at her scientific use of his great friend. From the outset of her acquaintance with Felix she realized how important Paul was to him. As he wrote her in Vienna on August 15, 1911, while still in Munich himself: "Paul is coming—to which I am very much looking forward: at least one human soul in whose presence at last I can come out of my shell a little bit."

Paul was Felix's ideal brother; identical in age, they went through school together, shared mutual interests (such as dueling), traveled in each other's company, and grew into adulthood as soul mates. For all they had in common, they were radically different as men. Paul, who was strikingly handsome and well developed physically, became a Don Juan. Helene thought that in all he had four wives, as well as many other women in his life. Given his friendship for her husband, in addition to his character and career, Paul was bound to fascinate Helene.

In her 1965 lecture Helene was talking about the capacity to identify with others, "as if" they were oneself; one of her most famous clinical contributions, originally published in 1934, had been her conception of the "as if" personality.* In 1965 she mentioned Paul in connection with the way actors create their talents from their power of identification, and use this capacity in the service of their art.

> An example par excellence is a friend of mine, a great and famous actor. He always identified so intensively with the figure he portrayed that he had difficulty finding his own identity when not on stage. I have seen him in his dressing room after a Faust performance (he was a famous Mephisto), free from his makeup and looking in the mirror in a kind of trance, unable to identify himself. When playing the same role in a long run, there were only two methods of finding himself again: by drinking or by making passionate love to a woman.

(Shakespeare's *Richard III,* and Lessing's *Nathan the Wise,* were two other plays in which Paul had played the leading role.) Helene knew about the gradations between abnormality and so-called normality: while a psychoanalyst does not have the actor's task of identifying with a figure he brings on the stage, any therapist must be able to enter into another's life; and yet, like an actor, a psychoanalyst must, in the face of shifting roles, be able to retain his or her own personality.

At the outset Paul seemed harmoniously friendly with both Felix and Helene. He customarily addressed Felix in letters as *gigerl,* a dandy; Felix was fussy in his dress, cared about how his clothes were tailored, and was generally fastidious. His shoes were always clean; the nickname *gigerl* referred to a lacquered pair of yellow shoes that he had had as a small boy.

In late 1912 Felix, on behalf of himself and Helene, sent Paul and his wife Lina a Christmas telegram. In high holiday spirits, Paul replied from Danzig:

> My dear Gigerl, dear Frau Halla!
> Hearty thanks, friends, for your telegram of greetings from home—it

* Cf. Part III, chapter 4, pp. 320–21.

was a most darling surprise! At our place it smells of marzipan, fir trees, sweetmeats, gingerbread, there is the aroma of secrets and in the pantry there lurks . . . ingredients for my new punch. Recipe: 1/2 bottles of best Mavaskiw, 1/2 bottle of best Avak, 2/1 bottles of light red wine, 2 liters water, one lemon. First bring the red wine and the water to a boil, then add Avak and Mavaskiw and lemon peel.—wonderful! Or—heaven help us—are you abstainers! I hope not!

Felix and Helene were, as Paul knew, not drinkers, but the account of his punch was his festive way of greeting them in friendship.

In the spring (end of May) we will be in Vienna, and then our dear wives can become just such friends . . . as we are! Really, even if so seldom, but you don't know how glad I am today of your thought! And today we will drink a "devout" glass to you, to your health, to your well being, your friendship, our love. *Yes,* a glass! My wife is playing theater at the moment, I have brought in for a visit some children of a doctor who is a friend of ours, and we have been playing.—Lord God! How well-behaved the children are nowadays, disgustingly well-behaved!—I am allergic to teachers' pets. This ambitious quality in these model children has something "old" about it, and "old children" . . . is disgusting.—We are young, we commit folly, we feel suffering and joy intensively, don't we?! We have after all remained for each other. Company is arriving to interrupt my writing this letter—Hearty here's-to-you for Christmas, and for a big letter—from you both to us! Yes!

> A thousand heartfelt greetings,
>
> Your
>
> Paulina

Dec. 24, 1912

The signature, an amalgam of his own and his wife's name, represented an effort on Paul's part to express unity of feeling as a couple toward Felix and Helene.

When Felix went away for his health in the spring of 1913, he immediately sent Paul a card. (The previous year, when Felix had gone away to recuperate from his liver disorder, he had written his best friend then too.) Paul replied:

Dear Gigerl,

It fills me with deep concern to hear that you are not well, and I would be really grateful to you or your dear wife if you would let me know about your illness in greater detail. When I recognized your writing and the postmark, I felt joy and a little bit of envy, but when I read of the reason for your trip, then I became very concerned for you, for you aren't one to complain at little troubles. Just take good care of yourself, and get better for me!

Paul babied Felix, as Helene did:

I'm looking forward so eagerly to our reunion, and to our wives getting acquainted with each other! So please—don't spoil my plans for me—at the end of May we're going to clink glasses, with excellent wine, to old friendship and new health, O.K.?! Write *immediately*, let me know what's the matter and how you're doing!!—Of us, I can only say the best!—"artistic-wise" and "human-wise."

Paul and Lina were theatrical successes in a series of different roles. But Paul was about to celebrate a momentous birthday: "My hair—you don't have to worry about this problem—is turning gray, but desire and courage for affirmation of life increase as I reach 'utterly' the staid age of 'thirty' tomorrow."

If Paul read a novel about the composer Franz Schubert, Felix did too; Paul sent Felix critical reviews of his performances, at the same time as he tried to extend himself to Helene as well. While she was away in Munich in 1914, Felix received a letter from Paul (which has not survived) that he thought was "psychologically very interesting and gives me much insight into my present and future." Felix sent it along for Helene to read, but wanted her to return it before he answered Paul, who he feared would not understand him. Helene (February 26, 1914) commented on Paul's letter; she too found it important and moving, if also worrisome.

> I fear for the future of his marriage—or is this just a mood? You know him better. In any case, he is a worthy friend to you, and I am very glad that you, that we, have him. I believe it is one of the great values in life to *possess* *totally* a friend—I do not know this happiness—and in truth it is not my fault.

At the time she was writing Helene was disappointed in her female psychiatric colleague who had come from Vienna to Munich; as Helene tried to explain to Felix, "she is not *the one,* the joyful unconditional friendship I had hoped to find." In 1932 Helene published an article on "Homosexuality in Women," and throughout her adult life had intimate female friends; but Helene never experienced the kind of selfless friendship that Felix and Paul had for each other.

Paul and Lina came to Vienna for two weeks early in June 1914, and invited Felix and Helene to join them in the Austrian Alps. The two couples went to a beautiful resort at Zell am See. Paul's sister Louisa, also an actress, and her boyfriend joined them too. After Felix and Helene left, Paul wrote him on July 5:

> My dear old friend!
> Have thanks for your letter, which heartily and truly gave expression to the feelings of us both!—As we parted, you said to me: "So—as ever!" That hits the nail on the head—or—strikes it even lower if possible. Our feelings for each other have been renewed and deepened, and our lives shall be enriched by our friendship!—Your hand! . . . To next year, old friend, to our seeing each other then!

Paul and Lina were heading back to Bremen, where they were planning to perform. Paul announced that his sister had gotten engaged—a third marital union. Paul also had words of unity about their respective wives. "You both were sentient of how I drew your dear wife to my heart like a sister. And Lina dotes upon you [Felix] in rare warmth and admiration." Felix had undertaken to send Paul some money, which Paul promised to acknowledge the receipt of. (From Bremen Paul explained that he was taking leave of his great-uncle, who had wanted to "control" him.)

Felix returned to Vienna, while Helene went to stay with Malvina, and then visited her parents in Przemyśl. In the midst of writing her about other matters, Felix communicated Paul's expression of brotherly feelings for Helene. Felix no doubt sensed that Helene was not entirely keen about the powerful friendship with Paul. Felix took some credit for the engagement of Paul's sister and thought that Paul in his "impatience" would on his own have wrecked the match. Felix too had his doubts about the nature of the tie to Paul. He wrote Helene (July 14, 1914):

> A ray of sunshine appeared in these days of disheartened waiting for your return, when I received from Paul a picture with some cordial words to you and me; I only fear that he is becoming inwardly closer and closer to me, as he becomes inwardly farther and farther from Lina. I am strengthened in this suspicion, through his not making any mention of her at all.

By the fall the war was in full swing, although it was too soon for any of them to realize how their lives would be permanently affected. Paul and Lina were working in Bremen, and a letter to Felix (September 1, 1914) expressed Paul's gratitude for the financial help.

> In these great times of war there were for me, too, always conflicts to settle, which I would like to write down, would like to pass on to you, but I lack (at the moment!) the time and patience needed to proceed from the thought to the written word. Now we have after all got an engagement in Bremen, with an extremely topical play. As chief producer, I am already enormously busy —decoration, costumes, etc. etc. Thank God, now I *do* have something to do, and don't need to putter around from extra to extra. Really, I had thought I would already be off to war. (Between you and me: I did go to the Consulate to volunteer here, but was not taken because of overfilling.) We now have, of course, a very modest income (200 M). But we are able to live without having to beg for anything. Of course, dear fellow, you were *the only one* who made himself immediately available to me in the difficult period, with word and deed.

Although Felix was a Viennese Jew and a Zionist, Paul identified with the cause of German nationalism. The Central Powers at that time attracted powerful allegiances, including even Freud's. But the pretentious language Paul used illustrates his particular penchant for the outward forms of heroism.

The prevailing feeling here is a wonderful sense of the certainty of victory. Only time is a question . . . He who saw the military march out here, his heart beat higher. Something . . . emanated from officers and troops, that one felt a warm sense of love for these people arise in oneself . . . One became . . . one with the people, and the whole rose above itself. And Kaiser Wilhelm!—You will be amazed, his picture is hanging in my room, adorned with golden laurels.—He has true heroism in himself . . . And then his breastplate! Now we are going to give them a thrashing. My dear fellow, you ought to see the warriors here! Men of brass! Old heroes have re-emerged from the books of legends. A mighty wonder has taken place, we have become *young*. In the dragon's blood a new Siegfried is horning himself.

Paul thought Felix and Helene were entitled to be happy in their profession, since they did good and were necessary, but in such times he felt superfluous as an actor.

As the years passed Felix and Helene were to grow devoted to the ascetic calling of psychoanalysis; Paul's bohemian life stood in contrast to the way they and their acquaintances lived. Standards of promiscuity vary from profession to profession, and although Paul was hard-working as an actor, Felix could once summarize Paul's conduct in a letter (1923) to Helene as a matter of "wine, women, and song." Yet something precious still remained to him from his friendship with Paul. They traveled together in Italy in the summer of 1924, and a letter from Paul to Felix afterward recalls not only their holiday but the time of their boyhood.

I am sitting in—our—former—room in Sorrento . . . The sea is breathing softly, and there is a light swell on the shore, like the gentle caress of a woman's bosom. The melancholy of the Neapolitan fisherman's song wafts over the sea, and soft oarstrokes are heard across the dark sand of the endless surface.

My old friend and brother—the leave-taking from you was not so easy for me as it seemed . . . Besides all the paradiselike enjoyment of nature, besides all the admiration of Rome and Pompeii, . . . those were the days of youth spent with you; an intimate band encircled us, a joyous, beneficent harmony surrounded us; it was—such a rarity—it was pure happiness.

The friendship was as unique for Paul as for Felix.

After my dear father passed away, you became my only friend and brother, my "elective kinsman"; never did I feel this so intensely as on our "Italian trip"! The old bond has endured and renewed itself. Since you have been away, I have lost the joy in enthusiastic high spirits. I have written much, even read. Tomorrow . . . we return, as per schedule, to S. Then onward, onward!—Where to? My body is going to Hamburg-Breslau. But my soul isn't going to the homeland. What does Schubert say? There, where you are not, there there is happiness!

Paul's final words in the letter were: "Stay well, don't let any woman command you, and greetings to you!"

After twelve years of Felix's marriage, Paul could afford wholeheartedly to take his friend's side. But the special circumstances of the friendship between Paul and Felix meant that Helene was an intruder. She was jealous of Paul, at the same time that she feared that he did not like or approve of her. Few wives would relish having to be a disturbing element in such an intimate relationship between two men.

Of the essence of the earliest love between Felix and Helene was the understanding that there be no secrets between them; just as he knew all about her involvement with Lieberman, so she learned about Paul's place in Felix's life. In a paper she published in 1930, about a manifest homosexual who becomes heterosexual, she put a paragraph about "another case" which described her version of the friendship between Felix and Paul. In introducing the "patient," she characterized him as being in "a state of intense self-satisfaction"; she knew that normally people only come as psychoanalytic patients out of discontent. Helene used technical vocabulary in order to picture her husband: "He was the type of narcissistically feminine young man with small capacity for love, for whom a relationship with a similar object was the only possible form of love relationship." In writing for a professional audience, she took for granted the premise that heterosexual love involves the ability to tolerate differences from oneself. The young man of her clinical report was strongly attached to a young actor.

In order to disguise her material, Helene introduced some changes; the "patient" aspired, not to be a musician, like Felix, but to become an actor. This alteration did not affect the reality of their both being artistic. The friend, a professional actor, was

> . . . a typical narcissistic object choice, . . . the embodiment of all those qualities which the patient would have liked to find in himself. He himself wanted to be an actor; his friend *was* one. His friend was tender like a woman and noble like a man, ready for every sacrifice, and yet in full possession of his personality, etc.[2]

Helene's use of "etc." is tantalizing; she did not venture further to describe psychoanalytically Paul's character. But she did conclude with a sentence to characterize Felix further: ". . . the patient bestowed as much admiration on his own person, and was as vain and self-satisfied as if he had actually possessed all these qualities he professed to find in his friend."

In connection with Felix's form of vanity, a letter of his (July 9, 1914) can partly illustrate what Helene had in mind. She had left for the trip to see her sister Malvina in Poland; Helene was unhappy back in her native land, and Felix wrote her joshingly, and yet with some truth: "I am in total agreement with your drinking the cup of boredom and misery to the dregs; for purely egoistic reasons—for my sympathetic personality rises thereby, without adding much of its own, in your estimation, and I gain the advantages therefrom." Felix went on half in jest, yet revealed a telling glimpse of an aspect of his personality.

> In general, I have begun liking my life up to now quite extraordinarily, and I could almost envy you the feeling of happiness at being able to live at my side. Fortunately I am so fully aware of my positive qualities that I don't need to have them brought to my attention by others, and I find my own sufficient satisfaction in this auto-eroticism. I pause simply to yield myself to a self-pleasing look at myself, like a peacock. I notice that I ought to do something for my exterior. I will see what can be done without breaking too many hearts.

Male homosexual love is at least as complicated as heterosexuality. Special possibilities of empathy arise between members of the same sex. The typical transiency of such love alone lends it a subtle and poignant air. Along with the crudeness of some male homosexuality can go a special sensitivity. While psychoanalytic theory cannot hope to "solve" the nature of such a bond, it was natural for Helene, within the limits of the concepts available to her, to try to come to terms with this aspect of her husband's past. She attributed it in Felix to an extreme attachment to his mother and sister; homosexuals look for protection in a man from too much mothering; any other woman in Felix's life would have been, she thought, a challenge to his basic loyalties. But in her 1930 paper she was describing clinically the kind of homosexuality that does not endure, but goes on to form a basis for later heterosexuality.

The homosexuality between Felix and Paul was only one component of their friendship for each other. According to Helene's later psychoanalytic thinking, when a mother's boy like Felix met what looked like a "real man," his passive longings were activated; in order to cope with such tendencies Felix had to play an active homosexual part in order to defend himself. From Paul's point of view too it was not "genuine" homosexuality. His behavior toward Felix was also defensive, a precaution against the loss of the friendship. Paul therefore had to comply; instead of being bereft or humiliated, he disappeared psychologically as a man. The signature "Paulina" in his Christmas 1912 letter to Felix and Helene had, then, an additional layer of meaning.

When Paul performed on the stage, he became so involved in his role that he felt he himself had disappeared; and his best friend had the same experience with music. Felix could play the piano for hours, almost in a trance. For all the differences in their personalities, the identification between them was, according to psychoanalysis, a "narcissistic" one. Felix too had been afraid of losing the full intimacy of his affection for Paul. A whole strain in German culture glorified friendship as an exquisite human emotion. The form of homosexuality that Paul and Felix knew together was part of their idealism and altruism; one friend would do anything for the other, since there were to be no limits to their love.

The German writer Friedrich Schiller, in his poem "The Hostage,"[3] had memorably celebrated such friendship. (In her mid-nineties Helene mistook Heinrich Heine as the author; she had thought the story was in "Nights in Florence.") A rebel against a tyrant is sentenced to death; the condemned man asks for three days' grace in order to travel to witness his sister's wedding. He offers to give his friend as a hostage; if the doomed man fails to return in time, his friend shall die in his place.

> His friend embraced—No word he said,
> But silent to the tyrant he strode.

A terrible storm, robbers, every conceivable obstacle arises to delay the friend's return in time; when he thinks he has missed the scheduled time of execution, he muses:

> "Too late! what horror hast thou spoken!
> Vain life, since it can not requite him!
> But death with me can yet unite him;
> No boast the tyrant's scorn shall make—
> How friend to friend can faith forsake.
> But from the double-death shall know,
> That Truth and Love yet live below!"

He succeeds in getting back before the hostage has been killed.

> Amazement seized the circling ring!
> Link'd in each other's arms the pair—
> Weeping for joy—yet anguish there!
> Moist every eye that gazed;—they bring
> The wond'rous tidings to the king—
> His breast Man's heart at last hath known,
> And the friends stand before his throne.

> Long silent, he, and wondering long,
> Gaz'd on the Pair—"In peace depart,
> Victors, ye have subdued my heart!
> Truth is no dream!—its power is strong.
> Give grace to him who owns his wrong!
> 'Tis mine your suppliant now to be,
> Ah, let the band of love—be THREE!"

Homosexual love, especially among men, is theoretically supposed to be ambivalent; Felix and Paul's conception of friendship was, at its best, unmarred by egoism; they were willing to reverse all roles.

In accepting his own bisexuality, Felix perceived that the person he loved was also partly homosexual. Helene believed that in overvaluing this form of love, Felix was also increasing his sense of himself. In the attachment to Paul Felix could persuade himself that he was like someone who was wonderful. At the same time, in his bond to Paul, Felix could become convinced of his future capacities with a woman. Sexuality with an intimate friend was meaningfully personal, not anonymous. Paradoxically, his relationship with Paul helped convince Felix that he was a man. In this way a form of homosexuality constituted a road to heterosexuality. Years later the American psychiatrist Harry Stack Sullivan would write about the frequency of such a "chum"; according to his biographer, "some sexual experimentation with a chum, in the late stage of preadolescence, could be a normal part of growing up and lead towards a heterosexual mode of interaction in adult life . . ."[4]

Felix was not generally interested in women, but was capable of maternal tenderness himself. Narcissus, in the legend, was so drawn by his own reflection in the water that he drowned; in Felix's case, he fell in love with a beautiful and attractive woman. He had some idea of what Helene's capacities were and was proud of her successes. Felix, a tolerant person himself, did not imagine that their relationship had to fit any stereotypes of how a man and woman are supposed to get on. Theirs was a union of friendship and comradeship, not passionate love; whatever its limitations, the marriage did last. Yet as a woman Helene was frustrated.

By the end of World War I she was seriously worried about the choice she had made. If she mistreated Felix, or got on badly with him, she could partly attribute this misfortune to an unfavorable contrast between Lieberman and Felix. At the same time, the worse things were between her and Felix, the more she could idealize Lieberman.

Helene's dissatisfaction with Felix did not, evidently, stop there. Her son Martin suspected that, in the context of her difficulties with Felix, she herself had had a sexual relationship with Paul; when interviewed, she chose not to deny it. Just as whatever went on sexually between Felix and Paul is less important than the emotional hold they had on each other, by the same token what might have happened between Helene and Paul is less significant than that she had come between the two men. She could rationalize what she did on more than one ground. She usually resented anyone in Felix's life who excluded her, and was subject to great mood swings; anybody who did not show her enough appreciation would be out as far as she was concerned. By the beginning of World War II she had succeeded in causing a rift between Felix and Paul. Felix was less than outgoing and generous toward Paul, although he was now safe in America and well off financially.† In letters to her Felix sounds more concerned about Reinhold's fate than Paul's; yet it is clear that it was Paul who felt he had some claim on Felix. No further letters

† Cf. Part III, chapter 2, pp. 300-2.

between the two men survive, although they met in Europe once in the summer of 1954.

In view of her past involvements with men, it is understandable why
Helene was attracted to Paul. She was susceptible to the attention of ladies'
men; the burning intensity of a good-looking and passionate man could overcome the barriers of her monogamous nature. She was neither as wild (nor as
chaste) as she feared, and liked to imagine; the fantasy of prostitution had
repeatedly come up in connection with Lieberman. Part of Paul's appeal to
women was the aura about him of the knowledge of hidden places and secret
delights. His career as an actor had a special meaning for her, given her own
interest as a young girl in becoming an actress and the man Mädi loved in her
journal; at the same time Helene would be threatened by him, since she
needed to be center stage herself. To the extent that she was in love with
Felix, an affair with his best friend was a distorted extension of an interest in
her husband.

Paul was proud of his capacities as an actor and got great pleasure from
his work; he had reason to be confident that he had a real human relationship
with Felix. He might have made love to many people who did not matter to
him, but Helene thought that underneath he was a decent person. Although
he tried again and again, Helene claimed he got no real satisfaction from
lovemaking. He needed sex, like his drinking, in order to feel more like himself; it was a measure of how much of himself he put into his art that he
needed such rituals in order to regain his personality. In the end his health
was undermined, according to Helene, by liver damage, although this ailment
was contracted differently from the similar affliction Felix suffered from.

During World War I Paul was an attractive figure in Helene's life. He so
wanted to be loved by women that he would use all his charm to be victorious, even with other men's wives. It can be exciting to a woman for a man to
be willing to risk getting murdered by a furious husband. Part of Paul's
fascination with married women was the idea of getting other men jealous. He
could prove the stronger, for he would have both the woman and his freedom
to leave. Cuckolding a best friend has a special meaning; Felix would have
been half disapproving and half envious, as well as deeply hurt. On Paul's
part, it meant an act of revenge on both the man and the woman. One
prerequisite to his success as a Don Juan was his ability at the same time to
identify with the woman. It may be no wonder that psychoanalysts have seen
a "latent" homosexual content in Paul's kind of avid heterosexuality. (Helene
accepted a lot of daffy ideas: for example, the notion that if two men talk
about sex together it constitutes a homosexual invitation. Other analysts too
could unnecessarily frighten people; they told male patients that if they
thought of another woman during heterosexual intercourse, that also meant
"latent" homosexuality.)

From Helene's point of view, the triangle with Paul and Felix was different from the one with Lieberman and his wife. Any such emotional sharing is

difficult and can be unstable. One of Helene's incentives to infidelity, however, was an excess of security with Felix as her husband. Her letters to him express how much she could miss him. That Martin did not physically resemble Felix deepened the inevitable mystery about the identity of his father. She deliberately tried to leave the issue up in the air, perhaps to make Martin wholly her son, as she had felt herself to be her father's child, or to take revenge on a child who was less lovingly understanding of her than she wanted. At the same time, if Martin were not Felix's child, it would rationalize to Helene some of her own behavior to her son; she once wrote about how a woman's tormenting doubt about the paternity of a child could interfere with mothering.[5]

Vienna was a cosmopolitan city, and the complicated world of the playwright Arthur Schnitzler was not simply the product of a writer's fancy. Helene's relationship with Lieberman might have been irregular by her mother's standards, but it had protected her from making even more daring human choices. In picking Felix she had gone to an opposite type of man. Yet each of her experiences, no matter how unusual or painful, succeeded in enlarging her as a person. Her capacities for human understanding were broadened, so that she could guide herself by the ideal of nothing human being alien.

It is conceivable that Helene was wrong about the full nature of the attachment between Felix and Paul: an allegation of active bisexuality might serve to explain away deficiencies she found in Felix and rationalize her own failures with him, as well as account for her disappointment in her marriage. Martin too, like his mother, might have been mistaken in ever thinking she had played such an active part in coming between Felix and his only friend; it would not be the first time a son has doubted his mother's fidelity, or even his own paternity. Helene's life, though, was a highly idiosyncratic one. As she took decisive steps toward Freud at the end of World War I, it was out of an awareness that her own unhappiness might be alleviated by psychoanalysis. If she came to romanticize some ideals of the relations between the sexes that now seem old-fashioned, it was due to a profound self-doubt about how she had chosen to live her life.

8

Analysis with Freud

As a result of the disruption caused by World War I the Vienna Psychoanalytic Society met on an irregular basis. Before the outbreak of war only a little over a dozen people regularly came to the Wednesday night meetings. Freud's name might be widely known, but he had not yet attracted the disciples who would later successfully create the psychoanalytic school of thought. Freud had brought his now legendary difficulties with Alfred Adler to a head in 1911; the upshot had been to split the Vienna Psychoanalytic Society almost down the middle, as members withdrew in protest against Freud's ideological intolerance.[1] In 1913 Freud broke with his Swiss heir-apparent, Jung.[2] Freud had written his essay "On the History of the Psychoanalytic Movement" (1914) in order to distinguish his work from that of backsliders.

Only fragmentary evidence exists about the tiny group around Freud during World War I. He mainly spent his time systematizing his ideas, since his clinical practice was virtually nonexistent under wartime conditions. (When the postwar inflation was over, Freud's lifetime's savings had been practically wiped out.) Helene once remarked that at the first meeting of the society she attended, Isidor Sadger gave a paper on flowers in dreams; he had gone overboard in emphasizing the sexual themes that Freud had introduced, and Sadger interpreted flowers as genital symbols. At the time Helene wondered to herself whether flowers could not also be just flowers. Among his Viennese adherents Freud put up with people he was dubious about: Sadger, for instance, had an almost pornographic interest in sex. (His own nails were dirty, and he would not even keep his analytic couch clean for a patient's head and feet.)

Helene's first formal contact with Freud's group did not impress her with the quality of his followers. In 1916 Freud chose her to comment on a difficult paper by Lou Andreas-Salomé, who was then living in Germany; the subject was "The Anal and the Sexual," but in contrast to the crudeness of Sadger's work this essay was a subtle bit of theorizing that gave Helene a good deal of trouble. The few surviving records indicate that she was more or less regularly attending meetings of the Vienna society in early 1918. She was formally elected to membership on February 13. On March 13, 1918, she presented her first paper, a short report on association experiments in melancholia; she drew on her unpublished work done at Kraepelin's clinic in 1913.

That spring of 1918 Helene made her arrangements to be analyzed by Freud beginning the next fall. Normally one would ask for an appointment to see Freud, known in his circle as "Professor," through a letter, and he would answer by mail; Helene never communicated with him by telephone. His procedure then was the reverse of what it became later, when a new student had to be analyzed first before becoming a member of an analytic society. Jung had been the first to suggest that all future analysts themselves be analyzed; in September 1918 Nunberg proposed that such "didactic" analyses be made the rule, but this change did not finally take place until 1925.

Helene's decision to come to Freud in 1918 represented a valuable acquisition for his group in Vienna; Felix by then was a respected diagnostician in internal medicine. (After the war Freud guaranteed the Deutsches' food supply by getting Felix a job as the physician to the English legation in Vienna.) When Freud accepted Dr. Elizabeth Révész as a patient—she was a Hungarian psychiatrist also married to Dr. Sandor Rado*—Helene thought Freud might take her too; in fact she replaced Dr. Révész, taking her analytic hour.

Helene had attracted Freud as a potential pupil precisely because of her involvement with Wagner-Jauregg's clinic. Yet entering analysis she realized that she would have to leave the clinic. Freud looked on official psychiatry as his enemy. The outside world had reacted with hostility to his ideas, and he turned away from it to his own group. Although he was flattered at an outsider's coming to him, Helene felt she had to cut her other ties. Freud wanted his teachings to penetrate the clinic, but at the same time thought that no one could serve two gods simultaneously. He was angered at his rejection at the clinic and held himself aloof from psychiatry; but he also wanted to change the atmosphere there.

Helene felt that Freud's attitude toward her was either/or. Others of Freud's pupils have reported that they were obliged to renounce psychoanalysis if they had interests in other fields. In Helene's instance pressure from within the clinic also pushed her into leaving. A friend of hers, Dr. Paul Schilder, had come back from the war, and she knew that Wagner-Jauregg

* For a discussion of Rado, cf. Part II, chapter 11, pp. 203–06 and Part III, chapter 1, pp. 281–84.

really preferred him to her. So for Schilder's sake, as well as for her ambitions with Freud, she left the clinic when she became Freud's disciple.

Within ten years Viennese analysts were so secure as a unit that in a reversal of Helene's direction some of them (like Anna Freud) asked for, and received, permission to see clinical material at the clinic. As Helene left the clinic, she received a two-year appointment as an assistant in Professor Karplus's neurological department. The position was one she could hold as a woman; and neurology, having nothing to do with psychoanalysis, would be less threatening to Freud. The new appointment was, however, close to Freud's own earlier interests, since neurology had been his field before he founded psychoanalysis.

As Freud's difficulties with Adler and Jung had already amply demonstrated, psychoanalysis at that time had the overtones of a religious sect. Logically it might seem good for Freud to have had Helene remain in Wagner-Jauregg's clinic. But Freud did not like the prospect of split allegiances, and had reason to fear he might lose out in a contest with academic life. In surrendering to Freud, Helene obeyed as if to a demanding love. If she at that time wanted a figure in her life who wanted all of her, this submission had something to do with her current misgivings about her relationship with Felix, as well as memories of her happiness with Lieberman.

Historians of ideas have been tempted to challenge Freud's originality; and in reality many of his concepts can be fitted into intellectual history. But the method of treatment and investigation that he had evolved was uniquely the product of his own personality and experience. Patients, for fifty minutes a day, lay on a couch, with the analyst out of sight, and they were obliged to obey the "fundamental rule" of analysis—free association. If the ideal for the patient was to express all thoughts and ideas, the analyst was supposed to remain opaque.

Freud did not believe in burdening the patient with extraneous issues but was committed to discussing those problems which the patient chooses to bring up. By the analyst's remaining cool, distant, and neutral, the relaxed patient is allowed to develop fantasies and expectations about the analyst. The emotional reaction of the patient to this analytic setting (the "transference") would reflect, Freud thought, the patient's past conflicts. (He ignored the possibility that the peculiarities of the therapeutic setting might itself distort the clinical material.[3]) By first evoking, and then interpreting, the transference reactions of patients, the analyst was supposedly able to contribute to a rational understanding of the patient's difficulties. This insight would, according to Freud, enable the patient to dissolve nonrational patterns that had interfered with his or her life in the past.

Helene had no need to undergo a conversion experience with Freud; she had been a partisan of his ideas at least since 1913. Perhaps, had the war not given her an unprecedented arena for her talents within Wagner-Jauregg's clinic, she would have gone to Freud for training sooner. In the fall of 1918 she was coming for therapy as well. According to psychoanalytic principles, only an analysis undertaken for the sake of alleviating neurotic suffering can hope to achieve a genuine emotional impact; according to the line of thought that regards suffering as necessary to produce insight, any other purpose will lead merely to intellectualization.

Whatever the theory of analytic technique might have been, Helene and Freud were real people to each other. She regularly shared her goats' milk with Freud's wife on the way to her analytic hour. Freud occupied the whole of one floor of the small apartment building he lived in. Helene would bring half a quart of goat's milk, ring the doorbell of the private apartment on the left of the hall-way, before entering the waiting room to Freud's office on the right. (Wagner-Jauregg used to joke, with his dry humor, about Helene's having a relationship with those goats, as he teased her about her "ambivalence" toward the clinic she had supposedly taken leave of.)

Although for special favorites, or with those who had made some prior contribution to his movement, Freud accepted patients free of charge, Helene paid a fee of about ten dollars an hour. Freud had had a penchant for a narcissistic type of woman who is very attractive to men; Helene felt an active, questing element in his behavior, and responded with the devotion of an adoring pupil. She was well read in psychoanalytic literature before her analysis, and studied anything further she wanted during the course of her treatment. At this stage, and with a pupil he liked, Freud practiced unlike some later analysts who infantilized patients and mobilized magical expectations by imposing absurd restrictions on their curiosity. In contrast to others who came to Freud, Helene was leaving behind a successful career; her psychiatric profession, however, did not give her the literary latitude of psychoanalysis. Now she could look forward to seeing individual cases intensively, and to comprehending them psychologically; she would have a wealth of material, based on direct observation, to write about. The analysis with Freud capped years of prior preparation.

Although Freud believed that his therapeutic approach would help people to change themselves, his chief objective was understanding, not healing. He thought he could reconstruct the role which childhood continued to play in adult life. People are, of course, different in different situations; still, each person has a recognizable center of gravity. Freud used his theories to generalize about the origins of individual symptoms, yet at the same time his whole clinical approach was dedicated to the proposition that each person brings a unique life story.

An analyst does not even have to leave his home to encounter fascinating human dilemmas; he sits and waits for patients to bring up their most painful human conflicts, and gets paid for the combined talent of empathy and confidentiality. For Helene the craft of being a psychoanalyst came at a time in her life when she felt frustrated and blocked in her private world. If she did not know what to do about her marriage and was unhappy with herself as a mother, psychoanalysis offered her a different and elevated sphere in which she could test herself. Now the complicated world of Schnitzler could be held at a distance.

For Freud, too, psychoanalysis had been a sublimation of human drives. He had once been passionately in love with his wife, Martha, but around the time he invented the technique of psychoanalysis, in the late 1890s, his physical relationship with her came to an end. According to his own words, in letters to his intimate friend Wilhelm Fliess, from about forty-one on sexuality was of no further "use"[4] to him. Instead of turning to another woman, Freud, already the father of six children, discovered psychoanalysis. Helene detected in him a man of immense self-control, who had been able to master his own strong passions through analytically participating in the lives of others.

As an analyst of future analysts, Freud could sublimate his human involvements even more. The man who made so much of the role of infantile sexuality, and who was condemned by many as a corrupter of the young, himself ended up sacrificing his own erotic life as the price of his creativity. In attracting Helene as a disciple he won someone who shared his experience that work could flourish at the expense of conventionally defined love. Freud was in the process of creating a new church; just as monks and nuns have been able to assist others in areas of their own limited experience, so analysts aspired to a similar high ideal of dedication and service.

In everyday life Freud was thoroughly bourgeois, and his system of ideas incorporated many characteristically middle-class elements. Although he was socially conventional, nonetheless Freud saw himself as a great revolutionary. For he taught that whatever we might think about ourselves consciously, in the end we are subject to all kinds of self-deceptions. These tricks which the mind plays on itself, revealed in slips, symptoms, as well as dreams, stem from the realm of the unconscious. For Freud, real truths were always things expressed unconsciously.

Freud had a cause for which he fought. In his writings he sounds like an embattled leader, and Helene was attracted to this side of him (as to Lieberman); in his office, though, he could be a masterful example of Old World charm. In behalf of his movement he used every device at his disposal. Yet it is unlikely that Freud was ever fully aware of the special seductive impact of his treatment situation. Lying on a couch, talking about themselves, patients were encouraged in their sense of self-importance; anyone who shared in their private drama was the recipient of naturally exaggerated feelings of significance. In the 1930s Freud admitted that in his earlier years of practice he had been unlikely to try to mobilize in patients negative feelings toward him. Since he was in reality a genius, it was natural for him to accept even the most extravagant estimations of him as fully justified by the reality of his achievements.

Although in his life Freud was, at least by the time Helene knew him, remarkably puritanical. (Elsewhere I have discussed his relationship with his sister-in-law Minna.[5]) In effect he became a spiritual Don Juan. He sought to win disciples, to proselytize even among those who came solely for therapy, and in the end he succeeded in winning to himself members of both sexes. His followers became thoroughly devoted and loyal. If Freud needed them to make for himself a large extended second family, they in turn found the security within his movement that they had lost in terms of their natural relatives. For Helene, as for others, psychoanalysis became a second and ideal home, in addition to its being a new profession.

One of Freud's favorite operas—he usually made a great parade of his distaste for music—was Mozart's *Don Giovanni*. The theme of the great seducer had a special attraction to Freud. Mozart's Don is finally dragged off to hell through a handshake; it is easy to forget the impact of Freud's own handshaking. Before and after every analytic hour, in accord with European custom, Freud shook hands with his patients; in this way, whatever the theory of analytic neutrality might have been, Freud and his patients stayed in touch with reality. Freud never, however, fully appreciated the suggestive impact, not only of the analytic setting but of his own way of practicing treatment.

Helene had come to Freud with both feet on the ground; nevertheless, her emotional transference to him was immense. Like other patients she became temporarily convinced that her analyst was in love with her. She once put an experience from her own analysis into one of her clinical papers. Although this "woman patient" could not remember anything from her analysis with Freud, and "especially the oedipal character of transference had escaped her memory,"

> she retained the recollection of an episode which happened outside the analytic room and which convinced her of this transference. She remembered that once she left the analytic session very excited—she did not know why. She stopped in front of a store window and experienced a tormenting thought: "What is poor Frau Professor going to do in *this* case?"[6]

In the course of Helene's reminiscing about her contact with Freud in her old age, isolated comments of Freud's could come back to her. For example, hostile things might be said about Freud at the clinic. In order not to have to repeat such remarks in her analysis, she informed clinic officials that she had begun her analysis with Freud. When once in an analytic hour she referred to the fact that she never produced unpleasant stories about him in her free associations, he simply said: "That is because you are too decent." Freud could be complimentary, and throughout the analysis he emphasized his sympathy and her importance; decency was one of the standards he tried to live by.

Freud was not enlivened by any accounts of her psychiatric cases; but as far as she could tell he paid attention to her realities. She was an interesting person to Freud, although not a remarkable "case." Neither her childhood in Poland, nor even the attempted seduction by her brother—Freud and she spent time on such issues—seemed especially noteworthy to him. The story of her relationship to Lieberman and her marriage to Felix held him; but details about her small child and difficulties with her nursemaid bored him.

Twice Freud fell asleep during her analytic sessions; she noticed his cigar fall to the floor. They had such an easy, friendly relationship that they joked about it. Once she forgot her handbag on the couch; when Freud shook hands after the analytic hour, he held on and gazed into her eyes. She was momentarily confused about his intentions, until she realized that she had committed what Freud would regard as a symptomatic act. According to his system of thought the forgotten handbag represented a symbolic sexual invitation.

Freud spoke much more freely with patients than analysts of a later generation. Some have said he chattered; he could be garrulous. Frequently troubled by his prostate during the year of her analysis, Freud had to get up many times to go to the bathroom.

In the course of Helene's analysis no repressed childhood memories were recovered. Whatever the abstract goals of analysis, in practice Freud had limited aims. With Helene his interpretations focused on her straightforwardly oedipal relationship to her parents, her love for her father and her antagonism toward her mother. Freud did not expect an analysis to be an upheaval in a patient's life; and with Helene he did not challenge her basic attitudes. His outlook confirmed her in her feelings, and gave her renewed grounds for old affective reactions. (Nowadays analysts would think that any oedipal constellation has to be shaped by pre-oedipal conflicts, which would be of an opposite nature to the ones Helene was conscious of.)

Freud could even offer Helene advice. Once, when Felix was out of town, she picked one of his colleagues to take her out; he had a car, and she was eager to take a trip. Helene sent him to Freud; but Freud found him a boring person, and thought she should give him up as a friend. He basically approved of Helene's marriage to Felix; although Freud would be intolerant of certain human diversities, and was especially threatened by male homosexuality, he could be wise and accepting as long as there were no secrets between husband and wife. Freud cherished confidences, at the same time as he did not like keeping secrets. (His *The Interpretation of Dreams* remains an invitation and a challenge to historians of his own life.) At times Helene found him indiscreet; so did someone like Ernest Jones. She soon found out which of his earlier followers in Vienna he found it difficult to put up with. If there was one lesson Helene took away from her therapeutic contact with Freud, it was that an analysis cannot be conducted according to any rule book.

Toward Freud himself Helene had feelings of religious awe. He remained a godlike figure to her for the rest of her life. To be sure, she might joke among friends about his inadequacies as a therapist, but her devotion was never in doubt. He was the thinker who provided her with the whole framework for her life's work. She knew Freud's writings by heart and would not even have to underline her edition of his works; she remembered details of his case histories, and recalled Freud's constructions, as if the patients had been living people in her own life.

Helene found it easy to idealize Freud. She admired his modesty, which stood out in contrast to his pupils' arrogance about how much they thought they knew. He was in reality an old gentleman when she started her analysis. (According to Helene's autobiography,[7] by a remarkable coincidence her father left Vienna to go home to Poland at the outset of her analysis with Freud.) To Helene, as for others in his circle, Freud was so much a hero that he had to be free of their own imperfections; if any of them still had oedipal conflicts, he was supposedly already freed from such feelings. For the sake of their own idealizations of Freud they would suppress whatever signs of neurosis they might see in him. None of them would ever have dared use Freud's psychoanalytic techniques in order to dissect the master's own personality.

Freud was a spellbinder, not just figuratively; as an orator he could enthrall. For Helene it was not like listening to Lieberman speak in behalf of the suffering masses or preach about socialist hopes for the future. Rather Freud's approach was a matter-of-fact one, as he brought new psychological truths to light. One of Freud's pupils, Abram Kardiner, thought that except for Winston Churchill Freud was the best speaker he had ever heard. The consecutive powers of Freud's mind meant that extemporaneously he spoke like a book. For Helene Freud had a very agreeable voice, and as she listened to him she "forgot the world."

In the fall of 1919 Freud suddenly declared that he wanted to give Helene's analytic hour to a former patient, the "Wolf-Man," who was coming back to Vienna. (To the end of his life this Russian prided himself on being Freud's famous case.[8]) Foreigners were now filling Freud's practice; he preferred patients who challenged his curiosity, and in his view Helene was able to do without further analysis. She was unhappy about having to give up her analysis with Freud; nor was she unique among Freud's disciples in being suddenly terminated. (Later, in 1923–24, she went to be analyzed by Abraham in Berlin.†) She felt she had bored Freud, and that he was not primarily interested in therapy.

In retrospect, Helene was convinced that in the brevity of her treatment

† Cf. Part II, chapters 11–12.

Freud had failed to analyze her unconscious fantasies of bisexuality. The concept of female castration anxiety,‡ or "penis envy," as it became known, was not yet widely endorsed within psychoanalytic circles. Followers of Freud, such as Abraham, were to make much of the idea; Freud himself had so far merely enunciated it in some of his earlier writing as a key theoretical principle. Although Helene later thought that for her sake Freud should have been more interested in her conflicts over masculine strivings, at the time she was unable to make him change his decision to put an end to the analysis.

After the conclusion of her analysis with Freud Helene soon began to suffer from what she considered transference depressions. The loss of Freud as her analyst left her discontented. Freud dismissed other patients, in similar circumstances—when he found himself unable to make further discoveries, and if he was confident that the interruption would not cause too much suffering. For Helene there were some compensations; she could now have more personal contact with Freud; he told her she could come to him anytime she needed him. As a matter of course he sent her more patients.

Freud concluded Helene's analysis with the suggestion that she stay on the road of her identification with her father. At the time she was shocked by the idea. She had come into analysis partly out of the desire to be more of a woman; but Freud seemed to be saying that she was feminine enough to be able to tolerate her own masculinity. Freud was convinced that her relationship to her father, whatever its oedipal roots, had been beneficial, and at the same time he was encouraging her to remain a follower of his own. Freud saw himself as a surrogate for her father. Whatever Freud's limitations as a therapist, he viewed Helene's identification with her father as a source of great strength. When, after her subsequent analysis with Abraham, Helene pointed out to Freud that certain dreams of hers in the analysis had been expressions of what was then known as unanalyzed castration anxiety, he maintained that the problem had been handled in the discussion of her tie to her father. According to Freud a patient did not have to be "purified" of neurosis. Without her relationship with her father Helene would not have become a professional woman. Freud believed in leaving alone and unanalyzed conflicts that did not interfere with a patient's capacity to love or work.

Freud's approach as an analyst at this time was to unscramble the patient's problems, give a glimpse of the existence of the unconscious, and then let the patient work things out alone. Whatever this limited technique failed to cure, it did help preserve a patient's independence. And the bigger Freud's turnover in pupils the stronger his movement became.

The help which Freud was able to offer Helene had little to do with the specifics of his therapeutic technique. As a disciple she took him as a model, never forgetting that her reality as a person was the most significant element in the impact which she could hope to have on patients. In her own experi-

‡ For a discussion of this subject, Cf. Part II, chapter 13, and Epilogue.

ence Freud's sheer existence in her life had made all the difference; and his assistance had come at a time when she needed it.

Freud succeeded in awakening Helene's creative energy, and he did so in accord with what she later thought was a pattern.

> Looking back, I see three distinct upheavals in my life: liberation from the
> tyranny of my mother; the revelation of socialism; and my release from the
> chains of the unconscious. In each of these three revolutions I was inspired
> and aided by a man—my father, Herman Lieberman . . . , and lastly
> Freud.⁹

Helene continued to pay deference to Felix's role in her life: "My husband had his own unique place in my heart and my existence." But her autobiographical discussion of Felix was compounded of nostalgia and sentimentality.

It is impossible to overemphasize the effects that the warmth of Freud's genius had on Helene. Not only was he the commanding figure in her life until his death in 1939; even afterward she so identified with him that she sometimes jokingly described herself as Freud's "ghost." Her attachment to him could be eternal and yet not erotic. The profession he had created turned out to be an ideal compromise for her. Within her role as a psychoanalyst Helene's talents were freed.

Helene could describe herself as an adopted daughter of Freud's. She knew that from Freud's point of view, she could never succeed in taking her place as a daughter; a rivalry later grew up between herself and Anna Freud.* But Helene could still legitimately feel like a daughter to Freud; for he had treated her as an assistant, and assigned to her a definite position within psychoanalysis.

In terms of what Freud meant to her, his universe was as much a court as a family; he was the reigning monarch. (Political systems have an inevitable impact on how people think about themselves, and the Austro-Hungarian regime of her youth had been an empire.) When Helene first began to publish psychoanalytic articles, she would show them to Freud first; as an editor of the journals he would be bound to see them anyway, but it was more a matter of his being the audience for whom she wrote. Even after she stopped presenting him with material that she had decided to publish, his towering presence remained the inspiration behind all her work.

For others in the history of psychoanalysis, particularly his exceptionally talented male pupils, Freud could be a burden; for Helene he managed harmoniously to release her creative talents. She could write as Freud's adherent, and at the same time fulfill her own needs for self-expression. Her professional audience responded to her work as that of one of the most prominent

* Cf. Part III, chapter 1, p. 287.

leaders in psychoanalysis. She was no mere imitator of Freud's, but within his system of thought she managed to express her own individual outlook.

The 1920s were Helene's most creative period; not only did she make some of her most notable psychological contributions during that decade, but she emerged as one of the most successful teachers in the history of psychoanalysis. As the first director of the Vienna Psychoanalytic Institute's training program, she left a permanent impact on the future of Freud's movement. At the same time the success with Freud highlighted the inadequacies of her personal life, and in particular her choice of Felix. The more her career flourished, the harder he had to struggle in her wake, and the more she came to resent the prior private failures—and the subsequent compromises—that had made her career as an analyst possible.

Freud won the Goethe Prize in 1930, and it was always natural for Helene, like other Central Europeans, to think in terms of the great German poet. Faust sought to abandon his boundless striving; and he was willing to pay with his soul for fulfillment. In retirement, Helene was reminded of Faust's words, as she tried to explain how it was she had come to be so thoroughly possessed by Freud. She thought that Goethe's wisdom expressed the spirit of her own involvement with Freud.

> Faust. If I be quieted with a bed of ease,
>   Then let that moment be the end of me!
>   If ever flattering lies of yours can please
>   And soothe my soul to self-sufficiency,
>   And make me one of pleasure's devotees,
>   Then take my soul, for I desire to die:
>   And that's a wager!
>
> Mephistopheles. Done!
>
> Faust.   And done again!
>   If to the fleeting hour I say
>   "Remain, so fair thou art, remain!"
>   Then bind me with your fatal chain,
>   For I will perish in that day.
>   'Tis I for whom the bell shall toll,
>   Then you are free, your service done.
>   For me the clock shall fail, to ruin run,
>   And timeless night descend upon my soul.[10]

For Helene to see herself as Faust, with Freud in the role of Mephistopheles, was to make a peculiarly safe figure of him, since in the end Goethe's devil gets cheated of his due by the eternal feminine.

Victor Tausk's Suicide

Helene's analysis with Freud was intimately touched by one of Freud's most senior followers in Vienna, Victor Tausk. Helene had been with Freud for about three months when, in January 1919, Tausk began to come to her for analytic treatment. Freud himself had refused to analyze Tausk but tried to work out a compromise; Freud recommended that Tausk go to Helene while she was in analysis with Freud. Tausk was Helene's first psychoanalytic patient. The circumstances surrounding his treatment, however, were to affect her for life, and the deep impression that Tausk's death made on her is an example of the trauma many psychiatrists bear from a suicide early in their training.

Tausk was born in Slovakia in 1879. Like Helene, he grew up on the cultural outskirts of the Austro-Hungarian Empire; as an ambitious young man he had gone to Vienna in 1897 to study law. Tausk married at the age of twenty-one; his wife-to-be was already pregnant; they then returned to Sarajevo, where he completed his training as a lawyer. He received his doctorate in 1902. Although he had two young sons, he and his wife decided to separate in 1905; she went back to her family home in Vienna, while Tausk moved on to Berlin in 1906.

Tausk was young and talented, and his aspirations disillusioned him with the life of a lawyer. He complained about not wanting to defend scoundrels; money-making was not enough for him. Law had merely been the shortest and cheapest academic study leading to a professional title. In Berlin he embarked on the new career he had longed for. Using his multiple gifts, he wrote poetry, practiced his violin, and drew charcoal sketches. The necessity of earning a living, however, forced him to struggle at journalism, which for him was demeaning. He yearned for creative work, at the same time as he felt guilt-stricken about his sons. Although he wrote reviews and even whistled in cafes, he had financial difficulties.

Tausk's life in Berlin left him run-down and exhausted; no matter how hard he struggled, he could not rise above the most insecure existence. Physical illness (as well as inner turmoil) preceded a few weeks' stay at a sanatorium, where he slid into depression—self-reproaches, sleep disturbances, along with fears of impoverishment. Like Helene during her interlude at Graz, Tausk was an original person whose conflicts went beyond the range of the statistically normal. Despite his brief period of intense self-deprecation, Tausk roused himself and tried something new. In the fall of 1908 he came to Vienna to study medicine; he already planned to become a psychoanalyst. While enrolled again at the University of Vienna he held a job on a newspaper. In November 1909 he presented his first paper to the Vienna Psychoanalytic Society.

Tausk had Freud's personal support, and the rest of the Viennese psychoanalytic group did what they could to smooth his way. (The society had been founded by Freud in 1902, but written records of its proceedings date only from 1906.) It was immediately obvious to all the members of the group that Tausk had superior abilities. Tausk was not the only pupil of Freud's to abandon his previous profession to become an analyst. The first generation of analysts typically came to Freud with the bravado of someone with a frustrated or failed career. In those early days of psychoanalysis it took someone at odds with himself to be able to see the relevance of Freud, beyond the barriers of convention.

In 1909 the circle around Freud included almost as many literary and humanistic students as it did physicians; when Tausk decided to become a doctor, from the outset he may have envisioned a special role for himself, for unlike Freud, Tausk chose to become a psychiatrist. His most original achievements were to be his clinical studies of schizophrenia and manic-depressive insanity. He had a post at Frankl-Hochwart's neurological outpatient clinic. Like Helene, he also worked at Wagner-Jauregg's psychiatric facilities. In 1911 Reinhold had introduced Felix and Helene to his intimate friend Tausk. Reinhold had, for a time, changed careers, too, in entering Freud's circle, leaving philosophy for psychoanalysis. Reinhold, however, came to feel that the Vienna Psychoanalytic Society was too narrow, and to escape being stifled, he gradually drifted away. In the years before World War I, though, Reinhold was as much swept up by Freud's ideas as was Tausk. Tausk and Helene had shared many professional discussions, but unlike her, throughout his years of studying medicine he was part of Freud's inner group.

Tausk was exceptionally handsome and attractive to women, and after the breakup of his marriage had many affairs. Helene knew several of the women. One was a famous actress, Lia Rosen (later a patient of Felix's), who, even though Tausk ultimately refused to marry her, saved his love letters to her until her death in Israel in 1972 (they were subsequently destroyed by her executrix). Another was a physician, Dr. Ilse Zimmerman, who was—like Lia Rosen—thrown into a terrible depression after Tausk broke his engagement to her.

The most notable woman in Tausk's life, and one who inevitably aroused Helene's fascination, was Lou Andreas-Salomé. She and Tausk were lovers in 1912–13. As Nietzsche's expositor (according to Lou, he proposed to her), she came to Freud in the fall of 1912 with a background of the best of European culture. She was still on close terms with Rilke, whose lover she had been and whose development as a writer she had encouraged. (Lou introduced Rilke to Freud in 1913.)

Lou was fifty-one when she came to Vienna; however attractive she might once have been, she now had to rely on her psychological resources to arouse the attention of any potential conquests. Vibrantly responsive to ideas, Lou possessed an extraordinary flair for identifying with men, especially with the creative part of them most subject to inner uncertainties. In 1912 she had actively set out to seduce Tausk; he was exceptionally good-looking, with blond hair, blue eyes, and a mustache. He might be eighteen years younger than she, but Lou thought he had the best mind in Freud's society. To a friend like Helene it was strange, if not offensive, to see him involved with a woman so much older.

Freud took Lou into his confidence to an extraordinary degree. In his letters of later years he discussed with her the emotional problems of his daughter Anna, whose psychoanalytic therapist Lou became for a time. In 1912 Freud courted Lou, sending her flowers and walking her home in the early hours of the morning. While on Tausk's part his love for Lou ended in physical revulsion and distaste (he used the expression "vomit" when he described to Helene how he felt about Lou's breasts), for a time he had hoped that being accepted as Lou's lover might make him to psychology what Nietzsche was to philosophy and Rilke to poetry. For 1912–13, however, Freud, Lou, and Tausk had established a triangle that had advantages for each; and the involvement of the three of them was bound to fascinate Helene.

To Helene, Lou was the personification of a *femme fatale*. Such a woman makes so much an impression on men that she becomes their destiny. The power that a woman like Lou had was not necessarily attributable to physical beauty. In an irrational way, Lou probably felt some responsibility for Nietzsche's later insanity. She was like the proverbial spider catching flies, not for the purpose of torture but out of the need to exist. She did not consciously and coldheartedly land her men.

Helene was impressed that Freud should have attracted such a woman, although the founder of psychoanalysis did not have to fear cannibalization. Lou added importance to Freud's person and glory to the circle around him.

But Helene did not like Lou; from her point of view, Lou's relationships to people were not genuine enough. With Freud, and even in the case of Tausk, she seemed to want to collect one more great man. Perhaps Helene saw Lou as a rival, since she was able to move so deftly in the professional world of men. Lou ended up as a practicing psychoanalyst in Germany. To Helene, she represented a species of nymphomaniac. (Helene could never forget that at a dinner party that Tola Rank and her husband Otto gave in 1921 for Lou, the Freuds, and the Deutsches, Lou flirted with Felix.) Helene was so intrigued by the relationship between Tausk and Lou that in 1965 she mistakenly recalled that their affair had only recently ended at the time she analyzed Tausk in 1919.

As the first in Vienna to give lectures on psychoanalysis for the lay public, Tausk was deeply identified with Freud. To Helene, Tausk was no mere imitator of Freud's but a real personality in his own right. While she was still admiring Freud at a distance, Tausk was already established with him. In her view Tausk was the "genius"[1] of the group in Vienna around Freud; doubtless each of these people were prone to exaggerate the others' significance; still, in terms of the history of ideas, they all were remarkable individuals.

While World War I had had a beneficial impact on Helene's psychiatric career, it had had an adverse effect on Tausk's professional advancement. No sooner had he completed his medical studies in June 1914 than patients grew scarce and the practice of psychoanalysis almost impossible. Tausk was called up for the Army in August 1915 and served as a military psychiatrist. Throughout the war he managed to visit Vienna occasionally, often to discuss one of his new papers. Whatever feelings of inward despair he might have had, he possessed the resources to produce his best psychoanalytic writings during this trying war period. He presented an important paper on war psychoses to the Vienna society, and one on the "influencing machine" in schizophrenia—which by itself established his psychiatric reputation.[2]

Helene was present at the discussion of Tausk's paper on schizophrenia on January 30, 1918. In his published article he alluded to some of her remarks. To her, he was a preeminent leader of the Vienna society of which she was about to become a member. He always had struck her as jolly and sociable, and she sensed no great pathology in him. A brilliant analyst and a trained psychiatrist, Tausk seemed to others as well someone of great importance in Freud's world. Earlier he had proposed an amplification of Freud's developmental model of personality growth; according to Tausk, compensation played a role, since people do not emerge from one period of development unless they experience the pleasures of the succeeding one. Now, in his paper on schizophrenia, Tausk had discovered the role of projection. While Freud had hypothesized the regression of libido back to primary narcissism in psychosis, Tausk was elaborating the significance of projection within a concrete psychotic syndrome. Helene's first (1919) paper[3] as a psychoanalyst, published at the same time as Tausk's own on schizophrenia, was designed to provide clinical confirmation of Tausk's views.

In the shrunken Vienna psychoanalytic group of the war years, Tausk loomed even larger for the future of Freud's movement. Right after the end of the war, however, external conditions for the practice of analysis were unfavorable. The city was no longer the center of a great empire; in a disorganized social situation, few patients were in a position to undergo formal analysis. In those days an analyst did not practice a little psychotherapy, with a few sessions over a short time, in addition to full-scale psychoanalyses. An analysis was then supposed to last for at least six months or a year. (Even as late as 1938, for a candidate in the Vienna Psychoanalytic Society to undertake psychotherapy on the side would have been considered an interference with his training.)

Postwar Vienna was not an easy place for anyone, and particularly for those without an established occupation. Tausk's only specialty was Freudian psychology, which was still an insecure profession; he had no medical standing in an accepted field like internal medicine. While many of Tausk's friends and associates shared some of these problems, most of them did not find themselves in as vulnerable a position. Helene, for example, when she resigned from Wagner-Jauregg's staff still retained her connections with the University of Vienna; her husband had his practice as well. Tausk sought an academic post in psychiatry, even though being an adherent of Freud's was no asset in the university circles in Vienna.

Within a month or so of returning to Vienna, Tausk went to Freud to request an analysis. Tausk's great dream now was to be analyzed by Freud. For those, like Tausk, who had come so early to Freud, more informal methods of learning, talking to Freud and each other, had been deemed sufficient to enable one to practice analysis. For Tausk to come to Freud to be analyzed represented even more of a personal submission on his part; no other analyst would be senior enough for him. Almost forty, he still had to live like an impoverished student, while trying to help support a family. Tausk had enough substantial work behind him to feel entitled to the privilege of an analysis by Freud.

Freud's answer was no. Tausk might well have had anxiety that Freud would not take him into analysis. While he recognized the persistence of his own inner difficulties, he must have known that his presence had long caused Freud's discomfort. Lou had seen as early as the Munich congress of analysts in 1913, when Tausk had loyally attacked Jung in behalf of Freud, that Freud had "plainly held him off."[4] Freud may have harbored old jealousies because of his suspicions that Tausk had been intimate with Lou. (Some years later Freud acknowledged envying Rudolph Loewenstein for his affair with Marie Bonaparte.) But realistically, Tausk at the end of 1918 had nothing, and he had come back from the war needing help.

Instead of accepting Tausk himself, Freud suggested that he go into analysis with Helene. Sending Tausk to her as a patient, Freud had to explain something about the case and his reasons for not taking Tausk into analysis himself. Freud told her he felt inhibited in Tausk's presence. He was restless and uncomfortable with Tausk and had no tolerance for this sort of discomfort. Unlike later, when his daughter Anna delivered papers for him at meetings, Freud was still coming to his society with his ideas in flux.

Freud told Helene that it made an "uncanny" impression on him to have Tausk at the society, where he could take an idea of Freud's and develop it before Freud had finished with it. Lou had noted before how Freud disliked being forced into premature discussion. The tension between the two men at the meetings of the society would only be heightened were Freud to become Tausk's analyst.

Freud complained to Helene that Tausk would not merely accept ideas but would come to believe they were his alone. A struggle over priorities, any contest about who originated which concept first, was extremely distasteful to Freud. Tausk was the only one in Vienna brilliant enough to be such a rival, although earlier, with Adler and Jung, Freud had found his relationship to students marred by his concern with originality. The issue has bothered others who write; depth psychology, moreover, is a field in which little can be objectively proven. Innovations come mainly in how we think about mental processes. Freud thought he still had discoveries to make, but he might be so convincing that Tausk could believe he had thought of them first. Tausk might elaborate Freud's ideas with his own clinical material, without making the distinction between what was his and Freud's.

Freud did not need someone in analysis who might argue with him— Helene would be no such threat. So he refused Tausk; he was as honest as he could be about his reasons, and sent him to a psychiatrist he already had in analysis. The referral was flattering to Helene but a terrible insult to Tausk. Despite her psychiatric experience, as an analyst Helene was a nobody. Both she and Tausk knew that he had done much better psychoanalytic work. Sending him to her only underlined Freud's refusal of an analysis; it emphasized that Freud was accepting other Viennese psychiatrists as patients.

In retrospect, Freud's proposal that Tausk go into analysis with Helene appears bizarre. Tausk, of course, need not have accepted the arrangement. He was, however, obsessed with Freud, and the master's self-sufficiency was especially attractive to Tausk. Freud had been partially rejecting Tausk for some time; this gave Tausk that combination of support and distance that he seemed to need.

Tausk swallowed the insult and entered into analysis with Helene. She could be a bridge from him to Freud. He would lie on her couch six days a week, knowing she would be with Freud just as often; Tausk could be analyzed by Freud through her. At the same time Tausk would be reestablishing a triangular relationship with Freud through a woman. Once more, as with Lou, an attractive woman would be the channel between the two men. Tausk knew that a woman would be far less threatening to Freud, and through her he could plead his case.

Whatever his inner conflicts, the economic chaos, or his strained relations with Freud, Tausk did seem on the way to building up a practice. He was able to see seven patients a day and one free of charge. According to the analytic rule Tausk paid Helene a fee. She thought nothing more serious than a neurosis troubled Tausk, part of it centering on Freud. Perhaps she did not know enough to be able to diagnose Tausk's troubles. Certainly Freud had not given her any special warnings. Never in three months of analysis was he for a moment suicidal. Tausk's relations to people were not restricted; he was a warm and dynamic person, in good human contact; and in his work he was objective and scientific. Knowing him as a living man, full of activity and love of life, Helene never guessed any melancholic past.

In his analytic sessions with Helene, Tausk talked almost entirely about Freud. Whatever Tausk's deeper difficulties, they now all focused on Freud. Tausk did not rage against Freud; he just grieved over Freud's attitude toward him. Tausk thought that the trouble between them lay in Freud's own difficulties. Tausk felt that he had had certain ideas before Freud did but that Freud would not acknowledge them. Tausk was capable of originating concepts of his own that could in fact correspond to what Freud might eventually think. Freud had a great need to arrive at any new point in his own way, by the continuous development of concepts already assimilated. He could not accept the ideas of others, but first had to transpose them into his own manner of thinking. Freud's mode of working was bound to elicit Tausk's resentment because it prevented Tausk from ever gaining credit for asserting himself in an original manner.

In the overheated atmosphere of Freud's circle it was often very difficult to tell who had which idea first. Years later Helene made the point that at times Freud may have only considered an idea in his mind, but seeing it in print he would conclude that someone had stolen it. He may well have had illusory memories about what lay behind the contributions of Tausk that he felt were taken from him. The theme of plagiarism can be found almost everywhere one turns in Freud's career.[5]

For his part Tausk would also have liked to have discovered all of Freud's ideas. One of the gratifications in being a disciple of Freud's was the possibility of fancying oneself in Freud's position as the inventor of psychoanalysis. But because of the way Freud's mind slowly enveloped alien ideas, Tausk feared he would never be able to get credit for something new.

Freud and Tausk shared a similar reproach. Part of Helene's fascination with the Freud-Tausk struggle stemmed from the similarity of their personalities. Each felt the other was taking ideas without due acknowledgment; and each had good grounds for this belief. To Freud it seemed that anything his pupils thought of was ultimately his. And to Tausk it appeared that no matter how far his mind ranged, ultimately Freud would put his own imprint on Tausk's contributions. Each was inhibited in the other's presence. Each man felt he was unique and a genius, and feared being destroyed by the other. Tausk, however, was the one who sought treatment. Having heard complaints and accusations from both sides, Helene—who could see above the conflict between them—thought there was reality to what each felt.

During Tausk's treatment Helene was naturally trying to continue her own analysis with Freud. Every time he sent her a patient she took it as a demonstration of his affection; sending her someone like Tausk reflected his immense esteem for her talents. The training of analysts was, of course, less systematized than now. If one had Freud's favor, that was all that was necessary. Nowadays, partly as a result of Helene's subsequent efforts, a structured procedure has been developed for an inexperienced analyst to get supervision on cases. Then, however, it was customary to go to Freud for advice on a case from time to time, but on the whole he encouraged his disciples to use their own judgment and trust their knowledge of the clinical material.

Even for those days, however, sending Tausk to Helene while she was in analysis with Freud was unusual. Helene never questioned Freud's reasons for sending Tausk to her; she simply assumed that Tausk, who had a high opinion of her as a clinician, would go to no one else. From her point of view, Tausk came as a patient in need of help. It was normal that he should come from Freud, since all the analysts relied on him for their cases. Freud had such confidence in Helene that later the same year he sent her a member of his own family. It never crossed her mind at the time that Freud might have had some old scores to settle with Tausk—over Lou, for example.

Whatever Freud's motives in sending Tausk to her, or Tausk's in accepting the humiliation, the arrangement proved unworkable. Helene learned Tausk's side of his struggle with Freud. Impressed with what she considered Tausk's genius, she spent a lot of time discussing him during her analytic hours with Freud. Tausk began to interfere with the conduct of her own analysis. Near the end of March, 1919, after three months, Freud called a halt to the whole situation.

He explained to Helene that Tausk had caused an interference in her own analysis, and that Tausk must have accepted her as his analyst with the intention of communicating with Freud through her. The burden was put on Tausk, not Helene. Tausk's success in fascinating her threatened the progress of her analysis with Freud. She felt Freud was acting like a demanding lover, as he had when he insisted that she leave Wagner-Jauregg's clinic.

Freud made Helene choose between terminating Tausk's analysis with her and discontinuing her analysis with Freud. To her it did not constitute a real choice but an order. With her unquestioned devotion to Freud she unhesitatingly communicated his decision to Tausk. Tausk's treatment ended immediately. In those days such instantaneous terminations of analytic therapy were not as suspect as they would be now. Helene told Tausk Freud's opinion and her own decision, and that was the last she saw of him as a patient. He listened and accepted, and was in no doubt from whom the rejection had really come.

Freud may have thought of sending Tausk to Helene as a compromise. It had not worked out, and he felt entitled to demand that she break it off. At that time far less was understood than today about the transference relationship between patient and analyst. It would seem obvious now that to send Tausk to Helene while she was with Freud would only encourage his preoccupation with Freud, as his analyst's analyst.

Freud was through with Tausk, no matter how difficult it might prove for Tausk to accept the rejection. This whole period after World War I marked as decisive a shift in Freud's fortunes as the earliest stage when he had emerged from his isolation and founded his school, just before Tausk entered the scene. Now, as at the Budapest congress for analysts in 1918, Freud's work had been hailed for the first time by public officials. And with the end of the war itself, foreign students could think of coming to Vienna to study psychoanalysis; by the end of 1919 they had become a steady stream that lasted until the Nazis occupied Austria in 1938.

Tausk continued to make presentations before the Vienna society; on April 16, 1919, he gave a paper on problems connected with psychoanalytic technique. Yet a rebellion against Freud was slowly taking shape within Tausk. He wrote to Lou about his resentment at Freud's attitude toward Tausk's work on the war neuroses:

> A paper on war neuroses Freud spoilt for me by assigning the subject to the dignitaries of the international association. "They are the group leaders; it is a matter of officially representing psychoanalysis," he said to me when I remonstrated because though a war-psychiatrist I was not made one of the speakers.

At Budapest there had been a symposium on war neuroses at which Sandor Ferenczi, Karl Abraham, and Ernst Simmel made contributions; these three papers, along with one delivered by Jones in London, were published in a small volume (1919) to which Freud wrote the introduction. (Tausk delivered a paper at Budapest on "Psychoanalysis and the Capacity for Judgment.") Tausk allowed himself to believe that, partly as a result of his analysis with Helene, he had overcome his dependency on Freud. As Tausk wrote Lou on March 26, 1919:

> Freud shows esteem but little warmth. Our relations have nevertheless improved since I no longer seek them. They are not likely to become much better, he continues to exclude anything personal. But I have at last been cured of my desire for them.

Freud's rejection had been so personal that it was difficult to rationalize on any scientific grounds.

Contact with Freud meant more to each of his pupils than to Freud himself. Nonetheless, Freud's response to Tausk also had its neurotic aspect. While a son may hate a father surrogate, it is equally likely for an older man to be jealous of a younger one. The Oedipus complex should not be presented only from the point of view of the son. Helene may not have questioned Freud's (or her own father's) seductive attitude toward herself, but she saw how Freud could view younger men as potential threats to him. From her perspective Freud had been much too involved to be objective; Freud saw in Tausk only a danger to himself, so he was unable to consider that Tausk was disturbed and in need of help.

The precipitating cause of Tausk's suicide was his inability (once again) to go through with a new marriage; unlike Lieberman, Tausk had failed at both work and love. Between the end of Tausk's analysis and his death on July 3, 1919, he met Hilde Loewi, a concert pianist sixteen years his junior. His elation at falling in love may have masked grief and mourning, and it would not be surprising for a patient to act out his emotional conflicts after the sudden blow of an interrupted analysis. Hilde may have been partly a substitute for the lost Helene. Tausk had first met Hilde as a patient who came to him for therapy.* For an analyst to marry a patient was to commit a great crime of his profession; in his choice of a former patient, which could have contributed to Tausk's disturbed feelings, can also be detected his growing resentment at Freud.

Tausk's suicide was a particularly cruel one: he tied a curtain cord around his neck, so that after he shot himself in the head, as he fell he strangled himself. But the surviving suicide note[7] (he also wrote one to Hilde) to Freud was tranquil, filled with devotion and gratitude for what Freud had meant to him. Yet Tausk did not give the reason for his suicide; he left Freud in the dark as to his motivation.

Freud's obituary for Tausk, the longest one he ever wrote, put the blame for Tausk's death on external circumstances.

> Among the sacrifices, fortunately few in number, claimed by the war from the ranks of psychoanalysis, we must count Dr. Victor Tausk . . . All those who knew him well valued his straightforward character, his honesty towards himself and towards others and the superiority of a nature which was distinguished by a striving for nobility and perfection . . . He is sure of an honorable memory in the history of psychoanalysis and its earliest struggles.[8]

* If, as has been proposed, Hilde was pregnant, Tausk's promise to marry her may have been prompted more by a sense of honor than his real wishes; the similarity of this situation with that of Tausk's first forced marriage, which ended so unhappily and with so much guilt, must have weighed heavily on him.[6]

In blaming Tausk's death on the war, Freud was not consciously dissembling. He really wanted to believe he had played no part in Tausk's final tragedy. Tausk was, as Freud put it in a letter to a Swiss follower, "a victim of fate, a delayed victim of the war."[9]

To Sandor Ferenczi, a Hungarian analyst who was also a special favorite, Freud wrote that the etiology of the suicide was "obscure"; then Freud conjectured: "Probably psy[chic] impotence and last act of his infantile fight with the father ghost."[10] In a letter to Lou, who had loved Tausk, Freud did not speculatively cast aspersions on Tausk's manhood, but he was open concerning his relief that Tausk was finally gone.

> Poor Tausk, whom you distinguished a while with your friendship, put a thorough end to his life. . . . His farewell letters . . . are all alike affectionate, attest his lucidity, blame no one but his own inadequacy and bungled life—thus throw no light on the final deed . . . So he fought out his day of life with the father ghost. I confess I do not really miss him; I had long taken him to be useless, indeed a threat to the future.[11]

In contrast to Freud's obituary, with all its public praise, in private Freud was left with only pity for Tausk.†

With Helene, as with Lou, Freud could count on her understanding the nature of his competitive struggle with Tausk. She was away in the country when Tausk died. Afterward she said to Freud that perhaps if she had kept Tausk in analysis and not sent him away, he would still be alive. Freud dodged her remorseful suggestion by saying coldly—"But you made the right choice, you chose for yourself." He gave her implicit permission not to be guilty, not to grieve. On the other hand, perhaps he was trying to protect her from feeling too blameworthy.

For Helene had played a greater part in Tausk's undoing than she was aware. Of course she was new and inexperienced as an analyst. Like others who have first started to practice analysis, she was stunned to find out how much the clinical picture fit Freud's account of the stages of an analysis; with her first patients she could get up between sessions and exclaim to Felix: "It's all true!" And she had her own analysis to take care of. Since she was so deferential to Freud, and also his patient at the time, it seemed to her as if the suicide were not her responsibility but Freud's. Just as Freud put the blame for Tausk's death elsewhere—on the war—Helene put whatever blame there was on Freud.

It was not surprising that Helene considered her own role negligible, herself a mere mediator between Freud and Tausk. On the surface, little emotional transference was ever established between Tausk and Helene. But in a subtle way Tausk had been wooing his analyst with the story of his conflict with the master. The tale of his difficulties with Freud was the most

---

† In her mid-nineties Helene agreed that Freud could have allowed himself to be more human in his reaction to Tausk's death.

seductive power Tausk had at his disposal. Tausk's resentment at Freud was an exciting contrast to Helene's own adoration; she could indulge her interest in this rebellious student without acknowledging to herself that she too might have critical feelings about Freud. All her own negative impulses toward Freud could be isolated in the person of Tausk. Going to Freud with Tausk's story, Helene was unintentionally betraying her patient; she was showing herself as the good pupil, not like the assertive and troublesome Tausk. She may even have implicitly encouraged Tausk's interest in her own analyst, and in his expressions of rivalry.

As different as their relationships to Freud were, both Helene and Tausk were obsessed with Freud. Although she had Tausk in treatment for three months, Helene learned nothing about his spending twenty-five days in a sanatorium in 1907. She remembered his closeness to his mother, and especially to one sister, without understanding his dependencies on women and the anger this passivity could awaken in him. Although such a short period of treatment was not enough for her to come up with anything very reliable as to the sources of his troubles, she had never even guessed that he could harbor intense self-accusations. She did not consider him a depressive, and had not the slightest inkling that he was a potentially sick man. A fine person, though temperamental and neurotic, Tausk shocked her as well as other acquaintances by his sudden death.

Helene, at least in 1919, had a weak spot as a therapist: she was susceptible to the attractions of a ladies' man. Tausk was a poet as much as a scientist, and he had the emotional fire of Lieberman. (Tausk, like Lieberman, had been expelled from school as a young man because of his political activity.) Artists are apt to have a rich and seemingly promiscuous sexual life—as in the instance of Paul Barnay—so Tausk was a striking contrast to the austere Freud, who so successfully sublimated his love life into work. Consciously or not, Helene may have anticipated that her relationship with Tausk was going to come to a bad end; and this would have encouraged her decision to terminate his treatment.

Tausk's analysis itself had done him harm. The treatment was supposed to activate conflicts for a constructive purpose. A patient is especially vulnerable in the early stages of an analysis, and just at that point Tausk was abruptly dismissed. Having permitted the three of them to become so close, Freud suddenly tried to be distant. It is possible to conjecture that from Tausk's point of view it was as if father had rejected him for interfering with mother's relationship to father; and in the end father took mother away, keeping her for himself. Helene and Freud had first mobilized Tausk's magical expectations, and then interrupted his analysis without finding any other compromise.

Helene chose to exaggerate the effects on Tausk of Freud's refusal to analyze him, at the same time minimizing the impact on him of her terminating his treatment. Since Tausk had changed his whole career in order to become an analyst, in later years she worried about others who might be tempted to leave their professions to become psychoanalytic therapists. Yet Freud's willingness to keep her and reject Tausk was bound to boost her self-esteem. In protecting himself from Tausk, Freud was acting to protect Helene's analysis as well.

One of Helene's Polish analytic friends, Ludwig Jekels, resented (like Tausk) the way the internationalization of psychoanalysis had affected Freud's relationship to his Viennese disciples. In 1910 the meetings of the Vienna society were moved from Freud's private apartment, where according to Jekels "the atmosphere was on the whole a rather agreeable, instructive one and full of enjoyment."

> Unfortunately, this changed markedly when the sessions were transferred into the hall of the Vienna College of Physicians. There differences came to the fore which to my mind had various personal motives as their basis; above all, there was one to be the favorite son (of Freud) and to cut out others who were in favor with him. Sad to say in this attempt the usual parliamentary forms were often greatly transgressed. Most often this happened between Stekel and Sadger, later Tausk also entered the lists who loved to assail the two of them. This went so far that Freud asked me after one of the sessions: "What does Tausk want from Sadger; he is indeed a serious scholar!" Besides, Freud thought very highly of Tausk's analytical talents yet refused firmly to analyze him although Tausk had asked him repeatedly to do it; I too asked Freud to do that, but he replied: "He is going to kill me!"[12]

It was tempting for Helene, as well as for the whole inner circle around Freud at the time, to attribute to Freud the power of life and death. Helene thought that Freud's attitude to Tausk had been the "last straw," and that Freud could have saved him had he so chosen. Paul Federn, another early (nonpsychiatric) analyst, even more bluntly thought that the motive for Tausk's suicide was "Freud's turning away from him": "If Freud had shown him a human interest, not simply recognition and support, he might have continued to bear longer his martyr-like existence . . . That we could not keep Tausk is our shame."[13] Tausk's struggle with Freud became a psychoanalytic family secret, on which Helene was known to be the expert. Others in that tiny subculture readily believed that if Freud dropped someone it could lead that person to self-extinction.‡ Exclusion from the revolutionary community was an annihilation as great as any death. Tausk's suicide became one of the early legends among Freud's followers, helping to bind them together into such a tightly knit community.

For Helene the Tausk story was all the more intriguing in that it highlighted Freud's problems with other key male disciples. As much as she knew that Freud was attracted by brilliance and consciously sought the best possi-

‡ Many other suicides took place in the history of Freud's movement.[14]

ble disciples, at the same time he needed yes-men. Although she had come to Freud's circle after the quarrels with Adler and Jung were over, she thought she knew, after her analysis of Tausk, the basis of Freud's troubles with his most talented male adherents. When he spoke of a "heretic" like Jung, he was specifically referring to how Jung had taken Freud's ideas. Tausk, compared to Jung, was merely a nuisance to Freud. But Helene appreciated how hard it could be for creative men to get along with a genius like Freud.

Helene so identified with Freud's power that by 1966 she did not even remember the obituary of Tausk, and before being shown that Freud's editor James Strachey (she did not own his edition of Freud's writings) had unquestionably attributed it to Freud, she tried to argue that it did not bear the stamp of Freud's style. It was not like Freud, she thought, to be so superficial and attribute Tausk's suicide to the strains of starting a new life after the war. Freud's human feelings at Tausk's death were, according to her, blocked by his guilt. (In writing to Ferenczi Freud had said of Tausk's suicide: "despite acknowledgement of his endowment, no adequate empathy in me.") According to one of Helene's versions of what had happened, Tausk had killed himself rather than Freud. For Freud to have fully reacted to what he had done to Tausk, in her view, he would have had to have gone off and killed himself.

In exaggerating Freud's role in Tausk's life, and by seeing herself as an agent of Freud's message to Tausk, Helene was continuing to evade her own moral responsibility. She was, to be sure, still in analysis with Freud, and he was at the time her conscience; but she was also a mature woman of thirty-four. Just as Tausk had so deeply identified with Freud that he had not known which of his ideas were Freud's and which his own, so Helene lost track of the proper boundaries between herself and Freud. (In addition to being the first analyst to invoke the concept of "identity," Tausk had also introduced the notion of "ego boundaries.") Helene admitted in old age that the amnesias she still had about some of the events connected with Tausk must have been due to the persistence of her own guilt feelings. Yet, like Freud, she distanced herself from Tausk's death in order to avoid emotional turmoil.

Helene had at best failed to help Tausk, and part of the problem lay in her readiness to throw herself into his dilemma. The best advice for Tausk would have been to leave Vienna; if he could not face going back to Belgrade, where a psychiatric appointment awaited him, Berlin was another possibility. If only Freud had not been so involved himself, instead of dismissing Tausk through Helene he might have suggested Abraham as an alternative analyst for him; Helene would make that choice herself only a few years later. But Tausk was as if bewitched by Freud, and Helene was too; instead of helping to detach himself from Freud, unwittingly she fed his problem. Like him, she found Freud too fascinating ever to have detached herself from him while she was in Vienna. In the course of her own analysis, and in the midst of her thoughts on her troubled relationship with Felix, she once contemplated going back to Lieberman. She was a married woman and hesitated to take her child from Felix; but Poland was now at last free, and Lieberman lived in the capital at Warsaw; nevertheless, she could not face giving up Freud's Vienna for an alien part of Poland that had once belonged to Russia.

Neither Freud nor Helene had been able to react with full human sympathy to Tausk's plight. For different reasons they had helped exploit his dependencies. Tausk's death, however, was self-inflicted; to blame anyone would be to detract from the genuine tragedy of his fate. Both Freud and Helene had acted as they did to the best of their capacities, even if neither of them had been able to give of themselves fully. They were as helpless, in terms of their own personalities, as Tausk himself. If in the end the outcome was catastrophic for Tausk, Helene had learned forever the limits of psychoanalysis as therapy; and she could acknowledge to herself some of Freud's human fallibilities.

10

Early Contributions

The years immediately after Helene's analysis with Freud were professionally full and exciting. The Tausk episode, instead of alienating Helene from Freud, bound her more tightly to him. After Freud brought her own analysis to a halt in the fall of 1919, she received four or five patients from him; many of them had already been in treatment with him for as much as a year. She flourished as a psychoanalyst, rapidly becoming an outstanding figure in Freud's movement. The case material fascinated her, and she so enjoyed her work that there seemed almost no limit to the number of patients she could treat without becoming fatigued.

The world of psychoanalysis was a special spiritual haven, even if it became customary for Freud's followers to emphasize the costs of their discipleship. Helene, in an article published in 1940, shortly after Freud's death, chose to recall the sacrifices of becoming an analyst: ". . . he who attached himself to Freud at that time knew that he was going into exile, that he would have to renounce his career and the usual gratification of professional ambition."[1] Yet Helene's own productivity was heightened by her contact with Freud; only long after his death did she come to realize how she had depended on him for inspiration.

By the end of World War I Freud's adherents were establishing devoted groups in the major European capitals. An analyst in good standing could count on a friendly reception wherever he or she chose to travel. The Viennese society in particular stuck together, and its members characteristically took their long summer vacations in the same place. (Some patients continued their analyses during the summer, moving to wherever the analysts had chosen to live.) The opposition of "official" medicine reinforced the ties binding the analytic movement together. As another early analyst, Franz Alexander, recalled: "One felt that whatever one's contributions were, one lived for a worthy cause and that the results of one's efforts would continue to live."[2]

In entering Freud's movement Helene had enlisted in a cause that had aspirations to be as international as socialism. Starting in 1908 Freud had begun to hold regular meetings about psychoanalysis (each called a "congress") with participants drawn from as many different countries as possible. In 1910 he founded the International Psychoanalytic Association, with Jung the first president; at that time Adler became head of the Vienna society, one of the branches of the new international organization. Four congresses were held before World War I, and then another (the one in Budapest) just before the conclusion of hostilities.

The first congress that Helene attended was that held at The Hague, September 8–12, 1920. On the way there she shared a train-compartment with Hug-Hellmuth. Her first congress always stood out in her mind. The Dutch had responded positively to Freud's ideas even before the outbreak of the war; analysis subsequently flourished in the Netherlands more than in any other European country. Along with her associates coming from Vienna in 1920, Helene was impressed by the warmth of the local reception for the visiting analysts. Wartime restrictions on travel were now entirely gone. Helene had her first chance to present a paper before an audience of her peers from beyond the confines of her previous analytic acquaintances. She had first tried it out before the Vienna society.

Her presentation was a clinical contribution, like her first paper as a newcomer to Freud's circle, "A Case that Throws Light on the Mechanism of Regression in Schizophrenia" (1919). In 1919 Helene had been combining her psychiatric training with psychoanalytic concepts in order to describe a psychosis.[3] She tried to show, by means of a concrete illustration of a patient who had been blind since her second or third year of life, the correctness of some of Freud's fundamental ideas. Her account was one of the earliest attempts to understand delusions psychologically. She was explicitly following Tausk's lead about the role of ego boundaries in schizophrenia, and how inner feelings can be projected onto the outside world. She interpreted the patient's dreams of sight both as a response to living for the first time in a psychiatric hospital, and as a regression to earliest childhood. Although Helene was dealing with psychiatric material relatively unusual for an analyst of that era, she was supporting Freud's conviction about the importance of the earliest years of life and the nature of psychotic regression.

Her paper delivered at The Hague, "On the Psychology of Mistrust," was her first attempt to speak as a certified analyst. The basis for her presentation was four analyzed cases. Yet she aimed to talk broadly about the phenomenon of mistrust as a neurotic symptom, a character trait, a concomitant of deafness, as well as a feature of mass psychology. Since suspicious people are afraid of unreal dangers, Helene sought to find the explanation in unconscious mental forces.

Each of her different cases supported her conviction that neurotic processes, however they might highlight in exaggerated form the nature of "normality," were separate from the psychoses. Helene explicitly emphasized the distinction between mistrust and paranoia. Suspicious people are perpetually on guard against imaginary threats; since they do not know where they are coming from, the mistrustful look for such dangers in everyone and in everything.

According to Helene, the projection of inner dangers, and in particular of ambivalently hostile feelings, formed a common core in instances of pathological mistrust. If feelings of anger are intolerable, for example, it therefore makes sense that a weakened ego take recourse to suspicious fear to cope with impulses that are not securely mastered. Disappointment with love objects, as well as the revival of infantile identifications, also played a role in encouraging a predisposition to mistrust.

Unlike some of her subsequent publications, Helene's paper at The Hague never became a classic in the literature. (In contrast, for example, Tausk's paper on the "influencing machine," which appeared in the same issue with Freud's obituary of him and Helene's 1919 article on a blind schizophrenic, would be repeatedly cited for over sixty years.) Yet Helene's talk, subsequently published, had been orderly, gave good clinical examples, and was thoroughly integrated with analytic thinking at the time. (She discussed, for example, the similarities between projection and anxiety hysteria, and the differences between suspicion and doubt.) If Helene, at her first congress, was making a modest clinical contribution, it was in keeping with her status as a novice on the international scene. In the list of abstracts of the proceedings of the congress, though, her article[4] came second only to that of an important paper by Abraham, Freud's leading follower in Germany.

Helene's lecture had been so successfully received that after she gave it she went to a park and sat by herself, crying. She sent a telegram to Vienna to make sure Martin was still all right. She remembered that in writing the paper, Martin had once been in her lap; he pulled at her chin, wanting to look at her, but she could not participate; analysis then meant so much to her, she felt she had to fulfill herself creatively. After her presentation at The Hague it seemed to her that her ambitions for a career were succeeding at the expense of her femininity, and that she was psychologically abandoning her small child.

One "patient" she spoke about at The Hague was a "highly ambitious and intellectual" woman who "since the beginning of her marriage . . . had lived in a constant state of conflict between her strong masculine aspirations and the feminine role she had assumed as housewife and mother." This so-called patient, in terms of what was customary for those who underwent analysis at that time, had so little motive for treatment that one suspects a disguised bit of autobiography on Helene's part. A central later contribution of hers was to describe how a woman's career may flourish at the expense of her emotional life.

Some months later, on March 30, 1921, Helene presented a paper before the Vienna society entitled "On the Pathological Lie (Pseudologia phantastica.)"[5] Like mistrust, lying plays an obvious role in everyday life; yet the objectionability of untruthfulness has to be qualified by the so-called white lies necessary in civilized human contact. Freud's analytic approach rested on the unique professional ideal of the truth-telling of the patient being reciprocated by the analyst's honesty. Freud knew, however, about the elusiveness of "truth."

In 1921 "Pseudologia phantastica" was a thoroughly original topic for an analyst. Helene was attempting to come to terms with a traditional psychiatric topic by means of the framework Freud had initiated. Kraepelin had in fact written on pseudology; he put the category of the "morbid liar and swindler" under the general heading of Psychopathic Personalities. In a paper for analysts, however, Helene could hardly begin by footnoting one of the leading figures in classical psychiatry who was also a critic of Freud's. To Ludwig Binswanger, a Swiss pupil who had tried to mediate between psychoanalysis and psychiatry, Freud had written in 1911: "I really look upon your expectation as heretical."[6]

Those used to studying schizophrenia would be attracted to the phenomena of pathological lies; a schizophrenic develops a pseudo-reality in which the distinction between fact and fantasy becomes at best unclear. In adolescents especially a psychiatrist might wonder whether the appearance of pseudology prefigures schizophrenia.

Precisely because pseudology (like mistrust) was beyond the bounds of both neurosis and psychosis, Helene could make a contribution by writing about it in terms of depth psychology. Instead of treating pseudology as the product of malingerers or the feebleminded, as even the early Jung did, she wanted to understand these fantastic lies in terms of a patient's individual history. Although within psychiatry she had long accepted the distinction between psychosis and neurosis, as an analyst she wanted to talk about an in-between area. Lying could be for pleasure and not for gain, and might not only occur in otherwise truth-telling personalities but be a platform for highlighting honesty. Yet to understand the wish-fulfilling component in pseudology required a sensitive handling of the pleasure-pain processes that Freud's system of ideas had revealed. Helene was operating on the principle that lies can betray concealed truth.

Throughout her career as an analyst Helene remained convinced that the real clinical issues lie between pre-existing categories. In her previously published "Two Cases of Induced Insanity," which she cited here, she had—like some of our own contemporary critics of undue diagnostic name-calling—

hesitated to label disease entities. If not all "castles in the air" are the same as delusions, neither do they snugly fit the classical theory of neurosis. In her later famous papers on "as if" personalities, *folie à deux*, Don Quixote, and imposters, Helene continued her interest in this area of disturbed identifications or so-called multiple personalities.

Freud had thought that women, with weaker superegos, were inherently more unreliable than men, which would be a paradoxical consequence of the traditional social insistence on female purity. But Helene, who soon would specialize in writing about femininity, did not think that pseudology was a specifically female trait. Pseudology means taking realistically something that has psychological truth. In *The Psychology of Women* in 1945 she cited Henrik Ibsen's Peer Gynt as the creator of tall stories. Whereas a lie is usually goal-directed and done for a reason, pseudology, like poetry, can be a gratification in itself. Pseudology occurs in various forms of neurosis, not necessarily hysteria; in obsessionals it can be accompanied by striking exactness about details. But whereas in cases of "as if" personalities someone unconsciously takes another's role, as if he were someone else, pseudology is less constant and can change from hour to hour. Being mystifyingly interesting can be part of the pseudologist's charm. Like the imposter the pseudologist tries to impose a new ego state on the outside world.

The young girl's pseudology that Helene extensively described in "On the Pathological Lie" was in reality harmless yet had its purposefulness. (Here Helene was drawing on her own adolescent experience.) Pseudology is a defense apparently full of conflict, yet as a self-creation it is free of anxiety; at the same time it can protect against present-day reality. Helene was anticipating her later interest in the place of denial in psychopathology; denial may seem a passive function, but pseudology is active in creating new conceptions. While a poet brings pseudology in the form of art, this young girl needed release from "an oppressive burden of memory." An incestuous threat from the past, reawakened in adolescence, can be repudiated by an elaborate fabrication. Or, as in the case of a young man who participated in a shared pseudology, a present-day reality can be responsible for reviving a past conflict.

As Helene noted when she briefly returned to the same subject in 1945, simultaneously the avoidance of a dangerous truth can be a kind of revenge for the deceits (imagined or otherwise) inflicted in childhood. The triumphant feeling of deceiving others can also be accompanied by a self-punishing uncertainty about whether the lying fantasy is true or not. Clinically an imaginary world of fantasied relationships can be more exciting, and preferred, to the pale reality of concrete experience.

Helene's 1921 concept of pseudology touched on the ego psychology of creativity, and for this reason she appropriately referred to Freud's essay "Creative Writers and Day-dreams" (1908). She considered pseudology as "an intermediary phase between psychical health and neurosis," which may be more common in artists than the literature even today has indicated. (Helene's view of pseudology fits Dr. Donald W. Winnicott's later concept of the psychology of "transitional" phenomena.[7])

The Bloomsbury novelist Virginia Woolf, whose etching Helene had on her waiting-room wall in the mid-1960s, suffered from the trauma of an attempted childhood seduction not unlike that in Helene's own history, described in this paper as a "case." But it would be mistaken to look on such traumas in a wholly negative light. Creativity, often linked to so-called schizoid processes, can also be seen in terms of the response to a traumatic past; it may even be the fate of artists to need to keep choosing traumas in order to continue to grow. Freud knew about the tragic edge to life, and Helene had been partly attracted to analysis by its sophisticated outlook on what extraordinary people can be expected to endure.

Creativity will remain a mystery, but because pseudology is an imaginative creation which, unlike the daydream, maintains an unusual contact with reality, this paper of Helene's represented a fragmentary effort to approach the enigmatic spark of artistry. Early analysts had a special respect for their patients as outsiders, so it may not be surprising that Helene's 1921 thoughts about pathological lying should remind us of the link between nonconformity and originality.

Pseudology had long played a role in Helene's own life, as in her fabrication of an adolescent romance; she raised her "tendency to fantasize" in her autobiography,[8] and traced it then, as in her "case" of the young girl in her article, to an actual attempt by her brother to seduce her in early childhood. One also thinks back, however, to one of Lieberman's 1911 letters to her, in which he exhorted her to conceal things from Felix, since lying could be "a human deed." Her exquisite tact was the product of a civilization that cultivated manners to smooth over even the most painful situations.

Clinical papers were an ideal form for Helene's talents as a writer. Any case-history writing for an analyst involves an artistic component, in that identities must be disguised without distorting the clinical material. In writing on pseudology Helene was, in relying partly on her own autobiography, using her inventiveness in behalf of science. She was not only giving creative shape to material in order to understand herself better but fitting her work within the contours of analytic thought.

Freud was absolutely delighted with Helene as a follower, which meant that he would couch whatever skepticism he might have in the most subtle terms. At a meeting of the Vienna society on November 9, 1921, she presented a "short communication"; it was "an observation" drawn from two of her nephews, children of Malvina's, although Helene did not publicly mention this familial connection. The boys were very different physical types, and the elder was the mother's favorite. He was killed in the war, however, and Malvina was grief-stricken; then, according to Helene, the younger boy began

to change physically, grew rapidly and darkened as well, until he came to
resemble his dead brother.

The proceedings of the Vienna society reported her account:

> Two brothers quite unlike one another, of which the elder dies. Later the
> younger brother comes to resemble both physically and mentally the dead
> brother in a quite remarkable manner; he wished to take the elder brother's
> place in his mother's estimation; this was the clear motive of his metamor-
> phosis.[9]

"If it were not Dr. Deutsch who reported this," Helene remembered Freud's
having remarked, "we would not believe it." In the light of her recent paper
on pseudology, and the autobiographical confession that Freud would have
been certain to detect, his double meaning may not have been lost on his
audience. Helene, however, took no offense. For Freud had gone on to say
that it was possible that the younger brother had been shaded from the mother's sunlight by the older boy, but with the removal of the overhanging tree
his mother's love had transformed him. Freud characteristically expressed
himself with such a visual image of a psychological process. It was also
typical of other loyal disciples to miss the trace of ironic reservation in his
appreciation of their work.[10]

The early 1920s were the years in which Helene felt personally closest to
Freud. Felix also joined the Vienna society; he gave his first paper, "Psychoanalysis and Organic Diseases," on January 4, 1922. Although Felix had been
fascinated by Freud's ideas since before World War I, the rule now was that
someone had to present a paper successfully before formally being elected to
membership in the society. Helene did not give a lecture before the next
congress at Berlin in September 1922, but she did report about its proceedings
to the Vienna society.

In Berlin that fall Dr. Eduard Hitschmann, a respected internist who
had joined the Vienna society as early as 1905, announced that the Vienna
society had finally succeeded in establishing a clinic called the Ambulatorium. This institution was the outgrowth of a couple of years' planning.
The Berlin society had opened an outpatient clinic in 1920; one of Freud's
wealthy backers had made possible this facility, which was in accord with
Freud's intent that analytic treatment be made available to larger sections of
the population. In his view, however, the opening of the Berlin "Policlinic"
meant that that city had become the chief center of the future of analysis.

All along Freud had been discontented with the quality of his Viennese
followers; he repeatedly sought to break out of the narrow confines of his
native city, as he sought the widest possible arena for his work. When Freud
had in 1910 made Jung, a Swiss, the leader of the International Association,
he appeased the natural resentments of the Viennese by retiring as president
of the Vienna society in favor of Adler. In 1920 the members of his Viennese

group were unhappy at the prospect that Berlin would become the best place to go for training analyses. Hanns Sachs, a Viennese (and later Theodor Reik as well), went there with Freud's blessings to teach in a new training institute.

Freud had originally been opposed to the idea of trying to get an analytic department as an extension of a general hospital in Vienna. He had the highest regard for Abraham's leadership in Berlin, but in Vienna he could not spare the time himself, and there was no one in his society to whom he felt he could entrust the management. Hitschmann, along with Paul Federn, pressed the plan, which according to Ernest Jones also had Helene's notable support.[11]

Evidently Wagner-Jauregg helped kill official approval of the proposal, although he himself moved to set up a psychotherapeutic outpatient department at his clinic. Freud was uneasy at Hitschmann's leading role in behalf of the society's ambitions, although on balance he thought it was better to have Hitschmann behind such a plan than on the outside as a critic. The Viennese society was determined not to slip behind their Berlin colleagues, and Felix Deutsch in the end found the premises for the facilities that were desired. On May 22, 1922, the clinic was opened with Hitschmann as the director. The public health authorities had stipulated that both the teaching staff and the students were to be doctors, and therefore with the exception of the patients, lay people were not to have access to the Ambulatorium. Freud, though, was not content with this arrangement, since he was convinced that analysis would benefit from an influx of nonmedical talent. For the time being, at least, Vienna was getting some institutional basis, besides Freud's personal presence, for the teaching of analysis. Each medical member of the society pledged to be responsible for at least one free treatment of a case from the Ambulatorium.

The Vienna society now met in the rooms of the clinic, and in the fall of 1922 Hitschmann gave an introductory series of lectures on analysis. Felix also gave a course entitled: "What Ought the Practical Physician to Know About Psychoanalysis." Yet Freud could hardly be satisfied by the way events had developed in Vienna. If the society was going to have its training institute, Hitschmann was not the one to lead it; he was without psychiatric training, which would be a drawback especially for foreign students, and he lacked the capacity to inspire confidence among the younger candidates in analysis. Freud liked Felix personally, but he was formally a newcomer within analysis.

In this context Helene emerged as the obvious future leader of the Vienna Training Institute, which was opened under her in 1924 and which she headed until she left for America in 1935. (By 1925 the British had their own training institute, and eventually each branch society developed along the Berlin and Vienna models.) The institute would be the teaching arm of the Vienna society, as opposed to the Ambulatorium with its therapeutic purposes; both institutions would be linked, since patients for the training of future analysts would be drawn from the Ambulatorium. Before undertaking this new role, Helene decided to go to Berlin to find out what its teaching arrangements were like.

Helene's letters from the summer of 1922 indicated her intention to leave Vienna for a period of study in Berlin. She then made arrangements to undergo an analysis with Karl Abraham, beginning in January 1923; at that time Abraham was, aside from Freud himself, the foremost training analyst. Abraham died prematurely late in 1925, but even so he succeeded in having had the most eminent future analysts in training with him: Sandor Rado, Alix Strachey, Edward and James Glover, Theodor Reik, Karen Horney, Melanie Klein, and Ernst Simmel.

Helene had work plans for herself, although in the midst of a glorious vacation she gave up the idea of preparing a lecture for the Berlin congress in September. Back in Vienna Felix was planning to present something of his own, but not without showing it to Helene first; in the end he spoke on the formation of "conversion" symptoms, an early term coined by Freud to cover somatic problems that arise from repressed affects. Felix was already seeking to remove some of the mysterious character from the processes of "conversion" between mind and body.

Helene, who was better at languages than Felix and already possessing some knowledge of English, thought it a good idea to try to learn English systematically, especially for purposes of future training analyses. In the hope of expanding his medical practice Felix was now taking English lessons in Vienna. The significance of the influx of American patients, with their wealth and solid currency, was heightened by the Austrian inflation. Helene was worried about what her role in the Ambulatorium would eventually be, as well as troubled by the uncertainties surrounding her stay in Berlin.

That summer she was living in the midst of a colony of analysts. As she wrote about an English colleague:

> Dr. Cole, my table companion, is a nice, clever person, with much understanding for analysis. She opened her eyes wide in amazement when she heard from my mouth the word "household economy." She had never had to do it for a single moment; she has a housekeeper who does all the housework, takes care of the Ordination,* keeps the clothes in order, shops etc.— as well as a housemaid for the "coarse" work. She resides in six rooms, and lives on psychoanalysis alone. She tallies up accounts for her housekeeper twice a month. Frau Dr. Abraham carries on her household in the same fashion. And poor me . . . How I would love to be free to divide my life between my love for you and my profession. But all the petty, means things of life . . . boo . . .

* "Ordination" meant office hours.

Helene felt isolated and yet refreshed. In the midst of so many of her associates she remained relatively aloof.

> You don't know how good it is for me, this aloneness—how wonderful it is to have a chance to get clear about things within myself. You are right: stay away from people; have connections within yourself, purely objectively, through outward interests, mentally or animally, but without bearing one's wounds, to air one's incognito and to wield one's soul. I believe it is going well with me. How good it is to be able to draw the balance, to shake off the dust of the past and to move toward new hopes.

Helene characteristically made a display of her disabilities, in order to help master them. In a letter (August 12, 1922) Felix encouraged her independence; at the same time he surmised, if only from her determination to have another analysis, that all was not right within her.

> Letters are expressions of moods, but when you write to me how good you feel being alone, and you undertake "not to expose your wounds to others anymore," then I wish that more would come of this intention than a mere mood. How often it has pained me when you betray your weaknesses to those whose business it is not . . . and after that you only suffer from the disappointment. My dear, when you find your way back to yourself, then my faith in you will be as unshakable as before. And as far as I am concerned, you are not again to suffer ruin from outward circumstances.

If Felix was worried about Helene, she was also concerned about him, in particular in connection with his career in analysis. Even in the face of her own gratification in the life of an analyst, she may have, as she sometimes later claimed, tried to dissuade him from becoming an analyst. If, however, Felix was going to be an analyst, Helene wanted to be sure that he succeeded in making a first-class contribution.

During August 1922, in a letter to Felix from Seefeld, a village high in the Tyrol, Helene reported a talk she had had with Ferenczi, who was well known to Felix. She and Hitschmann had been out walking with the Ferenczis, but she and Sandor

> got engrossed in a conversation, lost the company and remained for three hours in a very lively, almost purely scientific conversation. His phantasy goes in the same direction, his psychological method is introspective like mine, and so we understood each other splendidly. We also spoke about you, and F. quite spontaneously expressed his opinion, which corresponds to mine: in order to become a psychoanalyst, you would have to undergo an analysis, otherwise it would always remain a *half-thing* a *superficiality,* and that would be a great pity, for "such an internist" would be able to make a *great* contribution, given sufficient deepening of his psychoanalytic knowledge.

As a physician Felix was less attracted by the artistic side of analysis, and more interested in the so-called neutral, scientific aspect of Freud's work;

therefore he needed more urging about the necessity of a personal analysis. Helene went on in a way to accomplish her objective.

> Puschkuleindi, only my affective reactions are complex-determined, not, however, my concrete knowledge that your psychoanalytic ability is very slight, and that it will take you a longer time to be able to call yourself an analyst. What so offends and hurts me is that you are not even so far along as to realize that you still know little. I have the impression that F. is of the same opinion and that in the interest of psychoanalysis he is very anxious to see you undergo a didactic analysis. However, he had recognized the neurosis-lessness in your dear, distant, happy make-up, and realizes the difficulty of psychoanalysis resulting from this psychological healthiness. But he considers it necessary to overcome it, even at great sacrifice. He considers *Rank* most suitable, "even if the friendship should have to be sacrificed." What about Reik? For it is a matter of learning!

Either in reply to Helene's conversation with Ferenczi, or perhaps a precipitating factor in her worry, on August 17 Felix reported that he had sent an (unpromising) analytic patient to Hitschmann, after Freud, who was away on vacation, had chosen Felix to make the referral to an analyst. Freud had written to the patient that he was to have "complete confidence" in Felix since he stood "very close to analysis." More generally, Felix's letters to Helene reflected a broad absorption in analysis. (Felix's letters also were concerned with his medical practice, gossip about friends, and the complicated domestic negotiations he and Helene had to engage in.) By the summer of 1922 Freud considered Felix his personal physician, and when one of Freud's nieces committed suicide by poisoning herself (Federn had been treating her), Felix was automatically called in to help. Freud's oldest daughter, Mathilda, had asked a member of the family, already analyzed by Helene, to get in touch with Felix; three letters of his to Helene mention his involvement with the Freud family circle touched off by the suicide.

Helene had every reason to be concerned that Felix get proper professional analytic training. According to Freud's way of thinking, absence of neurotic suffering constitutes a stumbling block to a therapeutic analysis. But Helene was writing Felix at a time when it was more or less accepted that all future analysts undergo a training (or "didactic") analysis; in August 1922 she herself was conducting only therapeutic analyses, as she was now preparing to embark on a second analysis in Berlin.

Otto Rank, Ferenczi's suggestion for Felix's analyst, was a great personal friend of Felix's as well as Ferenczi's. Although Rank was almost a son to Freud, Felix was unlikely to be prepared to give up his friendship with Rank for the sake of a professional gain of an analysis. (As Freud conceived an analysis, it entailed an inherent inequality between therapist and patient, at odds with the give-and-take of friends.) Helene seemed to assume as much in writing Felix, and in recommending Reik as an alternative she knew that both

Felix and she considered Reik (who, like Rank, was not an M.D.) a poor therapist. But if Felix were to undertake an analysis for the sake of "learning," then a training analyst's therapeutic skills would be secondary. Reik was intellectual and scholarly, and in 1922 Freud held him in high esteem.

Alongside Helene's public reasons for planning to go to Berlin can be detected her private discontents. In her paper on mistrust she had cited the "case" of "a woman patient aged over thirty, engaged in an academic career" who "had not previously shown any neurotic symptoms"; Helene described this woman as torn by a conflict between her career ("strong masculine aspirations") and her home ("the feminine role"). The "patient's" identification with her mistrustful mother was one of the determinants of the symptom, but this regression had only arisen when the woman's "love for her husband began to wane . . ."

Helene's conflict was exacerbated by the reality of Felix's extraordinarily good relationship to Martin. He was a concerned and unusually tender father. Her letters about Martin exude her radiant joy in his uniqueness and talent; still Helene now doubted her own capacities as a mother, in spite of having broken with Lieberman to have a child. Just because of Felix's maternal affection for their son she may have been jealous. Martin fully responded to Felix's unusual capacity for communicating with small children, and reciprocated his father's immense love. On her side Helene would not only conscientiously report Martin's activities to Felix, but compose letters as if dictated by Martin, in order to give the spirit of the child's perspective.

Felix did not make the mistake of allowing his attachment to the boy overshadow his expressions of love for Helene. As he wrote her in Seefeld, shortly after visiting there:

> Now I have your dear letter in my hands and I look at it repeatedly. Is it a new springtime that awakens in me—such a warmth streams from your letter. Could it be that we should find each other after so many years? How different was my parting with you this time, so full of deep, unclouded heart-feeling, so totally without a trace of memories of bitterness, so full of hope *for you,* wife, my wife; are you full of longing, like me?
>
> How beautiful was our time together, and how much more so it could have been! A sound of jubilation is within me, as if from now on, for the first time, I should know all you are to me; may this sound never fade away.

Felix declined a dinner invitation because: "I don't want to disturb this harmony within me. It is rediscovery of the way back into long forgotten, purest, best feeling." No matter how warmly Helene might write him, nothing quite matches the poignant sound of his feelings for her. As he had once encouraged her to go to Munich in 1914, so he could tolerate the separation entailed by her planned analysis with Abraham: "Berlin too is part of that. But then you will find your way home to yourself and me."

It is never easy to separate in the lives of the early analysts their public and private selves; one of their attractive features is the way they wrote and worked out of their full beings. In arranging to go to Berlin, Helene knew that she had more in mind than simply being a distinguished visitor who came with Freud's confidence in her future. She consulted with Freud about whom he might recommend as her second analyst. He had first suggested Ferenczi in Budapest, but she ruled that out because of the difficulties her son might have with the Hungarian language; Freud then suggested Sachs, who was starting out as a practitioner in Berlin, but Helene thought she knew enough to be able to conclude on her own that Abraham would be best for her.

The Ranks were at Seefeld that August, and Sachs as well as Abraham and his family visited the village. Helene had a chance for a long talk with Abraham, and accompanied him (with his wife and children) to the railroad station. The formality of his North German manners might have put her off. Abraham was, she reported to Felix, a figure within the international movement: "colossally occupied with matters foreign. We agreed on January. Cold, objective, yet gradually thawing. Very precise in thought—a good school. How different from our dear Viennese."

In the same paragraph describing her first personal reactions to Abraham as her analyst-to-be, Helene injected her concern with how she could hope to work with Hitschmann in the Ambulatorium; it was not yet clear that it would be possible to divide a training institute from the pool of prospective training-analysands. Hitschmann was, in her view, notoriously stingy about money. She wrote Felix, who had to look forward with divided feelings to teaching in the Ambulatorium along with Hitschmann in the following fall, that "Hitschmann's reaction to my reservations about expenditures which await us in the Ambulatorium was prompt: 'Well, we'll just lock it up.' —That speaks volumes." Helene had a keen head about money matters, but analysis had to come ahead of account balances.

Evidently Felix had raised some points of his own about how he would fit into the Vienna society, perhaps in response to her suggestion that he undergo a personal analysis. She wrote back:

> We are in total agreement. You know how concerned I am that you should not depart from internal medicine and not fall prey to Hitschmann's fate (I mean this in the scientific sense). However, the example of Friedjung is not well chosen—for Friedjung produces practically nothing for analysis (scientifically). However, he does so in a practical sense, as a propagator. I believe you will find your own way yourself.

Helene did not want Felix to change his career, and become as inconsequential as both she and he considered Hitschmann, nor follow the model of the pediatrician Josef Friedjung. She sounded confident, at least in writing Felix, that he would successfully combine his medical knowledge with analysis in his own individual and productive way.

Helene's need for personal help had made her decide to go for another analysis. In reproaching herself that she would never be able to make Felix the "motherly wife" he needed, and yet at nearly the same time in another letter referring to Felix and Martin as her two "boys," she gives the impression that at bottom she thought that in her relationship with Felix their normal roles were out of joint.

11

Depression and Infidelity
in Berlin

Helene's decision to go to Berlin meant a separation from Felix that lasted for over a year. At the outset, not yet realizing how long she would be away from Vienna, Helene took Martin with her; but later on, for the second half of her stay, she left him with Felix. At the beginning of her time in Berlin there was no overt sign of any crisis in their marriage. Her first letter to Felix (January 5, 1923) gave news of her journey and details about the apartment she had rented. Inflation in Germany was so rampant that her food and lodgings came to five million marks monthly; even so these expenses were fixed only until April 1. What attracted her most about the boardinghouse where she planned to live, however, was that it gave

> an atmosphere of home for Martin—a lively dog, a nice chambermaid, a friendly lady and her grownup children. She too is looking for a kinder-fraülein. If a permanent one can't be found, then I will take on one for days . . . On the evenings when I am out, he will be cared for by the landlady and the others in the house. He is also looked after in other ways. It was this "domesticity" that moved me to make this choice . . .

Helene was naturally worried about her costs, but she was already assured of several analytic cases; an Italian who had been in analysis with her in Vienna* also came along, as did a Dutch analytic case. Her responsibility was to find suitable living quarters for such patients, but they could use their native (hard) currency. Throughout Helene's stay in Berlin, patients could

---

* This patient, a sister of a leader of the Italian psychoanalytic movement, had previously been analyzed by Freud. Helene thought that it was always difficult to make a diagnosis of neurosis as opposed to schizophrenia, and in later years the patient ended up in a mental asylum in Australia. Her brother once wrote about her case.[1]

pay in relatively stable foreign funds to Felix in Vienna, and he in turn would exchange the money there, sending along as much in German marks as she or they needed. Before leaving Vienna Helene had also scheduled some Viennese patients for analyses with her in Berlin; once again she could rely on Felix to help smooth the arrangements at the other end. Viennese intermediaries could, on trips to Berlin, get money for her or her patients. Entirely aside from cases she might expect to pick up from referrals in Berlin, Helene arrived in a self-sufficient condition. As it turned out, she got few new private patients but had to accept low-paying ones from the policlinic.

Helene might be a foreigner with a small child living in a city beset by wild inflation; yet the local analytic community did their best to make her comfortable, and to find her help. A Viennese, Walter Schmideberg, had met her at the railway station, and was "self-sacrificingly gallant." (He was later married to the daughter of the pioneer child analyst Melanie Klein[2]; both young people were to become analysts themselves.) Members of the Berlin society looked after Helene. A Dutch analyst in Berlin, Johann van Ophuijsen, had a son Martin's age, so Helene was sure of at least one playmate for him.

As soon as she arrived in Berlin Helene started her analysis with Abraham. In her earliest letters to Felix she made it apparent that she was not undertaking a mere academic exercise. "The analysis affects me severely. I always come away severely shaken and tired. Abraham is a very cleverly understanding, cool person—I believe I am in the right place." She could not participate in the first meeting of the Berlin society since it was too soon for her to have made arrangements for Martin to be taken care of. "It is said that these evenings are filled with pulsating interest and are very inspiring. I have found out that I am held in high regard here, and that people are looking forward to my working with them. In such situations there always comes a disappointment." The Berlin analysts were also, she claimed, interested in the direction in which Felix's own work was going.

If it proved more difficult to leave Martin in the evenings than she had anticipated, part of the problem was her own guilt feelings about having taken him away from Felix. All her letters to Felix touch on how Martin was doing. One of her earliest communications from Berlin expresses the tone of how she tried to keep Felix up-to-date.

> He is our well-behaved, sweet, endlessly clever little fellow, a little friend at my side. Of course, it is not without its traumatic side. He doesn't sleep well; his appetite isn't the best, he can't quite find himself. My good little fellow. This afternoon I tucked him into bed, for he had been sneezing and had a slightly reddened throat. In the evening, however, he was so active and jolly that I am not concerned. Now I hear him murmuring long monologues into the pillow. He's deeply offended at my writing the letter without him—unfortunately, I didn't have a chance to do this all day. Today we'll write together again.

Helene appreciated the intimate bond between Felix and Martin, and did her best not to disrupt it.

> Yesterday we were imagining what it would be like if the door should suddenly open and you appeared. Martin's phantasy: There is a ring at the door: "Good Day. Does a Lady with a Big (!!) boy live here? (What are their names?) Frau Dr. Deutsch and Martin. (Yes, they live here.)" Now the two of us (he and I) pop out. Outside, there stands our beloved Papa, and we both try to throw ourselves upon him. Both try to be first, and a tussle develops between the two of us. This situation is enacted; we start elbowing each other, until Martin, quite tired, with sad and disappointed face, declares "Yes, but he really isn't here; why are we tussling." He was also a little saddened by the fact that today is Sunday.

In Vienna Felix had devoted his Sundays to Martin.

Helene could cite the example of another female analyst in Berlin who had two small children and also was forced to live in a different city from her physician-husband, but for an indefinite period of time. The Deutsches were confident that in their case this interruption in family life would only last, according to her, for "a few months." Therefore Helene did not try to enroll Martin in any kind of school.

The arrangements for taking care of Martin proved to be more troublesome than Helene had thought. Even though her movements and professional life were therefore restricted, Helene's "main goal," the analysis with Abraham, was

> for the time being not in jeopardy. Abraham is very clever and quickly grasped the situation. We are in the midst of very intensive work. I am experiencing the remarkable state of isolation *en deux* with the analyst, and, my darling, don't be surprised if my letters should be short, with little content and impersonal. All my psychic energy must go into that, please understand this and wait until "our time" comes again.

She of course inquired how Felix was doing ("My poor old boy. My big, good, dear son"), and reassured him that they would "get everything together; everything will be fine." But her compositions of letters in behalf of Martin, expressing their child's reactions to Berlin, meant she had also found a way of being aloof about her own doings. She maintained that she was thoroughly satisfied with her work as an analysand: "The psychoanalysis with Abraham is grandiose! Totally objective, without any reeling experience of transference. One then sees what a good-for-nothing one is."

The contrast she drew between herself as an analyst and Abraham's capacities was only part of her dissatisfaction with herself. In Berlin she wanted to test whether Freud's recommendation that she stay on the road of identification with her father had been a sound piece of advice. She had somehow found herself depressed over her relation to Freud, even though she was not characteristically depressive. In spite of her career as an analyst, she still yearned for the satisfaction that Lieberman had brought to her life. Helene had the emotional and intellectual ability to perceive what she was missing with Felix. Although she had been convinced, with Freud's help, that she had reached a tolerable compromise, she had her gnawing doubts. Away from Vienna Helene could have the space she needed to be able to help figure out the situation for herself. After eleven years of marriage she never questioned that Felix wanted their marital relationship to continue; but she was concerned about whether it was enough for herself.

Going to Berlin meant not only a hardship for Felix but a cruelty to Martin. Over fifty years later he still resented the separation from his father. He was alone a lot for a child of his age, and the German governesses were stricter with him than he was used to. Even in the face of her guilt feelings, Helene had to test whether she wanted to continue the marriage. She went to Berlin, as she had originally to Freud in 1918, to find out whether she could fully live up to what she wanted for herself in life.

Freud may have been a holy figure to Helene, but she had her reservations about him as a therapist; he sought to teach more than cure. Abraham was Freud's trusted lieutenant, the leader of the Berlin society, someone in whom Helene (like others) had great confidence. Although she would not have gone to Berlin for treatment without the need for learning organizational matters as well, it proved a greater sacrifice for her than she had expected. Berlin had good music and was the center for the cultural life of the Weimar Republic, but she said she found it a cold, noisy city, lacking in charm, just as Lieberman had thought in 1908.

Early in her analysis Abraham showed her a letter from Freud in which he instructed his disciple that this was a marriage that ought not to be disrupted by analysis. Helene later declared that she had been less inhibited with Abraham than with Freud, and told her second analyst thoughts which had not come up in the presence of the founder of analysis. Nonetheless Freud's letter to Abraham had been, she later felt, a condition making an analysis impossible, and at best set a limit to what she could hope to accomplish in Berlin. Her original transference to Freud was such that she could never seem to develop enough of an emotional attachment to Abraham to succeed in changing herself as she might have wished. In having dismissed her so abruptly from treatment, Freud had not helped enough to free her from dependencies on him. In not taking her again into treatment Freud was implicitly trying to help her get free from her transference to him. Her own experiences with Freud had been such that afterward she concluded that it had proved impossible for her to be analyzed following Freud.

Subsequently Abraham told Helene that he had written Freud and Felix that he had not really been able to analyze her, since he had too much positive feeling for her. Some later analysts might think that the treatment had not worked because she had known him beforehand; and Freud, in termi-

nating his treatment of her, had told Helene she was not neurotic. She came
to believe her analysis with Abraham had been a failure; she knew he was a
bit too solid and straightforward for Freud's own taste, since Freud cherished
followers with more dash and fantasy. But to Helene Abraham seemed an
unusually harmonious person, uniting, as she expressed it, "a cool face with
the warmest heart," and she became close friends with him.

Soon Helene was finding reasons to explain the decreasing frequency of
her letters to Felix; she said she had an inner inhibition in writing, which she
had always been able to overcome as far as he was concerned. Outward
circumstances, particularly looking after Martin, made it hard for her to
write as often as she might have liked. The daily inflation was itself difficult to
keep up with. The price of her board and room was already being doubled, a
room was taken away in favor of someone with American dollars, and heating was inadequate. She had to search for another place, one that would also
reduce her travel time to and from her analysis. A different set of lodgings
had bedbugs. Finally she found a small pension right beside where Abraham
lived. (Its price would rise daily that spring; her cost of living could double in
a single day.)

Unlike Felix in Vienna, she had not been to the theater, and Helene said
she was living on the whole "outside Berlin." (Nevertheless she went to a
hairdresser early every morning.) Her analysis was, she reported, progressing
well.

> My mood is in equilibrium, calm—somewhat excited and tense immediately
> after the analytic session. Abraham thinks it would be good for you to have
> yourself analyzed (i.e. he backed up my opinion). Just think how disgust-
> ingly—unbearably—neurotically I smeared you there! My poor, little, moth-
> erless boy.

Her spirits were sufficiently high that she asked Felix to look in one of her
desk drawers for her course lectures; even if it was not imminent, she was
thinking in terms of using them after the expiration of the current Berlin
courses.

Gradually Helene was able to participate more in at least the social life
of Berlin analysts. Formal meetings of the society were part of the picture; so
was, for example, a large Saturday evening party at the Abrahams', and an
equally big Sunday reception at Melanie Klein's. Somehow, though, she
could not succeed in getting into her work, which was understood to be
something different from conducting analyses. Reading was difficult for her;
her letter writing, even in behalf of Martin, grew less detailed and more
infrequent. She admitted the onset of low feelings even in the face of good
weather.

> For the past few days I have been in a deep wave of depression. The spring
> makes me tired, sad, depressed, hopeless. This means nothing: it will have

changed in a few days. Don't be angry if silence is what reaches you from me in such a mood . . . Good, dearest—how good you are to send me the balsam of your kindliness in your letters.

In her depression it seemed to her, despite all her activities as an analyst, that hers was going to be a failed life. A gallstone attack reinforced her awareness that she was now more than thirty-eight years old.

It soon became apparent that Helene's stay in Berlin was going to be more prolonged than either she or Felix had anticipated. Felix kept planning a trip to Berlin, as Abraham became an intermediary between Helene and Felix.

A. is going to speak to you, and may have to reveal to you much about my complicated difficulties. If only one had such a clean, undivided existence as a certain dear boy has. If one could stand at his side and breathe the dust-free atmosphere that surrounds him.

Helene recalled the initial contrast between her involvement with Lieberman and her love for Felix: "Do you remember what I often said 'back then,' when we were still young and free: 'The air is pure'—how pure could it always remain for you, and how heavy did the atmosphere become which I breathed out."

Helene was letting Felix know that unexpected difficulties had arisen.

Puschkuleinderl, things are deep-rooted, and compulsion for repetition reigns with its dark power. And to say more would be a betrayal of Papa-Abraham. My master has not yet made any prognosis, but recently he let slip out: "If it should be successful . . ." Will it be successful? Yes!!

Helene was completely satisfied with Abraham as an analyst, but she made no pretense about its therapeutic purposes.

The analysis is progressing. One can't imagine such simplicity: technically uncomplicated, taken for granted—such classical perfection. Just like his scientific works. I am too much absorbed by the personal difficulties to think about the didactic advantages. But I do hope to make use of a great deal, "later."

Splendidly clear weather did nothing to alleviate her spirits, at least as she reported them to Felix. Her hopes and plans for the future alternated with "anxious fear, tormenting worry; renunciation and thoughts of death." She felt better, at least when she sat down to write Felix, but she thought that her "condition had not yet run its course." She invoked Abraham's authority in order to try to delay a trip to Berlin Felix had planned around Easter, although Abraham evidently thought that a visit from Felix was in principle a good idea. She complained of being sleepless and at times unable to stay home, even in the evenings; she also continued to admire the way the analysis with Abraham was going, and the enlightenment she derived. "You can't imagine this classic technique and grandiose superiority. One would like to relearn, and has the overpowering feeling that one only now has understood psychoanalysis. Oh, if only you could do the same as I!"

At other times Helene excused her silences and short letters by the ordeal of her treatment.

> I didn't know that psychoanalysis was such a difficult task. I never saw in my patients such a hard struggle, such a breakdown of all constellations, such a state of absolute dissolution . . . I live in neurotic isolation. I take a completely passive part in the active work going on here. I socialize quite a bit with the Abrahams, but go out seldom. I am chronically sleepy. I read aloud to Sonny and . . . I mope. The psychoanalysis is proceeding, so that there is no hour that goes by without productive work.

She suspected that Felix was angry with her, although none of his letters indicate the slightest reproach, except that she had not written enough. As she tried to explain, "You know that whenever I do anything to hurt you, it is always by way of my own pain." The analysis had become a central absorption of hers: "Now a small crisis has arisen in my psychoanalytic existence—there is a rock surrounded by waves of resistance that I must somehow surmount. All the psychic power that I possess must be mobilized—forces are doing battle and a chaos is going through my soul."

She felt free to characterize her troubled state of mind, but exactly what was bothering her most acutely she omitted to tell Felix.

> Someday when we have found our way back to quiet, intimate togetherness, and the devil has no more access to our hallowed halls, I will tell you everything.
>
> Now everything that goes on outside the unspeakable is such a dull likeness of existence that it appears impossible to deal with it in a letter to you . . . I always sit at home, and I spend more time in sullen introspection than in working or thinking.

She kept to the analytic rule of making her treatment private, but she continued to socialize with Abraham's family. "Monday I spent the whole afternoon with Martin at Abraham's—then I stayed for supper, to attend the evening session with Abraham. The sunny, free atmosphere of this house does me good."

Helene's work "inhibition" intensified in the course of the analysis. Before her depression had set in, she had been optimistic about the therapeutic course of the analysis; she thought it might take "a long time, considering the compulsive-neurotic character of my disturbances." She grew increasingly pessimistic. Springlike weather might temporarily revive her spirits, and a performance of Ibsen's *Peer Gynt* reminded her how little psychiatrists knew compared to artists; but no comparable period exists in which we have records of her sounding so conflicted and divided against herself.

I have had a few bad, melancholy days. I was in a stupor-like condition for days on end, standing beside the stove, in fantasies that could not be grasped, confused and tormented. Today I believe I have come out of it, after a very productive psychoanalytic hour.

My letters must remain empty and devoid of content as long as, persisting in my inverted condition, I have no relation to the outside world. My condition is a repetition-situation mobilized by the psychoanalysis, out of an early infantile period, the time limits of which have not yet been established, with change of decoration and with displacement objects.

You can imagine that in such a condition I am far removed from any ambition-plans, from desire to work and the like. The only positive thing still to have its place in a person is the wish to get out of the twilight. For the present state can only be compared to a condition bordering upon real twilight.

Nevertheless, I am absolutely optimistic, and take it for proof of the "attack," i.e., of the effectiveness of the treatment.

Your golden-sunny letters are for me always the dearest of sunbeams.

No matter how professionally designed her trip to Berlin had been, by the early spring of 1923 the analysis had temporarily swallowed up the other considerations behind her coming.

The main goal . . . , which had been forgotten over all our plans and hopes, is gradually becoming the all-absorbing nuclear point. My analysis devours all my psychic energy; it is becoming a great, deeply penetrating experience, and I make everything round about me into a secondary phenomenon.

Martin was, she thought, exempt from her new preoccupations with herself. Evidently her analysis with Freud had not prepared her for what she experienced in treatment with Abraham.

Her personal contact with Abraham, outside of her analytic hours, exceeded anything she had been used to with Freud. About a supper at his house she could write: "Abraham does not allow himself to be disturbed by resistances that possibly may arise from such situations." (A "resistance" was in principle any self-imposed obstacle to successful introspection.) Away from Vienna and Freud's dominant role, she felt a more honest, more "fraternal" atmosphere, freer from the "envy-infested" air she had grown used to. Her admiration for Abraham went beyond his conduct of her analysis, extending to his course of lectures as well: "brilliant, glorious, unpretentious." In such a context problems connected with the Ambulatorium in Vienna left her cold, but she still reminded Felix: "let us not forget that it was our work and that we must not leave it in the lurch."

Although she almost never had referred in writing to marital difficulties with Felix, by March 1923 she was determined to clarify things with him. She wished

at last to remove from you all the suffering that comes from me; to let you
sigh with relief, in utter happiness; to belong to you uninhibitedly as friend
and *wife*, and to put a triumphant end to the limping misery of our relationship. How close we are, as human being to human being—and how much
laborious work on the self is still necessary, in order to find oneself as a being
governed by drives.

Tactfully Helene was arguing that both of them shared in causing their difficulties, and that he as well as she needed analysis.

You see, my dearest friend, my knowledge has been enriched by this insight:
like a positive and a negative, our libidinous deficiencies toward each other
complement each other and cause our relations to become lamed by friction
one against the other. And this insight causes me to insist upon your psychoanalysis, since you will not come to health through my health, but rather
through your own work.

"Libidinous deficiencies" meant whatever was wrong with their sex life.

If Helene thought she had to overcome Felix's reluctance to undertake
an analysis of his own, she dissuaded him from choosing one of her own
analysts. As far as she was concerned Abraham was out of the question for
Felix. That "the master builder should construct the tunnel into the mountain
from two sides, until the dark ways should eventually find each other," was a
dismaying prospect even for someone with as much confidence in analysis as
Helene had. She wondered if he had decided on Jekels.

Felix was about to embark on his own analysis in Vienna, conducted—
on Freud's advice—by Siegfried Bernfeld. By the time of their eleventh anniversary (April 14, 1923) both were not only full-fledged members of Freud's
movement but were willing to submit themselves to therapeutic treatment. If
Helene's anniversary letter is to be believed, her affection remained undimin-
ished.

It takes so long for two lords to shake off original sin and find themselves in
freedom? Or longer? I kiss your dear eyes hotly, your sweet mouth—I press
you to my heart, and wish to both of us the fulfillment of all those hopes
which in happy youth seemed so easily attainable.

Felix had not yet, by then, decided on who would conduct his analysis, a
matter which Helene termed "the choice of the 'Father.'" (In deciding on
Bernfeld, a junior member of the Vienna society, Felix would in fact turn to
what he and Helene considered a "brother" figure.) For herself, in thinking
over their marriage, Helene exulted in Martin. She joyfully toyed with changing her destiny as her father's successor, a new "solution" for her: "must I be
'the old Rosenbach'—if a better edition grows for me here."

By the time of his long-planned trip to Berlin, Felix had completed his
arrangements to be anaylzed by Bernfeld. Helene was filled with mixed emotions after his departure.

> You have been here and I know nothing of it. Everything I had to say to you
> disappeared. All the kindness and tenderness I wanted to show you dissi-
> pated, and when the train was gone I wanted to run after it and make up for
> what I had missed. Thus one lives within oneself, beside oneself, past oneself.

She was still in a state of painful solitude. Her sadness was echoed in what she
detected in Freud's newest book, *The Ego and the Id,* which appeared in the
third week of April, 1923. "Do you know what pessimism it contains with
regard to our therapeutic efforts? If the sublimation value pales so much!"
(Felix thought she was wrong: "I maintain that the 'it' [the 'id'] is also capable of being educated . . .") Helene was also concerned about the state of
Freud's personal health, since Felix had reported to her on his trip to Berlin
about a growth in Freud's mouth which "Professor" had asked Felix to in-
spect.

Whether it was her natural recuperative forces, Felix's determination to
seek analytic help, the coming of springtime, or a combination of these factors, by May Helene was gradually able to turn successfully to the professional life she had anticipated when she came to Berlin in the first place. Her
capacity to read (her difficulties had never interfered with her studying
Freud's works) and to write started to return. Abraham had arranged for her
to give some lectures, and no matter how paralyzed she might have sounded a
little earlier, her analyst knew that she had the resilience to carry her through
becoming a teacher at the Berlin institute.

From now on the tone of her letters to Felix is different, as she flourished
with her enthusiastic reception:

> Now I have a favorable tide, which I must keep riding for the next few days,
> if I am not to abandon my scientific enthusiasm by Wednesday. I have
> already held my course lecture (in a completely altered version). It was an
> *extraordinary* success—the room was filled. Am I or am I not? I, this inter-
> est-less idiot—is it possible that I have spoken such "beautiful and pro-
> found" things?

Her success renewed her self-confidence; for the time being she was astonished at the return of her capacities that had been dormant in her since
coming to Berlin. Abraham responded by scheduling her for new presentations. At the time when Felix was experiencing the first disorientations and
self-doubts that accompanied his own analysis, Helene was enjoying a revival
of her career.

Helene now sounds more like her usual happy self, voraciously thinking
in terms of analytic concepts; in reading Oswald Spengler's *The Decline of the
West* she found parallels in historical events to Freud's concept of the compulsion for repetition. Her guilt feelings were allowing her more peace: "I have
already scolded the bad woman—now I wish her well." Her lectures were
attracting more of an audience; she spoke, for example, on the psychology of

the female revolutionary, thinking in terms of a possible publication. Her moods oscillated as she still felt isolated in Berlin. But her good relationship with Abraham meant, according to the analytic principle that therapeutic improvement is a result of first creating a transference neurosis and then subsequently dissolving it, that her therapeutic progress was not promising. "Too strong sympathy for Abraham, quite without fantasy formation, no resistance, thus frequently slow progress." Now that Felix was himself in treatment a further reason justified their continued separation. "Do you now understand the impossibility of staying together during analysis on both sides? Where everything is to be borne out and any betrayal comes out of resistance?"

After a summer holiday together with Felix and Martin, Helene had been planning—on Abraham's advice—to return alone to Berlin, leaving Martin with Felix in Vienna. A separation for a few months from Martin, who was ready to enroll in the first grade (which Felix arranged), would be an incentive for her to finish as promptly as possible in Berlin. During the late spring of 1923 she gave her first "reception," a dinner party for sixteen people at her pension; by then she owed a lot of social invitations and was preparing to live in the coming fall on "more of a student footing." As her normal exuberance reasserted itself, she spoke up for the first time at a general meeting of the Berlin society.

The analysis with Abraham inevitably involved a reliving of her childhood in Poland. As she anticipated a summer vacation by the sea, she mused about the possibility of dissolving some of her ties to the past. Martin could build sandcastles, "and his four brothers in Poland, these crude churls whom I tell him about (do you remember?) will be thrown into the water and will disappear forever. Only Abraham can understand this!"

In *The Psychology of Women*³ she explained her meaning in terms of her own sibling rivalry; Helene's account of a mother's storytelling only changed the location to Russia.

> She had an only son whom she loved very much. She was intelligent and intuitive and believed that she was not making any educational mistakes. She devoted much of her free time to her child and would tell him true and imagined tales about her life in Russia, where she was born. The untrue stories were always recognized as such by common agreement. One of these, usually told to the child when he was being fed, ran as follows: "I have three grown-up sons over there [in Russia]. They are three giants. They eat a whole ox and a pot of spinach as big as this room for every meal. They are enormously strong and perform all kinds of exploits."
>
> The accomplishments of these characters were described in detail, and the mother and son were greatly amused by them. The attitude of these three powerful but stupid fellows toward the little boy was naturally not very good, for they knew perfectly well that the mother loved him alone. Then the mother would tell him why she loved him so much, in such a special

way, in contrast to her feelings for the others: he was intelligent and refined and tender, and things of the spirit were as close and precious to him as they were to her.

In her published interpretation, Helene wrote that analysis of the mother revealed that in her sharing a triumph over these competitive siblings, she was re-experiencing a victory over the giants of her own childhood; she wanted Martin to be as happy with her as she felt the chosen one of her own father. According to Helene, she had

> overlooked one psychologic fact. If her grown-up sisters and brother had been a solved problem for her, she would not have needed to experience her triumph again and again. Actually they were still there, those giant fellows; they involved a danger for her and had to be conquered again and again. She recalled that despite her father's love for her she had felt very insignificant in her littleness and had been very jealous of the strength and accomplishments and potentialities of her older sisters and brother. They also tormented her and she was physically afraid of them. Since she had repressed that part of her memories in the stories she told her little son, she did not know that he refused to eat because he could not, after all, compete with boys who ate a whole ox, and that at night he was afraid because if they should come they would prove stronger than he. Thus the little boy sensed more of the mother's unconscious than she did herself, and against her will identified himself with the anxious component of it.

Malvina had told her stories, as a child, to make her jealous. Although Helene did not mention it, Martin was furious about his rivals and remained lastingly resentful at her storytelling about them. In her letter to Felix she had mentioned "four" brothers in Poland; perhaps she was then including her mother (who was still alive) among her old rivals. Although Helene at first had seen no dangers to Martin in these stories, she sensed the presence of unresolved infantile conflicts of her own.

As Felix was finding his analysis a trial, Helene encouraged him to endure the awakening of hidden memories. She herself had been through a bad patch of her own.

> Following upon an experience which, although unpleasant was not shattering, I fell into a state of compulsive crying lasting a full eight days without interruption. I cried in torrents night after night, so that the bed-clothes had to be wrung out—I cried at mealtimes, on the street, in analysis. The condition looked so serious that A. evidently thought it necessary to supervise me; he invited me to his place often, and was a kindly, understanding father to me.
>
> In the analysis today, the condition dissolved itself in the last round of compulsive sobs, in the memory of having been thrown out of the room, lovelessly, for the first time, by my father. I took on a defiant, uncrying pose: "It makes no difference to me," and suppressed the affect. Later life brought

me into a whole chain of similar situations, arising in compulsive repetition —until now the last one, called forth by psychoanalysis, led to the discharge of the whole horrible affect. Today it is like after a bath—feels good, restful, a sense of well-being.

Helene thought this incident was enough to explain why she had not written to Felix; yet nothing in the tone of her letter sounds as distraught as she felt during her depression earlier in 1923. One wonders if the tale were not mainly intended to justify her having ignored Felix, as well as to support him in his own pursuit of therapeutic insight.

She might have felt rejected by Freud's dismissal of her as a patient, and interpreted her current depressive problems as a delayed reaction to her first analysis. She suspected that Freud was now not overly concerned about her. ("Does Professor express no word of sympathy for me? For a simple word would have been caused by you to grow into a mountain and would have been transmitted to me. It doesn't matter . . .") The appearance of Freud's *The Ego and the Id* at the end of April, 1923, had been, as in the case of all his major publications, an occasion for enthusiasm on her part. She soon knew it "by heart." Immediately she had wanted to know if Felix had already read it (Freud had presented him personally with a copy), and she yearned to know what was being said about it in the Vienna society.

She also bought and read Georg Groddeck's *The Book of the It*, and therefore advised Felix not to buy it. (One of Freud's earlier friends had been the Berlin physician Wilhelm Fliess; since Abraham was, she said, "a strong adherent of the views of Fliess," Helene told Felix to "acquaint yourself with them.") Freud had partly derived his latest title from Groddeck. Helene's own imagery was marked by Groddeck's use of the concept of the "it," which Freud's English translators later turned into the "id."

So you are with Professor? How glad I am of this, for I belong to "I hate the profane mob." Who would not press such a dear, kind person to his heart? He must have had bad experience in his childhood and not be able to free himself from it. But then he locks you up all the more warmly within himself, and knows that human being finds his way to human being if it [id] wants to, and it [id] will soon want to.

As Freud had expressed himself in *The Ego and the Id*, Groddeck was "never tired of insisting that what we call our ego behaves passively in life, and that, as he expresses it, we are 'lived' by unknown and uncontrollable forces."[4] Groddeck, like Felix, was one of the pioneers in psychosomatic medicine, but Helene assured him there was nothing original or "scientific" in Groddeck's admittedly charming flights of fancy. If Felix had realistically doubted her involvement with him, their shared intellectual lives meant they were drawn tighter together than ever. "You are mine and remain mine for life," she wrote him. Although she did not like "sticky" dependency in people, she teased him about whether he would still want her after the liberation that would in principle be brought on by his own analysis.

For all the intimacy between Helene and Felix, she had deceived him during the early part of her stay in Berlin; she had embarked on a relatively brief extramarital affair. Later in the spring, when she referred to the way in which she and Felix had had "libidinous deficiencies toward each other," she was not using the concept of libido in its broadest sense. Felix was not a man who struck people as masculine; he lacked sex appeal for women, and although at the outset of her marriage he may have been what she wanted for herself, by 1923 she was actively dissatisfied. When he first started on his analysis with Bernfeld, Helene still had tender feelings for him; yet at the end of that letter in which she movingly described how she felt after his short trip to Berlin, when she had thought about running after the train carrying him away, she also wrote these enigmatic words about Felix's analyst: "Does he already know that you—no, I can't write it, even though a reproach appears in my heart." Felix understood her to have been referring to the problem of premature ejaculation.

Felix's naïve optimism—his belief in human perfectability—played a role in preserving the marriage. He wrote that he had not even been sure whether it was "by chance" that her analytic treatment was taking place so far away from him. But even he began to have his suspicions, which he voiced in a letter. Early on in her stay in Berlin he indicated to her that he was becoming jealous of "certain people." She played dumb, as if it were a mystery whom he could have had in mind. Might it be, she asked, her transference situation with Abraham that Felix was referring to, or even her involvement with Martin? She claimed that all her "sympathies are frozen in the cold breath of my *a*libidinous attitudes"; her loneliness was, she said, rooted in neurosis. But Felix had correctly divined that he had a genuine male rival in Berlin, and he specifically mentioned (February 2, 1923) his jealousy of Sandor Rado.

Felix may have correctly seen through to the realistic nature of the depression she had written about. The symptoms she had described—insomnia, fatigue, sadness, distraughtness—were too unusual for Helene to be ascribed to the analytic treatment with Abraham; Felix knew better than anybody the extent of her unhappiness with the marriage as well as how guilt-laden she would be if she were to take up with another man in Berlin. Though Helene thought herself emancipated from bourgeois norms, she accepted middle-class standards more than she liked to acknowledge. Precisely because the emotional bonds between Helene and Felix were built on considerations outside "normal" heterosexual relations, he had to be especially sensitive to what was going on in her soul. The precariousness of their relationship heightened his perceptiveness.

Although Helene's letters to Felix did not come anywhere near as often as his to her, even in the face of his steady reminders of how remiss she was being in not writing to him, she did mention the companionship in Berlin of Rado, a brilliant Hungarian analyst. Not formally a member of the Berlin society until 1924, Rado was already a star within analysis. He had been secretary of the Budapest society and in the future would become one of the leading theoreticians. Ultimately he led his own school in New York City.[5] Rado was to take Otto Rank's place in late 1924 as editor of the *Zeitschrift.*[6] He soon analyzed such people as Otto Fenichel, Heinz Hartmann, and Wilhelm Reich. In the winter of 1923 he had already been away from his wife in Budapest (also an analyst), for almost half a year. Rado was six years younger than Helene, but more established within Berlin analytic circles; his lectures were scheduled ahead of hers, although they both became "guests" of the Berlin society.

Doubtless Rado, like Helene, had been attracted to Berlin as a center of analytic learning; it is also plausible to suppose there was tension within his marriage, since his wife had remained behind in Budapest. In letters to Felix, Helene had indicated that she was seeing Rado socially, as a "companion in suffering." For example, they went to the theater together. At the bottom of a postcard that Helene, in behalf of herself and Martin, sent to Felix, Rado penned his greetings. (Paul Barnay† sent his regards to Helene at the end of one of Felix's postcards to her.) Rado's name appears in some of the letters Helene wrote in behalf of Martin, and she told Felix how Rado had helped handle some of her currency problems. In late January, 1923, Rado was called by telegraph to Budapest, since his wife had suddenly died; the death upset Helene, and she inquired of Felix what had "really happened." On a trip to Budapest earlier that month Felix had diagnosed "a severe anemia, but not a pernicious one"; he did not think "the prognosis is entirely bad." In retrospect, however, Felix emphasized the psychogenic component to her dying: "The stone was rolling and not to be stopped. The marriage to Rado finished her off. I believe death had cast its shadow on her years ago, when she was visiting in Vienna."

Rado was not just one of the most learned and intelligent of the post-World War I analytic generation (he had a photographic memory), but he was also, as Helene later put it, a "seducer" of women. According to her version, he got gratification from conquering women, and even took pleasure in breaking up marriages; she claimed he liked to torture women by making them jealous and betraying them with others.‡ Although he was not physically

† At that time Felix wrote Helene: "What I regret above all is that Paul is coming to Berlin and I won't be there. I had written to him at the same time as to you about my intentions of going to Berlin. But it is better thus, for I would not have been able to share between you and him." Felix said that Paul would look her up.

‡ In a 1926 paper Helene wrote about how "in the course of analysis the liberation of libidinal forces caused a hitherto strongly inhibited female patient to fall violently in love with an obviously unsuitable love object. Constant renunciations, necessitated by the love object's incapacity to love, made this strong and passionate relationship regress to a process of identification . . . I had the impression that she knew even before the man himself had become aware of it, that his previously platonic relationship with another woman had now acquired an erotic tinge . . . One

attractive, one of Rado's appeals to women, which mobilized their sexuality, was the intensity of his desire; although Helene could be level-headed about almost every area of her life, she—like others in their choice of love partners —was misled by her instincts and lacked sound judgment about men. Rado loved good food, had style and flourish, and other women besides Helene were enchanted by him. It would be hard to think of a greater contrast to her devotedly faithful Felix. Although she and Felix knew Rado personally and professionally for the rest of their lives, she always resented how little their affair had meant to him emotionally.

Although she rationalized not telling Felix about the short affair, on the grounds that it had not been humanly important to her, she was disturbed by her own behavior. Her anguish was deep; on the back of an anniversary letter from Felix to her, which exuded his thankfulness for her thoughts, she had written: "What has happened is now really 'the end of the world' for me. I know exactly what has become pretext—I know that everything is finished." In a letter to Felix she mentioned having had a "remarkable dream" which she wanted to tell him about sometime; she self-analyzed one dream in partic-ular, writing a two-page study of her introspective interpretation of her in-volvement with Rado.

On the right-hand side of the top of the first sheet she put the equation: "Felix = mother." It is not clear whether she had her own mother in mind, a maternal figure for Martin, or a combination of both.* On the top of the left-hand side of the page, she drew a diagram to account for how her emotions toward her father had come to be split between Felix and Lieberman.

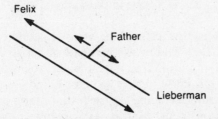

Afterward she added, in the short-hand language of psychoanalytic concepts, an attempt to account for her own conduct: "Father = Lieberman = wish-fulfilling and yet denying. Separation from the wife and yet not leaving her, no child therefore = fulfilling what he (the father) did not fulfill and denying

evening she sat at home in a state of utter despair, secluded from the world, and totally domi-nated by a single emotion . . . I believe that, by making a certain kind of object choice, this patient actually contrived to be disappointed in love . . ."[7]

* In *The Psychology of Women* she wrote about "the motherliness of the husband without whose active help that of the wife cannot function. In the life stories of such mothers one always discovers a strong infantile dependence upon their own mothers that has been transferred to their husbands."[8]

thus identical." Her attachment to Lieberman had been patterned on one
feature of her allegiance to her father, and yet was also part of her betrayal of
Felix.

> Father = Felix = infidelity committed = "because you did not love me I
> am turning away from you, becoming revolutionary, loving another *against*
> you." Infidelity tendency against F. as father imago to L. as away from
> father to L. Turning away from F. as imago of the inactive, not potent-loving
> father to L. as father imago = active, potent father.

Her relation to her father had led her to now having what she considered
"two sons," Martin and Felix.

Helene's reasoning to herself was in accord with the accepted analytic
theory of her time. She was betraying Felix with Rado as she had once
betrayed her father with Lieberman, in both cases because of a failure in her
father/husband. Helene was a believer in Freud's ideas; for these people analysis was a religiously held system of ideas, and she was engaging in a special
form of confession. The extensive material she went on to report, in connection with that one dream, was a mixture of her associations and interpretations, as she tried to explain (and rationalize) her fundamentally disturbing
actions. As far as Helene was concerned, Rado—although a talk with him
appears in her associations—was only a minor part of a larger picture. The
reality of what she had done sexually was mastered by an attempt to understand the psychology of her own childhood. It might seem that she was
taking flight from the present in order to hide in the past. But Lieberman was
still, after all the years of her marriage, a part of her soul; in her associations
to the dream, she had put "current infidelity tendencies against F. to L."
Before returning to Felix in Vienna in the spring of 1924 Helene would again
be in contact with Lieberman.†

There is abundant evidence of the unusual nature of the marriage between Helene and Felix. During the first part of her stay in Berlin she had
made a brief attempt to break free of it. It might look masochistic of her not
to leave Felix, but she knew what it had cost her to break with Lieberman.
One of the considerations holding her back was her appreciation of the affectionate tie between Felix and Martin. As she wrote to reassure Felix, "the
child is still from you—what speaks most of all for this is his great love for
you, as well as the purity of his soul and the sweetness of his temperament."

One other document exists to illustrate the tension in Helene's marriage;
it was written on an undated bit of notepaper that Felix must have saved. It
contains the flavor of Helene's temperament.

> I want to tell you everything, frankly and honestly, that tormented me as I
> thought it through during the past night. I am completely confident of hear-
> ing the truth from you, regardless of the great pain which you will suppose is
> in me. It must become clear to you that for me, loving you and uniting my

† Cf. Part II, chapter 12, pp. 223–28.

life intimately with you, means one and the same thing. Until today I haven't given this any form for myself, in my consciousness—I could take it so much for granted that I didn't need to reflect upon it at all.

I did not think, and will continue not to think, of "outward circumstances." I will always subordinate them to my content and to the true beauty and real richness of life, and I feel myself too strong and too proud to be able to do without.

By the time of the occasion for this particular crisis in their marriage, Helene had reconciled herself to her marital fate; but for once Felix had allowed himself to outwardly chafe at his predicament.

Yesterday I heard from you that I am superfluous to you, and that living together with me is not necessary to your future. If I am not dearer and more necessary to you than everything else which forms the content of your life—if you have not the intention, governed by nothing but your feelings, of joining your life with mine in total mutuality, then I believe it would be more worthy, for you and for me, that we should separate!

She thought she needed to allude to Martin.

Don't think one ridiculously small, obvious thought. You know I am too independent to think anything other than *You* in this matter.

In the years after 1923–24, Helene and Felix would have two other periods of geographic distance between them; but on her side the die had been cast. Once Helene's own fundamental ambivalences were under control, Felix had some opportunities to express his own doubts about their marital arrangement. (In Vienna he became involved for a time with Dr. Dora Hartmann, an analyst.) Helene had made clear that it was a life with Felix she had chosen, as opposed to a compromise for the sake of Martin. Outsiders to their marriage continued to see signs of conflict between them; on the whole, it looked, even to Martin, as though Helene willfully mistreated Felix. Some of her closest students did not even think the marriage was an exceptionally intimate one. Yet Helene and Felix continued to live together until his death in 1964; few people detected the exceptional kinds of emotional support they gave each other.

12

The Men:
Felix, Freud, and Lieberman

From the beginning of Helene's stay in Berlin Felix had to cope with loneliness. His busy medical practice (hospital duties in the morning, a cardiac
station in the evening) took up a great deal of his time; but he dwelt on their
analytic circle of friends in his almost daily letters. (Over one hundred of
Felix's from the first half of 1923 survive, while fewer than half that many
from Helene exist.) He could be sure that however alienated she might feel,
the discussion at the Vienna society would interest her, and especially any
comments of Freud's. Otto Rank's wife, Tola (also Polish), was an intimate
friend of Helene's, and even if she missed hearing from Helene directly, Tola
could be counted upon to look after Felix on a regular basis. Felix turned to
opera and concerts as well as theater for solace and diversion; poker games
among analysts were also a regular activity.

Both Felix and Helene, although she was allotted more space, were supposed to write articles for a medical handbook; their papers were due in
February 1924. Of more pressing interest to her, he knew, was the problem of
the Ambulatorium. The teaching setup and the outpatient clinic were, according to Felix,

> in total uncertainty. Hitschmann's leadership won't lead to the goal, I'm
> afraid. We see this again in the course arrangement; . . . besides other mis-
> takes of his, the announcements have appeared late, so that Nunberg has
> only four drummed-up auditors. Now they are coming to me to take the
> matter in hand. I have refused, unless I am officially entrusted with the
> matter. Why should I unnecessarily make an enemy of Hitschmann?

Felix came to regard his students as "adherents," and opponents of
Hitschmann, since the two men were more rivalrous than ever. Professional

problems could be a burden; Felix tried to think instead of Martin, and characteristically enclosed some stamps for him to collect.

When Herbert Silberer, a long-standing member of the Vienna society who was, however, no longer on good personal terms with Freud, killed himself, Felix alluded to it.

> A piece of news you are likely to have already heard, but which does not leave me completely neutral, is that Silberer put an end to his life by means of the rope—allegedly on account of "mental overstimulation," as I read. After his most recent confrontations in the Sunday and Monday papers with Loebstösell, this ending has had more publicity than is good for psychoanalysis. In any case, he was closely connected with the history of psychoanalysis.

Although Felix was not privy to the history of Freud's relationship with Silberer,[1] his letters to Helene reflected the shock within the Vienna society. A few days later he wrote:

> Among the psychoanalytic members there is a rather subdued mood on account of Silberer's suicide. And among the doctors there has been yet another suicide. Dr. Kahane, the electrotherapist, who once also belonged to the society, slit his Radialis—supposedly because of neediness. I knew him well—an elderly rather eccentric gentleman. I'm curious as to how Prof. takes these things.

Felix (who was still taking English lessons) reported a more favorable attitude toward him by people like Federn, Jekels, Nunberg, and Hitschmann; and he attributed this rise in his standing to the fact that some Americans had registered for his course. (In the end they did not come, since they wanted their introduction to analysis in English; Freud sent them to Federn.) Felix's doubts about how he stood with Helene increased, and he specifically wondered whether she had read his letters at all. (A few of his letters appear to have remained sealed and never taken out of their envelopes.) In honor of Martin's sixth birthday, however, Helene bought the present Felix had suggested; and Felix sent Martin poetry, with drawings for his son to laugh at.

Felix was on the lookout for a new apartment for them in Vienna, and wondered whether Helene would consider having her office separate from their living quarters. Domestic considerations were always discussed along with the part psychoanalysis, and Freud, played in their life. When Freud sent Felix an American (medical) patient, for example, it meant Felix's practice was improving. If Felix stayed home working on a Saturday evening, he might drop by the Ranks' as late as eleven o'clock at night.

> Annerl [Anna Freud] was there—she had been waiting for Prof., who was at the usual Tarok party. He didn't come up, fresh and merry, until 1:30. He has steered another American in my direction—the other one is completely

cured (40–50 dollars). It clearly gave him pleasure to get the case for me
. . . You see, I'm in his good graces at the moment, probably via Annerl.
But you know best how quickly this sun can cloud over.

Any contact with Freud or his daughter Anna, even on a walk, would
arouse Helene's interest. She was doubtless also amused by the rumor he
picked up among nonanalysts about her reason for going to Berlin: Felix was
astonished to report that she had supposedly gone to have Martin analyzed. If
Felix was nourishing jealous suspicions about Helene in Berlin, he had a
secret of his own. For two weeks he withheld the news that he was preparing
to deliver a lecture (January 31, 1923) before the Vienna society. Immediately
afterward he was delighted to share with her his success in detail.

Yesterday I gave a lecture at the society, "Psychoanalytic Illustrations."
Bernfeld engaged me, since no lecture had been scheduled. Tola, represent-
ing you, took the dress rehearsal, and was very satisfied. The lecture was
really good, about 3/4 hour . . . Prof. backed me up constantly and in
lively fashion against all attacks, and even accepted corrections of his own
previous views on the relation of experiences to symptom formations, favor-
ing my views. As for the rest, it was a generally friendly debate (especially
Schilder and Federn)—with the exception of Hitschmann, who again was
ugly, and, as usual, "stick-in-the-mud," and stupid. But my assured position
made me conciliatory. Prof.'s attitude is one of supreme benevolence.

Later that spring, anticipating a scheduled discussion by Federn of Freud's
The Ego and the Id, Felix expected a lively society meeting.

Much is unclear. Even Prof.'s personal position on these matters. He often
stresses that he has "only lit a tiny match in the dark"; this light could
totally disappear before the light of an arc lamp. He resists following it, but
is angry if anyone goes beyond him. Everything looks much more secure in
writing than when he is commenting on it.

However well Felix might manage on his own, his depressed moods
could not be brushed away; a quick weekend trip to Berlin late in February
helped strengthen him, so that he was able to comfort Helene. "Yesterday I
read your two items about distrust and psychopathology, and I think that
such a head cannot become empty all at once." He appreciated the extent of
her suffering, and told her how he worried about his own share in not having
succeeded in making her happy. As he better understood the crisis she
seemed to be going through, he was less concerned about the regularity of her
letter writing.

His missing Helene was one thing; but he naturally also worried that
Martin would gradually start to forget him: "His heart belongs to the one
who reads to him, plays with him, initiates him into the mysteries of the
world. We live to a great extent in the past; for him, each coming day is a
revelation." Abraham had thought that Easter would be too soon for another

of Felix's visits. But since Helene could not bring herself explicitly to enjoin Felix from coming, he overrode Abraham's hesitations in behalf of himself and Martin.

> sitting here alone at Easter, with the sky so blue and children's voices resounding everywhere; and knowing that not too far away there is another such little fellow running around—with no real reason for not being allowed to see him—all this is a sacrifice I cannot make for you. Therefore I am coming, and will disturb Abraham's circles as little as possible.

It was typical of Felix's playfulness with children that one of his short notes to Martin was written in half-a-dozen different colors.

In March 1923, Felix did not neglect to let Helene know how he still felt about her. As her self-confidence returned, he could let her know about his own guilt feelings.

> . . . twelve years ago, when there was still so much of storming the world in you, and when I was still unready, the two of us did not get in step—things went this way and that; sometimes there were real clashes. Now we have buried many vain hopes, and yet I still dream of a beautiful future with work and enjoyment.

Their professional lives bound them together. That month a close friend of theirs asked him to visit the sister of a Viennese political leader, Otto Bauer; according to Felix she had "a severe hysteria with organic symptoms," had been "in Freud's treatment twenty-five years ago, and has nothing good to say about analysis." The patient turned out to be "Dora," one of Freud's most famous published case histories; Felix reported having had "a momentous success" with her, as her acute symptoms dissolved after two hours of his "persuasion." (Later, in America, Felix published a paper about "Dora" as a postscript to Freud's account.[2])

Felix was, despite his periods of depression in that early spring of 1923, still fundamentally a contented person. His optimism led him to be hopeful about what he could bring to Helene's life.

> My love for you is young and new and springlike. And what of his love—the young gentleman! That must warm you! Halunin, the war has cheated us out of a great deal; there is much that must be recovered. But I don't want to live with you with my face toward the past, but looking toward the future— even if this should only mean the next day. No empty talk; I don't expect mountains of gold from life—I know my all too many weaknesses; I am prepared for much bitterness—but the day on which I should know you to be happy and contented, and I should experience it along with you, hold your hands and kiss them and think so much to myself that can only be felt and not be spoken—even if it were only that day—and then back to humdrum existence, until the advent of another such day—I would be contented and would have peace and joy in my work, and I would sun myself in that day. But there will be many of them, won't there, Mamuschkele?

As Felix finally made his arrangements for his own analysis shortly after their eleventh anniversary, Helene's own feelings for Felix began to return. He responded to her renewal of faith in their union with touching self-criticism.

> How can I express all the warmth which now promises to fill my existence through you? *That* is what spoke out of you when we met together in Munich, but I understood too little of it, the echo was too weak, which came from me—you overflowing with love, I overflowing with repression. What I could give out was only a glimmer—so that your flame went out, and burned into you.
>
> Now I am awakened—perhaps I have been for a long time, but it was too late; there was no echo from you. Now it will be different; there is no use in making accusations or in giving pardon. Two captives are stepping out into freedom, and breathing the delicious air. And in this freedom, we stretch out our hands to each other once more, firmly and knowingly, not inspired with unclear, intoxicating hopes, but sure of ourselves in action, and mature in love. Love, however, above all, which is yours from me as a human being and a man. That's the end of this wedding song.

In the same letter Felix reported that he had finally decided on Bernfeld as his analyst. It was an unusual choice (which "astonished" the Ranks, as well as Helene), yet not one made without a good deal of thought, including prior consultations with Helene. Freud lacked full respect for the older generation of analysts in Vienna; but for some reason Wilhelm Reich was not considered—perhaps because Freud did not like him—although Reich's work was closest to Felix's. In announcing the decision to Helene, Felix had put it: "I have left the company of the fathers and have chosen from the brotherhorde, and the younger one at that. Thereby I expect more of the analysis." (The imagery of a "horde" came from Freud's *Totem and Taboo.)*

In picking Bernfeld, Felix was following Freud's own advice to him; past active bisexuality in Felix might have in itself ruled Freud out as his analyst, although Freud treated foreigners with similar conflicts. Felix had earlier informed Helene of the nature of Freud's reasoning: "I was at Professor's last evening. First question: Please reassure me that nothing serious is happening in your marriage?! I gave him this assurance—rightly, I believe, for the present." Freud's own marriage was, by romantic standards, nonexistent, but his work flourished nonetheless. Felix had "explained everything" to Freud. "He believes the decision [to be analyzed] to be correct. The best thing would be: Ferenczi or Abraham." Felix "unfortunately" had to inform Freud that his first choices were "out of the question"; Felix could not afford, even over a three-month summer holiday, to abandon his medical practice to go to Ferenczi in Budapest, and Helene had already ruled out Abraham.

> He is not enthusiastic about Federn. He doesn't consider the technique flawless: too confused, too much love, highly gifted. But besides him, Bernfeld is

the only possibility—he named him the most suitable, even though he still does not have this experience.

Bernfeld was a newcomer as a practicing analyst (although he was a long-standing member of the Vienna society), without an M.D. and younger than Felix. Felix was strongly against "lay" analysis, since he did not believe in the duality of the mind and the body. At the time Felix went for advice to Freud, however, Bernfeld was brilliant,* needed patients, and very much in Freud's favor. (Subsequently he was analyzed in Berlin by Sachs in 1930–32.) Freud's daughter Anna was in love with Bernfeld, and Freud then considered him a potential son-in-law. According to Felix's account to Helene, Freud, besides Bernfeld,

> also thinks highly of Jekels, even if he is very embittered. Finally he settled on Bernfeld. It is out of the question for me, if only for reasons of space. So there remains the choice between Jekels and Federn. Before I decide, please tell me your opinion. It's no fun getting didactic material from secondhand, and moreover, having to say this to the analyst. Do you see a way out?
>
> Afterward I had supper with Prof.—very free and easy. Among other things, he said he thought that if more foreigners came to Vienna, they would only take the courses of Bernfeld and myself; he spoke scornfully of everything else. He thinks Berlin to be the coming center. I told him of your course, about which he was very happy; he spoke his greetings to you several times.

Helene did not have to write Felix her opinion of Federn, since she had first picked up her own reservations about him from Freud himself; and Jekels was her friend. Whatever Felix's difficulties in reconciling himself to the choice of Bernfeld (among other problems, Bernfeld lived on the other side of Vienna), ultimately Felix submitted to Freud's recommendation. Felix was pleased when he approached Bernfeld, since he was frank "about his inadequacies." Bernfeld said he only accepted Felix because Freud had sent him. (Later in the analysis Bernfeld told Felix that Freud had said of him that he was a very nice person.) Felix's intention may not have been to take analytic cases, and he undertook no further analytic training; until moving to America he kept up his practice as an internist, and within analysis he remained in a relatively unimportant position.

Although in later years Felix was contemptuous of what he had learned from his analysis with Bernfeld (in 1965 Helene called Bernfeld a "miserable analyst"), in his letters to Helene at the time he made no special complaints. Most of Felix's comments indicated that the analysis was proceeding well, and that he was learning from the clarification of his relationship with his analyst. (In the midst of feelings of inferiority and guilt, Felix could write:

* The first volume of Jones's biography of Freud was indebted to pioneering research of Bernfeld's into Freud's early life.

"the analysis is proceeding impeccably; I am working by the sweat of my brow.") Felix cared a good deal more about the prospects of the future with his wife than he did for his own analytic treatment: "My consciousness . . . has been extended through the analysis, and yet: everything streams toward you. I, the eternal beggar, and you, the sevenfold locked house. It will probably never be different. I am still more ashamed than angry."

The analysis, Felix thought, increased his loneliness, since it added to the emotional space between himself and Helene. The inner "tinkering" sometimes left him feeling topsy-turvy. The pressure of the analysis increased Felix's need for Helene's letters, although he felt "almost ashamed" of his "wheedling."

> Since I have been going through the pre-hells of analysis, and daily draw my hand over my head and venture a look into the depths—letters from you have become the straw to which I cling . . . The extensions of my consciousness through the analysis occur with experience of great shock—it often takes a great effort to remain in equilibrium. But *I* am *I,* and it will be completed. Only he who has experienced it can measure the attainment of being analyzed.

His experience transported him into the past; he hoped that he would grow through the liberation of his mental well-being, and that he would be strong enough for Helene.

After about two months of his analysis, Helene had ventured her ambiguous hint about Felix's inadequacies, which he took to refer to premature ejaculation. Felix said that he had just "spent the last week under a highly ambivalent attitude of rejection of the analysis, which had had a very unfavorable effect on my work-productivity and my relations with people." Her letter to Felix, which he understood to refer to his sexual performance,

> gave the occasion for B., given my preparedness to accept this reproach of yours as real, to answer the question that had kept tormenting me: "Have I a neurosis?" (without my having put the question explicitly)—his answer being that today, according to the results of the analysis so far, he could assert that there was in no way a neurosis present in me, even if neurotic tendencies, such as, according to his opinion—and yours and mine as well—are present in everyone, are not missing in me either.

According to psychoanalytic thinking of that time, a man might have a sexual dysfunction and still not be considered to have a neurosis. Felix wanted reassurance from Helene about *ejaculatio praecox,* a subject on which Abraham had written in 1917 (Tausk published a paper commenting on Abraham's approach).

> as far as the e.p. is concerned—please write and tell me if that is what you meant—that is, that there is a reproach in your heart about it—then possibly

such a thing could be present, in Abraham's extended sense. You see, I am being severe with myself, but I want to be honest, in order also to make Abraham's judgment on you easier for him. If anything more about me should come to light in *this* matter—which is hardly to be expected—the far-progressed analysis will do away with it. Then I would again feel confident about the two of us.

Apparently Helene never alluded to the subject again in a letter to Felix. In a couple of that age, experience, and sophistication, premature ejaculation could not be just a question of technique or ignorance.

As intimately revealing as Felix's correspondence with Helene could be, he—like herself—could avoid sensitive subjects with his spouse. At the time of his consultation with Freud about the choice of an analyst, Freud spoke to Felix, as his personal physician, about a growth in his mouth. Although it turned out to be a malignancy, Felix did not discuss Freud's medical problems with Helene; and he helped conceal from Freud the true nature of the illness. By the time Freud had been fully operated upon and had discovered Felix's deception, he was furious; a correspondence grew up between Felix and Freud that Felix wanted Helene to know nothing about.

Freud was to mind particularly Felix's indiscretions to Bernfeld about Freud's health problems and thought that Felix's medical judgment had been impaired by the analysis. Here Felix was in a box not of his own making. In the course of his analysis he naturally free-associated about so critical an issue as Freud's cancer. Since Freud had sent Felix into treatment with Bernfeld at the same time he showed Felix the malignant growth, could he realistically have expected anything else? Perhaps it was true that Felix, in the course of his being analyzed, lacked the objectivity that might have been ideal in Freud's physician. But Freud had turned to Felix for medical help partly with the confidence that this follower of his would be a tractable medical adviser. (Helene later said she thought to herself that Freud took Felix as his doctor for her sake.)

The worst of the problem for Felix, which in the end assumed the proportions of a trauma, lay in the future. For the time being he remained silent with Helene about the seriousness of Freud's health problems. For Freud's sixty-seventh birthday on May 6, 1923, Felix told her that he had sent Professor flowers in her name. Felix reported that Freud was insistent on paying for his treatment.

From Professor, after my reply to him in which I rejected his financial proposal, I have received a more recent letter in which he writes that if I place value on remaining his family doctor—as he very much desires—then I must act in a more business-powerful manner. So I will have no choice but to give in to him.

Before Freud left for his summer holiday in the Tyrol, Felix visited him and found him fit for "a stay at any altitude." "I already see the spark which will reignite his old creative powers."

Felix had correctly predicted that his analysis would create a new element of reserve toward Helene in him. It also served to estrange him from Paul. The friendship still continued; Paul announced that his arrival would be at six o'clock one morning, and Felix offered him lodgings and board "so that the little time I have will be spent with him." Felix also had the idea of asking Paul to accompany the Deutsch family to the seashore summer holiday on the Baltic they were planning to take. (In the end Felix decided against inviting Paul—". . . he is too restless and inconstant. Also, his relationship with his wife is not the best . . . he is enjoying life in his own way—with wine, women, and song.")

> I am still bound to Paul through the old common memories, but the bond has been loosened through the analysis. I can't talk with him about myself, so that he too is becoming more reserved. Nevertheless our relationship is most friendly.

It was a relief when Paul left.

> Although he stayed at our place, we didn't cramp each other. He's still the same old Paul, hungry for life and love, and never satisfied. Last evening we spent a pleasant time at a festival in Grinzing, and we walked home through the night. He talked and I listened. He didn't even notice. I thought a lot of good thoughts about you—about the time when it was going well for us together, and how I imagine it in the future . . . Paul has made a gift to Martin . . . He loves making gifts now just as much as he used to . . .

Although Felix had specifically asked Helene to comment about their sex life, she had successfully evaded his inquiry; he worried about being responsible for her waves of depressed feelings. Her analysis was in a tranquil phase, but Felix's had just begun to be troublesome.

> Now I am "cleaning out the stable." Phew, what a stink—it stinks to heaven! But it must be endured to the end. And one is not even allowed to hold one's nose. I think the dirt really is dung. Well, we'll see what the ground underneath looks like. Didactics! One tries to rub off the dirt, and believes oneself to be quite spick-and-span, and lo and behold, another layer. And if one didn't know that one's clean skin is underneath there, one would despair. I once said to Tausk, how good and wise and forgiving one must be after an analysis. This is the prospect that lets me endure it.

Felix's reference to Tausk had uncanny undertones; for Helene's problem in 1923, as in 1918 during her analysis with Freud, was similar to that of Tausk. For she, having entered Freud's circle, was faced with the prospect of defying Freud. He had left no doubts that he wanted her marriage to continue. Although he was in many ways emancipated from conventional values, when it came to the Deutsches Freud had felt confident about contributing his advice. (Freud had, to be sure, a special professional stake in their marriage in particular.)

By going to Berlin for a second analysis Helene was making an attempt to break free. Since Freud had never looked with favor on divorce in general, and in particular had thought that Helene should continue her marriage, by the spring of 1923 she felt more trapped than ever. Through her affair with Rado, she had made a try at liberation; afterward she had reason to return to the ease and comfort of Felix's love. Now that Felix was more a part of the Freud family circle than ever, and undergoing an analysis to boot, it was harder for her to follow her natural inclinations as a woman. Although, like Lieberman (and perhaps her father), she might think of her failure to divorce as her unhappy fate, and even develop a theory about the special form of masochism characteristic of female psychology, in the last analysis (as for Lieberman) it was good for her career to tough out her marital situation. Berlin confirmed how satisfying her profession as an analyst was going to be; and the prospect of being a leader in the training of the Viennese analytic community was alluring. Even as she was assuring Felix that despite everything she would be coming back to him, she also wanted to continue with her analysis in Berlin in the fall of 1924.

Meanwhile Felix was hoping to finish with his own analysis. He anticipated that by the time of their reunion, he would be more mature. Even before he undertook his treatment with Bernfeld, Felix felt he knew where things had gone wrong between himself and Helene.

> Now there is an end to my desiring well-being as your boy, or to my having desired it, when such a big boy grows up. I no longer need fear his competition. There will be room enough for both of us in your heart. What a fool I was to live ten long years in the wrong role! I am confident as never before. What are ten years, if even one day of fullest togetherness and belonging is ahead. When the veil over the past has been lifted totally, then a curtain will be lowered, and time between us will be measured from the year 1923. Only, his life is blessed from the *first* day onward.

Although Felix never mentioned it in letters to Helene, his career too benefited from the continuation of the marriage. Helene was to be his golden chariot within analysis, his "meal-ticket" as she and others uncharitably put it.

Felix had thought that the summer holiday would let them know how they got on together. Once again, though, their mutual involvement with Freud's life did not leave them enough room for themselves. Felix had approved Freud's own vacation, but Freud was so uncomfortable that his daughter Anna persuaded him in late August to ask for Felix's help before embarking on a further trip from the Italian lake country to Rome. At the time Freud had first shown Felix the growth in his mouth in April, Freud had said to him: "For what I intend to do I need a doctor. If you take it for cancer, I must find a way to disappear from this world with decency." For Freud, death was preferable to a life without dignity, and cancer could mean a painful and humiliating end. Before leaving for Italy, Felix consulted with Helene at Riga, their Baltic vacation spot on the North Sea, about Freud's meaning. There was no immediate danger from the cancer, but Helene agreed with Felix about the possibility of suicide.[3] They also feared that Freud might allow himself to die by refusing further surgery; at the time of Freud's first operation in the spring of 1923, a favorite grandson had died: as Felix wrote of the impending death of the child, ". . . it will be Prof.'s worst blow."

Felix did not like telling patients bad news, and believed in concealing things from dying patients. Freud's initial appeal to help him depart life with dignity had been all the excuse Felix needed. Freud's cardiac history might also have worried Felix, in addition to Freud's depression over the loss of his grandson in June. Freud had planned a trip to Rome with Anna, and Felix knew how much that meant to him. So although he perceived the necessity of a more radical operation, after making certain that Freud would be back in Vienna not later than September 20 Felix allowed him to continue on his journey. In Freud's absence Felix found an oral surgeon who performed the first of Freud's subsequent operations in October 1923. Although Helene had herself been a participant in her husband's decision to withhold the full truth from Freud (it is hard not to believe that somewhere Freud was denying to himself what he ought to have known on his own), she was angry with Freud for later speaking so persistently against her husband's conduct. And at the same time she was furious with Felix for being the cause of this new distance between herself and Freud.

At the time of Felix's trip to Freud in Italy it had seemed that Helene's husband was associating not only with the head of the analytic movement but its leaders as well; all the chieftains of the international movement (Ernest Jones, Sandor Ferenczi, Hanns Sachs, Karl Abraham, Otto Rank, and Max Eitingon) had assembled for a meeting with Freud. (They colluded with Felix in deceiving Freud about his illness.) Felix wrote Helene that when Abraham, for example, "mentioned the clarity and plasticity of your course and its favorable reception," "Professor in his quiet way remarked that it had been *the best* of all courses in Vienna." By the fall of 1923, when Freud had to undergo a far more radical operation, it was apparent that there was a dark underside to Felix's having been Freud's physician when he contracted cancer.

In letters to Freud in the summer of 1924, Felix defended his "white lies" to Freud as an important part of the treatment, and claimed that he had acted at all times "under the influence of analytic control" with Bernfeld. It would not be surprising, given the threat to all analysts posed by Freud's possible death, if Felix persistently though unrealistically believed the cancer could be successfully eradicated. Felix seemed to have hoped that with luck and successful surgery Freud could be spared ever knowing that he had had a malignancy at all.

According to Felix, Freud was a fighter who could not countenance weakness in himself any more than in others. It seemed to Felix that Freud was angry at him precisely because he had caught Freud in a weak moment. (To be sure, Felix was irritated that Freud had sent him to Bernfeld, and upset with himself for having accepted the humiliation.) According to Felix's interpretation, he had seen in Freud a man whose normal fear reactions had to be taken into account. The cancer was a sign of Freud's vulnerability. After Abraham visited Freud during his recuperation on the Semmering during August 1924, Felix wrote Helene on her holiday:

> I know how much all the details of my time spent with Abraham interest you. He left this morning. Last evening he was at my place. We spoke a lot about Professor—how he withdraws more and more from people, which A. had occasion to experience for himself when he was staying at Semmering. Up in his workroom Professor has a telescope with which he studies the moon and the stars, and by day he studies the hills and mountains of the region. He withdraws more and more from the world.

Freud would be permanently changed by the cancer, although he was writing again that summer. As chance would have it, it was the last time Freud and Abraham, who died in December 1925, would meet. (Felix went to visit Abraham as a physician on December 17, 1925.)

In August 1924 Felix took a tolerant attitude toward the alterations in Freud's personality: "How can one demand of this man that he bother about our affairs? It is said that his own family is already suffering from this withdrawal." Freud had not yet made up his mind who should succeed him as president of the Vienna society. Helene then intended a "demonstrative withdrawal from the society" of her own, which did not seem warranted to Abraham; Helene planned to write Abraham about it. When she was depressed over her relationship with Freud, after his falling out with her husband, Abraham wrote her in 1924 that she was exaggerating Freud's rejection out of her feminine masochistic feelings toward her father; he advised her to be more active toward Freud, who was then in the process of losing Otto Rank and therefore would have, in the terminology of that day, a surplus of libido for new objects in his life.

As far as his own relationship with Freud went, Felix thought he understood the nature of their difficulties.

> As always, Professor still speaks of the covering up of the truth concerning the nature of his illness, and the more firmly set he becomes in his injustice, the easier it is for me to get over the clouding of our relationship. But the more he ought to realize how his reasons don't hold water, the more he tries

to support them with other motivations. And finally: he who looks for the hair in the soup will find it.

During the illness his ego has not always proven constant and impermeable, and now that it—severely wounded—is raising itself up, it can only accomplish this task—given the severe organic damage that has remained—by drawing off the libido from the person who was witness to these weaknesses. He tries to establish as the cause of his inadequacy at that time, the uncertainty as to the nature of the illness. But someone must have been to blame for that uncertainty. He has to move me into a light that makes the withdrawal of his favor possible for him. There is nothing easier than that, for infallible I am not. And the surrounding world takes care of material for that noble purpose.

Felix had been afraid that Freud's resentment toward him might extend to Helene as well. (Felix mistakenly thought he himself would "soon be over this incident," which had ended in Freud's withdrawal as Felix's patient.) Helene, Felix wrote, could "go happily to work, for you have not lost Professor—and you have won Abraham. The latter means even more." Felix, trying to protect Helene's relation to Freud, had written him that he had never discussed Freud's medical condition with her, and that she knew nothing about the exchange of letters between Freud and Felix. It was typical of the gravity of what Felix chose to discuss with Helene that he did not want her to talk of these matters "even to Tola."

In the fall of 1923, when Helene had left Martin in Vienna with Felix, they both undertook to conclude their respective analyses. Felix had started conducting an analysis (without any fees) in January 1923; only later in America did they both have regular analytic cases. Helene repeatedly failed to receive satisfactory medical reports about Freud's condition from Felix. On October 4, 1923, she wrote, ". . . over my sky full of hope there hangs the painful black cloud of concern over Prof.'s condition. I just don't know what to make of it! Send me detailed bulletins!" Although Felix had mentioned Bernfeld's indiscretions about Freud's health, this "betrayal," as it seemed to Felix, would not encourage him to talk loosely even with Helene. Back in analysis once again with Bernfeld, Felix took some comfort in the vacation break: "Prof. was very happy when he found out by chance that I was not in analysis during his illness. It could not be pleasing to him, when no one had access to him, for me to bear out intimate matters." After Freud's operations later in October, Helene asked Felix to send "Professor a glorious bouquet of roses *from me*—and from the Abrahams a chrysanthemum (card enclosed)—send them with wishes for his recovery."

Helene thought that Freud's anger at Felix meant that "a newly gained father-transference" in Felix was being severely shaken, but he still refused to speak out to her. Freud's anger at her husband's deception, and the offense she perceived in Freud's treatment of him, united her more strongly with

Felix. On Helene's return to Berlin, Rado had met her by car with another female colleague; she admired his brilliance at analytic meetings but told Felix: "Rado is in the midst of a severe neurosis, and Abraham advised me to leave him alone, which I for my part am glad to do." Later that fall she wrote: "Rado has abandoned me totally for his Hungarian girlfriends."

She missed her little son ("may the 'history of the development of analysis' take it upon its conscience"), and also Felix; but she had little trouble returning to genuine work. In addition to her practice and meetings, in November she presented a short paper to the Berlin society on the psychology of sport. She also was taking daily English lessons, planning for a paper at the international congress to be held the following spring, and beginning to shape up a monograph on "the female sexual functions," which she completed in early 1924; it would be the first book ever published (1925) by an analyst on female psychology. If some projects, like a paper on the female revolutionary, did not see the light of day, that was par for the course in the life of a writer like herself.

In December 1923 a new book co-authored by Ferenczi and Rank evoked widespread dismay (especially in Berlin) among analysts more determined than ever to preserve the purity of Freud's teachings. Helene was also reading Rank's *The Trauma of Birth,* which came out that month too. She interpreted Rank's new thinking in the light of the changed circumstances brought about by Freud's cancer. At that time Rank was presumed to be Freud's successor as leader of the analytic movement: ". . . who would recognize, in this soap bubble around a true nucleus, the cool, critical mind of Rank? It is the deeply felt, neurotically experienced trauma of sickness and of that which lies ahead in the life of Professor!" For all analysts Freud's illness had called into question what they were working for; her own analysis was also taking place "under this sign." She reacted to the new uncertainty by devoting herself to her work more zealously than ever.

Her analysis was progressing at such a pace that it looked as though she would have to return to Berlin after the holiday break for Christmas 1923. Felix had written directly to Abraham, who on December 2, 1923, replied at length about Helene's condition.

Dear Herr Colleague,

I received your letter yesterday, and I understand your point of view thoroughly. In the meantime, your wife has written in greater detail about the question of her further analysis. I must confirm that the two weeks before Christmas are not sufficient for the conclusion of the analysis, but I think I am able to say favorable things to you otherwise.

The little manuscript that you recently received has probably furnished proof to you that the work inhibition is on the decline; also you will agree with me that the little article is quite a success. But what seems more impor-

tant to me is the development of her condition otherwise, in connection with
the progress of her psychoanalysis.

Abraham was not violating Helene's confidences, yet Felix could be expected
to accept his authority.

> The treatment has lately been having to go through a very difficult stage, i.e.
> through the analysis of the masochism which turns out to be a main source
> of last summer's crisis, but also upon which all other difficulties of the past
> years were based. It now seems to have been possible to put a stop success-
> fully to those tendencies.

Felix must have understood what Abraham meant by the "crisis" of the
preceding summer; as an extension of Freud's will, Abraham was working to
preserve the marriage.

Abraham was concerned about Helene's fluctuation in weight. (She had
written to Felix for advice about renewed gallstone attacks.)

> For the past week or so I observe, besides the psychic improvement, a re-
> markable physical convalescence. The reduction of weight which was striven
> for in the summer had succeeded *too* well, i.e. under psychic influence, a
> reduction occurred which went too far. Now, recently, the appearance has
> improved greatly, and I believe you will have a very favorable impression at
> Christmas.

Allowing for the three-month summer vacation, Helene had had about eight
months' worth of analysis with Abraham; and he cautiously predicted that if
things continued to go well

> the portion of the analysis lying ahead of us should be significantly shorter in
> duration than the portion up until now. I certainly know what each addi-
> tional month means for you, and also for Martin, but you "know the ropes"
> in psychoanalysis sufficiently to appreciate that the termination of treatment
> depends not only upon my efforts, but that we are dealing with a patient
> whose affect-life is laden with considerable difficulties. I *hope* we will get by
> with less than one year, which certainly is not long for such a difficult
> analysis.

Helene's own letter to Felix was briefer than Abraham's, but
unambivalently confident.

> While telling me the content of his letter to you, Abraham revealed to me his
> opinion on the duration of my exile. But I think he named the maximum, for
> at the present stage of my analysis something does appear to be visible,
> shimmering through the thick fog. You can't imagine what torments
> Mamuschkerl is experiencing. Longing for you, utter loneliness, little lust for
> work, bad physical state, difficulties of the analysis, hypochondriac fears for
> the two of you—worry about Professor etc. etc. Everything that the masoch-
> istic soul can dream of piles up into one big state of misery.

Despite how her letter might sound, her deeper convictions were supposedly settled: "For never was it so clear to me that behind the seven seals there is a magic garden, and in it I see, from a great distance, *three* people closely pressed to one another."

By early 1924 Helene was again giving a course of lectures for the Berlin society. She gave a talk in late February on the psychogenic causes of sterility before a general audience at the German Union for Sexual Reform. With Martin in Vienna, Felix could be confident of her eventual return. From the time of her coming back to Berlin in the fall of 1923 there had been no interruption in the flow of her letters expressing her ardent longing to be back with Felix in Vienna. The early months of 1924 are full of her successes at work. In finishing a paper Helene realized that its form was not yet first class: "Now I really do have great difficulty in expression—I, the old stylist. This must not stagnate and must be practiced. Don't worry, it will be."

At the same time, in the midst of runaway inflation in Berlin, a new note of her old social conscience began to resound. She still held the left-wing political convictions of her youth. "Dearest, don't get worried about news coming from Berlin—somewhere in the world there is need and hunger, somewhere innocent blood flows, somewhere clouds of resentment and protest gather—nearer or farther away; for those who hide, there is no danger." Helene's social guilt feelings were awakened.

> Don't let yourself be intimidated by false cries of alarm. Berlin is so unchanged, except for the many o o o o o's. There is no mood of panic, no barricades, no starvation (in the west). This personally. How it is fermenting and foaming down there, how people suffer, how the billows of the wave of social upheaval are towering—that is history—the individual remains—where he wants to. And the unsocial neurotic just remains introverted, and lets things be fine for him in his narcissistic castle.

Helene may have described herself in letters to Felix as living the withdrawn life of an old maid, but this revival of her social concern reflected the fact that she was now once again back in touch with Lieberman. The first letter of his to her that she had saved since her marriage was from Warsaw on the stationery of the Polish parliament (April 20, 1924).

> My Dear Halusia,
>   I was silent for a long time, I do not know myself why. And now I long for a talk with you.
>   Since my return from Berlin many things have changed in my life. Two weeks after I came back I parted forever from the lady I told you so much about. Since then I have lived in loneliness and I feel broken inside. I work a lot, and have been through many political fights, some of my experiences were tough and not without a certain amount of bitterness. When we meet, I will tell you about everything. I have an irrepressible desire to see you, to

> pour out everything that hurts in life so much; it is like a wave of sadness
> and longing from my youthful years.

The tone of this letter sounded so familiar to Lieberman that he was aware
how reminiscent it must have seemed to Helene too.

> Are you not laughing, Halusia? I must confess that I am afraid of your
> psychoanalysis. Perhaps you with your knowledge take as a symptom of a
> sickness this which we simple people consider as a feeling or longing?

Still the same dedicated socialist, Lieberman could not feel at ease with
Helene's new ideology.

> I must admit that I came back from Berlin completely confused about you, I
> had the impression of being an involuntarily turning wheel in the psychoana-
> lytic therapy system. This used to fill me with grief sometimes. Do not be
> angry about my writing like this, but because you have not ceased to be a
> holy person in my life I feel the need of being sincere with you.
>   Do not think I have forgotten you, after returning from B. On the
> contrary! Because of a variety of happenings I am in a strange psychological
> state; something still rebels inside me against writing to you.

Lieberman had no intention of their renewed contact being short-lived.

> I would like to hear many, many things from you. Write me how you feel.
> Are you over this crisis which you told me about, and which had a deep
> effect on me? I was thinking very much about your suffering. Are you well?
> Will you stay in Vienna? Will you come to Warsaw? I ask you please to do it!

Lieberman had to return to Przemyśl (and his wife) for a short period, but he
hoped to hear from her in Warsaw. He closed his letter by inquiring about
what Helene's summer plans might be.

Helene was planning to deliver a paper on motherhood before the eighth
congress in Salzburg: it became the nucleus of her first book. She was preparing to start life over in Vienna, in a freshly painted apartment that Felix was
fixing up for her so that she would feel like a queen returning to a completed
castle, but she had not been able to resist renewed contact with Lieberman.
She was excited about her forthcoming publications, and appealed to Felix to
help calm her down; she now begged him to answer her questions, as he had
once sought for news of her life in Berlin. But while she looked forward to her
new life in Vienna, part of her went back to Lieberman.

In October 1924 Lieberman wrote to her again; she had written him
from Vienna in September; evidently one of his earlier letters to her had
gotten lost.

> I could not believe it. I answered your three-month-old letter *the same day* I
> received it. Your letter was so moving, I felt such a warmth emanating from
> it, that I had tears in my eyes and answered you immediately. It has been so

long since I have felt such a moving feeling, such goodness, full of understanding of my soul and my longing, which do not leave me.

He had been eager for news from her; late in August, in passing through
Vienna, he had tried to reach her, but she was in the country. "Life is difficult
here," he wrote from Warsaw. "I had a year of hard fights, in which I was
very active. Maybe you read something about that in papers."

Lieberman had followed Helene's recent presentation on "The Menopause" at Würzburg, Germany.

> I was very happy and proud about your success at the conference of psycho-
> analysis, just like in the old times and just as if you still belonged to me. Do
> you remember, Halusia, your speech at that meeting in Vienna, about al-
> lowing women to study law? I was very proud of your success at that meet-
> ing then, and now I had the same feeling when reading the report of the
> conference.

He wanted news from her: "How do you look, how do you feel, how is your
life going?" He wanted, once his financial situation got better, to come to see
her in Vienna. He was confident and diffident at the same time: "Is that all
right with you? Will it be convenient for you? Or rather, will I be convenient
for you?" It had been "a year" since he had broken off with "Mrs. D."
Lieberman had discussed her with Helene, and she had advised him to stay
with her, but it had not worked out. Now Lieberman thought it was strange
that he did not resent that woman at all. "It was not so with Halusia, about
whom I still cry in the most secret depths of my soul, as the most wonderful
dream of my life."

In November 1924 she had written to propose they meet in the course of
a trip to Paris. He replied (November 22, 1924):

> Your letters emanate such a warmth! Their fluid penetrates me. You write to
> think about you warmly. I could not describe what I feel when I recall you.
> When I think about you, my soul feels this: (I am writing this to an analyst,
> which you are) a hot current penetrates my blood, my heart sinks, tears
> come to my eyes. In spite of all my misfortune and in spite of hurting you so
> many times, my feelings for you were the most beautiful, like the purest
> flower of my life.

Helene may have decided to spend her life with Felix, but she could not resist
toying with the thought of another kind of existence for herself. The great
love of her life was alive in Warsaw, a part of Russian Poland which was so
foreign to her that she had never even been there; the success of Polish
independence meant that Lieberman was working far from their old milieu in
Galicia. If she could not think of leaving Vienna, either taking Martin from
Felix or leaving the child behind, she still cherished memories of what Lieberman had meant to her. As he wrote, planning to meet her on the way to Paris,

A strange and irrepressible longing draws me near that wonderful past
where you were near me and with me, you would wake me up from my sleep
(do you remember once in Vienna when you woke me up with flowers and
strawberries?), we used to dream together, to go on faraway trips and you
had made plans for the future.

He tried to comfort her: "In your letter there is a lot of sadness and resignation—do not give in to this feeling." An aspect of herself could be truer with
him than with Felix. "Do not give up, Halusia, do not boast about your gray
hair. I have not found in my life a woman more beautiful, sophisticated, and
worthy of love than you."

Helene was more realistic, and therefore more difficult, than Lieberman
had once known her. Now she did not want a trip to Paris, but one to Rome
instead. He was against a January visit to Rome, and tried to see if she would
accept a more attractive setting. It sounds as though they did not meet again,
until by accident she encountered him in Venice during the summer of 1925.
In the meantime, she sent him a copy of her first book, which he acknowledged (June 15, 1925).

> I read it with great interest, pride, and great affection. Something in my soul
> overjoyed and kept on repeating: this is my Halusia, mine, mine, the one
> who represented my longing and dreams, this is her, this divine person that
> is mine, from years past, has flown far away from me but has reached great
> heights! Can this be true? This is my little dear, whom I have cuddled in my
> arms so many times, who became a scholar fit for the whole world. Can this
> be happening? Is this real?
>   Please forgive this tone, my dear Halusia, I have no right to it.

Lieberman had found out from her brother-in-law Michael Oller that Helene
had gone to Rome during the spring, but she had not tried to contact him. (In
the late summer of 1924 Felix went without her to Italy, when he had met
Paul Barnay; she traveled with women friends, and in the spring of 1925 she
journeyed to Florence, Naples, Sorrento, Siena, Capri, and Amalfi.) Lieberman wondered where she would be that summer, and said he would "of
course" try to contact her when he passed through Vienna. He had himself
recently written a short book, but he did not think it had much value. She
must have been touched by his continued expressions of devotion to her.
"You have not ceased to be the deeply loved sanctity of my life. So I thank
you from the bottom of my heart for this book and for the few words you
wrote about me in it."

In August 1925 Helene was in Venice with Martin and Tola Rank. As
she sat outside talking about Lieberman with Tola, wholly unexpectedly he
appeared. She arranged for him to meet Martin, then over eight years old.
Lieberman made a long speech to the boy about how unusual and wonderful
his mother was; he wanted Martin to be sure to remember that he had a great

woman as a mother. Lieberman also told the boy that he—a child—was the reason why she had left him long ago. Martin, however, did not understand a word of Polish, and deeply resented the exclusion of his father from the encounter; Martin always disliked the second life Helene seemed to have for herself in Poland, as if she were withholding herself from him. (One of Martin's playmates, Tola's daughter "Halusia," shared similar feelings toward her own mother.)

It never dawned on Lieberman that his Halusia's son would know only German. Polish had always been the only language between Helene and Lieberman. In Venice she was so startled, and enthralled, by seeing Lieberman that she failed to notice the antagonism Martin felt for him. Afterward, she and Lieberman went for a gondola ride. He then explained that her passive devotion to him had made it harder for him to break with Gustawa; and he claimed that his wife had threatened to murder his daughter, and Helene as well, if he did not give up his illicit affair with her.

Lieberman may have shed tears with Helene, but his departure from Venice was not romantically perfect; he had been accompanied there by a lady friend. As he wrote Helene from Montecettini on August 16, 1925:

> Do not be angry with me, because I left without saying good-bye. Something happened, I cannot give you more details now, and this forced me to leave suddenly, early in the morning from Venice, with the lady known to you.
>
> I have been through many hard experiences in the last few days, so that I am completely shattered, my nerves are worn out. I will spend a few days here to get a rest and then I will leave for Warsaw, because I had a call from there.
>
> My Halusia, you probably will react to that from a psychoanalytical position with a skeptical smile on your lips, that everything can be explained, but life is still a terrible suffering.
>
> If it is possible, Halusia, I will stop by in Vienna for a few hours, and then I will give you a phone call.
>
> Please give my regards to Madam Rankowa and ask her to forgive me for not saying goodbye to her.
>
> My dear Halusia, my only one, whose memory is holy and clean, I send you my warmest greetings.

Helene may have regretted what her life had become, but after her stay in Berlin there was no turning back. She could mourn Lieberman; but life is a mixture of choice and circumstance, and for her it meant Felix and psychoanalysis. However she sounded in letters to Lieberman, she had written to Felix exuberantly as she contemplated returning to Vienna from Berlin in the spring of 1924.

> I will bring along so much . . . tenderness for you two. Such hot tears flow from my eyes when I read that a poor little head is longing for my lap—I would like to take it to me and at last become to it that which I could never

manage before. A motherly woman. My dearest, what is this acquired capacity for work? I *must* attain another capability. Will I? Posing and phrases are nothing any more. The air is beginning to become clean, like twelve years ago. Do you remember how I used to say, "The air is pure"—oh, I didn't understand myself.

Her feelings for her own mother left her tortured by traditional conceptions of motherhood; an unresolvable insecurity had led her to end up with as respectable a man as her mother could have wanted. She thought she would try to outdo herself as a mother. Helene was full of hope, based on the turn she was about to give analytic ideology.

A trembling fear is in me. Can it really become as beautiful in life as it looks before me now? Will our Bunnykins become what he promises? My arms are empty and reach out for you—where are you, my sons? Puschkuleinderl, there is only one relationship of the woman to the man that is true, deep and full: the maternal.

She wrote Felix that she might have another child, perhaps a daughter. At the same time her Polish past flowed into her analytic present: "Aunt Lajka's spirit still speaks." (Aunt Lajka was an eccentric sister of her maternal grandmother.)

And the Pure Ones back home pray for the possessed soul of the granddaughter, and Abraham drives it out with holy water—I see how he twists and turns, how he still holds me in his clutches—Gloria, Gloria—the day is coming! Will you also torment me so? Are you also so full of hopes?

13

"Unappreciated Female Libido"

In Berlin Helene managed to ensure that her introspection was used for objective purposes. Away from Vienna she composed her first essay on female psychology, which she delivered at the Salzburg congress on April 21, 1924. (Abraham had been secretary of the International Psychoanalytic Association,* and was elected to the presidency, succeeding Jones, who had filled the office for five years.) "The Psychology of Women in Relation to the Functions of Reproduction"[1] immediately became a classic paper in psychoanalysis, and would be widely cited for the next sixty years.

Before leaving Berlin Helene had also succeeded in completing a draft of her first monograph, *Psychoanalysis of the Sexual Functions of Women;* it would be regularly referred to in the field[2] until the appearance of her two volumes, *The Psychology of Women* (1944–45), replaced it as the standard text. From 1925 on she became famous as a writer as well as a teacher; and feminine psychology remained her area of specialization.

Freud's own ideas had always been cast in the perspective of the male; this was true although most of his early cases were women. One of the weakest spots in all Freud's thinking was his outlook on women, which was later to be the point of departure for some of the earliest fundamental critiques of traditional analytic thought. Freud's implicit devaluation of women was matched by a tendency to idealization, and he was gallant toward them. Yet his concepts, which sound sexist, were separated by a wide gulf from his clinical practices. However much Freud's theories might reflect social pat-

* The IPA then had a total membership of 263. The breakdown of the membership of the component societies was: Britain, 49; Vienna, 42; Switzerland, 40; America, 31; Berlin, 27; New York, 26; Holland, 19; India, 16; Hungary, 13.

terns of sexist dominance of his time, in practice he could be remarkably
broad-minded. As another female analyst, also a former patient of Freud's,
wrote in 1934, protesting against his mature theoretical views on femininity:
"It is not a credible view of women . . . Freud himself has not always
looked at women thus."[3] Helene knew Freud well from her own personal
experiences with him; but it is too easy now to overlook how far ahead of
himself culturally he was in treating men and women as equals. To one highly
artistic male patient, Freud specifically linked creativity to femininity: "You
are so feminine you cannot afford to let it out," Freud told him, and Freud
intended this interpretation as a compliment. (Freud once congratulated
Marie Bonaparte on her "virility.")

The limitations of Freud's fundamental bias were at least implicitly
checked by the logic of his conviction that all people are inevitably bisexual.
Since Freud was a philosopher as well as a scientist, recent embryological
research on dimorphism cannot ultimately settle the matter for or against his
approach. Pleas in behalf of androgyny are as humanly relevant as any appeal
to early "nature." Ideally a theory of bisexuality should be used to encourage
toleration, not to reinforce cultural preconceptions about maleness and
femaleness.

In 1899 Freud wrote that he was accustoming himself "to the idea of
regarding every sexual act as a process in which four persons are involved."[4]
The notion that two people in bed ought really to be looked upon as four
should do something to dispel the myth that Freud was more staid than we
are today. The existence of feminine components in men, and a masculine
side to women, was entailed by some of Freud's most basic beliefs. In terms of
the history of analytic doctrine, however, only in the 1920s did female psychology begin to receive anything like its due.

Psychoanalysis of the Sexual Functions of Women finally appeared from
Freud's Vienna publishing house in 1925. (Helene sent inscribed copies to her
mother and sisters.) Karen Horney reviewed it in a lengthy essay.[5] Karen
Horney has been acknowledged as a leading figure in challenging Freud's
theories of women; and in their later works she and Helene would pause to
tangle with each other. Karen Horney took the initiative in criticizing
Helene's outlook, often taking her contributions for granted, while Helene
confined herself to brief defensive comments.† In Karen Horney's extensive
review article of this book, she might have had reservations about some features of Helene's work; but she thought that it was

> of the greatest value that an undertaking like the subjection of the whole
> range of female sexual functioning to psychoanalytic consideration should be
> attempted at all . . . One cannot do justice to a country-side if one only
> travels along its main thoroughfares, and in the same way this review which

† Cf. Epilogue: A Woman's Psychology, pp. 341–42.

has to keep strictly to the main ideas cannot do justice to the real wealth of observation and thought that this work contains.

Although the ideas of Karen Horney and Helene subsequently diverged and helped fuel an important controversy over female psychology that has preoccupied many analysts, it would be mistaken to read back all their later disagreement into the mid-1920s. (Melanie Klein, another analyst who differed with Freud's views on women, relied at various points on *Psychoanalysis of the Sexual Functions of Women.*) In contrast to the way in which Helene always camouflaged her modifications of Freud in the most tactful language possible, Karen Horney went on to develop her own independent school of thought; but by the 1940s Helene had her own qualifications and reservations about Freud's earlier theories.

At the time Helene was writing in 1924, Karen Horney had recently proposed that a woman's identification with her father was an explanation for a neurotic lack of femininity. Unlike Karen Horney, from the outset of her work on female psychology Helene Deutsch was trying to include an intimate tie with a woman's father as a normal source of personality growth, an enhancement of the ego. This original point of Helene's, part of the way she used the theory of bisexuality, is not easy to see nowadays, since throughout her book she expressed herself in terms of the then current libido theory. In effect she was using biological-sounding concepts for the purpose of female emancipation. She wanted to treat the so-called masculinity complex in women as a normal part of development. After the completion of *Psychoanalysis of the Sexual Functions of Women,* Freud published three short papers of his own about female psychology; the work of Karen Horney and Helene stimulated Freud into writing on femininity, since he did not want to be left behind.

In 1905 Freud had maintained that "libido is invariably and necessarily of a masculine nature, whether it occurs in men or in women and irrespectively of whether its object is a man or a woman."[6] As Helene wrote Felix with a sense of satisfaction on completing the manuscript of this book: "It brings something new to this *terra incognita* in analysis—I believe, the first ray of light on the unappreciated female libido." But she was a broadly cultured woman who knew that however important female sexuality was, it ought not to be treated as all that might be said about the feminine soul. Sex, no matter how broadly defined, is still after all only a part of life; and Helene had tried to make sure that in her book she had not made it "the central part of existence." (One of her protégés, Wilhelm Reich, would end up insisting on just such a significance for sexual gratification.)

Of all the early analysts, Helene more than anyone developed the implications of Freud's ideas for women. It is true that she remained a Freudian loyalist; but to the extent that his vision was a commanding one, she brought its advantages (along with its limitations) to bear on the problem of femininity. Whether she was talking about motherhood as a normal developmental phase, or the origins of the specific symptomatology of frigidity, at the time she was making original contributions. Although Helene continued writing within Freud's framework, she increasingly sought to draw on her own experience and outlook; cultural restraints, which bind us all and set limits on what we can accomplish, also make possible a measure of civility.

She confined herself throughout *Psychoanalysis of the Sexual Functions of Women* to theoretical concepts. After Freud first contracted cancer in 1923, he never composed another case history; the specter of his own death accelerated his speculative tendencies. Helene's book was written in the shadow of Freud's illness. In contrast to almost all her other writings, clinical illustrations, except for the last chapter, were left out. In the most sustained bit of theorizing she ever engaged in, she was explicitly addressing herself to a professional analytic audience.

Helene naturally began with an account of early childhood, since according to Freud it was the prime source of adult character. Psychoanalysis stressed the fundamental reality of human infantile helplessness. These stages of life had not yet been directly observed scientifically, but had been reconstructed from the dreams, memories, symptoms, and fantasies of analytic patients. She relied on Freud's model of childhood development, although such terms as "oral," "anal," and "phallic" may now have an archaic ring to them. They were, however, an essential part of the mythology in which all early analysts thought. The metaphysics of psychological stages corresponding to erotogenic zones eventually made an enormous impact, getting popularized, for instance, in the child-rearing handbooks of Dr. Benjamin Spock.

All the language of early analysis was stylized. Freud's terms distorted reality for the sake of heightening our perceptions; this approach is familiar in art, and if some of Helene's subsequent readers took her too literally it was because her work, as part of psychoanalysis, was presented as science.

The emphasis on the psychological significance of the penis, and the lack of it, was in the mid-twenties assumed by analysts to be basic to any discussion of femininity. With hindsight one can see that the early Freudians overdid the literal meaning of the anatomical differences between the sexes, and missed understanding how organs of the body could be used to symbolize powerful or weak social roles. "Feminine castration anxiety" was the technical concept for what became widely known as penis envy; it was a term designed to explain how it could come about that women were disparaged, resentful, or disappointed. Helene, like so many of her colleagues (including Abraham, and the early Karen Horney) concentrated in their theories on apparently innate developmental problems. Later writers, such as Erich Fromm, for example, would instead look for the cultural bases of psychological prejudices.

The notion of penis envy now seems an obvious outgrowth of the patriarchal bias Freud shared with his social order. Women's complaints of deprivation, conscious and unconscious, as well as the consequent desire for revenge, were realistic signs of social injustice. The tendency of women to identify their values and destinies with those of men, the figures of power in society, has been noted by many—and was to be analytically dissected by Karen Horney and other "dissidents" in analysis. She later proposed that penis envy was an early expression of the mysterious attraction between the sexes. In the context of the history of psychoanalytic thought, penis envy was originally used to coordinate female psychology with that of men. (In sharing Freud's view that as compensation for the acceptance of "castration" the young woman identifies with her mother in the craving for a child from her father, Helene had found an explanation for her own tortured involvement with Lieberman.)

Freud had long thought that castration anxiety, an irrational basis for contempt and derision of women, was a crucial aspect of male thinking. He had a powerful sense of the dramatic, and some of his case histories—the "Wolf-Man," the "Rat-Man"—sound misleadingly ominous. According to Freud's 1925 theory of normal human development, whereas in men the Oedipus complex was supposed to be overcome ("dissolved") by the threat of castration, in women the impact of the anatomical absence of a male organ preceded and prepared for the creation of an Oedipus complex. Although in one sense the idea of penis envy lowered women's standing, especially since Freud failed to emphasize male jealousy (or fear) of a woman's reproductive capacities, on another level Freudian theory was now attempting to put female development on an equal conceptual footing with that of men.

This early generation of analytic thinkers made too much of the cognitive perceptions of the differences between the sexes. Yet knowledge and enlightenment were at the same time viewed as powerful therapeutic tools. It was believed that neurosis could be averted by superior childhood sex education. Helene always remembered the case of an eight-year-old boy who had been sent to her for an explanation of where babies come from; he listened, asked intelligent questions, and accepted her account, but as he started to leave her office he stopped halfway out the door, turned and said: "But not Empress Zeita!" As she interpreted it, for him somewhere there had to be a pure woman—if not his mother, then the empress. (When she wrote this incident up later in America, she changed the Austrian empress into Mrs. Roosevelt.) The early psychoanalytic experience with such matters is still relevant to much contemporary thought about sexual learning. Within psychoanalysis it would take someone of Reich's daring to propose that what was necessary to abolish neurosis would be a fundamental rearrangement of Western middle-class family life.

The early chapters of Helene's book prepared the way for what she felt most at home in talking about as an original contribution: the significance of the functions of reproduction for feminine psychology. Her paper at Salzburg had encapsulated the ideas she developed in her first book. The official summary of her presentation is a good outline of how she proceeded in her more sustained *Psychoanalysis of the Sexual Functions of Women*.

. . . the speaker discussed the psychic reactions of women to the physiological processes which accompany the function of reproduction. These processes—the onset of menstruation, its periodical recurrence, pregnancy, parturition and the climacteric—involve powerful upheavals in the economy of the libido and assume the proportions of traumatic experiences, partly in the form of a "blow to narcissism" and partly as a result of the conflicts which arise between the individualistic (ego-libidinal) and the reproductive tendencies. The speaker described these conflicts and the manner in which they are normally surmounted. She gave special consideration to the possible fates of the libido during pregnancy and to the mother's relation to the child before birth. The process of delivery was defined as the final result of the struggle between different libidinal tendencies. The psychic situation of the woman after parturition was finally touched upon.[7]

As late as a case history published in 1918, Freud had held that the little boy's earliest, most intimate attachment was to his father. Although beginning in the 1920s Freud had been specific in suggesting that the Oedipus complex of the boy could reverse the "positive" feelings (attachment to the parent of the opposite sex and rivalry toward the parent of the same sex), he was loath to see boys experiencing a normal identification with the mother. Freud could concede the young man's passivity to a father; but an early identification with a mother meant more psychological frailty in men than Freud wanted to acknowledge. Male development is now seen as less straightforward than early analysis supposed; and "this vulnerability predisposes to the high incidence of gender pathology in men."[8] A young man, who is expected to be socially dominant and a leader, gets the message that he must break his ties to his mother; while eroticism may be easier for a man, his gender identity is now thought to be more fragile than Freud had supposed.

Freud understood the mother as an object of sexual desire and a source of sensual pleasure. But he did not emphasize the mother's protective functions, and he failed to mention the mother as a figure on whom the child at an early age establishes a legitimate dependency. By and large Freud took for granted the nurturing functions of a mother. He did not exclude the mother's part in the psychopathology of male patients; but he saw her mainly as either a seductress into an oedipal situation or the source of adult homosexual conflicts.

Helene was not the only analyst at the time who began to emphasize the neglected role of the mother. Rank, Groddeck, and Ferenczi were all coming to similar conclusions, although each did so in ways which were characteristic of his own point of view. Rank and Ferenczi, for example, were interested in new approaches to therapeutic technique. Helene was the one analyst, however, to look at motherhood primarily from the perspective of its significance for female psychology.

Her Salzburg paper, to her chagrin, was never cited by Freud, although she mentioned it at the outset of *Psychoanalysis of the Sexual Functions of Women.* (He was absent from that congress, and all succeeding ones, as a result of his illness.) Despite the warmth of Helene's personal relationship with Freud, the issue of priorities now arose between them. (In her writings she later touched on the problem of unconscious plagiarism.[9]) He saw her book before its acceptance for publication, and in his office they discussed her recent work on female psychology. Over forty years later she still remembered the intensity with which he told her that before reading her monograph he already had had some of the thoughts which appeared in her writing. At the time she was astonished, although her intimate knowledge of his difficulties with Tausk had prepared her for his competitiveness with men. Her book was scheduled to appear before his own first essay on femininity. She regarded her failure to insist on the relative independence with which she had arrived at her ideas as an abdication on her part.

She was disappointed when, in the fall of 1925, Anna Freud read her father's paper, "Some Psychical Consequences of the Anatomical Distinction Between the Sexes," and there was no mention of any of Helene's prior work. Her book had appeared on schedule, and she attributed it to Anna Freud's jealousy that there was no reference to her. In the published version of Freud's paper, however, a concluding paragraph, apparently not part of Anna Freud's presentation, acknowledged the work of others in this area. Knowing Freud's earlier anxiety that others might take from him without acknowledgment, one can see how muted the great prewar battles with Adler and Jung had become.

> In the valuable and comprehensive studies on the masculinity and castration complexes in women by Abraham (1921), Horney (1923) and Helene Deutsch (1925) there is much that touches closely on what I have written but nothing that coincides with it completely, so that here again I feel justified in publishing this paper.[10]

It is hard to know how realistic Helene's resentment against Freud was, and it may be that her reproach against Anna Freud was unjustified, since Freud's last paragraph might not have been written when she presented his paper. In keeping with her sense of being special, Helene did not like being cited with two others, although she respected them both as at least her equals. (She minded even more being later cited[11] by Freud in association with Jeanne Lampl-de Groot and Ruth Mack Brunswick, since she did not think they were on the same level with herself.) The incident was so emotionally charged that she suspected that in referring to her book Freud was ignoring her earlier

Salzburg contribution. Other pupils of Freud's last years felt he had lifted concepts from them without due acknowledgment. Yet these disciples were so close to Freud that it was all too easy for them to confuse their ideas with his.

Throughout her early thinking on female psychology, Helene took for granted Freud's own contrast between passivity (femaleness) and activity (maleness), which has continued to distress current thinkers about sexual distinctions. (At the end of his life Freud tried to qualify his earlier position; and Helene in *The Psychology of Women* took a different tack.) Creative acts especially seem to entail elements of the opposite sex.

But she compounded the issue, like Freud, by linking masochism with femininity (and sadism with masculinity). Aside from discounting the everyday overtones to the specialized vocabulary she was using, it ought not to be supposed that she was advocating one or the other for either sex. Analysts had regularly treated both men and women who, for example, needlessly blamed themselves. The unconscious self-infliction of suffering was a main object of psychoanalytic treatment. For women, masochism might mean sexual inhibition, or a passion for men who mistreat them. (In a 1930 paper Helene sought to understand more about feminine masochism—a problem she felt she knew all too intimately—and its relation to frigidity.)

With all the so-called advances since 1925, it is still true that evidence supports the notion that women more than men suffer from mental problems; they pay more visits to doctors, take up more places in hospitals, and use pills more frequently. According to Freud's belief, which Helene was elaborating, the differentiation between the sexes imposes a greater burden on the female, and leads to the unhappy state of affairs of women being more neurotic. In Freud's view, neurosis was a sign of civilization, and the Oedipus complex an achievement.

In keeping with the emphasis within early psychoanalysis on traumatic aspects of personality development, Helene sought to pinpoint those crises that were specifically female. According to her thinking, adolescence was the point at which "femaleness" gets established. It may well be, however, that she was mistaken in thinking that human bisexuality lasts as long as she supposed. Instead, as analysts like Melanie Klein and Karen Horney were afterward to postulate, early primary vaginal sensations may help account for later feminine characteristics. Although Helene had observed that "from earliest infancy distinctive features appear in boys and girls," she still stuck to the idea that femininity was some kind of retreat from disappointed maleness.

Development from the so-called phallic phase, which Helene, following Freud, had made so much of, may be relatively secondary. By 1932 she acknowledged that analysts had been too absorbed by the phase of phallic organization, which is identical in boys and girls, and she pointed to elements in her 1925 book which stressed earlier, uniquely female aspects of personality development. These may sound almost like theological points; but they had the implication that feminine castration anxiety must be relegated to a far lesser role. At the time of *The Psychology of Women,* and even more strongly in her mid-nineties, Helene could express her dislike for the whole notion of penis envy. If her work had unwittingly helped reinforce sexual stereotyping, it would not be the first time that an apparent innovation had unanticipated reactionary results.

Entirely aside from the issue of penis envy, in discussing the beginning of menstruation, still considered a special problem, Helene was touching on at least some of the possible unconscious fantasies. Much more is understood now than in 1925 about the psychology of menstrual tensions. But modern medicine has benefited from her particular use of Freud's ideas. For example, gynecological evidence has accumulated on the psychogenic components of absence of bleeding (amenorrhea), as well as excessive pain (dysmenorrhea); even organic gynecologic problems are understood to have secondary psychological aspects.

At least in passing Helene explicitly acknowledged the special role that "cultural conditions" play for women as opposed to men, in enforcing a long delay before the attainment of sexual maturity and the possibility of satisfaction. This would help account, according to her, for the exceptional place of fantasy life in the young girl's experiences. Although as a theorist her orientation was overwhelmingly intrapsychic, she realized the way a feminine code of abstinence could have consequences for the attraction of the forbidden.

Among the pubertal fantasies that still sound plausible Helene mentioned the "parthenogenetic" one of a self-produced child. Later she would use the idea of immaculate conception to help account for mothering, as well as illegitimate pregnancies. In general, she thought of intellectual production "in the male manner" as a sublimation of this aspiration for independence. She considered herself to have been spiritually fertilized by her contact with Freud, but it would have been better if she had been able to see how social forces could play a role in "the sporadic appearance of individual women whose intellectual achievements are completely original."

One chapter in her book, entitled "the act of defloration," highlights how different the world she grew up in was from our own. In late-nineteenth-century Poland, ritual defloration, especially among the peasantry, was still a common practice. In that whole era, of course, virginity had a value that may be hard to appreciate today. For certain social classes, for example, a woman would be considered unmarriageable if she was not a virgin. Shyness and reserve in a woman, and the need to be courted, could be especially attractive, making a man feel he was a conqueror in overcoming obstacles. What we know as the sexual double standard was firmly embedded in a whole psychosocial structure. Entirely aside from the specific horror of venereal infection, contraception was harder then and pregnancy (or abortions) relatively more dangerous. The so-called sexual freedom in our own time has to be put in its cultural context. For us to consider ourselves more cosmopolitan than the society from which Helene came would be to repeat the ethnocentric error of mistakenly believing in the superiority of a later culture to an earlier one.

In writing specifically about the psychology of the sex act, Helene emphasized that for the woman, unlike the man, coitus becomes part of a much broader process: pregnancy and labor are possible sequels. It is sometimes erroneously thought that it is a recent idea that processes of giving birth are an aspect of female sexuality. Maternity was, according to Helene, so crucial to femininity that she proposed a psychological explanation for the different reactions of men and women in postcoital relaxation. (She later extended the significance of a woman's simultaneously playing the role of mother and child to female homosexuality as well.)

Helene thought that sexual contrasts help account for the strengths and capacities appropriate for men and women. She would later propose that one of a woman's greatest sources of talent—and here she was speaking with pride of her profession as a psychoanalyst—lies in the ability to identify with people. She was living at a time when, at least for the middle class, women had to live primarily through others; yet motherliness and vicarious living are also intrinsically interconnected.

In writing a chapter on frigidity and sterility, she was breaking new ground—but also calling attention to some of her own personal problems. Frigidity was not a subject to which Freud ever paid anything like the attention he gave to the symptom of male impotence. Helene had all along in *Psychoanalysis of the Sexual Functions of Women* thought of the woman as potentially "a fully enjoying partner," whatever stereotypes there might have been at the time about female sexual coldness. By 1930 she had come to believe that sexual disturbance is "emphatically not in direct ratio to the severity of the neurosis"; according to her, in severe neuroses there can be no frigidity, and some "healthy" women are able to tolerate sexual inhibition well. (No doubt by then she was reacting to some of Reich's simplifications.)

Over the years some of her views changed significantly. In 1925 clitoral masturbation was implicitly being discouraged by considering it, in accordance with Freud's terms, a "masculine" trait in women; Helene joined Freud in hypothesizing the necessity of the mature woman's transferring to the vagina earlier pregenital trends. By 1945, six years after Freud's death, she held that with a clitoris and a vagina the woman possesses "two sexual organs."[12] Later on she evolved even further, consistent with the thinking of some other analysts; she accepted "the central role of the clitoris" as a "biological destiny."[13]‡

In 1925, however, frigidity, like any other neurotic symptom, was to her an expression of unconscious conflicts. This outlook would be at odds, for

‡ Cf. Epilogue: A Woman's Psychology, p. 340.

example, with those sex therapists today who insist on the power of ignorance and lack of communication; these practitioners would not consider frigidity as globally as a psychoanalyst, instead isolating it and breaking it down into discrete entities. In contrast, a Freudian like Helene interpreted frigidity as an outgrowth of basic psychological blockage. Psychoanalysis held as a matter of principle that the alleviation of any individual symptom was less important than a fundamental change in character. A successfully treated symptom could in theory simply be replaced by a substitute. Yet when it came in practice to handling sexual dysfunctions, Freud and his immediate disciples could be clinically down to earth. Freud is known, for example, to have prescribed contraceptives for the sake of providing more pleasure, and not to have ignored details connected with something as important as potency.

Whereas men characteristically can have a split in their emotional life, so that sex and love are separated, Helene proposed that women suffered from a different dilemma. Under the then "cultural conditions," she specified, women have difficulty maintaining desire where they cannot love.* If sex means different things to men and women, then according to the logic of Freud's concept of sublimation (a redirection of the aim of sexual energy), one ought not to be surprised to find them each seeking contrasting creative outlets. But Helene ignored the full implications of the issue of what social opportunities for work might be readily available.

Throughout the history of psychoanalysis, however, the therapeutic bias of an individualistic and rationalist treatment procedure has affected its theory. (One has only to think of the early use of surrogate sex partners by Masters and Johnson to dramatize the contrast between the "talking cure" and one early phase of sex therapy.) In large measure Helene too was guilty of isolating female development from that of men. She wrote, for example, how a woman's failure at the mother-child relationship could mean frigidity, without explicitly acknowledging that for a woman to consider a man as a child could be infantilizing for him, and lead in turn to frigidity. But there is just so far anyone can go in self-knowledge, and it would be inhuman to demand that she have full insight into the sources of what may have gone wrong between her and Felix.

A key to understanding Freud's whole perspective is that he saw sexuality in terms of the evolutionary value system of procreation. Helene made her basic differentiation between male and female accordingly. In 1925 she thought of the vagina as a "duplication" of the woman's ego, and talked about how the penis could "develop into an erogenous zone before the devel-

---

* In 1944 she developed this reasoning in a different and interesting way. She wrote that

> Men who cannot sexually desire the object they love, and vice versa, are numerous, but they are neurotic. The same split in erotic feelings is encountered in girls, but . . . rarely with regard to the love object. In them, this split affects themselves, that is to say, they either lower themselves to the status of a purely sexual object or raise themselves to that of an "unattainable."[14]

opment of its sexual function." In her view, to the woman the act of parturition becomes the conclusion of the sex act begun in coitus; she tried to account for neurotic fears and forebodings associated with childbirth, as well as certain graver postpartum difficulties.

Pregnancy itself represents a special emotional upheaval for the woman, and subsequent literature has followed up on her early suggestions; it is now considered a normal "maturational" phase. The birth of an infant, Helene had held, brings about in a woman "a change in the whole attitude toward life." The woman's relation to the child not only continues the bond to her sexual partner, but also revives the love for her father. The newborn child at the same time is the recipient of its mother's ambivalences.

In keeping with the state of analytic thinking of the time, Helene excluded the role of a woman's relationship to her own mother during this period of exceptional stress; later on, in *The Psychology of Women,* she explored this theme. But in 1925 she was ahead of her time in emphasizing the special preciousness of a child to its mother. The child can be such an immense gratification to a woman because it embodies her ego ideal, in a way which—since it is "biologically prefigured"—can never be exactly matched for a man.

Parental disappointments are inevitable. And from the moment of the child's birth the unity with its mother can never be completely peaceable. Without ignoring the big part which "physical factors, actual living conditions, etc." play, Helene concentrated on the independent role of psychological conflicts. While some women will never become full people without reproducing themselves, and reach physical and psychical prime in pregnancy, others suffer as an "uncomfortable appendix" of their child. Helene, although a pathfinder within psychoanalysis and psychiatry, did not discuss the possibility, bound to be unsettling to all Freudian theory, that some women might be better off not bearing children; to have pursued this point would have been to question her own urgent need to break with Lieberman.

In accord with some of the most recent arguments in behalf of natural childbirth, Helene proposed that the use of drugs to diminish birth pangs has unfavorable psychological results. Although narcosis may eliminate the phase of "emptiness and disappointment," it also entails feelings of strangeness; she thought it had the consequence that "the joyful new attitude to the child is not so ecstatic and not so surprising in its intensity as it is when birth takes its natural course." It is partly due to an appreciation of psychodynamic factors that the use of general anesthesia in labor has been restricted to surgical procedures, or as a last resort.

Although Helene did not touch on the man's possible feminine wishes, she was aware how the woman's relationship to her husband, in terms of her inner life, is necessarily complicated by the act of having given birth. Children do seem to involve a woman's sexual disengagement from her husband. The young child can become a competitor of hers, just at the time when her own maternal feelings are being withdrawn from her mate toward their infant. In her weakened state, and out of identification with her newborn, she may feel childlike herself. But Helene did not underestimate the impact of specifically chemical forces, especially in helping to account for the postpartum psychotic clinical syndromes.

It is odd that, in contrast to *Psychoanalysis of the Sexual Functions of Women,* so much theoretical work since then has sought to undermine the inevitability of bisexuality.[15] Of course the word "bisexual" has historically been used in a wide variety of contexts, from fetal development to manifest homosexual behavior; and it may have been put to authoritarian clinical purposes. Unfortunately, psychoanalysts have been apt to stigmatize bisexuality in women as a "phallic fixation" on the clitoris, or a consequence of the wish to reject femininity.

Although Helene did not, as she would in 1944, connect her psychological theories to any greater social premium on masculine qualities, her book had been an effort to demonstrate the exceptionally strong part played by bisexual trends in feminine psychology. She was trying to ensure a conception of normality that allowed for the existence of multiple possibilities in women. It should not be necessary, she thought then, to advocate the abolition of concepts of maleness and femaleness, in favor of uniformity, in order critically to scrutinize assumptions about sex-typical behavior.

In trying to assert the moral equality of women, writers may have involved psychoanalysis in new conformist uses. To the degree that people are held to be creatures of social forces, it becomes necessary to abandon the hope of instincts being at odds with culture for the sake of human autonomy.[16] Evidence for developmental differences in the sexes persists, and ought to be morally welcome. Any generalizations are bound to have their drawbacks; but if we have only begun to understand what might conceivably be innately feminine or masculine, and the role society can play, it would be perverse in terms of human freedom to try to obliterate the distinctions between the sexes. Furthermore, the concept of psychological "normality" is in itself an ethically questionable one, and Freud and his early followers could rightly be skeptical about the value of "health." At the same time Helene was resentful of Felix and grew contemptuous of his inadequacies; the reversal of the usual sexual roles and the violation of customary cultural norms became a grievance to her.

Malfunctioning is easier to discuss; and Helene wound up her comprehensive account of female sexuality by describing the way menopause can have special meanings for a woman. The "post-genital" period was, in her view, a second time in which, from an evolutionary perspective, male and female no longer exist. Yet her case material, which she allowed herself to use here, illustrated the special consequences for the woman of this particular stage in life.

It is impossible not to suspect that she was at the same time trying to account for her own extended residence in Berlin:

> . . . typical changes of behavior take place in which the parallels we have . . . established between the libido of the woman at the climacteric and the girl at puberty manifest themselves in emotional life. The renewed boost of vaginal cathexis at the first phase is felt by the woman herself to be a tremendous uplift. She feels like a young girl, believes herself able to make a fresh start in life, as she says, feels ready for any passion, etc. She starts keeping a diary as she did when she was a girl, develops enthusiasm for some abstract idea as she did then, changes her behavior to her family as she did before, leaves home for the same psychical reasons as girls do at puberty, etc.

Entering her forties, Helene had every reason to be concerned about the approaching onset of menopause; but her theories were multifaceted rather than deterministic. A woman at that time of life can have

> manifold and individually various forms taken by sexual feeling. Many women who were frigid during the reproductive period now become sexually sensitive, and others become frigid for the first time, generally in a hitherto monogamous marital relationship that can no longer satisfy their increased narcissism. Others who have put up well with frigidity now begin to demonstrate all its typical concomitant phenomena: changes of mood, unbalanced behavior and irritability set in and make life a torment for the woman herself and those about her.

Helene noted the narcissistically determined increase of libido, as well as the heightened need to be desired and loved. A woman's life, however, by no means has to be restricted to issues connected with childbearing, especially given the "biologically revived bisexual constitution."

Helene pointed out some unique possibilities for sublimation that arise after menstruation has ceased. She concluded her book on an altogether optimistic note about the efficacy of psychoanalysis as prophylaxis, which was in accord with the hopes of her new profession in the 1920s. Later clinical skepticism weakened her initial enthusiasm. With the faith that knowledge ultimately means power, and in the conviction that how we think affects our behavior, she had singled out femininity, then regarded by analysts as especially problematic, to be her specialty. Whatever the inevitable limitations to her pioneering ideas, her work still stands as a memorable introduction to her professional concern with the complexities in a woman's development.

14

The Movement

At the time of the appearance of *Psychoanalysis of the Sexual Functions of Women,* Helene was the first president of the Training Institute of the Vienna Psychoanalytic Society. Bernfeld became vice-president, and Anna Freud the secretary. All the patients who came for training in Vienna had to be interviewed by Helene; she looked for their empathy, their capacity to identify with others, as well as their control over narcissism. These ideal expectations were designed to ensure a measure of objectivity in candidates. Her students included the next generation's leading analysts, for instance, Ernst Kris and Erik H. Erikson. Until she left for America in 1935 she continued as director of the institute, and played a key role in Freud's immediate circle.

Feminist critiques of Freud's ideas have been abundant; but recently some feminist literature has adopted a different attitude toward psychoanalysis—it has been seen not only as a reflection of the psychological oppression of women, but a source of insight into their potential liberation. In terms of her life and career, Helene became a powerful leader, and an inspiration to many younger women colleagues. Some senior American analysts have reported that it is easier to place referral patients with women than with male therapists.

The exact steps by which Helene succeeded in becoming the leader of the new institute are not entirely clear. The need was obvious, especially given Freud's illness. (In his absence from the society, Rank, as vice-president, had been presiding over meetings.) With Berlin as a model of training Vienna needed its own teaching facilities. The Ambulatorium policlinic had about thirty-five to forty patients under treatment, but neither Freud nor the most talented younger analysts wanted Hitschmann to play a central future role.

Helene not only had a secure ally in Freud but also had the confidence of the potential staff she would need for teaching purposes. Her writing while she was away in Berlin sealed her self-confidence in the mission she undertook.

One of the younger analysts recalled in 1973 a version of the unconventional way Helene had undertaken to set the institute going. In contrast to the greater formality in Berlin, not to mention the future rigidities elsewhere, the Viennese then thought that one should become a training analyst for future practitioners when a candidate wanted to go to you for analysis. As Dr. Grete Bibring (later head of the Department of Psychiatry at the Beth Israel Hospital in Boston, Massachusetts) remembered it, she and her husband—and two other analytic couples—helped get things under way.

> In our juvenile enthusiasm, we set up an institute in a week. Helene Deutsch came from Berlin and told us about the institute there. I remember I was in the Ambulatorium listening to her story, and we decided that this was a good thing for us, too, and that Helene Deutsch was naturally the right person to be its first chairman, because she knew all about it.

Helene had six official documents prepared, for the Bibrings, the Sterbas, and the Waelders. According to Grete Bibring:

> We had certificates signed by Freud; I don't know how Helene Deutsch persuaded him into doing that. They were signed by Freud and by Helene Deutsch and stated that we had graduated from the Vienna Institute, which hadn't quite existed yet . . . So there were six certificates for the first graduates of the Vienna Institute, which we almost wrote ourselves because we thought we couldn't be teachers in an institute if we hadn't graduated from one.[1]

These people were among the newest adherents of analysis in Vienna. Robert Waelder, for example, was a Ph.D. who had come to Freud's circle while Helene was in Berlin; he became librarian of the society, an editor of *Imago,* and was immediately recognized as a promising theoretician. Subsequently all the members of this group became important figures in America: the Bibrings in Boston, the Sterbas in Detroit, Robert Waelder in Philadelphia, and Jenny Waelder-Hall in Baltimore. (According to the official membership lists, as opposed to Grete Bibring's memory, Waelder's future wife, Dr. Jenny Pollak, became an associate member—a new category introduced in February–March 1925—only in 1928. Both Dr. Edward Bibring, later treasurer of the Vienna society, and his wife, Grete, were also associate members in 1925, as was Dr. Richard Sterba, whose wife, Dr. Edith Alberti, became an associate member in 1926.) The phase of apprenticeship was ending, and a formal school now being set up; by the early 1930s, the number of candidates had grown from six (in 1924) to thirty-five, and no longer was the majority of students trained virtually free. Among these new candidates many more were foreigners than were Austrian.

Helene had succeeded in arranging things so that Freud's desire not to exclude nonmedical practitioners could be fully honored. His interest in lay analysis was in fact an excellent ground for setting up the structure of the institute side by side with Hitschmann's Ambulatorium, instead of amalgamating the two as in Berlin. By making Hitschmann (along with Federn) part of her teaching staff, Helene performed the appropriate gesture of appeasement toward the earliest generation of Freud's Viennese supporters; through adding Nunberg and the brilliant young Reich to her roster of teachers, she ensured a promising beginning representation among psychiatrists.

The Training Institute was officially inaugurated in January 1925, with fifteen students. As Helene announced:

> The purpose of the Institute is in the first instance to train future psychoanalysts and, further, to extend the knowledge of psychoanalytic theory, especially in its bearing on education. The training of psychoanalysts includes (1) their own analysis for purposes of instruction; (2) theoretical training by means of lectures, seminars, demonstrations and the use of the Institute's library; (3) practical training by conducting analyses under the supervision of the Institute. The patients so analyzed are mainly drawn from the clinic of the Vienna Psychoanalytic Society. The course covers two years.[2]

The training committee, besides Helene, was made up of Bernfeld, Anna Freud, Hitschmann, Nunberg, Reich, and Theodor Reik (but not Federn). Teaching continued at the Ambulatorium, and the Vienna institute never achieved the level of the Berlin one. Her post at the Training Institute was enough in itself to ensure Helene's place in the history of psychoanalysis.

Within the Vienna society Helene's title over the years was described in various ways: sometimes principal of the Training Institute, also director of the training committee, as well as president of the training committee. One suspects that "director" of the institute was not quite adequate since it was a sore point that Federn (and not Helene) had become vice-president of the society as a whole on October 28, 1924; since Freud retained the presidency but did not attend public meetings, Federn presided. For the small gathering of twelve analysts who met every few weeks around an oval table at Freud's apartment, Federn was in charge of selecting which half-dozen members of the society would occasionally attend. Helene had sufficient standing to ensure one of the six regular invitations. And by virtue of her office at the institute, she was automatically a member of the council of the society. (When Robert Jokl asked for a percentage of the fees from an analyst to whom he had sent a patient, the council—with Freud's help—had to decide on a superior ethical principle; even though Jokl could be described as a "servile" follower of Freud's, the master strongly disapproved of such conduct.)

Helene's position within the Vienna group also ensured her place within the International Psychoanalytic Association. She first reported on the activities of the Vienna institute before the ninth congress in Bad Homburg in September 1925. According to her then, the organization was officially founded in October 1924. She paid tribute both to the Berlin model as well as to the Ambulatorium's prior practical training of students. She stressed the institute's concern with the quality, rather than the quantity, of the candidates it accepted for training, and its openness for educationists to study there. Hitschmann, as a member of the training committee, could take part in selecting candidates.

In keeping with Freud's own concerns, Helene maintained as an objective that his "discoveries . . . be preserved from the effects of erosion or misuse"; a guiding principle was "depth before breadth." Of special interest to her, however, was the subject of supervised analyses. Freud might have had his own idiosyncratic ways of overseeing the work of his disciples, but Helene was trying to formalize these procedures.

> Like our colleagues in Berlin we attach special importance to the conducting of analyses under supervision. Experience shows that this is not only extraordinarily valuable for the beginner but also gives both the instructor and the student himself insight into the latter's mental attitude and capacity attained. Thus it was once found that a young student who was conducting an analysis under supervision had difficulties in carrying it through owing to his own unresolved conflicts. The insight thus acquired caused him to return to the analyst who had conducted his instructional analysis, and though this delayed his training it certainly made his later analytic work easier.[3]

At the next congress in Innsbruck in September 1927, Helene served on the International Training Commission, which was set up to maintain standards of the individual member societies. Max Eitingon, a wealthy Russian follower of Freud's who resided in Berlin, was the leader in this particular endeavor. Rado gave a survey of the building up of the analytic curriculum; Sach lectured on training analyses; and Helene spoke on the subject of supervised analyses, which were known as "control" analyses. Although it was intended that these three essays be published in full, they—along with the discussions—"remained behind the closed doors"[4] of the International Training Committee,* and none appeared in print. In 1935 she again returned to the same subject, at a conference held in Vienna. It was shortly before Helene left for the United States, but she was unable to attend the scheduled meeting because of ill health; Anna Freud then read Helene's paper "on the principles and practices of the Vienna society."

Throughout the period from 1924–1935 Helene was known as one of the greatest teachers in psychoanalysis. (Dr. Abram Kardiner recalled her from 1921–22 as a Helen of Troy, brilliant and beautiful, "Freud's darling".) For

---

* In 1929 she was nominated to a new subcommittee of the ITC, and was soon developing "a common training syllabus."[5] On these committees she worked with the Swiss Dr. Philip Sarasin, for years a lover of Helene's Polish friend Dr. Solomea Kempner, also an analyst.

young students of psychoanalysis at that time Berlin seemed a better place for training. Around Freud, the scientific-minded, like Nunberg, tended to be dull or crusty, whereas the more interesting people, like Wilhelm Stekel, were volatile and unorthodox. Helene and Felix Deutsch were probably the liveliest in the Viennese psychoanalytic circle.

In addition to her reputation as a writer and lecturer, Helene was much sought after as a training analyst and supervisor. Her own seminars (which started at nine-thirty at night) became remarkable experiences for students.[6] She could listen to a case presentation for hours, and then be able to pull the threads together, remembering details the candidate had reported. After a full day's analytic practice, she might conduct such a seminar until one-thirty in the morning, and have the stamina to revive and want to go on to another case. (As she reflected in retrospect, evidently she was not eager to go home.)

Her thoughts on supervision remained unpublished until 1983.[7] Even though she had her paper translated into English, she did not publish it in her lifetime. Perhaps it was a question of timing. Once she left for America there was a new social situation to adjust to; even within psychoanalysis she had to face the demands of a bureaucratizing movement. (Unlike in Vienna she eventually was obliged to keep written records.) But, in addition, she shared Freud's own reluctance to publish on technique. Although technical papers might appear to help beginners, they could also contribute, in the hands of the insecure, to unanticipated rigidities. Her immediate audiences, both in 1927 and in 1935, needed her ideas; but generally she thought issues involving training and control analyses had an illusory appeal to those who might be better taught by experience.

The record of the Innsbruck congress does report her as having given a bread-and-butter account of the activities of her institute. She concluded, however, on a note which underlay her similar concern for protecting the autonomy of candidates which can be found in her 1935 paper:

> Our Institutes are all built up on the same ideas, and in their most essential points their program is the same. Their international nature has not yet declared itself. It would be a great advantage if, by an interchange of students, this international character of the training could be expressed. By dividing the course into the students' personal analyses, their theoretical instruction and their practical training this contact between the different training centers could easily be established. For instance, they could be analyzed at one Institute, the second part of the training could be undertaken at another, and the third at yet another. This could be more easily arranged than an interchange of teachers, who are more or less bound to their centres of work.[8]

Her own past told her how geography can help reinforce independence, emancipating students from educational as well as therapeutic transferences.

Freud himself believed that promising candidates could derive special benefit from trusting their own judgment. As late as 1922 he had brushed aside the uncertainties of Bernfeld, who had joined the Vienna society in 1919, about whether to follow the Berlin example of a didactic analysis before beginning practice. Freud's answer was: " 'Nonsense. Go right ahead. You certainly will have difficulties. When you get into trouble, we will see what we can do about it.' Only a week later he sent me my first didactic case."[9] Although Helene had thought she benefited from an absence of undue supervision at Wagner-Jauregg's clinic during World War I, she had gone to Berlin for a second analysis. As she described the founding of the Vienna training program, "the Berlin institute, which was already extant, provided us with a lead for the first steps of our new venture. All that we had to do was to adapt the experience acquired there to local conditions."

As the head of an educational center Helene was acutely aware of student needs as well as the evaluative task of a supervisor. She thought that Freud had been forced to articulate ideas about technique in order to create a discipline; mainly he expected his followers to stick to free associations, not going into personal reactions too much. As an educator she remained convinced that an emphasis on technique might unduly gratify the quest of young analysts for the fantasy of certainty. In analysis, as in life, there are always going to be problems; since no analysis can be conducted according to a rule book, a place must be reserved for the artistic component to play its part.

Any jargon can undermine a student's self-confidence. In contrast to those analysts who felt that it was possible to construct a uniform method which would be teachable to others, Helene emphasized that good therapeutic results depend on the principle that "within the frame of the technique given by Freud, every individual has his own methods and variants which correspond to his personality . . . [T]he candidate should be permitted to fight his own way through any difficulties and thus retain the personal note in his analytic activity." Helene was therefore inevitably at cross-purposes with herself, as she tried to guide without stultifying. She did not like both analyzing and supervising a candidate, and as a matter of principle she did not do it.

Implicit in her stress on the significance of control analysis was her conviction that a check was needed on the tendency of training analyses to infantilize candidates. Transferences in didactic analyses have a special meaning, since the expectation of becoming an analyst serves as a compensation for a frustrating situation. In 1937 Freud proposed that "for practical reasons" a training analysis "can only be short and incomplete."

> Its main object is to enable his teacher to make a judgment as to whether the candidate can be accepted for further training. It has accomplished its purpose if it gives the learner a firm conviction of the experience of the uncon-

scious, if it enables him, when repressed material emerges, to perceive in himself things which would otherwise be incredible to him, and if it shows him a first sample of the technique which has proved to be the only effective one in analytic work.

The gradual lengthening of training analyses in later years would be hard to reconcile with Freud's 1937 recommendation that "every analyst should periodically—at intervals of five years or so—submit himself to analysis once more, without feeling ashamed of taking this step."[10] Helene shared the Viennese belief that after an analysis has been performed, its effects should be allowed to ferment in a candidate who has therapeutically been left on his own.

In America Helene became more skeptical of control analysis, since it also could become ritualized; a supervisor should not succumb to a candidate's desire to be told what to do. Above all she tried to remain a clinician, and in her discussion about the proper means of encouraging future analysts she felt the needs of the suffering patients ought not to be neglected. Freud's own way of proceeding lay behind her thinking. Her first patients had come from him; from time to time they would discuss these cases, not so much because of his interest in her learning but out of his concern for the patients. Her thoughts on control analysis were initiated by Freud's preoccupation with the welfare of the patients he referred to her. Freud would characteristically remark that if there should be difficulties, he would be willing to see her. Perhaps she saw Freud about a particular patient ten times. He rarely gave advice, on the ground that she necessarily knew the patient much better. If Helene came to distrust the way controls could prolong transferences, she remained in favor of consultations to unravel blind spots in a therapist.

As one of her pupils, Ernst Kris, remarked on the occasion of her seventieth birthday in 1954: "Helene Deutsch's place is a singular and clearly defined one: her work is that of the great clinician."[11] In her paper on supervision she worried about the danger of intellectualization in training. And although she thought she had succeeded in helping patients whom she disliked, it was easier for her to aid those she liked. She concluded that the therapist has to have a positive emotional identification with a patient. The idea that one should treat people one does not like can encourage bad things in a therapist. She thought that a reasonable (not messianic) desire to help need not interfere with the patient's recovery, and that those she had not been involved with she had not "cured." Any such conclusions have to be seen in the light of the typical Viennese skepticism about the limitations of psychoanalysis as therapy.

She ended her paper on supervised analysis with a reference to one of her own technical contributions to the training of analysts: "continuous group control seminars" still exist today. In Vienna Reich's innovations had aroused discussion and controversy about technique. As part of the problem of how to deal with Reich she, as a teacher in a seminar, in 1928–29 presented one of her own cases—that of the "Fate-Neurosis." (In 1930 she recounted publicly the practice at the Clinic of "reporting on the same current case history every week, besides giving single accounts of particular cases."[12]) It was such a wonderful case that she felt it disturbed her work with the patient; she had to have interesting material for the seminar, and she was not as relaxed with the patient as she might otherwise have been. But instead of sterile discussions over technique she thought it better to bring a case and let her students see what Reich would do.

A quarter of a century later she saw the same patient in America, and discussed the case in a paper on psychotherapeutic follow-ups. (She regretted that other analysts were not eager to make a practice of "follow-ups.") Whatever her own changing views, she always remained convinced, as in 1935, that it is a mistake for a control analyst to consider "it is his task to offer the candidate something which we have never had—and probably never shall have—in analytic technique: a complete, learnable entirety which can be taught by thorough and regular drilling."[13]

During the years she led the institute, Helene was able to cultivate a whole generation of analysts. One of the secrets of her success as a teacher was her ability to learn from those less experienced than she. Having already "arrived" herself, she was able to be a patroness for others. She founded a Saturday-night group, called the Black Cat Card Club, which met informally at her apartment once a week. (Her personal friends were now almost all analysts, although she got on well with the Viennese painter Joseph Floch;[14] she commissioned him to do a portrait of Felix, and other analysts purchased his work as well.) Those who came on Saturdays included the Bibrings, the Hartmanns, the Hoffers, the Krises, the Waelders, all of them about ten years younger than she, yet destined to be leading orthodox analysts in later years. She had the established reputation and an "in" with Freud. Although ultimately she survived almost every one of them—those who were still alive sent her a gift for her eightieth birthday in 1964—in the end she owed much of her stature to having been an inspiring figure in the early professional life of those who carried on Freud's school after his death.

Ostensibly they had gathered for the sake of a relatively simple card game—poker would have been too absorbing—but while playing they could concentrate on analytic problems. (Helene arranged for a big dinner to be served as well.) Perhaps the most notable aspect of this group was its exclusion of some of the older analysts, such as Hitschmann and Federn. She got on poorly with both of them, partly out of identification with Freud's view of their capacities. Federn preferred motherly women to career-oriented types; Hitschmann too resented her, and later accused her of "dictatorship" in the Boston Psychoanalytic Society and of being responsible for his exclusion from a governing committee there. In Vienna the younger analysts did not want to meet socially with the old-line analysts; they felt Freud was stuck with them because they had supported him so early. If Helene could be demanding she was always fun to be around.

Proud and aloof, Helene nonetheless joined in the celebration of Freud's birthdays; she and Felix would send orchids and a telegram on May 6. When Martin was old enough to go off to school in Switzerland at the age of seventeen (1934), it was considered fitting for him to say good-bye by visiting Freud beforehand with his father; Freud gave the boy a telescope and wrote something in a book for him. Afterward Freud reported to Helene about her son's activities in Switzerland, on the basis of what he had heard during one of his analyses.

Helene held it a matter of personal honor not to join in the kind of active adoration of Freud indulged in by some female rivals in the Vienna society, such as Ruth Mack Brunswick, who received one of the rings he bestowed on special favorites. Helene's self-preservative capacities prevented her from becoming as vulnerable as others around Freud, but she was still jealous of those who rose in Freud's special esteem. One blow for Helene involving Ruth Brunswick concerned Freud's patient the Wolf-Man. When in 1926 he returned again in need of treatment, Freud might have made amends to Helene for terminating her analysis on his behalf if he had sent the Wolf-Man to her. But now, in making a gift of this patient to Ruth Brunswick, who wrote his case up once more, Freud seemed to have compounded the initial offense to Helene. Even though she dedicated herself to forwarding his cause, in her own mind she did not want to be like the others. She could have had more direct personal contact with Freud in his later years had she so desired; she knew his dependence on women, and his ability to surrender to their power.

While Ruth Brunswick drew closer to Freud, Helene stood back; she had the better mind of the two, and a more stable marriage (Ruth divorced from her second husband twice and died under suspicious circumstances[15]). Helene could easily accept as a rival someone like Lou Andreas-Salomé, who had been a great beauty and had had famous lovers, or Marie Bonaparte, a royal princess; but she felt disdainful of less eminent women like Ruth Brunswick or Jeanne Lampl-de Groot, who, as members of Freud's court, developed toward him what Helene regarded as neurotic clinging transferences.

It may have been partly with her own quiet seclusion in mind that she later wrote of Freud's pupils:

> While the less gifted expressed their ambivalence in a reactively increased dependence and in the over-evaluation of analysis . . . , the more gifted denied this dependence in a more direct but still scientific form and separated themselves from the group in either a noisy and hostile or in a more veiled and passive manner.[16]

She watched from a distance as Ruth Brunswick, not entirely unlike Tausk before her, tried to draw closer to Freud personally. Compared to some mod-

ern analysts Helene may have been cool and distant, but compared to Ruth
Brunswick she seemed more the therapist than the psychological observer.
Ruth Brunswick knew that Freud did not appreciate Helene's kind of temperamentalism, but their scientific work was so considerable that there were
grounds for the women's jealousy of each other.

Helene communicated with Freud mainly for the sake of interviews to be
arranged about patients and candidates. Her reputation made her an obvious
training analyst to try to get; in the view of many professionals she was the
very best, assuming Freud himself was unavailable. She functioned for almost
eleven years in her official capacity at the institute without any bureaucratic
backstopping. When she came to the United States her successors wrote to
her from Vienna because they could not find any records; she told them that
they had been lost in the course of her departure, but they had never existed.

Although Helene had been a rebellious young woman, within psychoanalysis there never was a hint of doctrinal "unorthodoxy" attached to her
name. She remained firmly within the mainstream of Freud's movement. For
her, however, psychoanalysis was a broad church, as opposed to a narrow
sect. For some disciples, the absence of academic, psychiatric or conventional
moral legitimacy encouraged a special religiosity. Ever since the prewar battles over Jung and Adler the history of psychoanalysis has been marked by
controversies and schisms; analysts seemed to have as much trouble with
each other as with the outside world. Some adherents treated Freud's works
talmudically, as they identified with an unconscious need in Freud to be a
believer. (Helene later thought that Freud's atheism represented a struggle
with the "rabbi-voice" in himself.) Just as Helene did not react as a fighter,
even when her ideas were directly, and sometimes unfairly, attacked by
Karen Horney, so she maintained a broad tolerance toward different kinds of
people and ideas that grew up within the movement as a whole.

An emotional prerequisite to becoming an analyst after World War I was
a general acceptance of Freud's version of the earlier ideological struggles.
Helene, while studying at Munich in 1913, might have written Felix to borrow one of Jung's books from Tausk; but she made no effort to keep up with
Jung's later writings or developments within his school. It was hard enough
for Freud's disciples to keep pace with the changes in his own world.

In a vague way Helene knew that Jung had been especially perceptive
about mythology; in old age, when she wrote a book about Dionysus and
Apollo, she had occasion to look into some Jungian literature. She thought
her own knowledge of the difficulties between Tausk and Freud gave her an
insight into the more famous controversies in the history of psychoanalysis,
which she could disparage as of "adolescent" significance. If there were scandal in Jung's private life, such as his having had a long-standing love affair
with Antonia Wolff, a former patient, Helene did not know about it. But she
shared Freud's conviction that the Swiss were, in her words, "big and anti-

*Helene Deutsch in the early 1920s.
She was to be remembered from then
as a Helen of Troy,
brilliant and beautiful,
Freud's darling.*

*Anna Freud (1895–1982).
Freud's daughter and Helene developed
a long-standing rivalry.*

Helene and Martin Deutsch.

Helene and Felix Deutsch.

Felix and Martin Deutsch.

Sigmund Freud in London shortly before his death on September 23, 1939.

Babayaga Farm in Wolfeboro, New Hampshire, which the Deutsches bought in the late 1930s.

Helene Deutsch in 1967. (Credit: Photo by Egone, Boston.)

Semitic." Jung's complicated collaboration with the Nazis was easy to reduce
to an unarguably distasteful moral position; and she mistakenly thought that
none of his followers were Jews.

She felt, as did Freud, less passionately about Adler. In later years in
America she was on formal good terms with Adler's psychiatrist daughter,
Alexandra. Vienna had had an Adlerian school for children; and Helene was
reported by an American analyst to have said in the early 1930s that whatever their theories might have been, it was the best place to send children.
Helene prided herself (as did other adherents of Freud's) on not being a
fanatic, although she had some nagging sense that her ideological convictions
might be humanly damaging. If the Adlerians had succeeded with their Viennese educational experiment, she also knew that a Freudian in Russia, Vera
Schmidt, had made what she called "an absolute fiasco" of founding a school
built on psychoanalytic principles.

Within the Vienna society she disliked Federn and Hitschmann the
most. She had to concede that Federn, at least compared to his friend
Hitschmann, had a certain inner psychological richness. In her view, Freud
had a special affectionate weakness for talented but disorganized types.
Federn was famous in the society for his classic slips of the tongue; he could
invite people like Helene and Felix for dinner and then greet them at the door
with a remark about how nice it was to see them but what were they doing
there. She emphasized the high rate of suicide among Federn's patients, over-
looking the especially difficult kinds of cases he would accept; and she ignored his depressive qualities, which added a humanly attractive feature to
his personality. To her, Freud had a special penchant for unstable people;
what they said might be "crazy" but their sources, she quipped, seemed
reliable. In once claiming that Freud had offered her the position of vice-
presidency first, she maintained that she had protested that she was too young
and not sufficiently well liked by the older men in the society. If Federn knew
that she had turned down what he was so grateful for having received, he
must have resented her all the more. Her marriage to Felix did not inhibit her
from accepting the office; but she said that she did not want to get involved in
the fights that such a position would entail.

Hitschmann, a respected internist, remained another personal difficulty
of hers; she blamed him for envying the way her institute drained off pupils
from the Ambulatorium. Wagner-Jauregg's clinic and law courts often sent
Hitschmann patients who did not have the means to pay for treatment.[17]
Helene made a principle of separating therapy from instruction; ". . . the
Director of the Clinic is always a member of the Training Committee and *vice
versa* some of the members of the Training Committee are collaborators in the
Clinic."[18] She mistakenly believed that Hitschmann was the source behind
Jones's account of Freud's initial reluctance to found a teaching unit in Vi-
enna. She acknowledged that Hitschmann might have been a cultured, witty
man; he was, she remarked, 200 percent "normal", yet with "a small charac-

ter and of restricted intelligence." Helene was convinced that Freud, himself not established in medical circles, despised him; as far as she could tell from her own analysis, Hitschmann was *persona non grata* with Freud. Freud considered that, among other faults, Hitschmann was indiscreet. As chance would have it, Hitschmann ended up later in Boston too; he was to be the first analyst there to become senile, and was the occasion for the enactment a rule about the forcible retirement of future training analysts. (Felix continued to get on with Hitschmann almost as badly as Helene; Felix joked that in his senility Hitschmann had finally reached the core of his personality.) In Vienna Hitschmann "spread the news," Helene claimed, that through her Black Cat Club she was forming her own group. But Freud was told, and was pleased, that a gathering of young analysts met every week at Helene's.

Within the international movement Helene functioned harmoniously. Even though she had no personal liking for Ernest Jones, she admired him because his interests were less narrow than the local Viennese she dealt with. She refused, however, to cooperate with Jones in his biography of Freud. (Felix did.) Jones was a Gentile in a movement that, especially in Vienna, was mainly made up of Jews; and Helene, like Freud, worried about the lack of adequately talented analysts for the future. At the same time a sense of humility kept her from allowing her natural vanity to get out of line. She appreciated that Freud had managed to keep to the end some early pupils he did not admire; when she wrote her 1940 article on "Freud and His Pupils," she worried that it was too derogatory toward his first disciples.

If Helene had allowed her own personal preferences and dislikes to play too large a role, she could never have functioned as successfully as she did as head of the institute. One of the sources of her degree of administrative success was a capacity to function even-handedly. She was not such a believer in orthodoxy that she could not maintain good relations with someone like Schilder; although he was a member of the society, he was a critic of many analytic ideas, altogether more objective as a scientist than most of the others. He needed his hospital affiliations for his research; most of the others in the society considered neurosis a new discovery; they were so preoccupied with their private practice that few would have dared to take a psychotic into analysis. (Schilder went to America in the summer of 1929, at the beginning of an exodus from Europe; Rado became the director of the New York institute in 1931.)

Helene could maintain excellent relations with a wide variety of personality types. Robert Waelder, for example, became a long-time admirer, friend, and associate; she thought he had a remarkable memory and outstanding political acumen. Although she thought very highly of his intellect, she had serious reservations about his psychological capacity; he knew human emotions, she once remarked, "only by hearsay." She could be acerbic about other members of the movement. She considered Groddeck, for example, "a refined quack," and as for Melanie Klein, who had had no scientific training, Helene could dismiss her as a little "confused," or even "a housewife with fantasies." (While Helene was in Berlin, Melanie Klein had little standing, although in England she later—to Helene's mystification—had an enormous impact. Among other motives, Jones had needed her to counter Anna Freud's influence; the two women led rival factions in the British society, which almost ruptured during World War II.[19])

Reich was one of the most talented of the post-World War I students attracted to Freud's group; although he was involved in difficulties from the very beginning of his involvement with the society, Helene got along with him exceptionally well. She regarded him as a fine therapist (and also appreciated him as a good dancer); she welcomed him on her teaching staff. He was interested in developing analytic technique, and concentrated in particular on the importance of analyzing patients' negative transferences.

With hindsight, Helene thought that Reich's search for hostilities in analysands reflected a paranoid disposition on his part. Eventually, at the 1934 congress, Reich was driven out as an analyst; but his relation to Helene remained solid, as other leaders of the society (like Federn) helped force his resignation. Freud himself would not, at this stage of his career, have stooped to confront Reich's "deviating" ideas. In a sense Reich was like the sorcerer's apprentice, carrying out one side of Freud's early liberationist appeal. Reich justifiably contended that Freud's *Civilization and Its Discontents* (1929) was designed to counter the trend in analysis which Reich represented.

Reich tended to think that sexuality was biologically and psychologically identical. He accused the other analysts of being too bourgeois and, in particular, sexually inhibited. Reich's first analyst, Sadger, had also been exclusively preoccupied with the significance of sex. (Later Reich had been analyzed by Federn and Rado.) Reich was, however, no Don Juan; his theoretical views were abstract. Helene disagreed, among other points, with Reich's specific approach to adolescence; for example, Reich thought that when a young person reaches orgastic potency he should have intercourse. Helene was opposed to forcing people ahead of themselves; for her, true freedom was a matter of individual choice, not the result of group pressures. When the issue came up at one of the gatherings at Freud's apartment, he agreed with Helene's own reservations about the proposed advantages of free love. In her view, unfulfilled fantasies were necessary for growth; she thought it was damaging for adolescents to do without genital sublimation. Freud did not like the idea of Reich's being always on the side of full and free sexual gratification.

Reich had little sense of humor and took his own ideas very seriously; a skin disorder had left his face scarlet, in sharp contrast, Helene recalled, to his black eyes. Although his arrogance and self-assurance had long made Freud personally angry (Freud refused to analyze him), Helene not only managed to put up with this turbulent student but protected him. Helene agreed with Reich that the analytic material will change if the negative transferences get interpreted, but she thought that the analyst had to be less active and wait for the patient to bring it up. Analysis requires a working atmosphere, and therefore an analyst must initially nourish the positive transference; but Helene agreed with Reich that others, such as Hanns Sachs, went to the other extreme of avoiding negative transference. In 1934, when Reich consulted her about his problems with other leaders in the movement, Helene concluded he was having a paranoid attack. She thought he had had ideas of grandeur all along, and that his later orgone boxes represented a projection of his own inner feelings. She did not, however, consider him schizophrenic, since he knew how to disguise and control his suspiciousness.

One occasion when Helene did get herself involved in one of the famous controversies in the history of analysis concerned the so-called defection of Rank, a contemporary of hers who had been in Freud's circle since 1906. His wife Beata ("Tola") remained her closest friend both in Vienna and later in Boston. They met for the first time at The Hague congress; Helene was aware that Freud had already mentioned Tola in a footnote to a 1919 paper, as part of welcoming her into the psychoanalytic family. She and Otto had been married in 1918, and Tola was immediately treated as an adopted daughter-in-law. Tola's daughter (an only child, like Martin) became almost like Helene Deutsch's child as well. Both the Ranks had personal as well as intellectual ties to each of the Deutsches. They lived close together in Vienna, and saw each other summers, even after the split between Freud and Rank; by then the Ranks were living much better in Europe than the Deutsches.

Otto Rank had been a special favorite of Freud's since before World War I. In 1923, Helene—like Freud—had been tolerant of Rank's innovations (as well as those of Ferenczi), but she grew alarmed when it seemed that events could drive Rank out of the analytic movement. Freud might have wanted to keep peace with Rank, but some leaders of the International (especially Abraham and Jones) interfered with Freud's personal attitude toward Rank. Freud's cancer created a special threat to Rank's attachment to him. Rank had prepared himself to become Freud's successor, and then Freud survived the illness; after having emotionally detached himself from Freud, in anticipation of his death, Rank had to cope with Freud's continued existence.

Helene thought she should intervene on Rank's behalf with Freud. She never spoke with Rank about the breakdown of his relationship with Freud; she had more of a personal relationship with Freud than Felix did, and she felt it was a job for a woman to do. (Her own previous divided loyalties between her husband and Freud may have been a basis for understanding what was going on within the Ranks' marriage.) In a mission of reconciliation, she specifically went to see Freud; she knew how much both men had once meant to each other. At the time (1924 or 1925) Rank was on one of his trips to America.[20]

Freud, however, became angry at what he saw as Helene's misguided effort to plead on behalf of Rank because of his upset emotional state. Although at times Freud could be understanding of Rank's dilemma, Helene found him "cruel." Freud rejected other explanations on the grounds that the issue was simpler: money. Freud thought Rank was doing well by his theories in America, and that Tola's extravagance had been responsible for driving him to an independent course. Helene was astonished at the accusation, since the Ranks then lived so modestly; to her Rank was an ascetic, a thinker and a writer, for whom the world was one of ideas. (By the end of her life Helene came to share some of Freud's point of view on Rank.)

When she heard Freud complain about Rank, and how he had developed some of Freud's own prior ideas, Helene imagined Tausk standing there; she was reminded by Freud's problem with Rank of his earlier difficulties with Tausk. Freud had brushed aside Helene's intercession in Rank's behalf by the last words from a Jewish story: "Then why isn't he kissing the hot stove!" (A rabbi has a beautiful young wife, and students living in his house. One day the rabbi returns to find his favorite pupil kissing his wife. The rabbi turns on his wife, but she pleads with him that the disciple is sick, he didn't know what he was doing. "Then why isn't he kissing the hot stove!") From Helene's point of view, Tausk's suicide note to Freud had amounted to what Freud seemed to her to be now demanding of Rank.

Although Rank had settled permanently in Paris by June 1926, Tola continued on occasion to return to Vienna, where she visited both Freud and the Deutsches. She had become a member of the Vienna society in 1923, and remained one even after 1926; she stayed in Paris after Rank had finally moved to the United States in 1935. (Helene visited with Tola at least once in Paris before she and Otto were formally separated; by 1938 Helene had succeeded in making Tola a member of the Boston Psychoanalytic Society, where she was one of the few nonmedical people to qualify.) Helene grew appalled at the way some of Freud's loyal followers, out of jealousy of Rank's former standing with the master, tried to make him seem to have been psychotic; she had never even seen him depressed. But she ignored the original nature of his ideas after he left the movement. (He quietly resigned from the Vienna society late in 1928, taking no other analysts with him.) In Helene's view, Rank had given up on himself after the break with Freud; he died suddenly in 1939 of an allergic reaction to medication he took for a throat infection, only a month after Freud's own death; Helene chose to interpret his succumbing as a form of self-extinction on his part.†

---

† Rado had had a similar fantasy about Abraham's death in 1925; Rado thought Abraham had behaved oddly medically, endangering his life rather than risk a conflict with Freud.

15

Clinical Writings

Helene's activities as a leader within the analytic movement were only one aspect of her profession. As a clinician she could rival Freud's own capacity for hard work. Starting as early as seven in the morning, she saw eleven or twelve cases a day in Vienna, six times a week. She did not even need extra time to herself between cases—Freud took ten-minute breaks. She made another trip to Italy in late March 1926, and also went to Sicily. Felix was taking care of Martin, who was ailing from a childhood illness, and he wrote her (March 29, 1926): "Cast off your burdens and be well. Perhaps work plans will develop which lie far away from professional psychoanalysis." In late August that year, Helene went to Switzerland, where she saw the Ranks; she also took a trip to Zurich to see another analytic couple, the Oberholzers (Mira was Polish, and later analyzed Tola Rank as well as Martin Deutsch). Helene felt justified in her habitual hard work: an analyst could hope to see relatively few patients in a lifetime and therefore needed clinical variety; it was also not then taken for granted that analysis would endure, so cases had to be taken as they came.

Helene's livelihood and thinking took place within the concepts Freud had created; yet she had come to analysis as a grown woman, with her own experience of life, so she maintained a measure of independence within the confines of Viennese analysis. When Freud went to a concert, she went too; but she sat with her husband, apart from the women who flocked around "Professor" in his final phase. Every event in Freud's life had meaning for his immediate circle; when he coughed, as Helene once put it, they all knew it. But she did not so identify with Freud that she could not use her own judgment. Once a case of epilepsy was referred to her, and Freud feared that his critics would charge that analysis claimed to cure more than the neurotic side of this affliction. Helene listened to what Freud had to say about it, but decided to accept the patient. Her creative period coincided with her close contact with Freud; his presence had a catalytic effect on her work.

The satisfactions of her career made up for her felt inadequacies as a mother to Martin. When she had privately wept at The Hague congress in 1920, after making her first international presentation, she was only beginning to understand how her work was destined to conflict with motherhood. As a wife, too, her life as an analyst took precedence; after her return from Berlin in 1924, within psychoanalysis Felix became even more strikingly merely her husband. When he presented a paper in Paris in December 1926, he revised it along lines she had suggested; it was inconceivable that she defer to him in the same way. Throughout the 1920s and early 1930s he continued to speak before the Vienna society; he was also asked to contribute to the public discussion on the contested issue of lay analysis. But he was known as a specialist in sports medicine, and the high point in his role in the movement was his short period as Freud's physician, although much later he succeeded in becoming a leader in the Boston Psychoanalytic Society.

As a teacher Helene was one of those unable to separate instruction from writing; for her the two activities went harmoniously together. Her publications, fully as much as her teaching, helped establish her fame as an analyst. Like Freud, she was not a great enthusiast for the efficacy of psychoanalysis as therapy, although she always insisted on what an analyst could learn.

When she wrote anything, it was both for herself and for Freud. The early analysts who succeeded in being productive were those who could, within the structure of Freud's approach, succeed in bringing something of their own as well. In Helene's youth she had been fully able to follow abstract discussions, such as the socialist debates at the Copenhagen meeting with Lieberman in 1910; and in writing her first book she had demonstrated her capacity to transmute her life into theoretical work. Following her period in Berlin, however, her functions as head of the Training Institute allowed her to concentrate on observing cases clinically rather than to "speculate." She found analysis liberating in that she could write about people she encountered; between her return to Vienna in the spring of 1924 and her final departure for America in September 1935 she came into her own as a clinical writer.

Two characteristic papers of hers appeared in 1925. The first, entitled "A Contribution to the Psychology of Sport,"[1] had first been delivered to the Berlin society on November 6, 1923. She described the case of a man suffering from impotence, anxiety states, depression, and multiple inhibitions, whose feelings of inferiority paradoxically led to an eagerness to engage in every possible kind of sport. Athleticism in adulthood was, in this patient, an equivalent of an earlier childhood phobia. By displacing inner dangers onto the outside world, in the pleasurable situation of games and contests, he was able to convert neurotic anxiety into real and justified fear, capable of being discharged and mastered in a form gratifying to his ego. Helene presented this case in an effort to elucidate the normal psychology of sport.

In a second 1925 paper, "On the Psychogenesis of a Case of Tic"[2] (first presented to the Vienna society on March 18, 1925), Helene described the appearance of a new symptom in the course of a patient's analytic treatment. The particular tic, a twitching movement in the area of the throat and nape of the neck, was a substitute for an earlier disturbing symptom that had brought the patient to analysis in the first place. As in her paper on sport, she wrote about a case because of the inherent interest of the subject matter. She was not purporting to describe the nature of therapeutic improvement, but rather to expand the understanding of unconscious psychology. The analyst's observational method was for her a kind of laboratory technique, although she directly traced her own understanding of this newly created symptom to a clearing up of the transference situation between the patient and herself.

Early critics of analysis could be remarkably prescient about the misleading tilts built in to Freud's approach. At the Berlin congress in 1922, Dr. Hattingberg of Munich, not listed on any membership lists of analysts, presented a paper called "Towards Analysis of the Psychoanalytic Situation." The abstract of his contribution sounds remarkably modern:

> The analytic situation, in common with every typical situation, is subject to the "Law of Position." That is to say, that when two people are engaged in analysis the mere fact of their having entered into this relation will cause their thoughts, feelings and actions to assume a certain typical direction, though for the most part they may be quite unconscious of the influence at work. If we examine a simple question of technique: whether it is better to make patients lie down, as Freud advises, or to let them sit opposite the analyst, we see how manifold are the considerations of this sort which combine to form the psychoanalytic situation. A deeper analysis of this situation may be made by applying to it Freud's method of regarding the phenomena of normal mental life from the angle of neurosis. The analytic situation then appears as the neurosis (place of retreat) of the analyst, as a situation created by him to protect himself: he makes use of it to defend himself when confronted with the interminable task presented by every form of psychotherapy, or with the problem of avoiding too close contact with the patient or of combating his own disturbing instincts. Nervous symptoms are represented in the analytic situation by theory—that which the analyst produces in the way of interpretation and theoretical speculation. It is "theory" which he interposes between himself and the patient: theory is the expression of his resistance. At the same time it affords a possibility of gratification for the analyst's repressed impulses (sadism etc.) Like the nervous symptom, it may serve as an end in itself (the mental gymnastics of abstract theorizing) in order to obtain some secondary advantage.[3]

Helene never publicly associated herself with such heretical reasoning, but in private she could be unblinkered. As she wrote Felix from Italy (April 5, 1926):

I am very sad, sadder than ever—but there is something beneficent and liberating in this present sadness. The future before me is still dark and blurred—the depreciated values of my yesterday life have not yet been replaced with new goals. One thing I know—I must free myself from what has been up until now, and only keep that which the two of us, the three of us, can use for comfort of existence: *material advantages.* It would be silly and adolescent to drop the practical point of view in favor of . . . strivings. But I don't want to practice my profession, as until now, with complete engagement of my personality, and above all, not with this rigid adherence to the phantom of "Freudian Method," which, as I now realize, I must regard as an *area of research* and not as a therapeutic method. The "swindle" is based on the fact that certain people (Professor himself!) in full awareness, for the purpose of scientific and material (sic!) exploitation, do not openly disavow the therapeutic—whereas others, on the one hand out of identification, and on the other hand out of the narcissistic need to have some special ability, unconsciously elevate psychoanalysis to be their battle cry, to be the one and only path to blessedness. If Stekel were not a shallow scoundrel, how right he would be! I myself no longer wish to be the servant of my own errors. To give psychic treatment, yes—but with full awareness that success is only minimally connected with the uncovering of infantile libido fixations and with transference agencies. The shortsightedness of these established views is clear to me in a theoretical sense as well. And above all—away with the odious pseudo-community of family life in the "movement"—but slowly, tactfully, unnoticeably! How glad I am—back then it was still intuitive— that I preserved you from sinking totally into psychoanalysis. Just as it happened: application of what is useful for *medicine* is the right way for you. No, your clear, kindly soul is too good for you to be an analyst by profession, as far as I am concerned.

In her consulting room Helene could be herself, although it took her another nine years before she broke away from the Vienna group; by the 1950s it was Felix who was still determined to evolve a science of therapeutic technique.

In 1926 Helene published one of her most original papers, "Occult Processes Occurring During Psychoanalysis."[4] Freud had been intrigued by the phenomenon of telepathy; some in his world were repelled by his fascination with the occult, while others tried to follow his lead. In Helene's instance she sought to understand telepathy by taking some examples from her own clinical practice. (Freud would later cite this paper of hers.)

In her approach to the occult, she made a contribution to the clinical understanding of the interaction between analyst and analysand that lies outside conscious awareness. In her view, an analyst's intuition is one of the most powerful therapeutic assets; unlike those in psychoanalysis who chose to em-

phasize the scientific side of this kind of therapy, Helene readily acknowledged the artistic component in her kind of work.

In contrast to Freud's growingly outspoken convictions about thought
transference—he once wrote, "If I had my life to live over again I should
devote myself to psychical research rather than to psychoanalysis"[5]—publi-
cally he stuck to his rationalistic guns. In 1921 he did write, in connection
with the problem of identification, that "empathy . . . plays the largest part
in our understanding of what is inherently foreign to our ego in other people."[6] But in 1927 he argued:

> The riddles of the universe reveal themselves only slowly to our investiga-
> tion; there are many questions to which science today can give no answer.
> But scientific work is the only road which can lead us to a knowledge of
> reality outside ourselves. It is once again merely an illusion to expect any-
> thing from intuition and introspection; they can give us nothing but particu-
> lars about our own mental life, which are hard to interpret, never any infor-
> mation about the questions which religious doctrine finds it so easy to
> answer.[7]

By 1932 he went so far as to deny the legitimacy of intuition in psychology.

> . . . there are no sources of knowledge of the universe other than the intel-
> lectual working-over of carefully scrutinized observations—in other words,
> what we call research—and alongside of it no knowledge derived from reve-
> lation, intuition, or divination . . . Intuition and divination would be . . .
> [methods of research] if they existed; but they may safely be reckoned as
> illusions, the fulfilments of wishful impulses.[8]

To link intuition with "revelation" and "divination" was to damn it as a
species of hocus-pocus. Yet the older Freud grew, the more he committed
himself to an almost mystical belief in thought transference as a "fact."[9]
Helene thought that Freud had had to emphasize the rational so much because elements of the irrational were so strong in him.

According to her, the analyst's intuitive empathy springs from unconscious sources; it is the special "gift," she wrote in 1926, of being able to
experience another person's life by means of an identification that takes place
within oneself. While patients develop transferences to analysts, the analysts
themselves must also have an unconscious relationship to the patients. Helene
was innovative in that she did not regard this involvement as a contamination
of the analyst's neutrality. Instead, an analyst must maintain an unconscious
receptiveness to a patient's needs; and this should, according to her, entail a
renunciation of the analyst's real personality, in order to identify with the
transference fantasies of the patient.

Telepathic processes could be partially understood by the example of
extraordinary analytic intuition; Helene offered illustrations from her own
clinical practice. In one case her fascination with a problem resulted in the
uncanny appearance of anticipated material in a patient's associations; her

own needs were met by infantile patterns of the patient. But in another case, a patient suffering from Helene's kind of miscarriages dreamed about Helene's sadness at her own "psychologically determined" childlessness; it seemed more than a coincidence that the patient accurately dreamed of Helene's feelings, somehow knowing in her dream that it was Helene's wedding anniversary. Helene concluded that transference of thoughts could sometimes take place, without sense organs, as a manifestation of greatly strengthened intuition which is rooted in the unconscious. In attributing telepathy to the affective process of identification, she was trying to render intelligible what otherwise seemed like mysticism.

At the tenth congress (September 1, 1927) Helene presented a paper, "On Satisfaction, Happiness and Ecstasy."[10] If Freud could be too rationalistic about intuition, other emotional moods were also beyond his ken. While he had emphasized the splits within the psyche, Helene sought to explain how normal happiness springs from an inner harmony of all the components of the ego. She even touched respectfully on the blissfulness of religious communion. (Freud dismissed religion as a universal obsessional neurosis.) The striving for unity she talked about stemmed from a permanent tension of human wants. Although her article had theoretical purposes, she used two cases to illustrate how both sexual satisfaction and sublimation could involve phases of dejection. She accounted for the sense of ecstasy by the temporarily undisturbed unity between ego and non-ego.

On March 16, 1928 (and then again during her 1930 trip to America) Helene presented a public lecture in Vienna, "George Sand: A Woman's Destiny."[11] This paper about a great French writer and novelist filled out some of Helene's purposes as a thinker; in the course of making the subject of women her specialty, she had to come to terms with the life of the woman she credited with being "the first systematic feminist." With the inevitable limitations of such a pioneering application of analysis to a nonclinical subject, this article stands as a precursor to much of what today comes under the heading of "psychohistory."

Helene had had a lifelong interest in George Sand, which endured into extreme old age; almost forty years after her paper first appeared, one good friend who knew of her fascination with the subject sent as a present a copy of a recent biography of George Sand. Throughout all these years the Frenchwoman has continued to attract critical attention from a wide variety of sources. Writers as different as Dostoevsky, Henry James, and Proust have been among her ardent admirers. Perhaps Helene's preoccupation with the career and writings of this brilliant woman began with an appreciation of the music of one of George Sand's many famous lovers, Frédéric Chopin. The history of women, however, has had its lapses: George Sand herself,[12] like Helene after her, has been attacked in our time for not being a feminist.

Helene saw masculinity as a disturbing influence on the development of

George Sand's femininity, as well as a secondary reaction to the failure of her feminine aspirations. The bold spirit of Gustave Flaubert's memorable words about his friend is pertinent here: "One had to know her as I knew her to realize how much of the feminine there was in this great man, the immensity of tenderness to be found in this genius."[13] Helene did herself espouse certain conventions of her time about the nature of maleness and femaleness. In reflecting on the debate that began among analysts in the 1920s over the nature of female psychology, it is fairer not to pretend that what we may now think could have been magically foreshadowed in early psychoanalysis.

In spite of the cultural changes since 1928, it is unfortunately still true that talented women characteristically have an exceptionally hard time of it emotionally. Perhaps the childhood tendency to idealization, in Helene's view so important to creative development, is inextricably associated, for members of both sexes, with later self-torments and disappointments. Helene was working again from the premise of the universality of bisexual trends. She believed (like George Sand) in a "primordial original unity that survives as a bisexual constitution in everyone," and that men and women become differentiated without being distinct.

From today's perspective Helene appears to have overemphasized George Sand's loneliness and divided soul. One of Helene's themes was the twisted course of mothering in George Sand's life; she was contrasting George Sand's sublimations with her unhappiness as a woman. But Helene was not crudely reducing a famous writer to the level of a neurotic; in talking about "destiny," instead of symptomatology, she was trying to discuss character structure rather than isolated syndromes (like a tic). In investigating the sources of the formation of George Sand's conflicted personality, Helene was also self-critically reflecting on the underside to her own immensely successful career. She revealed two autobiographical elements in the paper. Her account of the death of George Sand's mother's infant boy is reminiscent of a feature in Helene's reaction to Lieberman's son's dying.

> A disastrous bond between her and her mother arose . . . The formation of her feminine ego-ideal required her to identify herself with this mother who was later devalued in her eyes, but this she could not do. But the two were identified with each other in a crime which, though uncommitted, nevertheless burdened the unconscious.

Her tie to Felix is illuminated as well; she wrote that George Sand's

> disastrous affair with Alfred de Musset . . . started as an affectionate friendship between a brilliant boy and a kindhearted mother. She always called him her good or bad boy and she felt in no sexual danger in his presence . . . Her mother had cruelly abandoned her, and she too had cruelly to disappoint and be disappointed in turn.

Helene's major publication in 1930 was her second book, *Psychoanalysis of the Neuroses,* which was first issued in English in 1932.[14] (Jones once compared this book to the textbooks by Nunberg and Fenichel.[15]) It was, like Freud's own earlier efforts to explain psychoanalysis to the general public, in the form of a series of lectures; Helene was addressing herself specifically to the education of future analysts, and hoped to supply—through typical case illustrations of patients she had analyzed—a substitute for clinical demonstration in medicine.

Her introductory remarks were devoted to the part played by the "actual conflict" in the creation of neurosis; by "actual" she was referring to the immediate exciting event, although she acknowledged the role of "fixation" and "regression." Unlike those who theorized about earliest childhood, Helene chose to begin by stressing the current problems which distressed her patients. To be sure, she maintained that "the inability to resolve a real conflict was conditioned from the outset by internal motives." She believed that "every civilized person is really in a state of *latent conflict . . .*" Analysts would, however, be making a "crude mistake" in ignoring how patients can use infantile material defensively (a point Jung had made before World War I). According to her the analyst should modify neutrality to accord with real injuries to the patient from the outside world: the therapist "will manifest his human interest and desire to help the patient even though he holds up the analytic situation for a period by so doing." But "one cannot find a rule for everything."

She proceeded to deal with hysteria, and in particular with what she called a "Fate Neurosis." Here she was talking about tragedy, not symptomatology, the way individuals can appear to be involved as the victim of repeated external disasters. The patient she described was her father's favorite, struggling with a hopeless love for a married man. In her account of this woman's so-called repudiation of her femininity, her inner dependence and masochism, Helene was unknowingly mirroring her tie to Lieberman. In her own life too something seemed repeatedly to interfere with her achieving happiness.

Helene went on to discuss examples of hysterical symptoms—night terrors, bed-wetting, impotence, paralysis, speech defects, gluttony, fits, and trance states. She defined a conversion symptom as one that occurs when a psychical process gets transferred onto physical sensations. In terms of analytic theory, such problems were the result of unsuccessful repression; at one and the same time they serve forbidding tendencies, as well as the impulses seeking gratification. She held that in terms of treatment of conversion hysteria, "we can lay it down as an axiom that the *symptom* is easy to get rid of, but the *neurosis* difficult." By means of enabling people to withdraw from life tasks that are too difficult for them, conversion symptoms (like inhibitions) lead to freedom from anxiety.

She talked about various neurotic fears (phobias)—a case of cat phobia, one of hen phobia, and then the anxiety associated with open spaces. While hysteria fettered anxiety, the clinical picture of phobias was the opposite: dreads and avoidances. Each phobic symptom was a warning against the outbreak of anxiety; in accord with analytic thinking at the time, Helene held that these symptoms were more regressive, in the sense of defending against aggressive drives, than with hysteria. (According to an interpretation of hers that became well known in the literature, in the case of an agoraphobic the individual whose presence is required in order to prevent an attack of anxiety in the street is the parent whose image the patient has introjected because of excessive hostility.)

Helene turned finally to the way obsessionals resort to ceremonies, acts, and ideas in order to control repressed sadism. By obsessionality she meant the separation of a conscious content from its affective element. Inner indecision is due to ambivalence between tenderness and cruelty; it is possible to satisfy an unconscious tendency and then try to revoke and annul it. The real issue may have been displaced onto a trivial object, as with the inability to tolerate clocks in a room. According to Freud's kind of reasoning, the more aggressive the suppressed wishes the more severe did the superego become. (In an appendix Helene touched on the problem of loss involved in melancholia.) Like Freud, she traced superstition, distrust, and doubt to the obsessional's fear of the omnipotence of wishes and thoughts—especially bad ones. She illustrated how pedantry and rigidity could be a reaction formation by the case of a patient who after analysis chose to enter a convent; Helene thought that the analyst "too must at times be content with having found a *modus vivendi* for his patients equal to their task of adaptation."

In 1930 Helene also published specifically on the issue of frigidity ("The Significance of Masochism in the Mental Life of Women").[16] At the Oxford congress in 1929 she had spoken on the same subject; her stature at the time can be inferred from a group photograph in which she and Anna Freud are seated on either side of Ernest Jones. Freud later summarized some of Helene's theories about female development. She was convinced that love involved pain and worry, agonizing about things that are unreal. She admitted that "the analyst's most important task is, of course, the abolition of the sexual inhibition in his patients, and the attainment of instinctual gratification." Nonetheless, she urged, "when the patient's instincts are so unfortunately fixed and yet there are good capacities for sublimation, the analyst must have the courage to smooth the path in the so-called 'masculine' direction and thus make it easier for the patient to renounce sexual gratification." Helene was not content with a conformist view of so-called normality: ". . . the sexual disturbance is emphatically not in direct ratio to the severity of the neurosis."

Motherhood was a central feature to Helene's thinking on women. In trying to account for female homosexuality (1932),[17] she described a case sent from Freud who became, as the result of the analysis, no longer guilty or anxious about lesbian tendencies but manifestly "perverse." To her surprise Helene found that Freud had no objection to an end of analysis: the woman was discreet and her husband now wanted only a marriage of social convenience. Helene interpreted the homosexuality not as a matter of the woman's Oedipus complex, but in terms of a continuation and reaction to a "pre-oedipal" rivalry with her mother. (By 1932 the notion of early stages, before the oedipal one, was fashionable among analysts; it helped incorporate some of the insights of those who had rejected Freud's exclusive interest in the role of fathers.) According to Helene's reasoning, her patient was motivated by a sense of guilt toward her mother, as well as by a dread of disappointment and frustration.

In a paper on motherhood and sexuality (1933)[18] Helene pursued one of her favorite insights. According to Freud the existence of opposing forces characterized the normal psyche, and in women a conflict between mothering and eroticism was, Helene held, inevitable. She used one of Honoré de Balzac's pieces of fiction to illustrate how mothering can lead to a renunciation of erotic fulfillment; he had described two women, one of whom is a mother longing for passion, while the other is a devotee of love who longs for motherhood. (The movie *The Captain's Paradise*, starring Alec Guiness, turned this conflict into a comic situation.) According to Helene, a profession was a legitimate outlet for maternal feelings. "I have come to know many professional women who were able to satisfy very warm and intense maternal feelings in their work, but who were prevented from having children of their own by a repudiation of their mother's sexuality together with their own."

It is questionable whether Helene realized at the time the extent to which she was using her own life. In a 1933 article, first presented at the Wiesbaden congress, "The Psychology of Manic-Depressive States, with Particular Reference to Chronic Hypomania,"[19] she talked about the human propensity for denial. It is possible for people to blot out not only features of external reality but the existence of inner states as well. In contrast to acute mania, Helene wanted to discuss a nonclinical problem, the phenomenon of so-called chronic hypomania. Euphoria can nip in the bud any reaction to loss. Helene described a woman who "in spite of her exuberant activity" had something "lifeless and cold in all her liveliness." Mania was, instead, a direct response to a melancholic provocation. Yet one suspects that Helene was being self-observingly hard on herself as she gave an account of her own kind of self-protection against disappointment, and at her consequent aggressiveness.

> We are shown that we are dealing with a defense mechanism by a surplus, an excess of expenditure, an exaggeration and restlessness. If we look more closely at the real nature of the values in this manic industry, we note the hollowness of their success in comparison with the energy expended, how the love relationships lack warmth, in spite of their apparent passion, how sterile the performance in spite of continuous productivity.

Her hypomanic energy helped make Helene the force she was, although at some level she knew how hard to live with it made her.

The last congress Helene attended before leaving for Boston was at Lucerne in 1934, when she presented a lecture on Cervantes's *Don Quixote* and the theme of Don Quixotism.[20] She spoke admiringly of the Don's "delusion" of immortality, which she positively described as "the courage of the young child"; she contrasted him to Sancho Panza, who was a bridge to reality—"instinct-accepting rather than instinct-denying." In this clash between two eternal aspects of the human personality Helene looked with favor on "the eternal quixotism of the human spirit. It is in poets, artists, and in fanatics that it is particularly well-developed." When she showed this paper to Freud, he was as pleased and delighted as if someone had given him a present; he wanted to know how she had become interested in the subject. Nonetheless, within a year she had gone against his wishes and, despite what he had come to mean in her life, had gone to practice in the United States.

PART III

Cambridge, Massachusetts

"Now, of course, Puschkuleindi, the decision must be left up to you. If you come here in a mood of crisis, with a 'need for importance' and with the 'masculine protest'—with the ridiculously narcissistic question: 'Who am I there'—you will suffer here. But if you come with an attitude identical to mine: 'out of that stupid, stuffy atmosphere at last, and for once let us experience something freer, something that is extraordinarily relieving in its very uncertainty,' and with complete inner courage and with joy in work without regard to 'position,' etc.—then you can be very happy here. I am very happy myself, and only my longing for you, and the feeling that something is incomplete, disturbs me. Otherwise, come what may, it is such a joyful liberation, such a lust for work and an urge to work, such an intense interest—as I have not felt for at least fifteen years."

Helene to Felix Deutsch, October 7, 1935

"I saw the dear, quiet, modest boy with his face distorted by hate lugging heavy beams for the building of the wretched quarters in which death and desparation will prevail. And I remember how he came for a few hours from Craców to Przemyśl to talk with me: he was interested in allergy and his dream was to come to America for a year and to learn certain things. Could I help him with that? He said that in his wildest dreams he wouldn't think of staying in America.

I did nothing—out of that evil, passive *misanthropy* which 'simply ignores.' "

Helene to Felix Deutsch, Fall 1939

1

"Out of the Magic Circle"

During the 1920s Americans constituted the steadiest stream of lucrative foreign analytic patients in Vienna; they seemed rich and eager to be treated as well as trained. Especially in periods of inflation the dollar became an attractive hard currency, and Americans could afford to live cheaply throughout Europe. At the time of Freud's 1909 visit to the United States, he was an old-fashioned gentleman from an alien civilization who found himself unable to adjust—to the manners, sexual hypocrisy, the general lack of culture, or the brash wealth. In 1927 he was deeply offended by the decision of the American Psychoanalytic Association to limit practice to medical doctors; his own dependence on clientele from the States reinforced his prejudices against the North American continent.

Helene's own case load became two-thirds American. She took some American candidates for half a year, and then later they would come back for another several months; if Freud had done the same thing himself she would not have worried about it so much. She even turned aside the novelist Thomas Wolfe, whom Freud once sent her, because of his inability to pay her customary fees. (She charged about ten dollars an hour, which was a lot; if she had been less expensive, patients would have considered her not as good a therapist.) As Rank's career had already demonstrated, an analyst might live in modest circumstances in Vienna and be welcomed as a celebrity in America.

From May 5–10, 1930, the First International Congress of Mental Hygiene was held in Washington, D.C. President Herbert Hoover was the honorary president, Dr. William A. White the president, and Clifford W. Beers the secretary general of the inviting organization. Beers, author of *The Mind that*

Found Itself, put up much of the money for the congress; his doctor, Frankwood Williams, was an analyst who chiefly organized the meetings. A few European analysts were given grants to attend: in addition to Helene, Rado, Rank, Van Ophuijsen, Dr. Franz Alexander (a Hungarian, the first student at the Berlin institute), Dr. René Spitz (another Hungarian from the Berlin society), Dr. Oscar Pfister (from Switzerland), and Mary Chadwick (an English nurse). Helene traveled first-class, and when she arrived in the United States she received a Hollywood-like impression of American life.

Helene commented on four papers. She addressed herself, for example, to the problem of training psychiatric social workers; although she sounded on the propagandistic side, she wanted to be sure that they did not give up their own field. She also spoke on adolescence, as well as "the profession of parenthood." On this last subject Helene was able to be more flexible; she thought psychoanalysis was "still far from having framed an educational scheme that can be taught to parents," and in terms of therapy she saw analysis "as the last possible resource."[1] Sometimes she used German, and her remarks were translated or presented in an abstract; on other occasions she lectured in English. Her verbal command of German had remained as idiosyncratic as her English; yet her limitations in both enabled her to achieve a poetic effect.

On April 29, 1930 the New York Psychoanalytic Society had arranged a banquet at the Academy of Medicine in honor of the European guests; Helene gave her paper "On the Genesis of the 'Family Romance,'" previously presented in Vienna in 1928. (She lectured again in New York later in May.) The mental hygiene congress was to be a milestone in the reception of Freud's ideas in America. The meetings of both the American Psychiatric Association and the American Psychoanalytic Association, with a membership then of fifty-six, were timed to coordinate with it. The entire psychoanalytic program was taken over by the visiting analysts; Helene presented a paper in English on the "actual conflict," the first chapter from her *Psychoanalysis of the Neuroses.* In America she fretted about the delay in her receiving page proofs, blaming Felix for his ambivalence about her successful career.

Fritz Wittels, who had once left the Vienna society in a conflict over Stekel and then later had been accepted back, was already in New York; he placed articles about Helene in newspapers, one of them describing her as "Freud's foremost feminine disciple."[2] She said he also staged a kidnapping for another analyst (Dr. Olga Knopf) in order to get her established in practice. Helene was amused by the reports of how well she had been dressed. (In that period she preferred fitted silks; as she sat down, the stays—where they began and ended—of her well-corseted figure could be seen, which might be distracting. The Viennese women analysts typically were well tailored, chic, and inconspicuous. Helene would have looked international, maybe Parisian, except for the visibility of the stays through the soft fabrics.) When she returned to Vienna, where she had a waiting list of candidates to be analyzed, she spoke before the society about the impressions of her American visit.

One meeting at the congress was the occasion for a particularly brutal assault on Rank, still residing in Paris, who had come to talk on "The Development of the Emotional Life." Miss Chadwick accused him of presenting "a museum piece," pasting fresh labels on known analytic concepts ("new lamps for old"), and echoing the earlier heresy of Adler. Abraham A. Brill picked up on Rank's admission that he no longer was a psychoanalyst; he proceeded to reason along *ad hominem* lines, alluding to Rank's "own present maladjustment." Brill commented: "A deep conversion invariably involves a deep emotional upset . . . It is this emotional upheaval that is responsible for his present confusion." Brill's remarks were punctuated twice by laughter from the audience, and greeted with applause at the end. Alexander, and Isidor Coriat from Boston, joined in the attack.[3] At a meeting of American analysts the same day, Brill proposed—and was seconded by Dr. Harry Stack Sullivan —that Rank's name be dropped from the list of honorary members.

In her old age Helene recalled that once Freud and Rank had had their falling out, Rank's former friends "fell on him like dogs." Felix had written to her from Paris on December 24, 1926:

> Tola was in Paris until yesterday, i.e. until before the lecture [Felix's]. Then she left—she was as nice as ever, and of course she got some George Sand books for you . . . I only speak of her, although Otto is also in Paris but I don't see him. Why? Because this fool is jealous of the Deutsch family, because he believes the world is persecuting him, or God knows why. In short, when I was with Nunberg at the Hotel Copres, he didn't come down from his room.

By 1930 Helene had herself joined those who thought it necessary to repudiate Rank. She began her lecture before the American Psychoanalytic Association (the day Rank's name was expunged) with a special introductory paragraph:

> In 1913 at the psychoanalytic Congress in Munich, Jones in a lecture produced his arguments against Jung, considering the question of the current conflict. Since that time the problem of the current conflict has been discussed over and over again. Recently Rank has accused psychoanalysis of neglecting the current conflict in favor of the historical past of the individual. Let me review very briefly the position of psychoanalysis in regard to this question.[4]

Rank's 1931 published retort to her challenged the way she proceeded to choose a quotation from Freud.[5]

Helene was acting as an emissary of Freud. He had given her money to buy a present for Brill as a gift from himself; she bought a piece of silver, realizing that such a secondhand present meant that Brill, in whose house she stayed for a while, was really no special favorite of Freud's. (She took back to Vienna two boxes of cigars, one for her husband and the other for Freud; when one of them was stolen she was faced with a dilemma, but Felix told her to give the remaining box to Freud.) In America Helene found Brill fatherly. She kissed him after he gave a paper, and he turned purple; she had not had any erotic feelings in her, but thought it tactful of him to respond that way. America was still under Prohibition, but she reported that Brill usually had a flask in his back pocket.

Helene's letters to Felix from America reflect her excitement. On May 17 she wrote:

> My room is so full of flowers that for lack of space I must write on my knee. Interviews on board [ship] and here. According to a newspaper report an agent was awaiting me to arrange my trip to Yokohama. Then right after the congress—so says the newspaper—I am going with Prof. Weygand to Yokoh. That is a piece of America! . . . [F]or now I too plunge into the ratrace—but with the feeling of an interesting experiment, inwardly armed and protected. I am a bit curious and in a light mood: on the eve of the battle.

Tola Rank was evidently still trying to be loyal to her husband; she departed from New York two days before Helene's arrival. "She left me a letter full of sadness, and I am compulsively running away from the thought that she seems to be very unhappy. What I have heard about her here unfortunately confirms this suspicion."

Before the rise to power of the Nazis in Germany Helene had already been looking around for a new position. As she changed the dates of her travel plans, she wrote: "I must stay here to put out feelers, and to find out what there is here for me (for the three of us!!!)." Rado, who had accompanied her on the ship to the United States, had already sailed for home; he sent Martin a postcard from the ship, and undertook to call on Felix with mail. On May 13, Helene claimed already to have had enough of the United States; she said she was prepared to miss "a few 'important' lectures."

> The initial intoxication of suspense has faded; the whole torture is useless and one sees no real motive for suppressing one's desires. I am totally satisfied, even if at the moment the material side seems to be fruitless, yet I have managed to leave my calling cards in many very good places.

To her chagrin, Alexander (analyzed by Sachs) was about to become the first visiting professor of psychoanalysis at the University of Chicago; he offered Helene some courses, and after she refused he turned to Karen Horney, who accepted the invitation.[6] (Alexander was also soon a training analyst in Boston as well.)

> Immediate, well-prepared success really only fell to Alexander, who is esteemed *much* higher in America than Freud, and in spite of the bad lectures

that he gave, he had a magic power that made all homosexual men in highest places his slaves. He is also considering a terribly favorable professorship in Chicago. Healy [a Boston analyst] and Williams are angling for his favor— one must have been in America to understand such a thing.

She was planning on returning to the United States "because one is so anxious not to neglect the 'possibilities.' " She reported again about the Ranks: "I hear a lot of bad about Rank—he suffered a real calamity at the congress, and I felt very sorry, for I see a fate holding sway here, and Tola's future really worries me."

Family considerations intruded themselves into Helene's work. As she wrote Felix from New York: "I got a very reproachful letter from my mother, and I would like very much for the three of us to go to Poland for Pentecost. By car or by train . . ." She telegraphed Martin, who was thirteen years old on May 2: AMERICA IMPOSING REALLY NEW WORLD EVERYTHING GIGAN- TIC MAD TEMPO MAMA GREAT SUCCESS BUT LONGING NO TIME FOR LETTER WRITING MANY HUGS FOR MY DARLING. She also sent (May 10) Martin a picture postcard of the Capitol building in Washington:

> A bad Mama keeps thinking of her two dearest ones, and with everything going in circles, she doesn't find time to write. The congress was grandiose, and the country is terribly interesting. I passed by Edison's house. In the midst of it, surrounded by greenery, is his laboratory, from which the earth- shaking "rays" are sent out.

Martin was already interested in science.

On May 13 she wrote Martin a letter:

> Don't be angry with me for having written so seldom . . . I have seen and experienced terribly much—and I had no idea that America is *so* interesting.
> In order to enjoy everything that there was, I flew in a real airplane. I got a little airsick—but after that it was great. And the noise was terrible. Now, aren't you impressed with your old Mama? You would hardly recog- nize me—so bold and enterprising I have become.
> Today I even boldly looked the biggest dinosaur in the world square in the eye. Did you know the biggest specimens in the world are here?—I didn't know until today.
> The gigantic buildings are not, as we believed, simply "big buildings"— they have a totally different character, and in places, especially as dusk settles, they are the most beautiful architecture that one can imagine in modern style of building.

She explained her eagerness to get home, and also about her plan for a trip to Poland: "Poor Grandma is so offended, and she is so old." Four days later she again telegraphed Martin: PLEASE EXCUSE NO LETTERS. AMERICA EATS UP MY TIME. SEE YOU SOON. HAPPY KISSES.

Felix came over to America in 1933; he addressed the New York Psychoanalytic Society on April 29, and spoke to other medical groups. Hitler was now in power in Germany. Nunberg had left Vienna for Philadelphia, and Karen Horney had moved to Chicago; Sachs was in Boston. William Healy invited Felix to Boston, where Helene already had admirers. (She had trained Healy and his friend Augusta Bronner during summers in the late 1920s.) Part of Felix's professional problem was, though, that his work fell between psychiatry and internal medicine.

While Felix was away, Helene went to Switzerland with Martin; he was going to take a skiing course. Even though Freud had no intention of leaving Vienna, others in his circle were apprehensive; as Helene wrote (April 8, 1933):

> In the center is now the idea of founding an international institute in Paris— that is where we are all to go. The matter is to be proposed to Professor. Discretion, please.
>
> We (the Deutsch family) won't be going there. Just think of the hell of hatred and competition which will come into being there.—Puschkuleindi, how my thoughts are of love and tenderness, and how much I have only the *one* wish about your trip: that you should feel free and happy. Please, *don't burden yourself with the idea that I should expect anything else!!!*

Her injunction reinforced the reality of who was wearing the pants in the family. She had made notes for Felix about whom he should not neglect to see in America. The political news from Germany was alarming. "Yesterday, the first Jew to utter a harmless criticism of the persecution of the Jews was sentenced to a year's hard labor." She sent Felix a clipping from a Swiss newspaper "without party ties." Vienna was "still peaceful, but the atmosphere is full of suspense."

On April 12, two days before their anniversary (which she celebrated by a cable to Felix), Helene wrote about the rise of fascism: "Everything remains consistent—on the way into the abyss. In Germany the old orders and titles have been restored—reaction is victorious on all fronts . . ." Martin added his own letter to hers; but he wrote more about politics than sports. Felix and Helene were alarmed by his left-wing political affiliations and feared for his physical safety.

Helene made a trip to Zurich; Mira Oberholzer was about to leave "to go to Tola. It is said that there is 'trouble' there again. Oh, Pusch.—why so much suffering and sorrow, when the world is so wonderfully lovely? Poor Tola is causing me painful concern, and I would go there at once if it weren't for Martin." Zurich was still a great psychiatric center. Mira was an intimate personal friend (she had been analyzed by Freud), and her husband, Emil, was a major figure within the movement. Yet Helene found that there was no hope of the Deutsches' moving to Zurich: Mira

> complained bitterly about the decline of analytic practice in Switzerland, and considers it totally impossible for anyone from outside to get permission

to become established—or for any gainful activity, for that matter. The word
is that Switzerland is on the brink of the outbreak of a great financial crisis!

Helene had brought money with her to Switzerland; Felix was, she thought,
too introverted to think about such things, and like others she decided that
although interest rates were nearly zero, a Swiss account was safe. Helene had
a good head for money, and concluded that they were "tolerably well taken
care of and almost independent."

Martin was to enroll in school in Switzerland. The headmaster of his
Gymnasium in Vienna, a classmate of Felix's, had encouraged the Deutsches
to get their son out of potential political trouble. During the socialist uprising
in Vienna in February 1934 Martin was actively involved in fighting in the
trenches; the Dollfuss regime was authoritarian as well as anti-intellectual,
and it violently put down the Left. Helene grew so hysterical about the military action that Felix, for the moment at a loss, asked Martin to go into her
room and see if he could control her. Instead of appreciating that her agita-
tion was a result of her worry over her only child, Martin thought he had
finally called her bluff as a socialist. His political resentments reflected his
more general intolerance of her as a mother; it was hard for him to forgive
her for being so distant throughout his childhood. In his upbringing "neurotic" was a fancy—and confusing—term for naughtiness. Helene had been
convinced of his brilliance, and must have helped communicate to him a
sense of uniqueness. But she had also belittled Felix's family; and it seemed to
Martin that there was nothing in his father's life, compared to hers, that she
did not disparage.

For a time Martin lived in the Oberholzer house. As early as 1933 Helene had wanted Mira's help; both women had then thought it was worth
waiting for Felix's impressions of the prospects in America. Analysts were
competing for the available positions, and Helene felt she knew the people to
trust. She advised Felix that he should "naturally do nothing without Brill
. . ."; and she still recommended Healy (head of the Judge Baker Foundation) and Williams.

Boston increasingly seemed like the best place for the whole Deutsch
family. Dr. Stanley Cobb (1888–1968)[7] was founding a psychiatric department at an old and famous hospital, the Massachusetts General; with the
support of a Rockefeller Foundation grant it was to be the first full-time
psychiatric unit in the medical wards of an American general hospital. Cobb
came from an old New England family, and led a prominent neurological
school; he was later considered for the presidency of Harvard, and was to
write the 1944 Foreword to Helene's *The Psychology of Women*. Cobb also
had a special interest in psychosomatic medicine. Despite the opposition at
his own hospital, Cobb was tolerant of analysts. In 1938 he allowed the first
black physician to be on the house staff.

As recently as 1933 the Boston Psychoanalytic Society had had too few members to qualify as a member of the federation of the American Psychoanalytic Association. Ten "properly qualified" members were required, and Boston only could come up with six. The Boston society was reorganized to suit ideological needs; some members (analyzed by Rank in Paris, for example) temporarily resigned on the understanding they would be reaccepted once the national leaders were satisfied. Some Jungians, like Professor Henry A. Murray, were to leave the society for good. The plan of a few puristic activists was to move the society beyond inviting visiting teachers from New York City, and to open a fully functioning institute in the fall of 1935.

Before finally deciding to leave Vienna, Helene had consulted with Freud. Felix left the decision up to her, even though he was hoping there might be an opening for him as head of a medical clinic in Vienna. Freud did not want her to go, any more than he had approved the exodus of others who were personal favorites. But he refused to put the case for her staying in terms of his personal needs, which was the kind of appeal she would have liked. Instead he argued on professional grounds, claiming that the society in Vienna would suffer from her loss. She thought she knew the local analytic community better than he; although to her it seemed like an order that she not go to America, she left Freud's office hurt and more determined than ever to leave.

At the same time, Helene was experiencing some problems with her health. She had had trouble with her gall bladder until it was removed in 1925; now she had to go to a sanatorium, and she chose Reinhold's in Gräfenberg. She was thoroughly examined there; in February 1935 they made some studies of her upper and lower gastrointestinal tract, both of which were normal. She also had a gastric analysis done by methods current at that time; the hydrochloric acid content of her stomach was normal. She did have an EKG taken on May 14, 1935, with a summary diagnosis of normal and no evidence of any myocardial damage. (When she was examined in Boston in 1936 she was five feet four inches, and weighed 143 pounds.) In June she had to miss an analytic conference in Vienna; but Reinhold, like Felix, was opposed to a further operation. As she recounted the details of her therapy, Helene exclaimed in a letter to Felix: "Good God, I'm becoming like your mother-in-law!"

By early 1935 Helene planned to move to Boston in the fall; Felix headed back there for interviews. (Helene had already made an impact on the Boston Brahmins; in Vienna she had analyzed Dr. Molly Putnam, the daughter of one of Freud's most eminent early followers in America, Dr. James Jackson Putnam, the first Professor of Diseases of the Nervous System at Harvard. Molly Putnam was also Mrs. Cobb's closest friend, a second cousin. When Helene finally arrived she had a great entourage of patients, almost a full case load.) Before sailing, tourist class, for America, Felix stopped off in Zurich to see how Martin was getting on; Martin was then in analysis with Mira Oberholzer. Felix wrote Helene (January 21):

> Room as untidy as ever . . . I didn't talk with him about the analysis. His plans are: after the *Matura,* a short stay in Vienna, then for a time to Cambridge, to get the study material—then on his trip to America he will study English thoroughly.
>
> The evening with Mira was quite long. I was able to learn that the analysis is going quite well—no more than that, and that her words, "He leads us around by the nose" were coined about his relations with girls, told by him, i.e., it's no big deal. As for the rest, I have the impression that for the time being, at least, we know him better than anyone else, including, to this point, Mira. She knows more details.
>
> Well, Muschkuleindi, was I thorough?

From on board ship Felix let Helene know how he was doing; he worked on his English, and made plans for what he would do on his arrival. He said he would reject invitations to analytic parties and avoid contact with Judge Julian Mack, Ruth Mack Brunswick's father, who was a rich philanthropist and a friend of President Franklin Roosevelt's. If worst came to worst, Felix would confine himself to taking care of their immigration papers. Within a day, however, he was troubled about the absence of any word from Judge Mack. The Rados and Helene's analyst friend Dr. Dorian Feigenbaum planned to meet Felix at the pier in New York; Wittels also telegraphed the ship.

Judge Mack had arranged for someone to help Felix through customs inspection; he felt he was being patronized as a needy immigrant. Mack himself showed up at Felix's first hotel on Fifth Avenue.

> At 5:30 Judge Mack came, visibly fatigued, and preoccupied with himself and his wife. He is not conversant with matters of immigration and permits. He is a publicity man, and one can't ask a general how to clean a gun—one must ask a subordinate officer at best.

Mack was a distinguished jurist, someone considered plausible for an appointment to the Supreme Court. Felix was more at home with European analysts (Wittels, Rado and his wife, the Nunbergs), whatever stresses old friendships might entail. (Nunberg was very isolated in New York; he was usually sour-tempered and captious, and his "dislike of America" was, according to Felix, not helping him either.) Felix went to one party and was filled in about intrigues within the New York society—problems between Brill and Dr. Gregory Zilboorg, for example. "One thing for certain—all of America has nothing good to say about Europe—a European is a red cloth." Felix relied on his New York contacts to help him in Boston: Dr. Leonard Blumgart, a New York analyst treated by Freud, had a brother, Herman, who was an important figure in internal medicine at Boston's Beth Israel Hospital. Herman Blumgart was also Ruth Brunswick's first husband; Felix's reservations about Judge Mack may have stemmed from how helpful that acquaintance might be: "He is a poor, plagued human being, who moreover does nothing that the outside world doesn't know about. Nevertheless I will try to take advantage of his connection with the Beth Israel Hospital."

As soon as Felix got to Boston (February 6) he was welcomed by Sachs; he then had some discussions with Blumgart about a position at his hospital. Erik H. Erikson, then a child analyst recently graduated from the Vienna society, and known by his stepfather's name, Homburger, was already enormously successful; in Vienna he had been considered a protégé of Anna Freud's. As Felix wrote (February 9):

> I am trying to take up connections with a great variety of people, so as to get to know the lay of the land. For this reason I was at Homburger's today, to see how a man who certainly did not have the best pre-analytic qualifications, is able to make his way here. And he has done it! The means may not have been totally clean, but it can be excused by saying: the purpose sanctifies the means. He is now *the* child analyst. But he is working with utmost energy, and on the side he is completing the examinations for his doctorate in philosophy. I can forgive him for everything, for he has two charming children, who can only be compared with Hartmann's boys.

(Erikson, who had been a young artist before training as a child analyst in Vienna, later flunked out of Harvard's Ph.D. program in psychology.[8])

Erikson was helpful in orienting Felix to Boston; at the Vienna Institute Helene had been Erikson's first teacher, and she was immediately impressed by his inner charm. Dr. M. ("Moe") Ralph Kaufmann, an analysand of Reich's, was described as "ambitious, a leader, dangerous." Kaufmann worked at the Beth Israel, and later became a great friend of both Deutsches. Dr. Joseph Michaels, also analyzed in Europe, cooperated with Felix as well. Cobb was still the key, since he held the professorship; he had succeeded the famous Dr. Elmer Southard in the neurology chair, and for years had had contacts with Rockefeller Foundation money. The Boston City Hospital was also a possibility for Felix. Blumgart offered to help Felix get a medical license (as solely an analyst Helene needed none), and an assistant professorship at Harvard Medical School; but Blumgart held out no hope for a salary.

Boston was a great teaching medical community, and Felix tried every possibility he could think of. Cobb was relying on Dr. Alan Gregg's support at the Rockefeller Foundation, and intended to include Helene in his training program. Evidently Cobb had planned for Felix to start at a salary of three to four thousand dollars, which he could supplement with consulting work. But Cobb thought that Helene could expect as an analyst to begin earning about twenty thousand dollars a year.

By late February Felix thought he had succeeded; he telegraphed on February 28: COBB OFFERS 5,000 FOR MY WORK AND YOU TRAINING ONE OR TWO DOCTORS PRIVATE PRACTICE FREE. Helene's analyses would be the basis of her income. Felix once again sent Helene a telegram (March 4): COMBINED ENGAGEMENT AT PSYCHIATRIC AND MOST ELEGANT MEDICAL CLINIC WITH MOST FAVORABLE WORK CONDITIONS FOR THREE YEARS. HALF TIME RESERVED FOR PRACTICE. BLUMGART, HEALY, BINGER [Dr. Carl Binger was a Harvard classmate of Cobb's] CALL THIS OFFER EXTRAORDINARY. So did Rado; he cabled Helene on the same day: FELIX HAS RECEIVED ASTOUNDING OFFER THROUGH ACCIDENT OF LUCK. GATES ABOUT TO CLOSE FOR EUROPEANS. WARN AGAINST MASOCHISTIC ATTITUDE. Since Felix was proposing to come permanently, he faced greater obstacles than he would have as a "guest."

Within a week the deal for Felix had collapsed: COBB HAD UNEXPECTED DIFFICULTIES GETTING MONEY. FACULTY REJECTS ENGAGEMENT OF FEMALE ANALYST. NEGOTIATIONS ON NEW BASIS. SITUATION UNCERTAIN. Cobb (who stuttered) had had to disappoint Felix:

> In a letter you wrote: one should not trust a stutterer. Perhaps I am unjust to him . . . And now, stuttering, he begins: the "university" colleagues had spoken out against a woman's "training" the students; moreover, since Sachs was there [at Harvard Medical School] anyway, he would have to undertake the "training," and would receive, as far as necessary, the money earmarked for Herman. [Dr. William Herman, a local analyst, had just died.]

Cobb had only been able to secure one thousand dollars for Felix's laboratory work; Cobb further explained that Blumgart had already accepted half-a-dozen German refugees at the Beth Israel. Although Cobb tactfully linked the failure of his proposal with difficulties for Helene too, it was clear that the problem lay with finding enough of a position for Felix, not her. In the meantime, Felix—still working at his English—had at least succeeded (March 17) in solving the immigration problems for his family: "I have already sworn not to be an anarchist, not to engage in polygamy, etc." Martin now had a two-thousand-dollar bank account, and a paid-for round-trip ship passage.

In September Helene and Martin sailed first-class for the United States; she thought they were getting on fine. Mira Oberholzer told Helene that she had no objection to a "fairly long interruption" in Martin's analysis. He was prepared to stay in the United States if he was accepted at a good university, which was still an uncertainty. By September 24 Helene and Martin were in New York; the Rados, Wittels, and Nunberg met them at the pier.

She found Rado in a crisis over his relationship with Freud and European analysis. At the January 9 meeting of the Vienna society, Jeanne Lampl-de Groot had presented a critical review of Rado's monograph on feminine castration anxiety. Rado had, in her view, oversimplified the complexities in terms of an "unproveable" "trauma theory" involving the ego's struggle against masochism. The need to seize on only a fragment of the truth had already appeared in charges against earlier analytic "deviators," and Rank, Rado's predecessor as editor-in-chief of the *Zeitschrift,* had also used a "trauma theory." When she published her review later that year, Lampl-de Groot expressed not only her own opinions but also critical comments raised at the meeting of the Vienna society. Rado was offended at the insult—that Freud would permit her to write such a review. After all Rado's work for analysis, Freud seemed to be treating her with more respect. (She later claimed that Rado wrote Freud about the review, and that Freud had then shown her the letter and his reply.)

As with Rank, in good measure it was Freud's followers who led the attack on a former favorite of the master's; Freud resented the way Rado had helped and encouraged some Continental analysts to leave for America. In addition, Anna Freud had not approved of the warmth of a memorial for Ferenczi that Rado had published in 1933; she and he had quarreled over the report of the 1934 congress. Like Helene, Rado thought a "camarilla" now surrounded Freud; the faithful—out of jealousy, he held—would try to make him out to be a traitor. With Jeanne Lampl-de Groot's review he felt that the Vienna group was triumphing over him.

In March 1935 Felix had reported to Helene from New York:

> Sandor is dictating to Emmy [his wife] a long letter to Anna.—Now in the evening it was read to me; under my influence, as far as necessary, everything aggressive was deleted. I cannot express an opinion about the merits. In any case, it is certain that Sandor is led by the most honest of intentions. But ask Anna for yourself.

Helene's first letter from New York expressed her alarm at the possibility that Rado might leave the movement. (In 1944 he was dismissed as a training analyst by the New York society, although he remained a member; he headed Columbia University's Psychoanalytic Institute, and when he retired in 1957 he helped found the New York School of Psychiatry at the State University of New York.) Helene shared too many of Rado's feelings about Anna Freud's new role in Freud's life to want to speak to her herself; Felix, who had remained Anna's physician, got on much more smoothly with Freud's daughter. Helene wrote Felix (September 24) that she was afraid Rado was

> in the beginning phase of a psychosis. He is obsessed with Lampl's report— in fury-filled hatred against everything and everyone connected with it. So far one would think only of an excessive reaction of someone severely narcissistically offended. But this hatred extends in a paranoid manner to the rest of the surrounding world: the society, the city of Vienna, all of Europe. All cultural values that are "European", and which in him were so pronounced, meet with furious disdain, and are contrasted, in ridiculous chauvinism, with America. And all this, again and again, goes back to that one tiny nucleus of the Lampl report. Professor becomes an evil old man who wants to destroy him (Rado) with his hatred. All of us around him are either

crooks, or mental cases under Professor's spell and in his service, etc. There is no topic—not even the most remote—that doesn't finally lead back to this sphere of ideas.—Can the outbreak still be forestalled by withdrawal of the report? Puschkuleindi, speak with Anna, but not with the full diagnostic content of this letter!

Felix, however, thought that nothing further could be done (Freud had become embittered about Rado); Felix replied to Helene (October 5):

I think it is quite useless to speak with Anna about it. What could she do? The essay will appear; this cannot be changed. This, however, as you yourself have seen, is the central stumbling block. At noon I just received a letter from Rado, in which he brushes aside the matter with embittered superiority; he enclosed a "photographic" copy of Lampl's letter to him, and also his reply to the editorial office. A few days ago I was able to find out from the Bibrings how people think about it here. I won't even mention Federn's evil blabber. It is like the bursting of a balloon filled with hydrogen sulphide; it makes one feel sick. Mr. "Editor" Edi [Bibring] gives a long talk, dry and using many words, precomposed and inaccessible . . . Waelder quotes that it gave him pleasure when once he was attacked in the periodical. I was able to prove to him that his orientation in the matter is quite deficient—but there is no thought of putting the matter aside. The gentlemen on both sides are too busy playing offended. There will only be the vanquished.

A short while later (October 13) Felix rejected her suggestion that he speak to Freud himself; Hartmann too was said to be "inaccessible." On November 6 Felix wrote that Anna had

brought up the question of Rado. Last week there was an editorial session with Professor, in which I believe she undertook to write to Rado herself—which she has done. But sentiments are unknown: since he is in the wrong, there is no mercy. Moreover, the editors have no interest in changing anything in the matter—and Professor? He who staggers shall fall! So Bibring has been suggested as successor to Rado [on the International Training Committee] . . . I discovered that when I said to Anna that a sign of clemency from Professor might still save him (Rado), and suggested to her that Professor himself should ask him to take up the position again, as a token of his desire to retain him. Now it is hard against hard, and Rado will come out of it the loser.

Helene's letters to Felix were filled with news of her invitations in America: parties, meals, appointments, proposed lectures. Still she was worried about how she would be received in Boston. But everything reinforced her dim view of the European future.

People here are highly interested in European politics, and they are 100% pessimistic, concerning Austria just as much as concerning the threat of war. For the foreseeable future, there can be no thought of any Americans undertaking trips to Vienna. In general, as an analysis town Vienna has a colossally bad name here—at least in New York—largely Rado's propaganda. (Please keep this discreet.)

In reality Americans continued to go to Vienna for analysis until Freud left in 1938. But in Helene's world, Martin had decided to stay in America if he could get into a good university; he was thinking of Chicago, Harvard, and the Massachusetts Institute of Technology as possibilities. Given the political situation, Helene told Felix that "people" were "very surprised" that he had not come. Assuming that Martin remained she was determined to extend her stay until he was settled. She even spoke well of Nunberg; she later found him so angry and egocentric that she saw him no more. Felix shared her usual view of Nunberg, and would have discounted her overenthusiasm.

> I have spent an evening with Nunberg—he is the one that I like best of all here! Since his practice has improved . . . , his mood is better, even if his contempt for Americans and his burning homesickness for Europe persist. Nor am I fond of this land and these people—but half of my heart must remain tied here—will I be able to manage at home with the other half?

Helene oversaw Martin's college plans; through the help of a Boston analyst with connections, Martin's early preference for Harvard was satisfied with admission. MIT, however, allowed him more credit for his previous work. As she told Felix (October 2):

> So now it looks as if the way is paved for Martin's future. His intellectual qualities give assurance of this, and are highly admired here. But . . . oh, Puschkuleindi, my heart is numbed with fear . . . Martin is more neurotic than I ever thought, I believe he is more neurotic than he ever was. Besides murderous, hate-filled aggression against me, which even outsiders notice, he shows such strong masochistic tendencies that it fills one with fright.

She was so distressed by the details of Martin's behavior that she wound up exclaiming: "I don't believe in analytic therapy!" Later on in Boston she reported getting on better with him; he saw her once a week, or as her dinner guest.

Helene looked on the bright side of American life, even culturally.

> People speak of great unemployment and poverty—but there is something else as well—and in the whole mood there is a hope and a striving forward. Analysis is constantly pushing its way into the clinic and into the other sciences. Perhaps at the expense of depth? Maybe, but *that* is life!

Although a few of their old friends (like Schilder) were exceptions in being cautious about Felix's coming over, Helene had decided to stay for at least a year.

> One thing is certain: *anyone,* whoever he may be—you, I, famous or obscure —must make his way here from the very beginning. The most glorious a past is only a visiting card, which is more likely to cause difficulties, because it

raises expectations and makes one more critical. One must close the curtains on one's European past and build only on what one *is*, what one is *capable of*. The whole problem, discussed hotly in Vienna with friends, of "position" appears ridiculous to me here—as well as the idea of achieving something here which is not worked through and accomplished on the spot. Puschkuleindi, that goes for me too! Of course, for a small circle I am Helene Deutsch, with 20 years of fame behind me. But this brings only *distrust* and criticism. Only strenuous work by night and day can wrestle down a bit of future. My name is *only* a springboard, just as yours is.

She might have been about to turn fifty-one, but she remained as bold and confident as she had been at earlier turning points in her life.

In contrast to the New York analysts (she acknowledged her "anti-Semitism"), Boston's society meant she was dealing with relatively more Gentiles. Cobb had arranged for Martin to enter MIT as a junior; and Helene was negotiating with Cobb on Felix's behalf. She admired in Cobb the naïveté of a thoroughly decent and honest person.

You had no blind faith in this man? Puschkuleindi, this is 100% reliability, and if you sometimes thought you saw a certain inconstancy and uncertainty, this was just the tact that the New Englanders have when they can't or don't want to say something, because they don't want to hurt the other person. Cobb doesn't want to "abuse" his high position, i.e. he has to take the mood of his surroundings into consideration. He did not "change his mind," but it is plain that the situation forced him to go back on our "call" in favor of Sachs.

Sachs had analyzed Cobb for a while (Helene afterward treated him informally), and got the five thousand dollars from the Rockefeller Foundation that Felix had been hoping for. Since, as Helene explained, Sachs's grant meant three analyses, for five fifty-minute sessions a week, nine months a year, it came to fifteen dollars an hour. Cobb undertook to write Felix a letter, with a fresh proposal, but promised to show it to Helene first; she admitted to Felix that she had "exaggerated" his Vienna position to Cobb.

Helene was impressed with American egalitarianism: "There is no talk of hierarchy. Even the 'boss' regards himself as one of the working colleagues. Everyone emphasizes to me that working together with Cobb and the connection with Harvard is of great importance."

For your orientation—before you reply to Cobb—you should know that I gave as the motive for your hesitation: 1) Your relationship with Professor, 2) the completion of work begun, 3) the psychological motive of financial "dependence" on my person. Of course these neurotic men understand this very well. He countered this with the argument that this would only be a temporary state.

Now, of course, Puschkuleindi, the decision must be left up to you. If you come here in a mood of crisis, with a "need for importance" and with the "masculine protest"—with the ridiculously narcissistic question: "Who am I there"—you will suffer here. But if you come with an attitude identical to mine: "out of that stupid stuffy atmosphere at last, and for once let us experience something freer, something that is extraordinarily relieving in its very uncertainty," and with complete inner courage and with joy in work without regard to "position," etc.—then you can be very happy here. I am very happy myself, and only my longing for you, the feeling that something is incomplete, disturbs me. Otherwise, come what may, it is such a joyful liberation, such a lust for work and an urge for work, such an intense interest—as I have not felt for at least fifteen years.

Helene retained her youthful outlook until her mid-nineties; she was also trying to free herself, as well as Felix, from their Viennese ties.

The past several years have been a dull, weary sickness, and Puschkuleindi, believe me, if fate should force me back to Vienna—I would never again engage in society and institute work! Only now in retrospect do I see how everything there, imprisoned in dreary brooding, turning around its own axis, is drying up and withering. I feel very sorry for my friends left behind —whom I personally love and esteem.

Helene failed to get a small apartment she wanted in Brookline, as a result of anti-Semitic discrimination; but she soon established herself in a suite at the Commander Hotel in Cambridge. Her practice was promising, although she reported some problems with Sachs; he was recommending "solvent" patients to her, but with the fee of ten dollars an hour. (On other occasions she stressed Sachs's "impeccable" behavior.) Sachs had been one of the small group appointed by Freud before World War I to a secret committee to forward the cause of analysis. He had been invited to Boston from Berlin in 1932 as a desperately needed training analyst; he had to be guaranteed eight patients a day before he agreed to come, but they had not been difficult for local analysts to find. By 1935 he was already established in Back Bay, and had a butler. As a lay analyst, he had been worried about Helene's attitudes on the subject and been relieved by Felix's reassurances in early 1935; nonetheless, in a medically traditional city—even in the face of his medical school appointment—Sachs encountered problems. Helene was confident she would soon be "independent" of him, and did not need to fear him as a rival in the institute; she functioned better on committees than he did. She told Felix she intended to write "to Professor, Anna, friends, Federn officially. Without the slightest guilt feelings!!"

That fall Felix was being frequently invited to the Freuds' for supper, and afterward to the family tarock game. Felix had been obliged, in mid-September, to regularize Helene's position at the institute. During a meeting of the training committee, at Anna Freud's request he signed a letter of separation to Federn as vice-president over Helene's name; Anna was to be in charge of the business of the Training Institute, and Edward Bibring would take care of the functions of Helene's job in connection with the Ambu-

latorium. When Helene cabled in early October that she was staying "indefi-
nitely," the institute proposed that she be renominated as director; her seminars were divided between one led by Jeanne Lampl-de Groot, and the other
by Anna Freud and Edward Bibring.

Although the issue never came up in documents, evidently Helene had
earlier surmised that Freud wanted her to share more of the work at the
institute with his daughter Anna. The ambivalent rivalry between them was
of long-standing; although Anna had had no academic education, by the mid-
1930s Freud had succeeded in building her up as his successor within the
movement. Originally Helene had affectionately identified with Anna, view-
ing her as a pupil; yet she always remembered how coldly Freud had turned
aside her compliments on Anna's first presentation in 1922 before the Vienna
society. On Anna's part, she admired Helene and yet feared that she would
never be as good. But by 1935, as during the trouble with Rado, Anna had
built up her own following; and Freud was increasingly dependent on her.
Anna had acted as the gatekeeper for access to her father ever since his first
illness.

Anna's closest friend had become Dorothy Burlingham, a rich American
who had been analyzed by Freud. Anna helped raise Dorothy's four children,
humanly as well as therapeutically. (Anna herself had been reared jointly by
her Aunt Minna and by Martha Freud.) On September 26 Felix wrote Helene:

> Dorothy is back from London. I find she is not in the best psychic condition
> —the analysis is finished, and the transference is unsolved. She is now hav-
> ing me treat her organically—a feeble substitute. A poor shadow creature:
> can't live without the light which Professor infuses into her. It will be no
> different with the children.

Freud's disappointment in his sons had heightened his responsiveness to
Anna and her friends; Felix reported, for example, that Ernst Freud had
failed to be admitted to Palestine "because he neither knew who Herzl was
nor had any geographic idea" of the place. Felix discussed not only Freud's
family, but also sent to Helene accounts of meetings of the Vienna society.[9]

Cobb finally wrote to Felix on October 15; he tried to understate his offer
to Felix. "My feeling is that the only thing to do is to face this difficult
situation, and see what it might mean at the worst, and then hope for better."
Felix was to be a "Research Fellow in Psychiatry" at the Harvard Medical
School. Cobb thought that Felix would never equal in Boston the position and
income he had in Vienna: "this is because your chosen field is fairly well filled
here with able men. With your wife the case is different, hers is a narrow field
in which she can attract special patients wherever she lives." Cobb thought
within a few years Felix could expect to build up a small private practice,
especially if he used psychotherapy "as well as medicine." In terms of research, Cobb offered opportunities for both clinical and laboratory work; but
for the coming year Cobb could only offer Felix five hundred dollars. Cobb

said he was painting the picture as black as possible rather than risk Felix's disappointment; but he was obviously looking forward to Felix's coming.

Shortly thereafter (October 18) Helene wrote one of her most ecstatic letters about her new life.

> We here prefer the restless life to the glorious contemplating of the Viennese circle. I personally have more and more the feeling of being released from many years' imprisonment, and from a twilight state.
>
> Whatever may be my opinion of America and the Americans, one thing I know; *here is life,* and there is dull, narcissistic brooding round about people's own intellectual fog. What is good for Freud's genius and his age, and for Anna's yielding herself up to the paternal idea, is becoming for others a mass neurosis.

She reported that people in Boston admired Felix, and were awaiting his coming; she said she could not understand why he had not stayed earlier in the year. "You are going to receive a very remarkable letter from Cobb—I have a copy with me. Don't be frightened, this is only the reaction to my portrayal of your colossal position in Vienna (!?) He is afraid of responsibility . . ."

Later (October 30) she exerted herself once again to persuade him to come over.

> If I only knew in what direction your "considerations" are going! I am angry at you, for I know that you are not making decisions *according to yourself,* but according to the opinions of others. I am out of the magic circle of personal weakness, and nobody can lay down the law for me—I no longer even know what it is to allow oneself to be influenced. Every situation in life is a totally personal experience, and calls forth a different reaction in each individual.
>
> *I,* for example, can absolutely not understand why you were so distrustful in Boston—suspecting competition everywhere, instead of mobilizing confidence in others along with your confidence in yourself.

Felix did think of himself as cunning; in the meantime Helene had warmed up to American national character.

> The Americans are much kindlier than we are, when they say their stereotyped phrases: "I was glad to meet you—when can I see you again?"—that is formally also true; they are more positive toward people; and above all, they are more positive, more affirmative toward life. Culturally they are on a lower level, it is true—Martin says according to his studies, they lack the synthesis—but I personally feel that this is an advantage, since I myself set less store by culture.

Felix was more the healer than she; she continued to tell him of her amazement: "Great God, we are the doctors in the hospital, interested in helping the patients! How they lunge upon analysis—*in order to be able to help*—and how sad and disappointed they are, when they don't get that which they hoped for there." She was attending Cobb's rounds: "Heavens, where is the darkness of European authority with its rectal cringing servility? Here there are only those that know more or less, and C. is glad to let his youngest student teach him something." She sent Cobb a case from his own outpatient department, in order to round out his experience from his analysis; she wanted to teach him, by giving a liberal education, even if he was the head of the department. Cobb not only took the case, but according to his widow would come home and say with wonder: "Do you know what I learned about today!" (In 1965 Helene recalled her years at the Massachusetts General, despite how she is reported to have flourished there, as the hardest, unhappiest time in her life; such a discrepancy is typical of how hard she could be to interview.)

On November 3 Felix announced that he would be coming at the beginning of January; transatlantic mail was slow, and he also wired his decision on November 16. He intended to stay at least until the summer, to see if the working conditions turned out to be suitable. His career at the Massachusetts General never got very far, although Helene held an important position throughout World War II. In 1935 she asked for a copy of Felix's acceptance reply to Cobb; Felix said to Cobb that the "difficulties" lay "above all in two directions; firstly in the discontinuation of my personal relationship to Professor Freud and his home and secondly in financial considerations." To Helene, Felix wrote (November 13): "People are concerning themselves with me. They are particularly gracious in high places. Frau Professor allowed me to examine her! She has found her way back after thirteen years. What do you say now? Oh, Muschkuleindi, how cold this leaves me! *That* sun no longer warms."

By the end of December Felix was at the Freud's three or four times a week; Felix was free of any guilt feelings about leaving. As he wrote Helene (December 31):

> I didn't send New Year's wishes to Professor, because I didn't know if you were doing it. Moreover I see him so often. Also, I haven't told him myself anything of my trip to America. But it is plain that he has something on the tip of his tongue, for now he sometimes gets personal. His whole family's emphatic expressions of liking for me seem to have warmed him. But when I cast my eyes on him, I am looking into the past; not a trace of the former paternal bond is present. I admire the 80-year-old in his freshness and greatness, but I can leave him without sorrow. Why do I write this? Well, because there are others who are being left as well. And yet, how light is the weight of this, when I am coming to you and Martin. Together again!

On a short trip Helene and Felix returned to Europe for the congress in Marienbad in August 1936; Felix saw about getting their possessions out of Vienna, and Martin Freud helped dispose of the apartment. Freud's wife was politically so naïve that she thought their leaving for America was "pure high-spiritedness," an adolescent act. The Deutsches were to suffer no material or professional losses from Germany's annexation of Austria less than two years later.

2

Separation

Life in Boston meant a new cultural setting, but because of her profession Helene could continue Old World ties. Freud kept minimally in touch with her. He had been angry with Helene for leaving Vienna, but she could discount his reaction in view of his general distaste for America. She knew about his clinical prejudices; he was harder on his American patients than on any others. Once in Vienna he had recommended to her a candidate from the United States who, Freud said, had a bad reputation about money—and for Americans, Freud added in his note, such a rumor is usually justified. Freud harbored the most negative feelings for patients whom he primarily accepted because they could afford his fees; she thought he had had people in training whom he despised. She could not afterward remember a male pupil from the United States toward whom he was truly favorable.

Freud's anti-Americanism extended to (and was promoted by) what he thought of the branch of his own family there. In 1930 he had commemorated the death of his mother, at the age of ninety-five, by writing in English to a newborn American niece, Anne Bernays: "Welcome as a new output of life on the day great-grandmother was buried. Great Uncle Sigmund." Freud had taken this momentous occasion to make a historic circle, encompassing past, present, and future. Yet at the same time he was defying propriety and convention; he did not himself go to his mother's funeral in Vienna, instead sending Anna to "represent" him. In his writings he described[1] the mother-son tie as a perfect human relationship, the least affected by ambivalence. If he chose to stay home, and composed a family letter that day, he may also have been protecting himself from experiencing too much emotion; his feelings were intense, and the cancer made his own mortality loom larger. He liked to think he could dare to say anything; in the act of linking his grand-niece in a chain of generations, Freud also—by condescending to write in English and characterizing her as an "output" of a civilization he hated for its commercialism—was putting in a nutshell what he thought of the North American continent.

In Boston Helene was to be sending patients to American analysts, and she thought that if she had needed his help Freud would not have referred people to her. As he aged he had grown increasingly intolerant, harsh toward himself and standoffish to new people. In this context he personally inscribed (May 1936) three words to Helene at the bottom of a formal card printed to acknowledge greetings sent him on his eightieth birthday: "Loving but unrec-onciled." Affection was enough for Freud then; he did not need to forgive her for what he understood as a form of desertion. In 1938 he wrote her not to feel too guilty about having left against his will; he said that he believed and trusted she would remain faithful to psychoanalysis.

Edward Bibring maintained contact with Helene through birthday greet-ings to her on October 12, 1936; like Freud she took such occasions seriously. He was a leading orthodox theoretician of the future, and she treasured his note as testimony of how the Viennese group felt about her. He and his wife Grete later emigrated with the Freuds to London, and then to Boston (1940) where the couple soon became a rival to the Deutsches within local analysis; Helene maintained good relations with him, however, and admired how he coped with Parkinson's disease at the end of his life. When he wrote her in 1936, however, he was a symbol of the world she had left behind; she was still living at the Commander, before buying a house on Larchwood Drive. (The Deutsches, who had owned no property in Austria, had saved enough to need no mortgage.)

> Dear Hala,
>
> Our original intention was to telegraph you, but because of the high costs such a telegram must be very short, and in the final analysis it is unsatisfactory for both parties. For us, because we can't say what we want to say, and for you, because telegraph style does not convey the personal feel-ings. Moreover, with a telegram, you will find it much easier to send only a very short reply, or perhaps even none at all. We don't want to make that easy for you. If you don't reply, then at least you ought to have a bad conscience.
>
> After this long preface, now we can begin with the actual theme. We thought very cordially of you on your birthday. But not completely un-grudgingly, partly because you have left us, and partly because, off there in the distance, you are beginning to leave us inwardly as well; perhaps not always, perhaps only sometimes, perhaps only a little bit, but just enough for us to imagine with doubled intensity how lovely it would be if not even that little bit existed.
>
> However this may be—having spent so many long years together, years that were not marked by undisturbed calm and happy security—we feel we

have ties with you that are capable of resistance. And out of this obligation, we wish to you everything that you could wish to yourself in your situation: lust for work, friends, and all other satisfactions that one needs to live in happy and serene calm.

He thought he should bring Helene up to date about the Vienna society.

There is not much that is new here. As in many years previously, we again have our general meeting before us, we are beginning our courses and seminars, our society evenings and guest lectures, our discussions of scientific and administrative questions, and we take all this just so seriously as it is necessary to take seriously, when one is identified with a cause, and on the other hand, so little seriously, because the rather disturbed times do make one tired and sceptical. But this cannot mean that we have abandoned our tradition of devoting, with energy and passion, too much to work and too little to pleasure.

Bibring told Helene exactly who had lectured, and what the upcoming program was like.

Helene also shared the legendary Viennese tact. From a European perspective, America was a relief as well as a shock; Continental culture could be too mannered. For example, it would be a dreadful offense to step on someone's toes in a crowd in traditional Germany; but in Boston such an incident would be considered trivial. From the point of view of refugee analysts, Emily Post, in teaching a certain code for all American classes, had made a signal contribution to democratic behavior. But even in the refined atmosphere of the Boston aristocracy Helene was distinguished for her charm and directness.

On July 10, 1940, Helene wrote Stanley Cobb and his wife, Elizabeth (she had been in formal analysis with Helene in Boston; "Babayaga" was the name of the farm Helene started in New Hampshire):

Dear Betty and dear Stanley,

For a psychoanalyst who is struggling with human discords, and whose relation to married life is that of a patcher, (?) it is a lovely and unusual gift from life, to have a glimpse of a marriage which has no need of such patching.

I take today's occasion to thank you for having given me an opportunity to observe—how shall I say it?—"love" is too complex, "successful conquest of ambivalence" is too professional . . . I shall disregard the nomenclature, and merely affirm that you are one of the few couples whose marriage was not founded upon "error." I am completely sure that the path to the golden anniversary will be still more beautiful and more intimate.

My intensive efforts succeeded in finding one *"weak* point": that is the *coffee.* For this problem, I offer a modest contribution by trying to correct Betty's coffee by good cream. This old silver pitcher serves this purpose—first-class cream (!) can always be acquired from Babayaga.

My wishes to you both, and come from one who hold you both very dear.

Hala

P.S. The crown and the monogram on the pitcher do not pertain to my own family (hélas!)—

Felix added his own postscript to this letter: "Nor to mine. I join Hala in her wishes."

Letter writing was an art decreasingly practiced on this side of the Atlantic, and over the years Helene absorbed New World ways; telephone calls replaced more traditional means of communication. But if she chose to, Helene could still rise to the occasion. When she thought Martin's wife Suzanne (they had married in 1939) might be pregnant, Helene wrote to an imaginary grandchild. She never sent the letter, but put it in an envelope marked "to the mandatory Suzanne" (Helene started off with feelings of rivalry for her daughter-in-law). Helene had just received some money as an advance for her *The Psychology of Women;* she played with the theme of bisexuality.

Dear grandchild! This check came to-day—the first since you have announced your existence. Your sex is already known to you, but not to us. Suppose you are a girl: it will be of great interest to you to know your grandmother's books and to take *all* on spiritual and *material* advantages it brings. Suppose you are a boy: how nice to know more about the women— they will play a great role in your life! But *you* will be probably more interested in this part of her writings which never meant much to your grandmother: the financial one. It would be much nicer for you both—whoever you are—to have a knitting type of grand mother. She is very, very sad that she is not—but for her work your Mommi may buy for you plenty of things. So here it is!

Helene's mental stylishness, combined with the force of her personality, meant that within Boston analysis she attained a unique position. The most long-standing member of the society—Isidor Coriat—could be easily dismissed, though he was a kind and warm person, as someone of no account; she recalled he had told her where she could find good ice cream. The analysts involved in setting up the Boston institute had been students abroad when she was already established. Among the European refugees, Grete Bibring and Tola Rank later played important roles: but Helene prided herself on not needing high official titles. If she served for a short period (1939–41) as president of the Boston society it was because she was sorely needed. Her stature went beyond organizational connections: in Vienna she had had Freud's support, and now there was Stanley Cobb. Cobb had repeatedly remarked about her: "You have to believe in a woman with such magnificent eyes!"

She attracted a host of admirers from various walks of life. When Norbert Wiener, the founder of cybernetics, who had been a child prodigy, needed someone to go to for help, Helene assisted him informally. (According to his autobiography, he had earlier been treated by one of the undistinguished early Boston analysts.) By the early 1940s Helene's pupils in Boston were already enough for her to have made an impact on the development of American psychiatry. For example, she analyzed (1937–38) Dr. John C. Whitehorn, later head of the Department of Psychiatry at the famous Phipps Clinic at Johns Hopkins University. (In 1942 she asked him if he minded her having given his name as a reference regarding "professional standing and personal character" to obtain a certificate from the American board for specialization in psychiatry and neurology. She wrote: "As far as 'professional standing' I really think you can consider me to be a quite experienced and reliable person. As far as 'personal character' I am deep under my ego ideal but relatively not worse than the greatest part of certified people."[2] Earlier, she had had to take her medical exams over again; she had always kept up her interest in endocrinology and pushed it to the forefront whenever possible.)

Felix, however, had not succeeded professionally in Boston; that the city was such a medically strong center of training influence only made his situation more frustrating. In the late 1930s Felix impressed people as a "sweet guy," but not a strong personality in dealing with colleagues and friends; he seemed to handle his loneliness and anxiety by being charming. This gave the unfortunate impression of his being something of a "clown," which is the word serious leaders of Boston medicine used for him. Helene's reserve and personal dignity meant by itself that she would be taken more seriously.

Whitehorn had been invited to head a Department of Neuropsychiatry at Washington University in St. Louis, and Felix accepted an appointment from him as the first professor of psychosomatic medicine. In St. Louis he had an opportunity for research, earning money as well as academic status, unlike what he could attain in Boston. Helene could rationalize staying behind in Cambridge on the grounds that the society needed her; in any event, she was not about to give up her friends, old as well as new, for an uncertain future in the Midwest. During this, their last professional separation, which lasted from the fall of 1939 until the spring of 1941, Helene and Felix once again exchanged letters; she made one visit to see him, and he returned to the East for vacations. But their correspondence, though steady, did not equal in intensity or eloquence their earlier struggles to keep in touch by mail; their marriage was now settled, with shared concerns in their professional, personal, and political lives.

Many of Helene's letters to Felix were concerned with the plans and arrangements connected with her fascination with a farm she had started in North Wolfeboro, New Hampshire. She had called it "Babayaga."[3] Babajaga was a Polish witch who rides on a broom and sits in a basket; Helene had changed the "j" to a "y" in order to make it sound more like an American Indian name, giving the farm an incognito as she did with patients when writing clinical papers. The Polish witch was a bad one, never associated with good magic; she imprisoned children, and even ate them. A Russian Babajaga was a kind witch who told children stories. Since Helene had psychologically eradicated her mother as a bad fairy, she always worried about the impact she was having on people; at the same time she also identified herself with the little girl who, according to the Polish legend, could outwit danger. If Helene owned a farm, it had to have an original name, whose meaning not even Poles could immediately understand.

Like other Europeans then Helene felt the need for land; with the approach of war a secure supply of food had its realistic advantages. Dr. John Murray helped find her the property. Throughout 1939–41 Helene often wrote about caretaker problems and construction difficulties, as well as specifics in connection with the cows, hens, sheep, and gardening. Yet it was Molly Putnam who had the practical sense about farming. Helene had something of a Marie Antoinette attitude toward the farm; neither she nor Felix even felt at ease using fireplaces. But in later years she and Felix spent summers there with their grandsons. Martin and his wife enjoyed it too, although in the early 1940s Helene had to be restrained from building them overly elaborate accommodations. In Vienna Helene and Felix had grown used to a weekend resort in the countryside, and for extended vacations patients were able to live around them in New Hampshire. While Felix was away Helene learned how to drive herself back and forth from the farm, about a three-hour trip.

Helene as well as others found that Boston, with its Puritan heritage, was a particularly receptive place for analysis. Its background of seventeenth-century theological thought offered, in its particular conception of God, an expression of the enduring human belief in the reality of what Freud had called the unconscious.[4] Transcendentalism, and then Unitarianism, had been subsequent forms of idealism that paved the way for the acceptance of psychoanalytic ideas. By the beginning of World War II, proper Bostonians were family-minded, introspective, truth-loving, and loyal—also more than a little suspicious of Jews. It was one of those pleasurable paradoxes that Betty Cobb, for example, was a Cabot; her mother—with over sixty first cousins in Boston—looked on Helene with the suspicion due any foreigner, not just a Freudian. (Betty Cobb's uncle had founded the Watch and Ward Society, which arrested people for breaking the Sabbath.)

Helene's reactions to European events entailed reflecting on the past she had left behind. For in the fall of 1939 Poland was to be divided between Hitler's Germany and Stalin's Russia. Helene was worried about her family; as she wrote Felix on September 20, 1939:

> From Poland, still no word. How should there be? It will still be a while before "order" prevails. Today America's decisive "declaration of neutrality" is expected—a new victory of Hitlerism—*without* really sparing us "Americans" the war.

One lives in a dark cloud, automatized in all functions, with the same little problems and worries as if one knew nothing. Just the same way as in our being attuned to eternity while in full awareness of death . . .

Professor is very sick and dying from X-ray burns. Schur sits by his bed day and night. Poor old man. To die now, right at this time, is terrible.

One plays around with worries about the fate of mankind, Poland, etc. But what chokes one up most of all are tears shed for our youth.

Helene thought longingly of their past (September 28).

Do you remember autumn walks in the Vienna woods? With new ideas in our heads, and with the impatience to realize them—with overflowing and the feeling that "you don't understand me," because everything was so happily narcissistic that one was deeply insulted when a demand for clarification came from the other party? Where is all that now?

Since she was professionally unhappy, for the time being Helene decided to take no new patients; "for decency's sake" she reduced the number of old ones.

Sitting for hours on end behind someone whose talk is so empty and barren because one has heard it so many times before; immobility with inner restlessness; and above all, the futility of earning money—these things make it *impossible* to practice one's profession. So I shut myself off, I don't listen, I stare incessantly at the clock, etc.

Farming was continually on her mind; in animals she could see everything which in humans was a perversion. But politics kept intruding on her thoughts.

I wish I could go to an agricultural school, to polish myself up a bit in this direction. If it weren't for the peril of war, which keeps putting one in a condition of paralysis. In the White House there is unofficially no doubt that America will very soon be "in." With the German-Russian military alliance, the fate of democracy seems to be sealed. Are we yet to experience the change of fronts: Fascism vs. Bolshevism? (Perhaps an alliance of Germany, France, England). If one were not so tired of life and close to death, one would find the world very "interesting." Yesterday I was at the Red Cross— via Switzerland, inquiries can now be begun. I hope that Przemyśl is Russian —What tragic complications in individual fates would result from one part of the family's being in Russia, the other in Germany . . . So the personal becomes more than ever interwoven in the general. No sooner do I begin writing about personal matters than I am back at world events.

The partition of Poland left Przemyśl in Russian hands, and Stalin, after being attacked by Germany in June of 1941, would join the Allies. But the Soviet Union was far removed from the socialism of Helene's years of political involvement.

They each exchanged news from Europe, but since Felix's sister was now in New York it was Helene's family which was the one in immediate jeopardy. She reported that she had read about Lieberman's career in the newspapers.

> Lieberman is a member of the new Polish government in Paris—that is what I call perseverance in idealism (read: "hero fantasy").
>
> Did you hear Hitler's speech? Such lying hypocrisy and transparence! Unfortunately he believes fanatically and magically in his good star. And magic combined with a good army is very dangerous. Events will now come thick and fast.

Helene now more or less accepted that Cobb would never fully welcome Felix at his department; but the absence of word from Poland was more immediately worrisome: "This, and Professor's death make it seem as if the whole past lay in ruins. And if it were not for Martin and Suzanne—life would not have the slightest hint of a future for me . . ." World politics for Felix too meant that they were thoroughly putting Europe behind them: "It really takes great enthusiasm, in the face of these events," he wrote, "to be interested in ego-id-and-superego."

> After so many years of married life Felix still sent Helene flowers weekly. In October 1939 she made a strenuous trip to see Felix in St. Louis; as she had put it,

> I would like to have a look at your existence, for you know that I am not satisfied with platonic knowledge. For a few hours: the room, the views from your window, your work rooms—then I will be able to see you more concretely when you phone or write.

Helene's train trip left her only a little over a day with Felix, and others wanted to see her while she was in town. Felix had one complaint afterward:

> As you left, you told me I need a mother. Now, that's utterly wrong! What I need is to live together with you again like man and wife—the mother has been overcome. Back to you, not as a boy, but as what I am, have become. That is why I took the separation upon myself, went away—in order to prove that the "boy" is no more.

Helene hastened to try to defend her parting comment.

> No, Puschkuleindi, you are wrong in saying that you don't need a caring mother. From birth until death, hated or loved, feared or blessed, a man (as boy and father) *needs* his mother. Only the degrees and phases of the relationship change, and the wanderings and confusions make it necessary to flee or liberate the self from the mother in the woman. So let us both welcome this liberation from the one armed with the knife, and let us think of the one who will provide "light and coffee" in the near future.

On November 3 Felix accepted her clarification, explaining that he had been dragging his heels "against the mother, but not against the motherliness. . . ."

On returning to Cambridge Helene heard that Rank had fallen critically ill; although he had been divorced from Tola, and had recently remarried, she went to New York City to be with him. After a three-day illness Rank was dead: "Tola returned . . . with Halusia from the funeral: profoundly broken, for she still loved him. So once again we are mourning a piece of the past together." In contrast to Helene's success, Tola always seemed to be in a jam. When Otto died, Helene wanted Betty Cobb to go visit Tola, even though they were divorced. Events in Poland reinforced Helene's sympathy for Tola's loneliness and suffering.

Newspapers were full of stories about pogroms against the Jews of Poland. "The children of Jewish parents are forced into orphanages—the men are sent away and the women left to starve. Usually, people lose the traces of their loved ones. Do you feel this sadistic orgy of a government which in its own country pays premiums to the women for motherhood!" Whether it was due to outward circumstances or inner inhibitions, Helene's work was not going well.

> I have always imagined that when I am old, I will draw on the reserves of my "masculinity" and write thick books. All is in readiness. I have freed myself entirely from "social life"; no one disturbs me; but my Muse is not present. Do you remember how, during the time of my friendship with Tola in Vienna, I wrote nothing, and then had the feeling that even at a later date I would have written nothing either, if she had stayed in Vienna? In addition, there is Molly . . . In one word, productive work and women's love do not go together (for me as a woman!) But since I take these friendships to be very important, I am arming myself for a compromise, and setting out to write!

Felix was immersed in his research; he spent twelve to fourteen hours a day at work. That fall, when Cobb rejected two of his articles, Helene heard about it informally first. She was repeatedly telegraphing Poland (with prepaid reply) to no avail. She assumed that famine must prevail in Poland.

> How good it is that *emotionally* you are so occupied with your work. This is for me a song out of the distant past—today everything is so pale and devalued. I wish I could find the way back to intellectual things! For it is for me the sole and *natural* way to free myself from more personal matters.

Absence of specific news of her family left her (December 4) mournful.

> It's strange, how grief brings me back, beyond the years of separation and alienation, into the old past, causes my old passions to revive, and how after a phase of apathy I am deeply concerned and very, very sad. The grieving sense of "never again this and never again that" comes over me so frequently.

The *Christian Science Monitor* ran an article about the Jewish ghetto in Poland.

I saw the dear, quiet, modest boy with his face distorted by hate lugging heavy beams for the building of the wretched quarters in which death and desperation will prevail. And I remember how he came for a few hours from Cracόw to Przemyśl to talk with me: he was interested in allergy and his dream was to come to America for a year to learn certain things. Could I help him with that? He said that in his wildest dreams he wouldn't think of staying in America.

I did nothing—out of that evil, passive *misanthropy* which "simply ignores."

Helene also reproached herself for having done nothing earlier about one of her cousins. She made a resolution for herself: *"Where we can't or won't help, all right*—but from simple slovenliness, negligence—this must not happen again!" In December her brother-in-law telegraphed "all well," which was a temporary relief to her.

Old friends turned to Felix and Helene; they both read stories of Europeans who committed suicide rather than face Nazi terror. Paul Barnay had written Felix as early as July 21, 1939; he was in Budapest then, and he gratefully acknowledged thirty dollars Felix had sent him. Paul assumed that Felix could not have sent more, making a point of how many letters of "misery" Felix must be getting. (Felix saved no others.) Paul's money on deposit in Vienna, and royalties from song texts, were inaccessible to him, so he was hoping to get a visa by December or January. In Hungary he was not able to earn anything: "Now I am becoming young again—I am beginning to look for pawnbrokers." Paul had completed two books, and was hoping to "get somewhere with them" in America, either as a writer or a director. Felix had written Paul about Martin's marriage, but nothing about Helene. Paul replied: "Why do you write nothing at all about Hala? How is she doing in her profession; has she got used to things?"

In November Felix heard once again from Paul; he wanted to know if Felix could pay for his passage, but Felix was worried about how Paul would support himself in America. Paul was planning to come "with films, books, and good recommendations." Felix told Helene (November 6) that "as long as he sees his future in this direction it will be difficult to advise him. Before I reply to him, I will write to you." Within a day Felix had made up his mind to tell Paul that as long as Felix's sister, Else, was in need, and there was still uncertainty about Helene's people in Poland, it was impossible for Felix to take on this new responsibility. In addition to his university appointment that fall, Felix had three or four analytic cases in treatment; it was uncertain, though, for how many years his department would continue to receive its outside financial support. (Felix had been thinking, however, of buying a new car that fall.)

At the moment he is not in danger—he may be able to find a job outside his profession over there as well as in U.S.A. It hurts me to have to write that to him; but, much though we would like to, we can't shoulder new burdens. You surely notice how hard this is for me.

As the European situation grew grimmer, Felix felt guilty about Paul. In 1939 the Deutsches earned $2,600 in interest from $72,000 in capital. Felix also thought about Reinhold: "No sacrifice would be too great for me to save Reinhold. One would be saving someone not only for his own sake, but for others as well." Reinhold had left Czechoslovakia, as he returned to Poland to try and get his citizenship reinstated; he failed in this endeavor, although Felix sent Helene a clipping about a department for Polish doctors being set up in Edinburgh, Scotland. Reinhold had been Helene's special friend; earlier in the fall she had had her Boston lawyer, recommended to her originally by Sachs, draw up the necessary papers. She was the one in the family clever about handling finances; evidently she signed many affadavits for refugees with guarantees of money. At the time Reinhold's papers were first drawn up, "unfortunately" Helene preferred to spend the money for the house taxes in Cambridge and new farm debts. In the end she came through for Reinhold; Cobb had secured a position for Reinhold as head of a small psychiatric hospital. But his apathy prevented him from getting safely out.

Toward Paul, however, Helene felt differently. She forwarded a letter from Paul to her to Felix in St. Louis, commenting:

> His literary attitude toward America is very disconcerting. I think he ought to have used the waiting period to learn something more useful, with better prospects (for example, Hungarian swine-raising—I mean this seriously). Manuscripts of famous authors now lie untouched for years—especially in the film there is overproduction, the statistics of which I saw a few days ago. Frightening! If you give Paul regular support, he will have it better over there than here.

Helene was sending money to her family in Poland (as did Tola Rank to her mother); Helene told Felix she had answered Paul: "I made it clear to him that emotionally I am otherwise engaged, and I would have to leave this matter to *you*. Is this right? However, I will look around for possibilities for him."

Paul had four separate problems: (1) surviving in Europe—eventually he was to be put into a concentration camp; (2) getting a visa, and maintaining its validity; (3) securing the money for crossing the Atlantic; (4) supporting himself once he had made it abroad. Felix heard from Paul again in February 1940.

> I have received another letter from Paul, and I gave him an honest picture of the situation. Since he still has no visa, I am waiting for further word from him. I wrote to him that once he is here I will help him to the best of my

ability, but that this can only be limited help, and can only come from me
and not from you.

In October Paul was still in a fix.

> A few days ago a letter came from Paul. He writes that he had his visa, had
> scraped together the money for his trip, but then dollars had been de-
> manded. Now the visa has expired, and he is trying for a new one. But he
> needs dollars ($250) to pay for transport on a Greek ship . . . If it were
> only the $250 the decision would be easier—but the burden and the subse-
> quent responsibility. But I will send him some dollars, since, as he writes, he
> is already selling his clothes. I won't make the other decision before I know
> your opinion. The band of youth, and its meaning, insofar as it was embod-
> ied in Paul, has become foreign to me.

Helene remained unresponsive; as she wrote Felix on November 4, 1940, "I
must leave the matter of Paul entirely up to your feelings. That he will be
totally maintained by us here, there is no doubt. Now help from other
sources, jobs etc. for Jewish refugees have ceased completely." Felix's relationship with Paul was not over, but Felix seems to have wanted to be free of
him; and therefore Felix was less than enthusiastic about bringing him to
America.

Paul's sister Louisa had made it to England; but to her astonishment the
British Government had her interned. At Churchill's instructions, thousands
of German, Austrian, and Italian nationals were put in detention camps "at
His Majesty's pleasure." In this indiscriminate roundup Freud's son Martin
was also interned; the British subsequently shipped thousands of people,
mostly innocent refugees from Hitler, to Canada and Australia. Louisa had
been given Felix's address by her brother; she thought Paul might already be
in the States. She wrote Felix (January 25, 1941) from the Isle of Man:

> I was interned at the end of May. In October I was again before a tribunal
> and only then did I learn, to my great and unpleasant surprise, that I was an
> "enemy alien." Can you imagine that? The Nazis kill my family and chase
> me out of the country and to the English I'm an "Enemy"!

Felix forwarded Louisa's letter to Helene: "Read this letter from Paul's sister.
What all has taken place since Zell am See! I have had no word from Paul,
since I refused him the travel costs ($500), but also no confirmation that the
money I sent him has arrived."

Helene's own work commitments showed signs of reviving. Reading Polish literature helped her over her slump. In November 1940 Hitschmann,
who was thinking himself of moving to St. Louis, reported to Felix that
Helene had an admirable "whirl of ideas." While her own writing had been in
a fallow period, she had been pleased by Felix's research interests; he was
again playing in a trio, using music as a consolation, as he had when she went

to Munich in 1914, as well as during World War I, when she was so busy with her hospital appointment. Whitehorn had all along been asking Felix what might possibly lure Helene to St. Louis; she claimed that it was her involvement with building up the farm that more than anything held her back. She was capable at her peak of working clinically over ten hours a day. She was, she wrote Felix, "working like a horse—eleven analyses and one–three consultations a day."

The farm was a welcome regular weekend retreat. Helene composed both volumes of *The Psychology of Women* at Babayaga; she loved to swim there, and Felix was moved to paint. Even if there always seemed problems associated with setting up the farm, Helene was fascinated by what she was learning. In the winter of 1940, when her own work was not going well, she reported that

> Molly fell in love with a highly aristocratic cow (Fanny, $300) with a long family tree—but Mr. L. [the caretaker] and I decided to begin with a more proletarian one, which he will bring here this week. Especially because the bull in this region which is worthy of her is related to her in such a way as to make breeding impossible. You know, that is a complicated science! It is not a matter of the *closeness* of relationship but of certain kinds of relationship (e.g. Mother-and-son, or brother-and-sister are all right, but one must not be descended from a certain bull—etc.) Such a beast has whole books recording its ancestry, the quantities of milk in *generations*—one is obligated to carry on these books etc.

Molly chose cows by their eyes, and often had the responsibility for deciding on their names.

While Helene was feeling discouraged about her profession as an analyst, she determined not "to succumb to a new compulsion for repetition with the formation of a psychoanalytic group, didactic analyses, etc." If it turned out to be a necessity, she could accept being "a victim of circumstances" knowing others were worse off; but of her "own free will—no. I am through with that piece of life, and for that reason I could not produce *good.*"

If Whitehorn created a faculty position for her in St. Louis, it would be so she could continue his analysis and found a new institute there. As Felix toyed with the idea of possibly moving his practice to Chicago, she felt confirmed—whatever her expressed willingness to join Felix on a "sabbatical"—in her determination to stay put in Boston. For his part, Felix had planned to stay in St. Louis for a total of two years; the more he achieved there the more he thought he would be wanted elsewhere. Even as early as February 1940 he was already confident he would be returning to Boston; that March he was to lecture at the Simmons College School of Social Work. As Helene's own spirits were reviving, an issue of *Time* magazine published her picture; in an article on women doctors, she and Karen Horney were singled out as "the outstanding women psychiatrists in the U.S.""[5] The next month Felix commented that Helene seemed "once again full of ideas and joy in your work."

Martin's future had been a source of great concern to Helene as well as Felix; she regularly kept her husband up to date about their son's life and career in Cambridge. Toward the end of the war he joined the scientific community in Los Alamos (when she visited there she got to know J. Robert Oppenheimer); but while Felix was away in St. Louis, Martin had gone back into analysis. This time he went to a male therapist, Dr. M. Ralph Kaufmann; he was especially interested in psychosomatic medicine, and therefore close to Felix's own work. Later Martin would choose as an analyst Grete Bibring, who was on poor terms with both Deutsches.

Although at times Helene felt her son avoided being alone with her, the two got on as well as they ever did; Helene referred once to her daughter-in-law in terms of "the gold of her tenderness," and whatever doubts she had never got expressed in letters to Felix. She regularly referred to Martin and Suzanne as "the children," and saw a good deal of them at the farm. Helene was mildly worried by Martin's politics, which she once characterized as "Communist leanings"; Helene felt she had given up that sort of left-wing commitment. *"There* one no longer goes along. Age makes one into an adherent of 'ordered democracy'—which one will never experience." Although Felix and Helene both worried about the course of Martin's analysis (which Felix was paying for), and often felt encouraged by Kaufmann's various remarks to them, Martin's professional work took most of his time; sometimes he could be irritable because of overwork. Helene thought that she and Felix had tried *"so* hard to give him the freedom of *joy* in work!"

Despite the strength of Helene's constitution, occasionally she suffered from minor bouts of ill health. Dr. Louis Zetzel had been taking care of her and Felix ever since they had come to the States; Zetzel would give thorough reports about Helene to Felix, during this period stressing the one-sidedness of her diet. In the early spring of 1940 she staged a recovery, "through the magic effect of unopened medicine . . . don't tell Zetzel." Zetzel treated other analysts in Boston, such as Tola Rank and the Bibrings; and his second wife was a prominent analyst herself. A letter of Helene's to Zetzel (June 6, 1940) communicates something of her spiritual independence.

> Thank you for your letter, and I want to express on this occasion my great confidence and the high appreciation I have for you. This is not a manner of speaking, but a deeply sincere sentiment. My need to express it comes from the fact that I am a very bad patient, disobedient and undisciplined. This is not due to my lack of acceptance of the authority of the physician in charge, but to the fact that any subordination interferes powerfully with the way of my profession. I can only promise you that during my vacation, all your orders will be obeyed.

Zetzel had a patient in mind for analysis, and although Helene could not take him herself she undertook to place him elsewhere in the fall. (Helene, unlike some of Zetzel's other analyst patients, regularly paid him a medical fee; at that time Martin and Suzanne went to him as well. Only after Felix's death did she accept free treatment.)

Throughout 1939–41 Helene and Felix had a steady stream of refugees to worry about. Although in the end Anna Freud had decided to stay in London, other analysts were trying to get established in America. At one point while Felix was away she even had some needy (nonanalytic) refugees living in her house. As she remarked once in a letter to Felix, ". . . what does psychoanalysis have to do in all these mighty social upheavals." After the farm was more or less established, her concern for it began to wane.

> I absolutely have the impression that I must decide inwardly and I fear that the decision will turn out in favor of my vocation, or of a compromise which, while including the farm, still uses my energy in the old channel. Perhaps in a *programmatic* study of the animals' drives. However, for that one must be much better inwardly and outwardly equipped, must change over totally into the new area of work, or have reliable collaborators, etc. To be a farmer for a hobby—all right—but I am still too young and have too great a past to regard the hobby as filling out my life. For being *just* a farmer, I am too old, i.e. I can't make the thing work with all the depth and seriousness of function which has always been in my work, and *must* be in order to preserve my personality.

Helene thought the farm needed "a very adult woman as a ruling ordering spirit." She and Molly were not enough: "An intellectual Jewess and a compulsive-neurotic Yankee just aren't the right combination."

Gradually Helene wanted to get back to her former way of working. Earlier, when she was feeling dispirited, she had had only five paying analytic cases: "Life is empty when productivity lies idle. Then, not the objective value, but the subjective experience is of such great importance. I still don't know how I am now going to worm my way out of this emptiness of mind."

Even though, like others in Austria, Helene had seen the Nazis as an isolated German horror, she was generally pretty shrewd politically. Although she could not vote in the 1940 presidential election, it attracted her most intense interest. Helene was an enthusiast for Franklin D. Roosevelt; she was shocked by Cobb's support of Willkie, which she denounced as "a bit goyish-dumb" of him. (She could not appreciate the natural Republicanism of New England Brahmins.*) The Republican candidate seemed too reminiscent of European fascists; after listening to him on the radio, she wrote Felix: "The mass of cattle roared as loud as the Germans when Hitler speaks. The speech

---

* Cobb's mother detested Roosevelt. She put her own interpretation on a secret mission he made in 1945 to visit the training camp of the O.S.S. "Stanley has gone to Washington, and cannot say why. Stanley is a psychiatrist. Roosevelt is crazy. Therefore, he has gone to see Roosevelt."

was demagogic, of a quality that our proletariat wouldn't have tolerated even on its lowest level of development."

She was very excited about the election returns, pleasantly surprised by Roosevelt's re-election. (She had even canceled an analytic session to be able to listen to one of his campaign speeches.) On election night she had unsuccessfully tried to reach Felix by phone; ordinarily they telephoned at prearranged times.

> I wanted to share the joy with you, for—rightly or wrongly—this election matter seems to me of immense importance.
>
> It was so lovely, after our own political experiences, to participate in an action in which people can express their decision and choice really *freely! Freely!* Then did you hear the youngest, the oldest, the first and the last voter? Wasn't it beautiful to hear this serious boy, with such understanding and belief in democracy? Or the 120-year-old Negro who remembered slavery so well? Or this young official who came so late because she couldn't get away from her duties and who said so plainly that she had stormed for Mr. Willkie but she believed that nothing could happen to democracy: "we will work together."
>
> And did you hear that puffed-up balloon, Mr. Willkie, speak? Everything that feels decency in this country must turn away in disgust . . . But he remains—with his organized following—a grave danger. You know my theory—nothing is so dangerous as living above one's own status. And once one has been puffed-up, one doesn't steam off of one's own free will.

World politics was grim that autumn; to Europeans like the Deutsches it seemed like the last days of Pompeii. Even her good-for-nothing brother came back into her life. Emil—identified for Felix's sake as her "former brother"— had cabled for money, ostensibly for the sake of their mother; he used to do this for the welfare of his child, and Helene considered him "an anti-Semitic confidence man." She determined to get her mother's address from her brother-in-law.

By early 1941 Felix had decided to return to Boston; that spring he and Helene both got their citizenship papers. Helene tried once again to encourage him, as she had in the fall of 1935 before he left from Vienna.

> If you could only return so assured of yourself that your being is independent of the marks of outward recognition. Do not misunderstand me: I mean not resignation, but that certain outward attitude. Why not use the right word for it: freedom from fear.

From Helene's point of view, Cambridge life had turned out as well as she could have hoped; she had not had a chance to feel lonely, since so many people had rushed to take care of her. Her gaiety, combined with her professional talents, meant that she soon had friends who were possessive of her. If someone did not get enough of her, they could talk to Felix; the relationship between the Deutsches was no more eccentric than other arrangements, which could be accepted under the heading of a "Boston marriage." Boston was not only tolerant and a famous medical center, but it became a Mecca for candidates seeking analytic training.

3

Training Analyses

Even though Helene had been determined not to repeat her involvement with the Vienna society, nonetheless she found herself much in demand as a training analyst in Boston. Especially after World War II, when candidates flocked to be analyzed, she could not avoid training pressures on her time. She had acquired allies at the institute, like John Murray (she was his second analyst) as well as Kaufmann, who shared the ownership of the building at 82 Marlborough Street where Felix and others had their offices; later the society moved its meetings to 15 Commonwealth Avenue.

During the war, however, when people like Murray and Kaufmann were preoccupied with military service rather than institute politics, Helene thought she was being challenged. Originally she had been the institute's heart and soul. Although to close observers it still looked as though everyone was at her feet, she enjoyed less than undisputed sway and used it as an excuse to pull back from her teaching. Helene characteristically chose to withdraw rather than fight. In Vienna she had reacted similarly to Freud's desire that she share leadership with his daughter Anna; Helene still wanted to be first, effortlessly, as she once had been her father's favorite. Much as she was not averse to prestige and status, she would not manipulate to attain it. Long before she retired as an analyst she had ceased to lead seminars for students in training.

By the postwar period the Boston society had two well-defined rival factions, one led by the Deutsches and the other headed by the Bibrings. Almost from the outset Helene had felt threatened by the Bibrings; they were a formidable couple. In part Helene's fears were irrational; analysis is an unusual profession in that the larger the number of its practitioners in a city, the more likely it is that there will be an abundance of patients. The Bibrings had arrived while Felix was still in St. Louis. On his return, he led a clinic for nonanalytic patients at the institute; Felix was not a good listener and tended to hold forth on his own ideas. Both Bibrings hated Felix's clinic, and Felix and Grete in particular had problems with each other. She succeeded at the Beth Israel Hospital, becoming the first woman professor of psychiatry at Harvard, while Felix's academic career—partly because of his age—remained blocked.

Grete Bibring advanced herself while Helene remained standoffish. Grete was a gifted clinician who made her way not only within academic medicine but also trained prominent academicians (such as Talcott Parsons). In contrast to Helene's own kind of spark, Grete was aloof and proud. She was extremely talented at subtly flattering people about their own vulnerabilities; she praised people in such a way as to make them aware of their deficiencies. She sought the more conventional honors that Helene disdained, becoming, for example, the president of the American Psychoanalytic Association as well as an official figure in the international movement. Grete Bibring's English was easier to understand, and she assimilated (with private scorn) to American life. But Helene refused to believe that Grete was as good as others found her.

From the Bibring point of view, Helene had always been touchy and difficult; by leaving in 1935 she was seen as having deserted the Vienna group. Edward Bibring may not have been too tactful about his importance as a theorist, but he was more socially presentable than Felix. Official recognition meant little to Helene; she remained free of intellectual and cultural snobbery, and jokingly accepted the honorary professorship her students came up with for her. Helene felt no need to compromise with her own temperamentalism; she had enough charm and social ease to be able to walk out on fancy Cambridge parties as it might suit her.

Grete Bibring also flourished as an official adviser at Radcliffe College, a position Helene naturally envied; and Grete's chairmanship at the Beth Israel ensured her power in the lives of promising young residents. When in 1974 a small group of analysts broke away from the Boston society to found a new one, relatively more "orthodox," Grete Bibring went with them.

Helene had developed her own outposts of influence. One of her early protégés in Boston, Dr. Erich Lindemann, succeeded Cobb as the head of psychiatry at the Massachusetts General. Lindemann was an extraordinary clinician and teacher, although not equally good as an administrator; he was ahead of his time and paved the way for community psychiatry. (In the end Helene was disappointed in Lindemann; he hurt her feelings by not being devoted enough. He spread his interests and admirations among many people, and later moved to Stanford Medical School.) Helene also had her share of prominent academics of the future; Gardner Lindzey, for example, became head of the Center for Advanced Study in the Behavioral Sciences at Palo

Alto. Within Boston psychiatry Helene had her followers: Bernard Bandler, Lucie Jessner, Eleanor Pavenstedt, Gregory Rochlin; in Vienna Helene had trained Americans such as Flanders Dunbar and Helen Ross. Psychoanalysis was not an easy field in which to have pupils without founding a separate school; Helene tried to analyze individuals, and did not have disciples. When someone as talented as Dr. Elizabeth Zetzel, trained in England with Jones, returned to the States, Helene got on with her in Cambridge in spite of an aura of Kleinian ideology she brought with her; but Helene would, if anyone got too far ahead, cut them down. At meetings she could be merciless with a smile on her face.

Helene counted on Tola Rank as an intimate personal friend and loyal associate. She and Molly Putnam ran a center for disturbed children. (Molly was completely in the service of the Deutsch "party" in addition to her help with the farm; Helene relied on her as Freud had depended on her father.) Helene and Tola talked together every day; Felix was impressed with her, and also a bit jealous. Helene had brought her over from Paris with the idea that she would be an analytic social worker. But Helene got her to be an analyst; at first it was agreed that she treat children, not grownups. By 1936 she was acting as a control analyst for candidates in child analysis, and in the end she helped train every child analyst in the city.

Dr. Ives Hendrick opposed Tola, as he had Sachs, out of what Helene called "medical narcissism." Helene sent her patients, and in writings cited unpublished papers of hers. Tola suffered from ingrained insecurity, although she had a sense of beauty and understood art. Tola, an elegant person, also had a strong need to be loved; but after her husband she only had one romance, with a psychiatrist in Paris. Tola succeeded in competing with Grete Bibring in training academic candidates; but neither of them wrote very much, certainly when compared with Helene's output. (From the point of view of male candidates, the Boston society was run by a matriarchy.) Tola's attractive Central European complexities made an odd contrast with her co-worker Molly Putnam. This prim New Englander could not, for example, put a bite of food in her mouth until she had completely swallowed the previous morsel; while Helene and Felix consumed a snack in a hurry, Molly could spend an hour eating the simplest meal.

Felix grew increasingly self-confident within analysis, and attracted a number of devoted disciples. His interest in psychosomatic medicine, as well as a special interviewing technique ("associative anamnesis"[1]), helped him hold his own. Felix experimented with special sensory stimulation—an onion, or a noise—in order to demonstrate how material could come up around a focal point. He was attracted by clinical possibilities other than strict analysis, and he hoped to be able to make a science of technique. Helene, however, was always a bit dismayed at his therapeutic approach; he could be erratic, and did not have her own good clinical judgment.

Publicly, however, she wanted him to be respected, and fought his battles for him; he was president of the Boston society from 1951–54. Earlier she had shared in the tension at the Massachusetts General over who would be Cobb's favorite. Felix might be as good as Helene pictured him, and yet she never quite thought so; she protested too much about how others did not appreciate him, as she felt she had to build him up. Felix had a hard struggle, and in the end seemed overwhelmed by her stronger personality. Helene worried about having so much of the glory, and thought it was partly responsible for her bad relationship with Martin. In her bones she was convinced that a woman should not run the show, and so she (ineffectually) tried to arrange things differently; she still longed for a Lieberman-type situation. Not far below the surface her resentment at Felix showed through; she was irritated by him even though apparently she was secure within herself. Felix continued to worship her. After he had returned from St. Louis, she told friends how much she had missed him; at the same time she could reminisce on the "period" when she had been interested in marrying him.

While Felix made much of the "tactics" of psychotherapy, Helene's interviewing approach stemmed simply from her genuine interest in other people. She had an extraordinary ability to get patients to talk and open up; the way she threw herself into other's lives was more than a matter of intuition or empathy. She had a capacity for dramatically living with and being another person. Her understanding was without theory or complicated ideas. When she visited patients on rounds, her joyousness and robustness helped them unfold and come alive. She was not stuck in puristic analysis, and would look for the therapeutic direction in a case.

Helene succeeded in developing a capacity for winning an audience through her presentation and personality. She could envelop a group through a sublimated appeal for love. Her attractiveness was defined in terms of other people; through her warmth and outgoing manner they knew she was interested in their reaction, so her delivery was not an egoistic performance. She had chosen a profession which remained ideal for her; even in her old age, before presenting a paper at a meeting she would dress with great care.

As a supervisor she gave candidates in training lots of guidelines; she was more interested in helping to understand a patient than in defending her technique. Edward Bibring, for example, would be fussier, stricter about each interpretation to the patient, pointing out what a candidate had failed to see. He was more pedantic, the exact opposite of Helene, since she did not believe in getting people into an analytic harness.

Although Helene had early on been an advocate of control analyses, she was concerned that patients might be treated as guinea pigs. People who go to candidates in training have some money, are willing to make a sacrifice, but cannot afford someone who has completed formal training. Helene came to question whether such patients really get the best therapeutic deal. After a short time a supervisor may find the best therapeutic approach for such patients, but often psychoanalysis can turn out to be unsuitable. Yet by then the patient may have already started to develop transference. Under such circumstances it can be hard to decide what best to do. The conflict in her mind arose in the context of her enduring conviction that candidates need analysands for training purposes.

Helene might have been unhappy with institute politicking, but she was necessarily enmeshed in an impressively bureaucratic educational system. As opposed to her own informal beginnings as an analyst, there were now elaborate procedures to becoming certified. The initial acceptance as a candidate was only the beginning; one could be assigned to a "problem" status as well as a normal one, in which case the training analyst had special obligations about reporting to the local society on the progress of an analysis. The training analyst had to decide when a candidate was ready to take theoretical seminars, and also when clinical seminars were suitable. The training analyst then had a say in deciding when a candidate was ready for the first control case; it was not long before the Boston society required that each candidate analyze four control cases under supervision, which could entail hundreds of hours, but which also meant the training analyst had further decisions to make. For even mature people it can be tempting to develop the adolescent dependencies associated with such a prolonged training process.

In contrast to her practices in Vienna, Helene was now stuck with a series of letters associated with each candidate she trained; the final recommendation for termination of candidacy and graduation from the institute was the last phase in a complicated process of committee deliberations. When Helene was writing to her colleagues in Boston she could at least take for granted that they knew her style and would notice any warning signals she might send out. But later, if a successful candidate so decided, the further step remained of applying for membership in the American Psychoanalytic Association, which meant yet another letter from the training analyst. It is no wonder that candidates in this long process spoke of undergoing one analysis for the sake of the institute, and yet another later one for themselves. Since at the outset they were medically qualified and often therapeutically experienced, analytic training could, Helene thought, dangerously prolong their apprenticeship.

Helene's letters in behalf of candidates were models of brevity. Instead of going into details, she gave thumbnail sketches as character portraits; she rarely had to go into clinical details, or approach violating privacy, since she stuck to an artistic rendering of the people she described. She only reconstructed childhood when it was directly relevant. Each set of her letters about candidates communicated a different profile; if she was performing as a control analyst, she described the patient under supervision as well. Real people, with different individual characteristics and mannerisms, emerge from her files. She of course took for granted the analytic terminology of the time. As one reflects on her accounts of training cases, a fairly consistent picture of her clinical approach as an analyst emerges.

In recommending candidates for the American Psychoanalytic Association she frequently stressed moral assets: "Dr. Z. is a very intelligent and fine person. He has an excellent reputation professionally and is a man of integer character." Of another candidate she also wrote to New York approvingly: "Dr. Y. is a very intelligent, sensitive man, of great honesty and fine character." Regarding a candidate she was less enthusiastic about, Helene wrote: "Dr. X. is an ambitious young man with a great and honest zeal to improve not only his professional standard, but also his cultural and ethical qualities." The implication was that he was not as she might have liked; "ambitiousness" was not a good word to her, and to have to work toward such a goal implied some pre-existing inadequacy on his part. If Helene only had no reservation or objection in recommending someone for membership, it meant the candidate was not a special favorite in her eyes. (To the Boston society she had earlier been more outspoken about Dr. X.; he had made an "excellent adjustment in his professional and personal life," postponement of graduation would be "a terrible blow to his self-esteem," and she concluded that "he will always master his social attitudes according to the expectations of his environment and to his own ethical demands." Anyone who knew her would realize that such a description was less than wholehearted; respectability was not one of her key values.)

With a candidate about to go on to her first control case, Helene wrote that Dr. W. was "of great intelligence, culture, knowledge, and characterological integrity." She considered her sophisticated; still, she worried "whether her emotional restriction, her blockage of emotional expression will interfere with her analytical work . . ." Although Dr. W. remained, in her view, too prone to intellectualizing defenses (a common enough problem among candidates), Helene steadily recommended her through further stages of promotion. At termination she thought the analysis of Dr. W. was finished "satisfactorily."

> The basic personality, emotional restrictions and tendency to hide behind an intellectual façade is influenced highly by analysis but *not changed.* This certainly will have some interfering influence on her function as an analyst. Her positive qualities emphasized in previous reports will certainly make her a very valuable member of the analytic community.

Being a successful therapist was, in Helene's opinion, so close to functioning as a good teacher that Helene could identify with any patient who was able to learn from her.

If Helene did not like a candidate but saw no objective grounds for disqualification, a reader would have to pay close attention to the terms of her formal approval. One candidate she supervised under control had a patient who became engaged to be married. Dr. U. seemed to be too impressed by the patient's family's enthusiasm for the match. Helene's judgment of the candidate was, in terms of her own standards, qualified: Dr. U. "is a very intelligent, capable candidate—according to her temperament and whole attitude a woman of broad activity rather than an investigator of deeper problems."

As idiosyncratic as Helene could be in her procedures, she still was trying to work in behalf of a system beyond herself; one candidate in training started off by impressing the admissions committee as someone "unanalyzable." At the outset Dr. T. would not accept analytic interpretations of his life or problems, although, paradoxically, he sought help. Helene stuck by him partly because she considered him "well read and cultured, much above many of our candidates. He is not 'brilliant' but very promising." Helene anticipated on her side a "long and strenuous analysis." It continued in " 'small doses'; i.e. after long periods of resistance comes a drop of dynamically useful insight providing material." Gradually Dr. T.'s "devaluation" of analysis lessened. With time he gained "a positive relationship to psychoanalysis as such," which also meant that he believed "more and more the interpretations."

An interview with one candidate for admission to the institute went so badly that Helene could playfully describe the encounter: "It was evident I did not make a good impression on him." She recommended him for acceptance on a "trial" basis, essentially relying on the recommendation of his previous therapeutic analyst, whom Helene considered "an experienced man."

One of Helene's problems as a training analyst in America was that candidates could bore her; a young psychiatrist might be professionally promising and yet of little intrinsic interest to her. The more such people she treated, the greater the burden on her tolerance for their relatively standardized problems. (Others have reported a similar reaction.) In one case she began her report with an indirect form of criticism: Dr. S.'s "analysis does not present serious difficulties. But as the incentive of a neurotic suffering is missing, the goal is purely 'didactic.' " She could not put her finger on anything except the lack of excitement.

> There is a lively intellectual interest in the procedure and gratification of "insight." The personality problems are well defined and acknowledged, the transference is ambivalent but workable, and easy to handle. Dr. S. is a very intelligent psychiatrist, and has a good psychological understanding, but the whole analysis is remarkably undramatic, so to say *'flat,'* nevertheless it is in progress.

It would not have been beyond her to recommend such a candidate for advancement to seminars because she was hoping to be able to get rid of him. Even if such a person might not look like a good future practicing analyst,

Helene could still argue that he would make use of his training "in an honest and correct manner."

After the treatment was over, Helene's account of Dr. S.'s analysis became more elaborate but essentially unchanged. "The dynamic process stays on one superficial level with little flashes from the unconscious (or rather subconscious) . . ." Helene was convinced that Freud's essential recommendation about training candidates involved bringing them in contact with their unconscious; this had in principle little to do with the amount of time put into an analysis. But by qualifying Dr. S.'s knowledge as having come from "little flashes" from the "subconscious" rather than revelations from the unconscious, Helene was emphasizing the lack of depth of her candidate's treatment.

Helene was imaginative enough to devise something interesting to say about Dr. S.: his "transference is strong, fluctuating—so to say daily—between two levels: rich infantile elements appear constantly and are recognized by the analysand sometimes with amazement, seldom with evidence of a workable resistance and its resolution." Helene had proposed that Dr. S. give up the training, but he persisted. In the face of his determination there was nothing she could do.

> In all aspects of his life: love, family, profession, etc. Dr. S. is functioning extremely well and his neurosis—brought to light in analysis—seldom affects his existence. Speaking theoretically, this analysis could be effective only when the excellent structure of defenses would break down. This is not expected or desired.

She was not in favor of inducing artificial regressions. She proceeded "with this boring drop by drop procedure with the feeling that it is of great positive value for Dr. S., and I leave the question of his analytic career to the future." In his old age Freud too liked to leave it to the "future" to decide uncertainties. At Dr. S.'s termination, she reported that "as always in his life and in his analysis, the reality testing took over all his inner experiences and he successfully surrendered his emotional problems to an excellent adjustment to reality." Essentially she thought he was going to be all right with patients, but her reservations were obvious: "I believe there is a chance that he will become a good analyst and that his control work will be successful."

Psychoanalytic concepts gave Helene abundant ways of characterizing people she found tedious. About one such candidate who was to be in treatment for years, Helene's reaction was clear at the outset; the terminology was a means of self-control.

> Dr. R. is one of those obsessionals whose neurosis can hardly be labeled, because there were never symptoms. Object relations are strong, and often warm, the ambivalence not easy to discover.
>
> Aggressiveness is explosive but as a rule retained behind a wall of reasoning which is tiresome, exhausting, "killing" for the receiver.

With this method of defense he usually achieves justification but nevertheless every act of hostility and aggressiveness results in guilty feelings,
anxiety, and a need of endless rationalizations.

His pedantic punctilious way of speaking and extremely logical attitude
make free associations very difficult. In addition every attempt to interpretation is met as criticism and objected to.

Dr. R. is a very fine, intelligent, conscientious person, dedicated to his
duties and profession. Analysis moves very slowly but I do not consider it
hopeless.

The next year Helene claimed that the origins of Dr. R.'s behavior was
both "instructive and interesting"; but she conceded that "the analytic procedure is sterile and very boring." A year later Helene wrote: "Dr. R. is intellectually very sharp and his logic approach to everything is rather interfering.
Nevertheless I would say that the work with him is not as exhausting as it
was, and that with concessions in demands on the part of the analyst, the
analysis can continue." The didactic goal, as with other candidates, created a
special difficulty. Psychoanalytic training, as a step in professional education,
meant then an ultimate credential in a psychiatric career; by her early eighties
Helene came to question whether the idea of a didactic analysis had not been
mistaken. In the case of Dr. R. she noted:

The analyst is here not only the object of transference but also the holder of
the future destiny, a judge of qualifications for the most central ambition of
his professional life: to become an analyst.

The analytic situation is—and was all the time—not only the usual field
for transference with its characteristic ambivalence, etc., but also a kind of
professional ritual in which the patient tries in a way (typical for him) to do
his best, to make the greatest effort for achievement.

"Never in my work," Helene wrote, "was the didactic goal of analysis so
burdensome for the procedure." Her report took away with one hand what it
gave with the other: "Dr. R. has—no doubt—a degree of therapeutic results,
which I did not expect . . . This candidate certainly learned in his analysis
what psychoanalysis is *not.*" Helene sent his name forward positively.

With another candidate, however, an analysis ended with a mutual decision that he not become an analyst. After a year and a half Helene was merely
reserved in her judgment: she complained about an "attitude typical for him
and appearing in all spheres of life: a flatness, a superficiality of emotions as
well as of intellectual judgments." At that time Helene considered Dr. Q.
conscientious, though perhaps stupid: "By and by, Dr. Q. approaches the full
recognition of his difficulties and expresses a sincere desire to explore analytically the causes of this disturbance." Six months later Helene reported that
"this s. c. [so-called] analysis is still being conducted in a vacuum created by
the lack of free associations and of the expression of the unconscious." In

Helene's vocabulary she had met a "solid wall of resistance." Yet her account also had a commonsense description of the problem: Dr. Q.'s "chatter is intelligent but seldom amusing or interesting." Before long Dr. Q. agreed to be reduced to the status of a "problem" candidate.

Helene was still hoping not to "traumatize" Dr. Q. by recommending his rejection at the institute. But the end result was prefigured throughout Helene's reports.

> Dr. Q.'s analysis is a slow, monotonous drive through a desert. I cannot say that I have gained a very profound insight into Dr. Q.'s inner conflicts, neither has he.
>
> He is less detached than he was before, and with great effort and tolerance toward boredom one was able to reconstruct the development and fate of his Oedipal situation . . . and of the rejection of his identification with either of his parents . . . His self-image is so pale, so are all his emotional relationships. His marriage is excellent, his sexual life very satisfactory.

It took Helene a long time to understand the motive for Dr. Q.'s perseverance in analysis; the treatment turned out to be a protective shield against accepting his real limitations. Dr. Q. was finally put under the heading of "unanalyzable," even though at other times Helene thought the use of this category had often become an excuse for failure. According to Helene the outcome here was not due "to severity of his neurosis or defects of the ego, but to the motivation which made him wish analytic treatment and to persist on its continuation."

It is impossible to evaluate the inevitable personal component in Helene's clinical decisions. With some patients she did conclude that they would do better with another (often male) training analyst. People whom she found unacceptable might be approved by others. For example, another of her candidates was suffering from defects she too often encountered.

> The prerequisite for the establishment of a productive atmosphere—the neurotic suffering—was denied by the analysand. Since her childhood she was able to build up a continuous stream of narcissistic gratifications which kept her neurosis in limits. Her behavior was always rather stereotyped.

Academic achievement, combined with an ingratiating manner, constituted defenses she found "hard to conquer." At the same time, with a different candidate, Helene was not the kind of analyst who might be put off by the existence of what she openly considered "a neurotic personality."

> Dr. P. was a very unusual and interesting "case" of mixed neurotic manifestations, in which typical obsessional facets were superimposed over a rich, emotionally abundant hysterical personality. Dr. P. is psychologically very gifted, his understanding of analysis is deep and very serious. I am convinced that he will make interesting and original contributions to analysis.

Implicit in Helene's reports was the conviction that analysis was more than a science; she made no bones about the necessity for an analyst to go beyond "pure" technique for the sake of therapy. In one instance of a candidate she did concede that "this is an unusual case in which a perfect analytic technique can be applied"; on the whole, however, she emphasized how different from analytic "ideals" people could be. The majority of patients available to candidates for control analysis, for example, brought the "problem of suitability" with them. "I think that our candidates have by necessity to be trained not only in the analytic technique, but also in its modifications provoked during the analytic procedure." She had no anxiety about trying to be a neutral screen, and proposed that analysts, while striving to keep the analytic situation alive, make use of so-called parameters in their treatment. Essentially, however, she believed—unlike Felix—that a policy of maneuvering was bad, and that it was more important in therapy what one was than what one did.

Helene could acknowledge when she herself had failed. In one case she had hesitated about allowing a candidate to proceed to the phase of supervised analysis; she regarded Dr. O. as "analyzable (but very time absorbing)"; although Helene had been confident that the progress in analysis would continue, in the end she recommended with the candidate's agreement that a male analyst would be suitable. She had reached this decision "after long suffering on my part, but compensated by a great deal of insight into the structure of 'infantilism' "; it would be hard to imagine a less promising introduction to a case she was allowing to continue at the institute. A training analyst's power was checked by a sense of responsibility to others in the analytic community. Even in Helene's praise her distaste for this candidate was evident.

> Dr. O. is not only very intelligent and endowed with various talents, but he also seems to have an "empathy", which helps him work with patients. Sometimes this "empathy" is due to a projective mechanism of identification of others with himself. This is often easy, since the scale of his own multiple personality is very large.

Helene's report was almost catty; the candidate had only apparently "rich emotional experiences and interests"; but Helene thought she could vouch for the fact that "hate and dependency seemed genuine in relationship to me."

The intensely personal element in training was partly checked by the increasing rules and regulations of the institute. Although some restraint on the judgment of individual training analysts was desirable, the result was often an excess of bureaucracy. By the 1960s, for example, the preclinical seminars at the institute had become subject to general discussion; but these physicians were not experienced as formal teachers. As at some second-level universities it was as though nothing could be taken for granted. It might have been better for an institute to acknowledge openly that—as in the granting of Ph.D.s—candidates inevitably acquire backers and patrons in the course of their training. Given the kind of human material institutes set out to handle, however, from Helene's point of view analysis in America had surrendered to an excess of structure and organization.

4

"The Endless Continuity
of Personal Existence"

Helene's most famous clinical concept consisted in her notion of the "as if" personality. She first delivered a paper about this type of person before the Vienna society in 1934; subsequently she revised it, and gave another version of it in Chicago in 1938, finally publishing her polished views in 1942: "Some Forms of Emotional Disturbance and Their Relationship to Schizophrenia ('As If')."[1] The essay became so much a part of professional thinking that in 1965 a special panel was devoted to reconsidering Helene's topic at a meeting of the American Psychoanalytic Association; Helene once again spoke on the subject, but by then—when she was eighty-one—her concept had acquired a life and literature of its own.[2] Her early work had been succeeded by an efflorescence of interest in the self, authenticity, and identity. (Freud had originally disapproved of her using the expression "as if"; unknown to her, Freud was reminded of Adler's use of the phrase.)

In her concern with "as if" problems Helene was trying to describe a false affectivity that was neither neurotic nor psychotic. She had picked a rare pathology in order to say something general about people. For although she thought she was talking about an exceptional phenomenon hard to diagnose correctly, at the same time she held that as a transient experience "as if" is nearly universal. The patients in question make an impression of "complete normality."

> They are intellectually intact and gifted and show great understanding in all intellectual matters. When they try to be productive—and efforts in that direction are always present—their work is formally good but totally devoid of originality. It is always a laborious though skillful imitation of a model without the slightest personal trace.

Their relations with people are also intense, in terms of friendship, love, understanding, and sympathy, but still something is chillingly absent. True warmth and inner feeling are missing, although outwardly these people could "behave as if they possessed a fully felt emotional life." A key point of Helene's was that the patients themselves were not aware of any impoverishment, but believed that their empty performances were the same as the feelings and experiences of others.

Helene distinguished what she was talking about from old-fashioned instances of repression: those who hoard their emotions. The difficulty with "as if" cases lay not in the buildup of barriers against their instinctual life, but rather with the emptiness of their relations with themselves and others. Helene's concept of "as if" was designed to refer to people who are capable of powerful identifications which are peculiarly imitative and lacking in character.

> Their morality, ideals, beliefs are also mere shadow phenomena. They are
> ready for anything, good or bad, if they are given an example to follow, and
> they are generally apt to join social, ethical or religious groups in order to
> give substance to their shadow existence by identification.

Long-standing membership in an organization can be dropped in favor of another of opposite standards "without any change of heart." No disillusionment or internalized experience needs to take place, but rather a regrouping in the environment of the person's circle of acquaintances.

In terms of childhood development Helene traced the origins of "as if" personalities to the inability to develop a normal Oedipus complex. Freud's theory did entail that truly civilized conduct meant a degree of neurosis; yet many did not live up to that ideal of an inner life, with all its conflicts, and still could not be termed crazy. The phenomenon of "as if" was an expression of the human propensity to be imitatively suggestible, passively in wait of outside influences; such people "validate their existence by identification." This tendency toward mimicry was a substitute for genuine relations with people as well as causes, and a striking contrast to the utter single-mindedness of the Don Quixote she wrote about. One patient Helene described, for example, could "be anything or renounce anything, and her emotional life remained unaffected. She never had cause to complain about lack of affect because she was never conscious of it." Anton Chekhov had described such a woman in his story "The Darling."[3] To the extent that in our culture the concept of "as if" applied primarily to women, Helene was being implicitly critical of the conformism associated with the traditional conception of femininity. (Helene's paper on pseudology was an earlier account of how people can live fictionally.)

Helene's tolerance led her to broaden analytic concepts. In her "Absence of Grief" (1937),[4] which originally appeared in a *Festschrift* in honor of Reinhold's fiftieth birthday, she discussed remission in the work of mourning.

The refusal of someone to grieve can be a defense serving to protect a severely threatened ego. The omission of reactive responses to the death or loss of a loved one was to Helene as much a variation from the normal as excessive mourning, either in time or intensity. Such delayed mourning will, she held, seek an outlet; she proposed that grieving which can not be manifestly expressed may find vicarious satisfaction through identification with the sad experiences of others, which might also account for the existence of intuition and empathy.

In 1938 Helene's paper on *folie à deux* appeared, in which she distinguished between hysterical and psychotic clinical states; it continued her earlier interest in "induced madness," as well as illustrating the conviction she held that pathological attempts at identification "can also be found in a psychic state so universally human that its character of 'normality' cannot be denied—'being in love.' "[5] In 1939 she published a paper on certain defense mechanisms that can be a surprising resistance in analysis: intellectualization, rationalization, and turning to reality, as well as introspection.[6] The next year, timed with articles occasioned by Freud's death, her "Freud and His Pupils" came out.[7]

In the early 1940s she wrote up a paper on anorexia nervosa which she delivered before a seminar at the Boston society.[8] She was taking a typical case on a clinical subject that has long puzzled practitioners of every theoretical school. It describes how one compulsion—to starve—can compete with another compulsion—to overeat. In her understanding of the case she did not isolate the patient from her family background, or overemphasize the infantile history. Although not willing to go to any lengths to help this suffering patient, she was technically innovative within the confines of her professional identity. She did not hesitate to proceed in an unorthodox manner. Her special approach consisted of promising the patient that the subject of eating would not be brought up, but the patient had to agree to be periodically weighed. The treatment would only proceed if the patient undertook the responsibility for maintaining a constant weight. As part of her continuing interest in psychosomatic medicine, in 1942 Helene published a pioneering article: "Some Psychoanalytic Observations on Surgery."[9]

During World War II Helene had completed her *The Psychology of Women;* Volume 1 came out in 1944, and Volume 2 in 1945.* Her reputation with the general public was now securely established. Helene refused to revise, or add further volumes, to her books on women, but still she continued to publish on their problems. Yet in the years after World War II she wrote much less than earlier; the absence of Freud in her life weakened her creativity. She justified this decrease in her productivity in terms of wanting Felix's work to receive more attention. Whenever they spoke at the same time at a

* Cf. Epilogue: A Woman's Psychology.

conference, her room was packed while his was sparsely attended; she could always steal the show. In 1950 she published once more on psychosomatic medicine and women: "The Psychiatric Component in Gynecology."[10] Other essays complemented her earlier ideas. In a famous paper on "The Impostor" (1955)[11] she presented a striking case history of affective hollowness; unlike the "as if" personality, an impostor seeks to impose his pretending on others. Her interest in the issue of sham, or masquerading, can be traced back to her early paper on pathological lying.

In the period after Freud's death analysis became increasingly theoretical; Helene's papers, even if relatively infrequent, stood out because of her enduring interest in real people. She insisted on repeatedly quoting variations of one of Freud's comments in old age: "For a short while I allowed myself to leave the sheltered bay of direct experience for speculation. I regret it greatly, for the consequences of so doing do not seem of the best."[12] On another occasion she reported him as having said: "I have allowed myself to leave the pure empyrean of psychology, and I regret it."[13] Partly out of identification with the dying Freud, analysts trained during his final phase tended to neglect the more empirical side of analysis, and this theoretical bent accelerated over the years. Helene did not want to participate in neglecting "the more clinical aspect of psychoanalysis."[14] Even if she were to be mistaken about a patient, she was convinced that in thinking in terms of case histories she was being human not only in relation to the patient but to the reader as well.

In contrast to some of her colleagues, who emphasized the advantages of the length of analytic treatment and the depth of interpretations, Helene grew increasingly skeptical. Whatever lack of interest in therapy Freud might have had, she felt it was his right and not that of his students; she emphasized the significance of the supportive element. She had never been keen about technique, or the purely scientific side of analysis. Some of her worst analyses had had a good therapeutic effect, and some of her best analyses had yielded the worst results. She tried to follow the spirit of Freud's teachings rather than analysis as a bureaucratic movement. Prolonged treatment, she held, often serves regressive needs in patients. It was tempting for analysts to see themselves as godlike. Analysis was built on serious enough foundations to be able to do away with the unnecessary artifact of anonymity. Although too much reality can become an interference, she was confident that patients would have fantasies anyway; if an analysis becomes completely detached from reality, it is a consequence of a problem of the analyst's. Whatever the pros and cons of such issues, the need for ideological reflection helped keep her alive.

Helene couched her reservations about analytic therapy in a paper (1959) that she felt was inadequately appreciated: "Psychoanalytic Therapy in the Light of Follow-Up." Treatment could not insure future safety from pathology.

What we conquer are only parts of psychogenesis: expressions of conflicts, developmental failures. We do not eliminate the original sources of neurosis; we only help to achieve better ability to change neurotic frustrations into valid compensations. The dependence of psychic harmony on certain conditions makes immunity unattainable.[15]

The task of analysis was to teach how to compromise; the therapeutic situation gives the opportunity and the understanding, as the patient takes what is needed. Old World caution struck some Americans as undue cynicism; schools of psychology flourished which held out more optimistic, if not utopian, expectations.

On their seventieth birthdays in 1954, the Boston society arranged to honor both Felix and Helene; an appreciation of her by Ernst Kris, a former student, appeared in the *International Journal of Psychoanalysis.* Although she was outspoken in private, she was inhibited about attacking the abstract direction in which analysis had gone. She considered the theoretical neatness of Fenichel's *The Psychoanalytic Theory of Neurosis* as the "cancer" of her field. Despite the trend of analytic theory, she disapproved of the emphasis on ego psychology and was inclined to deny the existence, for example, of Hartmann's concept of "conflict-free" spheres. (She sometimes tried to speak within his framework, and in composing an essay in his honor she used his approach.[16]) Like other aging professionals, Helene had grown increasingly distant from the enthusiasms of the generation that had succeeded her in power and influence.

In 1962 she received the Menninger Award; her acceptance letter[17] epitomized her way of thinking.

> I must confess, although with some embarrassment, that the honor I have just received has made me very happy. It was a surprise for me, for I had assumed that such awards are made to younger people—to those who are in the midst of their analytic career, who are active participants in new, vital, and currently debated issues. According to my personal image of an award, it is not for those who have achieved something—for achievement is in itself an award—but it is given to those whose work carries a promise for the future.
>
> My observations on old people—especially, if I may permit myself for a moment to be subjective, my observations on myself—have led me to the conviction that age does not change that feeling of the endless continuity of personal existence, uninterrupted by death. We are all endowed with this feeling, in spite of the intellectual knowledge that our life is limited and short. There are certain deep-rooted currents in the psychic life of *homo sapiens* that are *timeless.* We carry them with us from early childhood until the day of death, even at a very advanced age.
>
> The timelessness of feelings of life without end leads me to the consoling thought that old as I am, I have been given this award for the sake of my achievements in the future.
>
> A second cause for my happiness today is a less personal one. This is

related to a trend among the younger generation of analysts. There is talk of "old" and "new" analysis, and one even introduces the term "modern" in contrast to "classical" analysis.

Indeed, one can hardly deny that in recent years there have been interesting developments in analysis. In this respect analysis shares the fate of other sciences which remain vital through progress.

Such a rigid separation of "old" and "new," however, appears to me to be an artifact. Many of the so-called "new" ideas are continuations and sometimes only reformulations of concepts originated by "classical" analysis.

The origins of the "new" are contained in the "old," and vice versa, the "new" carries the legacy of the "old." In the artificial dichotomy of old and new my work is certainly a typical representative of the "old." If, therefore, the award has the meaning which I read into it, the pleasure which it gives me lies above all in the fact that it acknowledges the value of the "old" for the growth of the "new."

Loyalties of friendship obliged her hesitantly to fit her thinking into fresh conceptualizations. But in the face of innovations she reaffirmed the elasticity of the practices of traditional analysis; above all she sought to preserve the patient's autonomy.[18]

The year 1962 was also Helene and Felix's fiftieth wedding anniversary; Stanley Cobb composed and had printed a sonnet for them.

> Vienna 1912 is like a dream
> Of life and love and beauty in old modes
> Before the Götterdämmerung benighted us
> And taught us things aren't really what they seem.
>
> Felix and Hala fifty years ago
> Began their union in felicity,
> But world upheavals brought them to our shores;
> What they have lived through we can never know.
>
> A quarter century we've had you here
> To warm our hearts and heal our troubled souls,
> A great gift to our land, but greater still
> A gift to each of us who holds you dear.
>
> No life of ease upon Elysian shores
> But a devoted victory is yours!

By 1962, however, Felix had grown old, while Helene still retained her zest. She thought he had behaved psychotically on a trip that year to the farm. His memory had begun to fail, and a committee relieved him of his standing as a training analyst. He would not accept or acknowledge that he had been forcibly retired. Helene was so offended at the decision of the Boston society that out of loyalty to him she herself resigned as a training analyst.

Helene and Felix would both have had their eightieth birthdays in 1964. But Felix died in January. He had been ailing for some time; an attack of jaundice had really weakened him. As he grew feeble, it was hard to know when Felix realized how sick he was. In replying to a letter of condolence Helene (February 10, 1964) described his last year to an Israeli associate of his; she sent Felix's library to the Hadassah Hospital in Jerusalem where he had worked.

> The last year had been very hard for Felix. Circulatory disturbances due to arteriosclerosis and a poor heart condition created a constant vacillating between difficulties, impairment in thinking, and recoveries, unchanged sharp lucidity, incapacity for work and great productivity.
>
> He fought with incredible will-power against his sickness, worked more than ever, and until the last moment denied his defeat.

In his last years Felix had grown difficult to handle. It was not just that eccentricities of his got in the way; his resentments toward Helene surfaced. As practicing analysts they had been able to discuss patients together; and she sometimes sent him cases. Usually she did not read his papers before publication, even though he tended to think what was clear to him was automatically understandable to others. They had such different minds that her comments on his work always ended in a quarrel; being in the same field did interfere with their marriage.

For years they had slept in separate rooms. But in his weakened condition he could hurt those he loved the most. Self-control had mattered so much to him that he appeared self-destructive when he underwent an operation for a severe hernia. Martin's wife, Suzanne, stayed with him at the hospital. It was terrible for Helene to witness Felix's confusion and paranoid states; her clinical training could only partially shield her from the pain she felt.

Felix's relationship with Helene was so strained that in 1963, after she had had an operation for a localized cancer, two friends of hers, Lucie Jessner and Eleanor Pavenstedt, took her away on a holiday to Greece. Felix was happy that she could have the pleasure of the trip; on their anniversary in 1963 he wrote her (Peter and Nickie were the names of their grandsons):

> Dearest. I hope this letter will reach you. Do you know that today is April 14th, the day on which we had our wedding fifty-one years ago? I am sitting here at lunch with Martin, Suzanne, and Peter. Nickie is in Washington with the school. Afterwards we all want to go to the concert of the Exeter school in the Symphony Hall. It is a lovely sunny day (9 a.m.), and we all hope it is just the same in Athens. Suzanne keeps me company every day, and protects me from invitations, of which there are too many.

Helene reacted with grief to Felix's death; it was the only time since she had been in the United States when her weight fluctuated sharply. (She lost seven pounds between 1963–64, but then gained them back.) She mourned his kindnesses to her. The loss of Felix was particularly difficult because she had so many guilt feelings about him; she regretted that he had not succeeded in getting more from her. Although while he was alive she could resent having overshadowed him, for the remaining eighteen years of her life Helene reacted by idealizing her union with Felix. She spoke of Felix as if he had been much better than she; his deficiencies, she claimed, stemmed from his having written on so many subjects. He had been a charismatic teacher, but Helene was unsuccessful in getting his former students to publish an appropriate memorial to him—a biography or a collection of his papers.

Helene almost immediately began to take steps to remake her life and prepare for her own advanced old age. She transformed Felix's consulting rooms at home into an apartment which could be rented out; ultimately it meant that she could have someone besides a housekeeper easily living in her house for company. She also altered her professional life. At eighty-two she cut back from five analytic patients to one, and took no new analytic cases; instead she devoted her time to consultations and short-term therapy.

Although she never wrote about a grandmother's anxieties, concern for her grandsons helped revive an old interest of hers in adolescence. She especially sought to treat young people, and evolved her own approach; she relished her practice because she felt she always learned something new from patients. In 1967 she published a monograph, *Selected Problems of Adolescence.*[19] (In 1965 her *Neuroses and Character Types* appeared, reprinting her 1930 textbook along with sixteen of her clinical papers; an even larger number of her essays remained untranslated and uncollected.) She was invited to give the Freud Anniversary Lecture at the New York institute, where she presented "A Psychoanalytic Study of the Myth of Dionysus and Apollo: Two Variants of the Son-Mother Relationship"[20]; it gave her a chance to expound on the way mythology illustrated the themes of bisexuality and immortality. For some years she also worked on her autobiography, which was finally published in 1973 as *Confrontations with Myself.*

Helene enjoyed an altogether remarkable old age. Her interest in other people helped keep her going. She retained her intellectual vitality; although she said she felt like an institution, she attributed her standing and the warmth of her professional reception to the comfort it was to younger people to see someone so old and active. She wondered whether the generations of analyzed people were any happier. Privately she often thought her own life had been a wreck, buoyed by too much denial. She considered she had failed as a mother, which caused her to redouble her efforts with her grandsons. She worried that she had not been fulfilled as a woman, and doubted whether her earlier choices had been right. Most people recognized none of her tragic feelings; they saw in her a joyful, fascinating, supercompetent woman with a seemingly inexhaustible supply of energy.

As she grew older she felt less close to death. Entering her early nineties, she was more serene and reconciled than in her eighties. As she aged she found it easier to accept the mothering of an Armenian housekeeper. The warmth and care she received enabled her to overcome her fear of showing helplessness.

Helene had experienced her share of ailments. A cancerous lump on a breast had had to be removed, and she also underwent surgery for a urinary cancer; treatment for a cataract was only partially successful; and she suffered from a painful form of arthritis in one hip. She maintained her humor about her frailties. Memory lapses about the recent past troubled her. For years she had dreaded the possibility of senility. (It usually has three stages she said: first one finds that something has changed, then other people notice the difference, and finally only others see it.) But at the age of ninety-four her physician considered her chemistries perfect. She had long been unable to go to meetings; she kept on reading although she could no longer write. (She always had felt bad about watching television.) She still could give interviews. She helped Nancy Friday with her bestselling *My Mother/My Self* (1977).[21] And Helene cooperated in a 1978 *New York Times Magazine* article about her career.[22] She cheerfully endured the loneliness of her situation, although sometimes she expressed the longing to see psychiatric patients again.

One of the most painful aspects of growing old was missing the friends who had predeceased her. Tola Rank, for example, although much younger, died tragically in 1967. Yet Helene retained many friends and acquaintances as well as former patients and students, who would arrange to stop by and see her. At her ninetieth birthday she was given a big party at a hotel which she thoroughly enjoyed. There was another, smaller gathering at her house in honor of her turning ninety-five.

Her grandsons were a source of immense pride to her. One of them as a schoolboy had been given a trunkful of objects and asked to write a story about it; he wrote one line: "I would seek the advice of my grandmother." She was proud of her ability to take a watch chain or piece of jewelry and reconstruct the whole human creature it had belonged to. The last love letters of her life came from this grandson; he sent exact physical accounts of his New York apartment so she could visualize a place she would never be able to visit. Martin remained absorbed in his work; having such a talented son had necessitated a special responsibility, but the ambivalence between them remained. Helene said Martin had preferred Felix to her, but would be kind to her when she was sick; however, she had described the positive elements in her mother's attitude toward her in exactly the same words. (Helene's bitterness toward Regina had been almost matched by Martin's feelings toward her.) She still brooded about her miscarriages and the abortion during her years with Lieberman. In her suggestion that Lieberman's baby boy had not died a natural death in 1905 but had instead been killed by Gustawa could be detected some of her own conflicted feelings about motherhood.

During her last two years Helene did not do well. She had always had

extraordinary recuperative powers; whenever she had shown signs of deterio-
rating, she had possessed the surprising power of coming back to herself. One
of the problems of her extreme old age was finding people who were enough
on her level to be able to stimulate her. Her daughter-in-law remained more
devoted than most daughters are to their own mothers, and from her own
house supervised Helene's care. Helene needed someone additional to live in
with her; she managed to endure being called "Hala" by a kind, uneducated
local nurse. Helene had such endurance that it seemed she would have little
trouble making it to her hundredth birthday.

Toward the end of Helene's life a Polish woman lived in Felix's old suite
downstairs. As Helene aged, her Polish past retained its meaning for her. In
1959 she had written a paper about Conrad's *Lord Jim* at a memorial meeting
for Edward Bibring.[23] In 1962 a New York analyst asked for her comments on
a paper of his about Conrad; she had written back (February 7, 1962):

> I only want to emphasize something which I consider neglected in your
> approach to Conrad's psychological personality. That is, his relationship to
> his fatherland Poland. He was born in an environment in which the patrio-
> tism had quite a special and unique aspect: love for the unhappy fatherland
> (conceived rather as "motherland" with Holy Maria the symbol) was an
> obsession, which started in earliest childhood. There was no other concep-
> tion of heroism than the sacrifice for the freedom of Poland and the revenge
> on the tyrants. This was a duty, an obligation, a centre of idealism, measure
> of individual value . . . I think that the main source of his powerful guilt
> feeling lies in the fact that he considered himself a traitor in the patriotic
> cause . . .

Her married name and the years in Vienna obscured the Pole in her. When
her autobiography came out in 1973, the first (and best) chapter was on
Przemyśl; she received letters from people who had once been associated with
it. And she heard from Polish scholars who were interested in Lieberman's
career.

In the spring of 1979 the housekeeper noticed that Helene now looked
and acted like an old woman; yet after a brief hospitalization she was herself
again. For some time she had needed help in getting up from a chair; the
problems became more complex. When Anna Freud got an honorary degree
from Harvard in June 1980, she paid a call on Helene. By the summer of 1981
Helene was still able to see people for short periods. Doubtless the fact that
she could afford to stay in the house where she had lived since 1936 prolonged her clarity and the will to live. She finally died at her home on March
29, 1982. According to Martin, toward the end she had had her father, Felix,
and Lieberman all mixed up; in the last week of her life Polish was the only
language she spoke.

EPILOGUE

A Woman's Psychology

"Any life when viewed from the inside is simply a series of defeats."
George Orwell

Every writer has to anticipate the likelihood of being misunderstood. Helene Deutsch poured the experience of her own conflicted femininity into her two-volumed *The Psychology of Women.* This set was to be so steadily reprinted in hardcover that it was not until three decades later that it appeared in paperback. The title itself attracted a broad readership.

Just as it has been easy to oversimplify Freud into his late categories of id, ego, and superego, so Helene's contribution on women could be crudely boiled down to the three concepts of narcissism, passivity, and masochism. It was like her not to highlight the way she intended to transform the meaning of each of these notions of Freud; however easily most have missed the nuances of her differences from Freud, nonetheless it ought to have been clear that like other psychologists she was describing as well as prescribing. *The Psychology of Women* was so encyclopedic in scope as to invite criticism from subsequent detractors of early psychoanalysis; it had established her as the leading proponent of the Freudian outlook on femininity. Whatever feminists of a subsequent generation were to think, Simone de Beauvoir's *The Second Sex*[1] treated Helene's books with the utmost respect.

In evaluating Helene's ideas it is important to recall the context in which she was writing. In the twenty years since her *Psychoanalysis of the Sexual Functions of Women* Helene's point of view continued to soften some of the most controversially sexist aspects of Freud's own theories of femininity. She concentrated on subjects that Freud had taken for granted. While Volume 1 of *The Psychology of Women* was subtitled "A Psychoanalytic Interpretation," she called Volume 2 "Motherhood." One of her central theses, which ascribed to motherliness "the highest degree . . . of altruistic emotion,"[2] implicitly subverted Freud's own skepticism about the genuine possibilities of altruism. (For example, Freud had insisted that the maxim "love thy neighbor" was both undesirable as an ethical principle and psychologically unrealistic as a human expectation.) If Helene's growing distance from Freud's own concepts might be hard for outsiders to detect, even a revisionist analyst like Dr. Clara Thompson could appreciate the value of some of Helene's case illustrations.[3]

When Helene composed these books she was almost sixty years old; she was drawing on her knowledge of a world unlike our own. In that period professional women were highly competitive with one another; but unlike today they could count on an abundance of available servants. Helene was trying to adapt her point of view to a new audience. It would not be unusual if she sometimes idealized what she herself had missed in life, or took for granted her own achievements as a woman. She already was consciously sorry about having had only one child, and later regretted that she was to have only two grandchildren. In writing about the conflict in women between motherliness and eroticism, Helene knew how much she had missed on both sides. To her mind inner preoccupation with her work had cost her a heavy human price.

Like even many contemporary writers about women, it is striking how—in spite of the experience of her own upbringing—she paid relatively little attention to the critical role which fathers can play. In evaluating what she added to that era's thinking about women, it is well to remember that we are now looking back forty years. As time passed, and cultural changes showed more of how many of her earlier ideas had been dated, she continued to adjust her thinking.[4] By the end of her life she was maintaining that she had never meant to suggest that women should stay home, but that they have a special relationship to domesticity. She nonetheless remained afraid that our culture is destroying the difference in the meaning of sex for men and for women; she thought it should be possible to speak of differences, even inequalities, between men and women, without implying any superiorities.

Beginning in the early 1970s the tide abruptly had turned against Helene's work. As feminists took a cold look at the import of Freud's system, Helene became the target for well-intentioned criticism; she, however, who had been a feminist long before entering Freud's circle, was so secure about herself that she scarcely showed any reaction to the attacks on her pioneering ideas. Helene looked on as it became undeniable that those within psychoanalysis who had publicly differed with Freud on women became more fashionable. Helene, who was known to have been personally involved with Freud, and never to have broken with the analytic establishment, paid the inevitable price of her own prior success. People who earn their living as so-called experts on the soul have to expect a natural resentment. Right now feminists are taking a more benign view of the meaning of psychoanalysis in the history of ideas⁵; but it has not as yet become widely known how distinctively her own—and unlike Freud's—Helene's approach was.

From her early years Helene's disdain for conventionality had helped her surmount obstacles in her path. The affair with Lieberman, an unusual marriage, and the devotion to a new profession of service, teaching, and care were of a piece: this was an unusual woman whose curiosity and imagination required her to push beyond the boundaries of stereotypes. Yet she paid the penalties of her originality.

With the advantages of hindsight it is remarkable to note the extent to which, by the time of *The Psychology of Women,* Helene had emancipated herself from theoretical dogmatism. She knew that previous criticisms had to be met, and in the preface she sought to restate, correct, and amplify her earlier views. As a sophisticated writer who carefully defined what she hoped to accomplish, Helene said that she wanted to use the psychoanalytic theory of instincts "to illuminate the biologic background from which the psychologic personality of woman emerges." Having grown up in Poland, practiced in Vienna, and emigrated to America, she herself brought up the inevitable significance of the social milieu. As a clinician, however, she could hope to describe "individual emotional experiences and the conflicts connected with them." She knew the minefield she was entering by daring to illustrate the "core" of femininity and the normal conflicts women endure. Despite obvious defects, she thought psychoanalysis had been "able to explore a dark region of the soul that has always been—and probably will always remain—inaccessible to more objective study."⁶

She decided not to try to describe a young woman's earliest childhood. She reasoned that it was so important a period that it would reappear in discussions of subsequent stages. She had a subtle understanding of early development.

> We tend to forget that in the wide range of child-parent relationships developed in the course of childhood there is no one single consolidated idea of the mother or the father. There is a beloved mother, and a hated mother; a sublime ideal mother and a disreputable sexual one; a mother who has castrated the father and another who has been castrated by him; one who bears children and one who kills them; one who nourishes them, another who poisons them; there is the rival, and the personification of security and protection. Similarly there are many different fathers creating a host of possibilities of identification.⁷

The choice of objects of identification in prepuberty, according to Helene, depends largely on these earlier phases.

Yet Helene's omission of even one chapter about the years before the age of ten meant that she was departing from the standard analytic approach. At that time, and subsequently, analysts engaged in metaphysical debates about even the preverbal stages. (As early as her *Psychoanalysis of the Neuroses* Helene had begun that book too with reality—the role of the "actual conflict" in the creation of neuroses; she was too much a clinician to want to delve speculatively into theories about infancy.) She herself had not treated small children; but she thought "direct observation shows that the girl from the very beginning has pronounced feminine traits." Even though it was at odds with conventional analytic wisdom, she began her study by talking about prepuberty, the years between ten and twelve, with the conviction that adolescence itself is "the decisive last battle fought before maturity."[8] (Nutritional advances have of course had their effect on the timing of physiological growth.)

Helene poignantly illustrated the strivings of a young girl's urge for independence; she herself had experienced what she called puberty's "normal revolutionary impetus." The attachment to the mother, Helene thought, represents a larger threat than that to the father, in that the mother presents a "greater obstacle to the girl's desire to grow up." On the other side of the coin, the "tragedy of motherhood" consists in the child's striving to break the tie, while the mother wants to preserve it. The struggle to achieve adulthood is often helped, however, by new people for the girl to identify with. Fetters of childhood dependency can be overcome through alter egos, or chums. As a therapist Helene believed that such young girls resist motherly women, and that "it is possible to achieve an intimate relationship with them only if one can assume the role of a 'girl friend.' " Helene proposed, in contrast to the dark forebodings of Freudian theory, that "the motive force in this phase is the inherent urge of the ego to grow up and achieve things."[9]

Helene emphasized the realistic conflicts of young women. Above all, she thought, "friendship between girls is of the greatest importance," although at that time analysts were not often discussing such factors. (Harry Stack Sullivan, in writing about young males, was an exception, and he has been suitably hailed as an innovator ahead of the Freudians.) Helene gave examples of how young women react to the loss of a friend through "separation or through her unfaithfulness in favor of another girl or boy."[10] Social workers had brought Helene clinical observations of what happened in the "lower social strata," so she did not have to confine her material to the neuroses of middle- or upper-class patients. Her books were filled with case histories that an analyst would not have been expected to encounter; in Vienna Helene had developed regular contact with more than one prostitute over a period of years.

According to Helene, it was characteristic of early puberty for girls to get involved in escapades not out of "genuine sexual need, but from the urge to show the grown-ups that they, too, were grown-up." The realities of World War II were a part of the background to the "sham-sexual actions" Helene was trying to describe. She was not afraid to sound old-fashioned: sexual experience "can take the place of love, and its consequences—prostitution, syphilis, and illegitimate children—often constitute an irretrievable disaster."

At the same time Helene stressed how important gratifications outside the home are: "to create a sense of self-responsibility and self-criticism, the approval of the outside world is at first urgently needed." Studying Helene's writings with care, it becomes clear she had moved far from an orthodox position: a young girl's hatred of her mother may originate "not so much in the Oedipus situation as in her anger at the fact that her mother prevents her from being a grown-up."[11] In unspecified contrast to Anna Freud's 1936 outlook on youth, Helene wrote positively about "ego functions," anticipating later ego psychology.[12]

> I wish to emphasize that certain developments of the ego are valuable because in an emergency they can serve as mechanisms of defense against dangers arising from sexual urges. I do not believe, however, that such defense mechanisms are created exclusively under the pressure of instinctual dangers, as weapons against them. In my view these mechanisms begin to develop before puberty, as offensive weapons for the conquest of reality.[13]

Although guilt feelings can harrow the lives of young women, Helene tried to concentrate on the scars of normal growth. For the time it was advanced for an analyst to insist that "in order correctly to understand pathologic behavior, we must realize what constitutes a normal development." Helene continued to argue that certain bisexual conflicts are typically recurrent. In unspoken contrast to Freud, who held that women are more bisexual than men, Helene proposed about male development that "a 'feminine' component perhaps plays the same part in his psychology as the masculine component plays in woman's. But the social valuation of these components furthers masculinity in women and discourages it in men." Helene's English was good enough for her to illustrate how young girls often had to be less repressed about their feelings than contemporary boys: " 'Tomboy' is often a compliment, 'sissy' always an insult."[14]

No matter how superior the earlier relation with her parents has been, a girl during puberty may need temporarily to reject them (as Helene had even her beloved father) as part of her liberation. In the meantime, others can fulfill the demand for ideal models or prototypes; Lieberman, and later Freud, had answered this requirement in Helene. With time, she thought, the heightened tendency to identify with others will weaken, as a woman's ego becomes stronger. Increased self-confidence accompanies the adolescent's solitude. The young woman is struggling to "harmonize her intensified ideal aspirations with her intensified sexuality." Inner restlessness, insecurity, irritability, and other emotional fluctuations characterize this vulnerable in-between period of life. Eroticism may remain separated from awareness of sexuality for a longer time than with boys. Platonic love feelings are a mixture of old emotions and new phantoms. Before becoming a "free human being," the young girl struggles with an overburdened fantasy life; at the same time she can have "the feeling of security and the conviction that nothing can happen to her that are typical of puberty."[15]

The thrust of Helene's argument, however, was that a woman's intensified inner life becomes a unique source of human superiority. During puberty a woman develops that greater intuition, subjectivity, and capacity for self-observation that Helene contrasted with the "primitive desire to get rid of sexual tension that more commonly characterizes masculine sexuality." She could write this without communicating any animosity toward men. In contrast to what some might think, she believed that "the road to the feminine woman as a sexual object leads through the psyche . . .." Helene was opposed to an emphasis on technique: "What is in question here is not at all the so frequently overstressed and even ridiculous demand made upon men by several sexologists that they heighten the woman's excitability (in the physical sense) by their dexterity."[16]

Helene ended up popularizing Freud's notion of female "passivity," elsewhere in her books described as the predominance of giving. She was, to be sure, writing in a society where career women like herself were rarer than now; she considered it "striking how many women engaged in active professional work await the moment when they will be supported by their husbands, and bitterly reproach a husband who is unable to satisfy this demand." But Helene was willing to invoke "receptivity" instead of "passivity," and also suggested substituting for Freud's idea of passivity the concept of "activity directed inward."

> If we replace the expression "turn toward passivity" by "activity directed inward," the term "feminine passivity" acquires a more vital content, and the ideas of inactivity, emptiness, and immobility are eliminated from its connotation. The term "activity directed inward" indicates a function, expresses something positive, and can satisfy the feminists among us who often feel that the term "feminine passivity" has derogatory implications.[17]

Whatever the terminology adopted, Helene was trying to use it to pinpoint the sources of a woman's capacity to identify with others, a feminine quality which, she emphasized, "shows great individual variations" in people. While completely preserving her own personality, a woman becomes especially capable of adjusting herself to others; at the same time women "possess solid, deep-rooted qualities that are almost inaccessible to outside influences, and they thus stubbornly resist assimilation."[18]

Helene contrasted her own concept of "as if" characteristics with Freud's references to the "multiple personality." While she said he had been referring to how "numerous identifications lead to a disruption of the ego," a "purely inner process of ego formation," Helene had wanted to highlight how "the ego constantly identifies itself with objects in the outer world instead of forming emotional relationships with them." Her theories helped her account for her own tie to Freud.

> Women are . . . frequently enthusiastic partisans of ideas that apparently have been given them by others. But closer inspection reveals that such ideas were previously conceived and developed in their own fantasy. The adoption or carrying out of these ideas is possible only through identification with other people. Even talented women are often uncertain of their own ideas until they receive them from someone else whom they respect.[19]

What she wrote about women has to be understood in the framework of her belief that "absolute originality is probably a quality peculiar to genius alone."[20]

Helene knew that there were different types of women, as she sought—unlike Freud—to sketch some of them; yet in ascribing a greater degree of the treasure of intuition to women, she was not denying its existence in men. "But a sensitive, intuitive man probably has a strong feminine component in his entire personality." A woman's greatest resource is her heightened inner perceptiveness. This is, Helene proposed, a preparation for her biological destiny; ". . . no human being has as great a sense of reality as a mother." Around this feminine core Helene acknowledged that "there are layers and wrappings that are equally genuine elements of the feminine soul and frequently very valuable ones, indispensable for the preservation and development of the core." So-called masculine qualities in a woman—her intellect and capacity for the objective understanding of life—frequently have a high social value, while femininity in a man makes him "ridiculous and even despised if it manifests itself too clearly."[21]

Helene was being true to Freud's heritage by emphasizing that specific human talents thrive at the expense of other capacities: ". . . in all fields of life progress is connected with regressive tendencies . . ."[22] This conception matched her own experience as well. She repeatedly emphasized the degree to which eroticism and sexuality, for example, can be at opposite purposes from the reproductive instinct and motherhood. Such polarities were, in her view, part of the human condition.

Helene cited not only examples from great literature, but also tried to rely on the enlightened opinion of her day. Freud may have had negative feelings about the sexologist Havelock Ellis, for example, but Helene could not write about irrational ideas associated with menstruation without using his illustrative material. She also paid attention to Margaret Mead's anthropology, as well as that of Bronislaw Malinowski and Abram Kardiner; she relied on J. J. Bachofen's theories of matriarchy, and Grantly Dick Read on childbirth. Like any other significant contribution, her books looked forward and back at the same time. Helene said she could not accept Freud's theory of a female castration complex, and tried to replace it with the milder term of a "genital trauma." She tried to down-play penis envy as a concept; she did not even regard envy as a specifically feminine quality. (She now dissociated herself from Abraham's theories about women which were, she wrote, "like any pioneer's . . . to some extent one-sided."[23]

Nor did she any longer accept Freud's Darwinian-like view of the relation between the clitoris and the vagina. She did think that women, faced with "the double function of the female as a sexual creature and as a servant of the species," tended "much more strongly than man in the nonindividualistic direction, that is to say . . . in favor of the reproductive functions." At the same she did not think that female sexuality needed to be defined in terms of the survival of the species.

> Freud assumed that the clitoris, which has become unnecessary for the mature sexual organization, transfers its pleasure sensations to the vagina and resigns in the latter's favor. But deeper analysis and longer experience seems to indicate that this transfer is never completely successful and that from the moment of her sexual maturity woman possesses two sexual organs . . .

"It is as though," she thought, "the biologic architect had planned two different organs for the two functions—the clitoris for sexuality, the vagina for reproduction—but later found it safer to attach the vagina also to the more selfish aim of sexual pleasure."[24]

Unlike Karen Horney, who long before her death had stopped writing about women, Helene continued to address herself to the perplexing question of frigidity. Because a woman possesses two sexual centers, "she often fares like the donkey in Aesop's fable, which starved to death between two full mangers because of its indecision: having two organs, woman often remains sexually ungratified." Later, at a professional panel in 1960, Helene amplified her position by declaring then that

> the clitoris is the sexual organ, the vagina primarily the organ of reproduction . . . The eroticization of the vagina is a job performed by way of the clitoris and by the active intervention of man's sexual organ. This central role of the clitoris is not merely the result of masturbation but is a biological destiny.[25]

In her The Psychology of Women, she held that the anatomic differences between the sexes, which Freud had made so much of, derives its significance from various physiological processes, particularly subjectively felt sexual excitation. Helene wanted in general to emphasize the influence of the emotions on the bodily functions; at the time pregnancy and delivery were subjects analytically untouched upon. Helene stuck to her long-standing conviction, however, that "the young girl takes her own body as the subject of self-love much more often than does the boy." This was, Helene wrote, a striking reversal of "the tendency to neglect personal appearance that is so typical of prepuberty . . ."[26] (It will be remembered that in 1913 she had written Felix about how she had once expressed her "outsiderness" by "unkempt hair and a dirty dress.")

In her account of the adult "feminine woman," Helene insisted on the greater inhibition in sexual life than with men; while this could lead to frigidity, simultaneously she was crediting women with a higher propensity for sublimation. She thought this was more constitutional than social, and that a woman may owe "many of the most valuable and interesting features of her psychic life to the processes connected with this inhibition." Women tended to subordinate sensuality to the "condition of love or longing for love." She quoted Freud as having remarked that "love for one's own person is perhaps the secret of beauty."[27]

By the 1970s narcissism had become the single most discussed psychoanalytic topic; the term "narcissism" may sound only like a pejorative Freudian term, but Helene was talking about both its positive and negative aspects. For example, the approach she was adopting held that "in the motherly woman, the narcissistic wish to be loved, so typical of the feminine woman, is metamorphosized; it is transferred from the ego to the child or its substitute." Although she never repudiated Freud's notion that women have weaker superegos than men, she did describe one "type" of woman "whose erotic enthusiasm can be kindled only by moral values, and it is destroyed by actions they morally condemn." Social conditions play a part; Helene had in mind a contrast between her own Polish background and, for example, parts of Germany: ". . . the feminine-erotic type is more frequent in Latin and Slavic countries, while the feminine-active-moral type is more characteristic of the Calvinist countries with their tradition of severity."[28]

If victimization is a danger of feminine narcissism, intensified self-love can be a self-preservative counterweight, protecting a woman from her masochistic potential. Helene specifically contrasted her views with those of Freud. She cited Natasha from Tolstoy's *War and Peace* as a "refutation of Freud's assertion that a feminine woman does not love but lets herself be loved." She was explicitly, if tactfully, trying to dissociate herself from Freud, who considered "only men capable of selfless love; in his view women do not need to love but only to be loved, and whenever they love in a selfless manner, they are loving 'according to the masculine type.' " Reluctant as she was to challenge Freud, still she wrote: "It seems to me that the form of relationship that appears temporarily in being in love is a permanent characteristic of genuine maternal love."[29]

Helene's mild-mannered way of expressing herself meant that only in the course of a footnote did she protest against Karen Horney's version of the import of Helene's ideas.

I should like to defend my previous work against a misinterpretation. K. Horney contends that I regard feminine masochism as an "elemental power in feminine mental life" and that, according to my view, "what woman ultimately wants in intercourse is to be raped and violated; what she wants in mental life is to be humiliated." It is true that I consider masochism "an elemental power in feminine life," but in my previous studies and also in this one I have tried to show that one of woman's tasks is to govern this masochism, to steer it into the right paths, and thus to protect herself against those dangers that Horney thinks I consider woman's normal lot.[30]

Karen Horney performed an immense service in challenging Freudian orthodoxy when she did. But psychoanalysis has been an extraordinarily sectarian field; and in time Karen Horney's polemical abilities were to prove more than a match for Helene's undogmatic defense of herself. The subsequent misreading of Helene Deutsch's position has constricted the range of her contribution to feminism, and obscured how both women, in their different ways, succeeded in attaining legitimate achievements.

For Helene it went almost without saying that "all those to whom the ideals of freedom and equality are not empty words sincerely desire that woman should be socially equal to man." When Helene appealed to the "feminists among us," in talking about the dangers of "masochistic subjection and loss of one's own personality," she was obviously thinking about how she had failed to exert her full claim on Lieberman. Every woman, she held, passes through a phase in which she unconsciously provokes mistreatment; "the attraction of suffering," she concluded, is "incomparably stronger for women than for men." This proposition represented her rendition of Freud's principle that masochism is a specifically female trait. But "badly managed feminine masochism," Helene thought, "is a serious psychologic and often sociologic problem."[31]

In order "to reassure the reader" Helene had prefaced her discussion of what she meant by "feminine masochism" by pointing out that "it lacks the cruelty, destructive drive, suffering, and pain by which masochism manifests itself in perversions and neuroses." Rather than aiming to put women down, Helene was trying to use Freud's work constructively, as she sought to elucidate what she called "a fundamental difference between man and woman . . ."

> what most contributes to the overflow of feminine masochism and gives it its self-destructive character is moral masochism, that is, the sense of guilt and its effects . . . When we encounter a passive-masochistic, feminine orientation in a man, we fairly always find that it came about under the pressure of guilt feelings and that his "moral masochism" acquired feminine erotic character only secondarily. This is reversed in women: in them feminine masochism is primary and moral masochism is secondary. The latter then sails under the flag of eroticism and appears as such, but its destructive character gives it away.[32]

Perhaps the whole psychoanalytic approach had the defect of undue complexities; and those who, like Freud, set out to emancipate may also end up unwittingly enslaving. But it would be wrong to suggest that Helene's own version of Freud's teachings ever meant to propose that women *ought* to love victimization.

Helene's early, overwhelming erotic experience with Lieberman had, she thought, helped interfere with her capacity for motherhood. Out of this tormenting experience she generalized that other women too knew a conflict between sexual satisfaction and their reproductive function. Nonetheless she had retained her warmth and harmony. If Helene had spoiled her own joy in her child, she was hardly recommending it to others; in her writing she maintained that the "essence of maternal love is that it demands nothing, sets no limits, and makes no reservations."[33] But Helene had sometimes overestimated her freedom, and the humanistic aim of being a woman and a professional had more problems associated with it than some might like to think. Whatever her success with Freud, she knew how—by ideal standards—she had failed with her husband and son.

Dissatisfaction with femininity she summarized under the heading of the "masculinity complex." These pages show how hard on herself she was capable of being. "Woman's intellectuality is to a large extent paid for by the loss of valuable feminine qualities: it feeds on the sap of affective life and results in impoverishment of this life either as a whole or in specific emotional qualities." Passages in Helene's books that critics have pounced on were originally written to express her own unsatisfied yearnings. "The intellectual woman of the non-feminine type . . . has no mother in the psychologic sense of the term." Helene's sister Malvina may have nurtured Helene, but in her account of thwarted femininity she sounds autobiographically self-revealing, reminding her audience of Pallas Athene, "the woman born out of her father's head."[34]

To the extent that she herself had become a so-called "active woman," she reasoned that she was bound to end up with someone like Felix: "Their choice of men is made difficult as a result of their preference for passive men, whom they furiously urge to become active and whom they persecute with the eternal reproach of not being sufficiently energetic." She therefore had partly accepted her society's expectations of what she had had to lose out on. Yet her need for loyalty and love to a series of father figures was at odds with her self-interest and her life instincts. Her commitments, and regrets, were inevitably those of a woman born in 1884. Some of her theories were a special form of self-condemnation: ". . . the girl's hatred and fear of her mother must yield to a feeling of love and tenderness."[35] If Helene had been more accepting of herself, it might have led her to ideas about human development and normality that would match the unconventionality of her own experience, and entitle others to feel more at ease in defying conformist pressures.

At the same time Helene felt inclined to assert the validity of her own life, even in terms that were at odds with what has been popularized as Freud's message.

Observation teaches us that a strongly sublimated daughter-father tie does not necessarily involve neurosis or feelings of frustration and privation, even if it impairs the girl's erotic life. Fulfillment of the positive goal of life is not necessarily connected with normal sexuality.

Whatever her reputation became, Helene's ideas do not fit the model of what an orthodox analyst should have believed.

Under certain circumstances, a type of behavior that stems from psychologically infantile sources, like rebellion against authority, may be more adapted to reality and more rational than so-called "adult" behavior that conforms to the demands of society. Immature individuals are often in the van of social development, and progress is inaugurated by the unsatisfied individual who strives for freedom.[36]

Motherhood may be a bourgeois concept, but Helene's private failures were intimately linked to her public successes; within the profession she chose for herself she became one of the best mothers in the history of psychoanalysis. In a field filled with ideological squabbles she never allowed an abstract controversy to be associated with her name. She wrote about the existence of

women whose motherliness is directed to objects other than their own children—i.e, to other women's children or to adults to whom they extend their motherly protection. Many such women choose professions that serve as outlets for their maternal feelings.[37]

As a teacher and therapist she urged others to independence.

In 1918 Helene Deutsch had originally come to Freud with self-respect and autonomy, and this pride endured throughout her years as a psychoanalyst. She grew by moving beyond Freud's specific conclusions, and therefore helped keep the Freudian tradition a live one. In contrast to the romantic notion, currently so pervasive, that feelings (even the most selfish) are inherently self-justifying, Freud's concept of the unconscious entails the conviction that we are all self-deceiving and benefit from rational self-criticism. Only the examined life is worth living, and in the spirit of that ancient conviction Helene Deutsch did her best.

NOTES

INTRODUCTION

1. Helene Deutsch, *The Psychology of Women,* Vols. 1 and 2 (New York: Grune & Stratton, 1944–45).
2. Cf. Elizabeth Badinter, *Mother Love* (New York: Macmillan, 1981); Susan Brownmiller, *Against Our Will* (New York: Simon & Schuster, 1975); Germaine Greer, *The Female Eunuch* (London: MacGibbon & Kee, 1970); Betty Friedan, *The Feminine Mystique* (New York: Norton, 1963).
3. "Introductory Lectures on Psychoanalysis," *The Standard Edition of the Complete Psychological Works of Sigmund Freud,* ed. James Strachey (London: Hogarth Press, 1953–74), Vol. 16, p. 330.
4. Helene Deutsch, *Confrontations with Myself* (New York: Norton, 1973).
5. Paul Roazen, *Freud: Political and Social Thought* (New York: Knopf, 1968; London: Hogarth Press, 1969); *Brother Animal: The Story of Freud and Tausk* (New York: Knopf, 1969; London: Allen Lane, 1970); *Freud and His Followers* (New York: Knopf, 1975; New York: New American Library, 1976; London: Allen Lane, 1976; London: Penguin, 1979; New York: New York University Press, 1985); *Sigmund Freud,* ed. Lewis Coser (Englewood Cliffs: Prentice Hall, 1973); *Erik H. Erikson: The Power and Limits of a Vision* (New York: The Free Press, Macmillan, 1976).

PART I POLAND

CHAPTER 1. "THE CENTER OF THE EARTH"

1. Deutsch, *Confrontations,* pp. 19–20.
2. Ibid., p. 20.
3. Ibid., p. 22.
4. Ibid., p. 21.

5. Deutsch, *The Psychology of Women,* Vol. 2, pp. 367–68.
6. Ibid. Vol. 2, pp. 383–85; Deutsch, *Confrontations,* p. 23.
7. Quoted in Helen Swick Perry, *Psychiatrist of America: The Life of Harry Stack Sullivan* (Cambridge: Harvard University Press, 1982), p. 63; Helene Deutsch, "Sublimation of Aggressiveness in Women" (unpublished). Cf. also Helene Deutsch, "A Note on Rosa Luxemburg and Angelika Balabanoff," *American Imago,* Vol. 40, No. 1 (Spring 1983), pp. 29–33. This issue contains four memorial tributes to Helene Deutsch.
8. Helene Deutsch, *Neuroses and Character Types* (New York: International Universities Press, 1965), pp. 244–45.
9. Helene Deutsch, "On the Pathological Lie," Introduction by Paul Roazen, *Journal of the American Academy of Psychoanalysis* (1982), Vol. 10, pp. 369–86.
10. Deutsch, *The Psychology of Women,* Vol. 1, p. 249.
11. Ibid., Vol. 2, p. 417.
12. Helene Deutsch, "Zur Genese des Familienromans," *Internationalen Zeitschrift für Psychoanalyse* (1930), Vol. 16, pp. 249–53.

CHAPTER 2. DIARY OF AN ADOLESCENT DOUBLE

1. *The Adolescent Diaries of Karen Horney* (New York: Basic Books, 1980); *A Young Girl's Diary* (New York: Barnes & Noble, 1961).
2. Roazen, *Freud and His Followers,* pp. 442–44; Angela Graf-Nold, "Aus den Anfängen der Kinderpsychoanalyse: Zu Leben und Werk von Hermine von Hug-Hellmuth" (unpublished).
3. Deutsch, *The Psychology of Women,* Vol. 1, p. 124.
4. Deutsch, "On the Pathological Lie."

CHAPTER 3. POLITICAL ACTIVISM

1. Artur Leinwand, "Herman Lieberman," *Rocznik Przemyski* (1970), pp. 171–212, and Artur Leinwand, *Posel Herman Lieberman* (Craców: Wydawnictwo Literackie, 1983).

CHAPTER 4. FORBIDDEN ROMANCE

1. Aldo Carotenuto, *A Secret Symmetry: Sabina Spielrein Between Jung and Freud* (New York: Pantheon, 1982), pp. 11–14.
2. Deutsch, *The Psychology of Women,* Vol. 1, pp. 201–2.

PART II VIENNA

CHAPTER 2. AN END IN MUNICH

1. Deutsch, *The Psychology of Women,* Vol. 1, p. 57.
2. *Letters of Sigmund Freud,* ed. Ernst L. Freud (London: Hogarth, 1961), p. 386.

CHAPTER 4. TWO CAREERS

1. Helene Deutsch, "Erfahrungen mit dem Abderhaldenschen Dialysierverfahren," *Wiener klinischen Wochenschrift,* Vol. 26 (1913).

CHAPTER 5. KRAEPELIN'S MUNICH

1. R. D. Laing, *The Divided Self* (London: Penguin, 1965), pp. 29–31.
2. Franz G. Alexander and Sheldon T. Selesnick, *The History of Psychiatry* (New York: Harper & Row, 1966), p. 163.
3. Quoted in Ruth Leys, "Meyer's Dealings with Jones," *Journal of the History of the Behavioral Sciences* (1981), Vol. 17, p. 465. Cf. Paul Roazen, "Book Review of Brome's *Ernest Jones* and Bertin's *Marie Bonaparte,*" *The Times Literary Supplement,* May 6, 1983.
4. *The Freud Journal of Lou Andreas-Salomé,* translated by Stanley A. Leavy (New York: Basic Books, 1964), p. 57.

CHAPTER 6. WORLD WAR I AND MOTHERHOOD

1. Paul Roazen, "Freud's Clark University Lectures Reconsidered," *Journal of the American Academy of Psychoanalysis* (1977), Vol. 5, pp. 447–58.
2. Paul Roazen, "Freud and America," *Social Research* (1972), Vol. 39, pp. 720–32.
3. "Memorandum on the Electrical Treatment of War Neurotics," *Standard Edition,* Vol. 17, pp. 211–15; Ernest Jones, *The Life and Work of Sigmund Freud,* Vol. 3 (New York: Basic Books, 1957), pp. 21–24.
4. Helene Deutsch, "Ein Fall symmetrischer Erweichung im Streifenhügel und im Linsenkern," *Jahrbüchern für Psychiatrie und Neurologie* (1917), Vol. 37.
5. Deutsch, "Two Cases of Induced Insanity," Introduction by Paul Roazen, *International Journal of Psychoanalysis* (1981), Vol. 62, pp. 139–50.
6. Helene Deutsch, "Occult Processes Occurring During Psychoanalysis," in *Psychoanalysis and the Occult,* ed. George Devereux (New York: International Universities Press, 1953).

7. Deutsch, *The Psychology of Women,* Vol. 2, pp. 145–49.
8. Deutsch, "Zur Genese des Familienromans."
9. Deutsch, *The Psychology of Women,* Vol. 2, pp. 417–18.
10. Deutsch, *Neuroses and Character Types,* p. 159.
11. Deutsch, *The Psychology of Women,* Vol. 1, p. 205.
12. Ibid., Vol. 1, pp. 203–4.

CHAPTER 7. THE FRIENDSHIP OF PAUL BARNAY

1. Helene Deutsch, "Clinical and Theoretical Aspects of 'As If' Characters" (unpublished).
2. Deutsch, *Neuroses and Character Types,* p. 93.
3. Friedrich Schiller, "The Hostage," in *Poems and Ballads,* translated by Edward Lord Lytton (London: F. Warne, 1887), pp. 113–17.
4. Perry, *Psychiatrist of America,* pp. 90–91.
5. Deutsch, *The Psychology of Women,* Vol. 1, pp. 207–8.

CHAPTER 8. ANALYSIS WITH FREUD

1. Roazen, *Freud and His Followers,* Part V.
2. Ibid., Part VI.
3. Paul Roazen, *Erik H. Erikson: The Power and Limits of a Vision* (New York: The Free Press, 1976), pp. 70–72.
4. *The Origins of Psychoanalysis,* ed. Marie Bonaparte (London: Imago, 1954), p. 227.
5. Roazen, *Freud and His Followers,* pp. 59–63. Cf. also Peter Swales, "Freud, Minna Bernays, and the Conquest of Rome" (Privately published, 1983). In my opinion Swales's otherwise interesting argument fails to consider the power of Freud's fantasy life.
6. Deutsch, *Neuroses and Character Types,* pp. 341–42; Cf. also Deutsch, *Confrontations,* p. 132.
7. Deutsch, *Confrontations,* p. 130.
8. Paul Roazen, "Book review of *The Wolf-Man Sixty Years Later,*" *New Society,* January 6, 1983.
9. Deutsch, *Confrontations,* p. 131.
10. Johann Wolfgang Goethe, *Faust, Part One,* translated by Philip Wayne (London: Penguin Books, 1949), p. 87.

CHAPTER 9. VICTOR TAUSK'S SUICIDE

1. Cf. Paul Roazen, *Brother Animal: The Story of Freud and Tausk* (New York: Knopf, 1969. London: Penguin, 1970. New York: Vintage, 1971. London: Pelican, 1973.) For further discussions of Tausk, Cf. Paul Roazen, "Reflections on Ethos and Authenticity in Psychoanalysis," *The*

Human Context (1972), Vol. 4, pp. 577–87; Paul Roazen, "Orthodoxy on Freud: The Case of Tausk," *Contemporary Psychoanalysis* (1977), Vol. 13, pp. 102–15; Paul Roazen, "Reading, Writing, and Memory: Dr. K. R. Eissler's Thinking," *Contemporary Psychoanalysis* (1978), Vol. 14, pp. 345–53; Paul Roazen, "Victor Tausk, Disciple of Sigmund Freud," *Historical Perspectives on Depression* (1980), No. 6, Hoffmann-La Roche; Paul Roazen, "On Errors Regarding Freud," *International Journal of Psychoanalysis* (1982), Vol. 63, pp. 260–61; François Roustang, *Dire Mastery: Discipleship from Freud to Lacan,* translated by Ned Lukacher (Baltimore: The Johns Hopkins University Press, 1982), Chapter 5; Marius Tausk, "Comments," in K. R. Eissler, *Victor Tausk's Suicide* (New York: International Universities Press, 1983), pp. 299–322; D. M. Thomas, "Fathers, Sons and Lovers," in *Selected Poems* (New York: Viking, 1983), pp. 14–17; Victor Tausk, *Gesammelte psychoanalytische und literarische Schriften* (Wien-Berlin, Medusa, 1983).

2. Victor Tausk, "On the Origin of the 'Influencing Machine' in Schizophrenia," reprinted in *The Psychoanalytic Reader,* ed. Robert Fliess (New York: International Universities Press, 1948), pp. 31–64.

3. Helene Deutsch, "A Case that Throws Light on the Mechanism of Regression in Schizophrenia," Introduction by Paul Roazen, *The Psychoanalytic Review* (forthcoming).

4. *The Freud Journal of Lou Andreas-Salomé,* p. 169.

5. Cf. Roazen, *Freud and His Followers,* Part V, Chapter 3.

6. Roazen, "Reflections on Ethos and Authenticity in Psychoanalysis," p. 584.

7. Cf. Roazen, *Brother Animal,* pp. 127–28.

8. "Victor Tausk," *The Standard Edition,* Vol. 17, pp. 273–75.

9. *Psychoanalysis and Faith,* ed. Heinrich Meng and Ernst Freud (New York: Basic Books, 1963), p. 71.

10. Quoted in Eissler, *Victor Tausk's Suicide,* p. 140.

11. Rudolph Binion, *Frau Lou* (Princeton: Princeton University Press, 1968), pp. 402–3. Originally the most offensive passage in the letter was censored, but in the English edition the cuts have been restored: compare Sigmund Freud and Lou Andreas-Salomé, *Briefwechsel* (Frankfurt: Fischer, 1966), p. 108 with *Letters of Freud and Andreas-Salomé,* ed. Ernst Pfeiffer (London: Hogarth, 1972), pp. 98–99. Even now Eissler cannot bring himself to quote the passage unabbreviated: *Victor Tausk's Suicide,* p. 158.

12. Ludwig Jekels, "Early Psychoanalytic Meetings," p. 11. I am grateful to Peter Swales for bringing this passage to my attention.

13. Cf. Roazen, *Brother Animal,* pp. 153–54.

14. Roazen, *Freud and His Followers,* p. 435.

CHAPTER 10. EARLY CONTRIBUTIONS

1. Helene Deutsch, "Freud and His Pupils," *The Psychoanalytic Quarterly* (1940), Vol. 9, p. 189.
2. Franz Alexander, *The Scope of Psychoanalysis* (New York: Basic Books, 1961), p. 539.
3. Deutsch, "A Case that Throws Light on the Mechanism of Regression in Schizophrenia."
4. Helene Deutsch, "Zur Psychologie des Misstrauens," *Imago* (1930), Vol. 7, pp. 71–83; *International Journal of Psychoanalysis* (1920), Vol. 1, pp. 343–44.
5. Deutsch, "On the Pathological Lie."
6. Ludwig Binswanger, *Sigmund Freud* (New York: Grune & Stratton, 1957), p. 37.
7. Donald W. Winnicott, "Transitional Objects and Transitional Phenomena," *International Journal of Psychoanalysis* (1953), Vol. 34, pp. 89–97.
8. Deutsch, *Confrontations,* p. 54.
9. *International Journal of Psychoanalysis* (1922), Vol. 3, p. 135.
10. Cf. Roazen, *Freud and His Followers,* pp. 327–28.
11. Jones, *The Life and Work of Sigmund Freud,* Vol. 3, p. 85.

CHAPTER 11. DEPRESSION AND INFIDELITY IN BERLIN

1. Edoardo Weiss, "Vicissitudes of Internalized Objects in Paranoid Schizophrenia and Manic-Depressive States," *The Psychoanalytic Review* (Winter 1963–64), pp. 69–70.
2. Roazen, *Freud and His Followers,* Part IX, Chapter 8.
3. Deutsch, *The Psychology of Women,* Vol. 2, pp. 319–21.
4. "The Ego and the Id," *The Standard Edition,* Vol. 19, p. 23.
5. Roazen, *Freud and His Followers,* pp. 506–9.
6. "Editorial Changes in the *Zeitschrift,*" *The Standard Edition,* Vol. 19, p. 293.
7. Deutsch, "Occult Processes Occurring During Psychoanalysis."
8. Deutsch, *The Psychology of Women,* Vol. 2, p. 273.

CHAPTER 12. THE MEN: FELIX, FREUD, AND LIEBERMAN

1. Roazen, *Freud and His Followers,* pp. 338–41.
2. Felix Deutsch, "A Footnote to Freud's 'Fragment of an Analysis of a Case of Hysteria,'" *The Psychoanalytic Quarterly* (1957), Vol. 26, pp. 159–67.
3. Paul Roazen, "Book Review of Schur's *Freud: Living and Dying,*" *The Human Context* (Autumn 1973).

CHAPTER 13. "UNAPPRECIATED FEMALE LIBIDO"

1. Helene Deutsch, "The Psychology of Women in Relation to the Functions of Reproduction," *International Journal of Psychoanalysis* (1925), Vol. 6, pp. 405–18. Reprinted in *The Psychoanalytic Reader,* ed. Fliess, pp. 165–79.
2. Cf. Helene Deutsch, "The Menopause," Introduction by Paul Roazen, *International Journal of Psychoanalysis* (1984), Vol. 65, pp. 55–62. Cf. Helene Deutsch, *Psychoanalyse der weiblichen Sexualfunktionen* (Vienna: Internationaler Psychoanalytischer Verlag, 1925).
3. Joan Riviere, "Review of *New Introductory Lectures,*" *International Journal of Psychoanalysis* (1934), Vol. 15, p. 336.
4. *The Origins of Psychoanalysis,* p. 289.
5. Karen Horney, "Book Review," *International Journal of Psychoanalysis* (1926), Vol. 7, pp. 92–100.
6. "Three Essays on the Theory of Sexuality," *The Standard Edition,* Vol. 7, p. 219.
7. *International Journal of Psychoanalysis* (1924), Vol. 5, pp. 391–92.
8. Ethel Person, "Some New Observations on the Origins of Femininity," in Jean Strouse, ed., *Women and Analysis* (New York: Grossman, 1974), p. 259.
9. Deutsch, *Neuroses and Character Types,* p. 252; Deutsch, "Clinical and Theoretical Aspects of 'As If' Characters."
10. "Some Psychical Consequences of the Anatomical Distinction Between the Sexes," *The Standard Edition,* Vol. 19, p. 258.
11. "Female Sexuality," *The Standard Edition,* Vol. 21, pp. 226–27, 241.
12. Deutsch, *The Psychology of Women,* Vol. 2, p. 78.
13. Deutsch, *Neuroses and Character Types,* p. 360.
14. Deutsch, *The Psychology of Women,* Vol. 1, p. 146.
15. Cf., for example, Sandor Rado, "A Critical Examination of the Concept of Bisexuality," *Psychosomatic Medicine* (1940), Vol. 2, pp. 459–67; Abram Kardiner, Aaron Karush, and Lionel Ovesey, "A Methodological Study of Freudian Theory: III. Narcissism, Bisexuality, and the Dual Instinct Theory," *Journal of Nervous and Mental Disease* (1959), Vol. 129, pp. 207–21.
16. Herbert Marcuse, *Eros and Civilization* (Boston: Beacon Press, 1955); Paul Roazen, "Review of Jacoby's *Social Amnesia,*" *The American Scholar* (Spring 1976).

CHAPTER 14. THE MOVEMENT

1. George E. Gifford, ed., *Psychoanalysis, Psychotherapy, and the New England Medical Scene, 1894–1944* (New York: Science House, 1978), pp. 360–61.

2. *International Journal of Psychoanalysis* (1925), Vol. 6, p. 528.
3. *International Journal of Psychoanalysis* (1926), Vol. 7, p. 139.
4. Joan Fleming and Therese Benedek, *Psychoanalytic Supervision* (New York: Grune & Stratton, 1966), p. 12.
5. *International Journal of Psychoanalysis* (1929), Vol. 10, p. 525.
6. Paul Roazen, "Review of Sterba's *Reminiscences of a Viennese Psychoanalyst,*" *Journal of Nervous and Mental Diseases* (January 1984).
7. Helene Deutsch, "On Supervised Analysis," Introduction by Paul Roazen, *Contemporary Psychoanalysis* (1983), Vol. 19, pp. 53–70.
8. *International Journal of Psychoanalysis* (1928), Vol. 9, pp. 146–47.
9. Siegfried Bernfeld, "On Psychoanalytic Training," *The Psychoanalytic Quarterly* (1962), Vol. 31, p. 463.
10. "Analysis Terminable and Interminable," *The Standard Edition*, Vol. 23, pp. 248–49.
11. Ernst Kris, "To Helene Deutsch on Her Seventieth Birthday," *International Journal of Psychoanalysis* (1954), Vol. 35, p. 209.
12. *International Journal of Psychoanalysis* (1932), Vol. 13, p. 259.
13. Cf. Paul Roazen, "Review of Malcolm's *Psychoanalysis: The Impossible Profession,*" *The Virginia Quarterly Review* (1982), Vol. 58, pp. 710–14.
14. Maximilien Gathier, *Joseph Floch* (Paris: Les Gemeaux, 1952).
15. Roazen, *Freud and His Followers*, Part IX, Chapters 1–2.
16. Deutsch, "Freud and His Pupils," p. 192.
17. *International Journal of Psychoanalysis* (1932), Vol. 13, p. 249.
18. Ibid., p. 255.
19. Roazen, *Freud and His Followers*, Part IX, Chapter 8.
20. Ibid., Part VIII.

CHAPTER 15. CLINICAL WRITINGS

1. Helene Deutsch, "A Contribution to the Psychology of Sport," *International Journal of Psychoanalysis* (1926), Vol. 7, pp. 223–27. Reprinted in *Motivations in Play, Games & Sports*, ed. Ralph Slovenko and James A. Knight (New York: Thomas, 1967).
2. Helene Deutsch, "Zur Psychogenese eines Ticfalles," *Internationalen Zeitschrift für Psychoanalyse* (1925), Vol. 11, pp. 325–32.
3. *International Journal of Psychoanalysis* (1923), Vol. 4, pp. 377–78.
4. Helene Deutsch, "Occult Processes Occurring During Psychoanalysis."
5. Quoted in Ernest Jones, *The Life and Work of Sigmund Freud*, Vol. 2, (New York: Basic Books, 1955), p. 392.
6. "Group Psychology and the Analysis of the Ego," *The Standard Edition*, Vol. 18, p. 108.
7. "The Future of an Illusion," *The Standard Edition*, Vol. 21, pp. 31–32.
8. "New Introductory Lectures on Psychoanalysis," *The Standard Edition*, Vol. 22, p. 159.

9. Roazen, *Freud and His Followers,* Part VI, Chapter 2.
10. Helene Deutsch, "Über Zufriedenheit, Glück und Ekstase," *Internationalen Zeitschrift für Psychoanalyse* (1927), Vol. 13, pp. 410–19.
11. Helene Deutsch, "George Sand: A Woman's Destiny," Introduction by Paul Roazen, *International Review of Psychoanalysis* (1982), Vol. 9, pp. 445–60.
12. Diane Johnson, "She Had It All," *The New York Review of Books* (1979), October 11, pp. 9–12.
13. Quoted in Curtis Cate, *George Sand* (Boston: Houghton Mifflin, 1975), p. 732.
14. Helene Deutsch, *Psychoanalysis of the Neuroses,* translated by W. D. Robson-Scott (London: Hogarth, 1932); Cf. Sylvia Payne, "Book Review," *International Journal of Psychoanalysis* (1933), Vol. 14, pp. 272–78.
15. Ernest Jones, "Our Attitude Toward Greatness," *Journal of the American Psychoanalytic Association* (1956), Vol. 4, p. 643.
16. Helene Deutsch, "The Significance of Masochism in the Mental Life of Women," reprinted in *The Psychoanalytic Reader,* ed. Fliess, pp. 195–207.
17. Ibid., pp. 208–30; also in Deutsch, *Neuroses and Character Types,* Chapter 13.
18. Deutsch, *Neuroses and Character Types,* Chapter 14.
19. Ibid., Chapter 15.
20. Ibid., Chapter 16.

PART III CAMBRIDGE, MASSACHUSETTS

CHAPTER 1. "OUT OF THE MAGIC CIRCLE"

1. Frankwood E. Williams, *Proceedings of the First International Congress of Mental Hygiene* (New York: International Committee for Mental Hygiene, 1932), Vol. 2, p. 417. Cf. also Franz Alexander, *The Western Mind in Transition* (New York: Random House, 1960), pp. 94–99.
2. Lola Jean Simpson, "A Woman Envoy from Freud," New York *Herald Tribune* (August 3, 1930), pp. 9, 20–21.
3. *Proceedings of the First International Congress on Mental Hygiene,* Vol. 2, pp. 118–50.
4. Helene Deutsch, "Concerning the Actual Conflict in the Neuroses," *The Psychiatric Quarterly* (1930), Vol. 4, p. 466; Cf. also Deutsch, *Neuroses and Character Types,* p. 11.
5. Otto Rank, *Will Therapy,* translated by Jessie Taft (New York: Knopf, 1945), p. 110.
6. Jack Rubins, *Karen Horney* (New York: The Dial Press, 1978), p. 128.

7. Carl Binger, "Some Random Recollections of Stanley Cobb," *American Journal of Psychiatry* (1969), Vol. 126: 2, pp. 131–36; Carl Binger and Wilder Penfield, "Stanley Cobb," *Harvard Medical Alumni Bulletin* (Summer 1968), pp. 78–79.

8. Roazen, *Erik H. Erikson: The Power and Limits of a Vision,* p. 8.

9. Paul Roazen, "A Note on the Vienna Psychoanalytic Society: Felix Deutsch's letters, 1923 and 1935," *Journal of the History of the Behavioral Sciences* (October 1984).

CHAPTER 2. SEPARATION

1. "Introductory Lectures on Psychoanalysis," Vol. 15, p. 206; "New Introductory Lectures on Psychoanalysis," p. 133; "Group Psychology and the Analysis of the Ego," p. 101.

2. February 2, 1942. (Archives of the American Psychiatric Assoc.)

3. Caroline Scielzo, "An Analysis of Baba-Yaga in Folklore and Fairy-Tales," *The American Journal of Psychoanalysis,* Vol. 43, No. 2 (Summer 1983), pp. 167–75.

4. Paul Roazen, *Freud: Political and Social Thought* (New York: Knopf, 1968. London: Hogarth, 1969. New York: Vintage, 1970), pp. 51–53.

5. *Time* (January 13, 1941), p. 54.

CHAPTER 3. TRAINING ANALYSES

1. Felix Deutsch and William F. Murphy, *The Clinical Interview,* Vols. 1 and 2 (New York: International Universities Press, 1955).

CHAPTER 4. "THE ENDLESS CONTINUITY OF PERSONAL EXISTENCE"

1. Deutsch, *Neuroses and Character Types,* Chapter 20.

2. Cf., for example, Joseph Weiss, reporter, "Clinical and Theoretical Aspects of 'As If' Characters," *Journal of the American Psychoanalytic Association* (1966), Vol. 14, pp. 569–90; Nathaniel Ross, "The 'As If' Concept," *Journal of the American Psychoanalytic Association* (1967), Vol. 15, pp. 59–82; Paul Roazen, " 'As If' and Politics," *Political Psychology,* Vol. 4, No. 4 (1983), pp. 685–92.

3. Anton Chekhov, *The Portable Chekhov,* ed. Avrahm Yarmolinsky (New York: Viking, 1947), pp. 396–411.

4. Deutsch, *Neuroses and Character Types,* Chapter 17.

5. Ibid., p. 247.

6. Ibid., Chapter 19. Cf. also Deutsch, *The Psychology of Women,* Vol. 1, p. 23.

7. Deutsch, "Freud and His Pupils."

8. Helene Deutsch, "Anorexia Nervosa," Introduction by Paul Roazen, *Bulletin of the Menninger Clinic* (1981), Vol. 45, pp. 499–511.

9. Deutsch, *Neuroses and Character Types,* Chapter 21.

10. Ibid., Chapter 22.

11. Ibid., Chapter 23.

12. Deutsch, "Freud and His Pupils," p. 193.

13. Roazen, *Freud: Political and Social Thought,* p. 102.

14. Deutsch, *Neuroses and Character Types,* p. xi.

15. Ibid., p. 352.

16. Helene Deutsch, "Posttraumatic Amnesias and Their Adaptive Function," in *Psychoanalysis—A General Psychology,* ed. Rudolph M. Loewenstein (New York: International Universities Press, 1966), pp. 437–55.

17. "From Helene Deutsch," *Journal of the American Psychoanalytic Association* (1963), Vol. 11, pp. 227–28.

18. Helene Deutsch, "Technique: The Therapeutic Alliance" (unpublished).

19. Helene Deutsch, *Selected Problems of Adolescence* (New York: International Universities Press, 1967).

20. Helene Deutsch, *A Psychoanalytic Study of the Myth of Dionysus and Apollo: Two Variants of the Son-Mother Relationship* (New York: International Universities Press, 1969).

21. Nancy Friday, *My Mother/My Self* (New York: Delacorte Press, 1977).

22. Suzanne Gordon, "Helene Deutsch and the Legacy of Freud," New York *Times Magazine* (July 30, 1978), pp. 23–25.

23. Deutsch, *Neuroses and Character Types,* Chapter 25.

EPILOGUE: A WOMAN'S PSYCHOLOGY

1. Simone de Beauvoir, *The Second Sex* (New York: Knopf, 1953).

2. Deutsch, *The Psychology of Women,* Vol. 2, p. 167.

3. Clara Thompson, "Review of Deutsch, *The Psychology of Women,* Vol. I," *Newsletter, American Association of Psychiatric Social Workers* (1944), Vol. 14, pp. 56–57; Clara Thompson, "Review of Deutsch, *The Psychology of Women,* Vol. II," *Newsletter, American Association of Psychiatric Social Workers* (1947), Vol. 16, p. 101.

4. Cf. Anne Roiphe, "What Women Psychoanalysts Say About Women's Liberation," New York *Times Magazine* (February 13, 1972), pp. 12–13, 63–66, 68, 70.

5. Cf., for example, Juliet Mitchell, *Psychoanalysis and Feminism* (New York: Pantheon Books, 1974); Nancy Chodorow, *The Reproduction of Mothering* (Berkeley: University of California Press, 1978); Luise Eichenbaum and Susie Orbach, *Understanding Women: A Feminist Psychoanalytic Approach* (New York: Basic Books, 1983).

6. Deutsch, *The Psychology of Women,* Vol. 1, pp. x–xi.

7. Ibid., Vol. 1, p. 7.

8. Ibid., Vol. 1, p. 280, p. 91.

9. Ibid., Vol. 1, p. 21, p. 8; Vol. 2, p. 302; Vol. 1, p. 15, p. 18.

10. Ibid., Vol. 1, p. 27–28.

11. Ibid., Vol. 1, p. 51, 53, 54, 55, 56.

12. Cf. Paul Roazen, "Introduction," *Sigmund Freud* (Englewood Cliffs: Prentice Hall, 1973); Paul Roazen, *Erik H. Erikson: The Power and Limits of a Vision;* Paul Roazen, "Erik H. Erikson's America: The Political Implications of Ego Psychology," *Journal of the History of the Behavioral Sciences,* Vol. 16 (Fall 1980), pp. 333–41.

13. Deutsch, *The Psychology of Women,* Vol. 1, p. 23. Cf. p. 109.

14. Ibid., Vol. 1, p. 74, 147, 85.

15. Ibid., Vol. 1, p. 111, 127, 107.

16. Ibid., Vol. 1, p. 186, 218.

17. Ibid., Vol. 1, p. 141, p. 190.

18. Ibid., Vol. 1, p. 131, 133.

19. Ibid., Vol. 1, pp. 131–32.

20. Ibid., Vol. 1, pp. 84–85.

21. Ibid., Vol. 1, p. 138, 140, 142, 147.

22. Ibid., Vol. 2, p. 278.

23. Ibid., Vol. 1, p. 318.

24. Ibid., Vol. 1, p. 172; Vol. 2, pp. 78–80.

25. Ibid., Vol. 2, p. 79; Deutsch, *Neuroses and Character Types,* p. 360.

26. Deutsch, *The Psychology of Women,* Vol. 1, p. 163, 25.

27. Ibid., Vol. 1, p. 185, 186; Vol. 2, p. 474.

28. Ibid., Vol. 2, p. 17; Vol. 1, p. 211, 213.

29. Ibid., Vol. 1, p. 187, 190, 266; Vol. 2, pp. 266–67.

30. Ibid., Vol. 1, p. 278. Cf. Karen Horney, *New Ways in Psychoanalysis* (London: Routledge & Kegan Paul, 1939), pp. 110–11; Karen Horney, *The Neurotic Personality of Our Time* (London: Routledge & Kegan Paul, 1937), p. 261; and Karen Horney, *Feminine Psychology,* ed. Harold Kelman (New York: Norton, 1967).

31. Deutsch, *The Psychology of Women,* Vol. 2, p. 487; Ibid., Vol. 1, p. 192, 274, 270.

32. Ibid., Vol. 1, p. 191, 271.

33. Ibid., Vol. 2, p. 265.

34. Ibid., Vol. 1, p. 290, 292.

35. Ibid., p. 294, 273.

36. Ibid., p. 248, 373–74.

37. Ibid., Vol. 2, p. 26.

ACKNOWLEDGMENTS

It is a pleasure to be able to thank those who were kind enough to see me about Helene Deutsch: Dr. Bernard Bandler, Louise Bandler, Dr. Doris Menzer-Benaron, Dr. Tully Benaron, Dr. Martin Deutsch, Nicholas Deutsch, Suzanne Deutsch, Mrs. Joseph Floch, Dr. Ingrid Gifford, Dr. Sanford Gifford, Mrs. Elizabeth Cobb Hall, Dr. Lucie Jessner, Dr. Arthur Kravitz, Dr. Gardner Lindzey, Dr. Alfred O. Ludwig, Dr. William F. Murphy, Dr. John Murray, Dr. Emil Oberholzer, Dr. Eleanor Pavenstedt, Dr. Leon Saul, Mollie Schoenberg, Dr. James Skinner, Helene Veltfort, and Dr. Louis Zetzel.

Those who helped on individual points in the text include Marie Briehl, Lydia Ciolkosz, Mrs. Irene Czarny, Dr. Artur Leinwand, Dr. Erna Lesky, Dr. E. James Lieberman, Leonard Oller, Dr. A. Polonsky, Dr. Karl Sablik, Dr. Irvine Schiffer, and Dr. Helmut Wyklicky. I am also immensely grateful for the translating assistance of Eric Mosbacher, Tom Taylor, Anne Szeftel, and Sophie Szeftel. For critical readings of the manuscript I am indebted to Mrs. Maxwell Geismar, Dr. Hans Mohr, Vivienne Holland, and Dr. Michael Rogin. Dr. Martin Grotjahn was kind enough to read an early chapter.

Professional talks about Helene Deutsch gave me a chance to try out my ideas before interested audiences. Therefore I am grateful for the invitations to speak at the Canadian Institute of Psychoanalysis (Ottawa Branch); the Clarke Institute of Psychiatry, Toronto; the Dutch Fellowship of Psychoanalysis, Utrecht; the Department of Theoretical Psychology, the University of Leyden; the Philadelphia Academy of Psychoanalysis; the Radcliffe Institute, Cambridge, Massachusetts; the Departments of History and Religion, the University of Rochester; the Southern California Psychoanalytic Society; and the Department of Psychiatry, St. Michael's Hospital, Toronto.

Grant support facilitating my research came from the American Philosophical Society, the Laidlaw Foundation, the Radcliffe Institute, the Faculty of Arts Minor Research Grants Programme at York University, and the Social Sciences and Humanities Research Council Small Grants Programme at York University.

My agent, Georges Borchardt, has been exceptionally understanding throughout the years during which this book evolved.

INDEX

A

Abbazia, 53, 69
Abitur, 47, 57, 63
Abortion, 237
Abraham, Karl, 18, 157–58, 169, 174, 178, 183, 187–88, 191–203, 210–12, 214–15, 218–22, 228–29, 232, 235, 256, 257n., 340
Adler, Alexandra, 253
Adler, Alfred, 92, 150, 152, 166, 174, 177, 182, 235, 252–53, 273, 320
Adler, Victor, 49
Adolescence, 236, 242, 255, 272, 327, 336
Adriatic, 64
Agoraphobic, 266
Aichhorn, August, x
Albrecht, Herman, 52
Alcoholism, 15
Alexander, Franz, 177, 272–74
Algeciras, 57
Algeria, 57
Algiers, 57
Altruism, 333–34
Ambulatorium, 182–84, 188, 197, 208, 243–46, 253, 286–87
America, 127, 147, 183, 213, 220, 233, 243, 246, 249, 254, 256–57, 259, 268, 270–72, 274–79, 282–84, 288, 290–91, 300, 319
American Psychiatric Association, 272
American Psychoanalytic Association, 271–73, 278, 309, 312–13, 320
Andalusia, 55

Andreas-Salomé, Lou, 121, 151, 163–69, 171, 251
Anorexia nervosa, 322
Anti-Semitism, 5, 11, 64, 96, 252–53, 285–86, 306
Archduke Francis Ferdinand, 125
"As if," concept of, 139, 180, 320–21, 338
Associative anamnesis, 310
Australia, 17, 302
Austro-Hungarian Empire, 3, 11, 105, 126–27, 159, 161
Autonomy, 247, 325

B

"Babajaga," 293, 295–96, 303
Bachofen, J. J., 339
Balabanoff, Angelica, 9n.
Balzac, Honoré de, 267
Bandler, Bernard, 310
Barcelona, 44, 48, 51
Barnay, Louisa, 141, 302
Barnay, Paul, 98, 98n., 138–49, 172, 204, 216, 226, 300–2
Bauer, Franz, 133
Bauer, Klaus, 133
Bauer, Marianne, 133
Bauer, Otto, 211
Beauvoir, Simone de, 33
Bebel, August, 100
Beers, Clifford W., 271
Belgrade, 174
Benedict, Ruth, 9n.
Berlin, city of, 18, 64–65, 83, 161, 174,

Meridian

READINGS IN PSYCHOLOGY

(0452)

☐ **THE PSYCHOTHERAPY HANDBOOK, Richard Herink, ed.** This unique guide brings together clear, concise articles on more than 250 varieties of psychotherapy practiced in America today, making it by far the best single overview of a complex and crowded field. (005256—$9.95)

☐ **FREUD AND HIS FOLLOWERS by Paul Roazen.** A comprehensive study of the founder of psychoanalysis. Based on extensive research and interviews with more than a hundred and twenty eight individuals who had associations with Freud, it explores the many facets of one of the greatest thinkers of the modern age. (007445—$12.95)

☐ **GESTALT PSYCHOLOGY by Wolfgang Köhler.** A penetrating and thought-provoking study of the Gestalt theory—now universally regarded as a classic text in modern psychology—how we see, feel, and hear as an integrated whole rather than as a combination of separate parts. (005310—$4.95)

☐ **STRATEGIC PSYCHOTHERAPY: Brief and Symptomatic Treatment, Richard Rabkin, MD.** Provides a clear and sympathetic view of this increasingly dominant approach to therapy, spells out exactly what brief and symptomatic therapy can and cannot do; what the roles of therapist and patient are; and how a course of treatment is begun, successfully carried out, and satisfactorily concluded. (006252—$7.95)

Prices slightly higher in Canada.

Buy them at your local bookstore or use this convenient coupon for ordering.

THE NEW AMERICAN LIBRARY, INC.
P.O. Box 999, Bergenfield, New Jersey 07621

Please send me the MERIDIAN books I have checked above. I am enclosing $_____ (please add $1.50 to this order to cover postage and handling). Send check or money order—no cash or C.O.D.'s. Prices and numbers are subject to change without notice.

Name_____

Address_____

City_____State_____Zip Code_____

Allow 4-6 weeks for delivery.
This offer subject to withdrawal without notice.